S0-BNB-916

"YOU HAVE GOT TO READ THIS BOOK."
New York Daily News

"One of the most unique baseball books ever written"
Baseball Bulletin

"Entertaining and informative"
Chicago Tribune

"Not only great for quick reference on the players of the era—but also plain enjoyable reading."

—Frank Messer,
Yankee announcer

"A valuable book"

—Mel Allen, Yankee
announcer

"Do yourself a favor—
read AARON TO ZUVERINK."
New York Post

AARON TO ZUVERINK

RICH MARAZZI
AND
LEN FIORITO

 AVON
PUBLISHERS OF BARD, CAMELOT, DISCUS AND FLARE BOOKS

AVON BOOKS
A division of
The Hearst Corporation
1790 Broadway
New York, New York 10019

The Stein and Day edition contains the following Library of Congress Cataloging in Publication Data:

Marazzi, Richard.
    Aaron to Zuverink: a nostalgic look at the baseball players of the
fifties.

    1. Baseball players—United States—Biography.
I. Fiorito, Len.   II. Title.
GV865.A1M33   796.357′092′2 [B]   80-5893
                                                                  AACR2

First Avon Printing, May, 1984

To our parents and our wives, who have supported
our baseball interests over the years

ACKNOWLEDGMENTS

We give special thanks to the following:

Ralph Winnie, for providing many anecdotes and current occupations of several players;

Foxy Gagnon, for providing several current occupations;

Russ Dille, for use of his collection of countless editions of *The Sporting News* from the 1950s;

Larry Donald, *Baseball Bulletin* publisher and editor, for supplying several pictures used in this book;

Tom Hufford, for supplying occupations of former players;

Loisann Marazzi, for typing the final manuscript and aiding in research on the nostalgia of the fifties;

Mike DeLeo, for reviewing the manuscript for historic accuracy;

Bill White, Yankee announcer, for providing anecdotal information on several players; and

Bill Crowley, vice president for public relations for the Red Sox, for supplying anecdotal information on several players.

Our appreciation goes to others as well, who helped with specific information and data on players profiled in this book:

Steve Cooper, Mike Somo, Tom Rogers, Bill Borst, Norman Jackson, Jeanne Kelly, Lauren Matthews, Tom Zocco, Bill Schmidt, Colin Connelly, Miriam Kelly McNeil, Bill Haber, the staff of the University of Washington Library, and the staff of the Ansonia, Connecticut, Public Library.

To those who replied on behalf of major league teams, we owe a particular gratitude:

Erma Cook, S.F. Giants; Fred Claire, Dodgers; Tom Mee, Twins; William Crowley, Red Sox; Burt Hawkins, Rangers; Dan Ewald, Tigers; Robert Brown, Orioles; Larry Shenk, Phillies; Jim Toomey, Cardinals; Richard Griffin,

Expos; Jay Horowitz, Mets; Roland Hemond, White Sox; and Dave Szen, Yankees.

Some of the material that follows in the text arose out of interviews with the following players: Hank Aaron, Roy Campanella, Bobby Thomson, Ralph Branca, Moe Drabowsky, Ralph Kiner, Dick Gernert, Cal Abrams, Robin Roberts, Joe Black, Ed Bressoud, Tommy Holmes, Jim Hearn, Don Mueller, Joe Torre, Frank "Spec" Shea, Sal Yvars, Roger Maris, Wally Post, Russ Meyer, Hank Bauer, Bob Balcena, Al Konikowski, Billy Loes, George Shuba, Duke Snider, Don Larsen, Joe Collins, and Art Ceccarelli.

Our original editor, Art Ballant, has shouldered more than his share of interest and support in this very long and sometimes frustrating project. We express to him a proportionate gratitude. We also thank our new editors, John Douglas and Chris Miller, for their careful assistance in the reprint of this book. Finally, we thank Dave Weiner for his interest and dedication to *Aaron to Zuverink*.

FOREWORD

Only in America can a boy realize the dream of growing up
and competing against the same major league stars whose
baseball cards he had once collected. For me, getting the
opportunity at a professional baseball career was a bless-
ing in so many ways. While I carved my niche in the history of the game we call our national pastime, the real
thrill for me was meeting the many players and fans
across this land. Yes, America is a beautiful country with
beautiful people.

My special thanks goes to my former skipper at Baltimore, Paul Richards, who gave me that all-important second chance when others thought I was finished. In giving
me another shot at the majors, Paul also renewed my self-
confidence. He made me believe in myself.

To baseball fans, thanks for the opportunity to seek and
discover this dream.

Reading *Aaron to Zuverink* brought back so many wonderful times for me. If you followed baseball in the fifties,
I'm sure it will do the same for you. To Rich and Len,
thanks for the memories.

George Zuverink

INTRODUCTION BY RICH MARAZZI

The vivid impressions of one's childhood are often indelibly etched throughout life. Born between the years of Pearl Harbor and Normandy, I came alive to the nightmare of World War II only through stuffy textbooks and actors turned war heroes at the local cinema.

In the late 1940s my intellectual skills were much too shallow to digest the complexities of international tensions in China. The baseball crisis between New York and Boston made more sense.

I cautiously admired the verve and tenacity of the "Whiz Kids" in 1950, but in all honesty, this band of National League mavericks wearing giant-sized numbers on their jerseys were a threat to my beloved Yankees. Baseball rebels like Ashburn, Sisler, and Seminick attempted an overthrow of established pinstripers, but as expected, the coup was thwarted in a four-game sweep.

It was during the fifties that John Cameron Swayze's professional journalistic approach launched the original "M.A.S.H." series with nightly reports covering the Korean conflict. But in the eyes of a nine-year-old baseball junkie, more important wars were being fought in baseball bastions like Yankee Stadium, Ebbets Field, and the Polo Grounds. Bellicose figures like Eddie Stanky, Billy Martin, and Clint Courtney demonstrated the American fighting spirit on the home front.

I journeyed to Yankee Stadium on a Y.M.C.A. bus trip and saw my first major league game at age 10. Armed with a brown sandwich bag and $2.25, I finally made it to Mecca. The sight of the stately stadium with its picturesque awnings and its sea of green seats dwarfed my dreams.

Inside this diamond pantheon, a young sinewy blond named Mantle, the heir apparent to number 5, was defying the laws of physics with his tape measure wallops and lightning speed. But to my chagrin, the visitors from Chicago with names like Nellie Fox, Chico Carrasquel, and Minnie Minoso handled the soon-to-be-dethroned champions with ease.

Across the river at 155th Street an ebony god named Willie was performing miracles in the garden of Coogan's Bluff, while at cozy Ebbets Field "Duke," "PeeWee," and "Campy" excited their Flatbush faithful.

While Bill Haley and the Comets were singing "Rock Around the Clock" in '55, the Dodgers rocked the Yankees for the first time in the autumnal classic. Johnny Podres and Sandy Amoros were lionized for their efforts. The cry of "Wait till next year!" was not heard this time.

In retrospect, life at that point was a bowl of cherries. School no longer seemed a chore and Little League success gave me identity for the first time in my life playing for the Pioneers in Ansonia, Connecticut.

Following the advice of Horace Greeley, the Dodgers and Giants packed their bags. The Yankees now had the Big Apple all to themselves. But I felt a sickening void. As in conquest, a mix of euphoria and emptiness was epidemic. Would I ever see Willie and Duke again? Or what about Aaron, Klu, Musial, Jeffcoat, and Repulski?

Granted, a "joint" no longer means a bar, and the supply of wax teeth is exhausted, but things aren't that different. Elvis Presley and Fats Domino remain boarders packed away in snug record jackets. Shows like "I Love Lucy" and "The Honeymooners" refuse to leave. The Cold War wasn't just a fad. And the flaming Yankee-Red Sox rivalry rages on.

The fifties—if I could only put time in a bottle!

INTRODUCTION BY LEN FIORITO

My earliest recollection of baseball is with the Seattle
Rainiers of the Pacific Coast League in the early 1950s.
The team's radio announcer, Leo Lassen, was already a
legendary figure in the Pacific Northwest at this time.
There was a special, nasal tone in his voice which was fre-
quently mimicked by youngsters on playfields in the
Seattle area, most notably his home run call of ". . . back,
back, back, and it's *over!*"

I'm somewhat hazy on the details of the first Rainiers'
game I viewed in person at Sick's Seattle Stadium; this
likely came in the late 1940s. I do recall protesting to my
father our early departure from a game with a batter still
at the plate with a bat in his hands. I can now assume a situation of the Hollywood Stars holding an 8-1 lead over the
Rainiers with two out in the home half of the ninth inning.
So much for the old adage, "The game's never over until
the last man is out."

In 1951 an announcer in far-off New York was screaming
over and over, "The Giants win the pennant! The Giants
win the pennant!" Although somewhat less dramatic but
with much significance in Seattle, it was "The Rainiers
win the pennant." A colorful outfielder named "Jungle"
Jim Rivera led the way in what to this novice fan was the
routine winning of a pennant. Eight-year-old fans have not
yet suffered through the losing seasons. Eventually I
would learn to adjust, not just to lost pennants, but to lost
franchises. As the American League would reappear in
Seattle in the late 1970s my main concern would not be
one of winning a championship but just keeping the franchise in town.

Along with becoming devoted to the Rainiers in the early
1950s, I came to accept that level of competition which was
above even my home-town favorite. The next several sum-

mers would be spent following the Rainiers closely and the major leagues from a distance. There are numerous fond memories of baseball in those years: collecting and trading baseball cards; playing the game enthusiastically if not proficiently; my brother idolizing a player named Andy Pafko; and searching for a namesake in the game like other neighborhood friends named Morgan, Pellagrini, and Torre.

But above any other summer, 1955 stands out. Not only did my favorite major league team finally make it to "next year," but home-town hero Fred Hutchinson returned to Seattle to manage the Rainiers to a pennant. "Hutch" had been a classmate of my mother's at Franklin High School, just beyond the centerfield fence of Sick's Stadium. I was fortunate enough to see a great number of Rainiers' games that summer, many of those from my Uncle Pre's box seats between home plate and first base. A trio of major league stars already aging in those years, named Vern Stephens, Ewell Blackwell, and Larry Jansen, contributed to the pennant. But the one player I recall with the most fondness from the team was a hustling little Filipino outfielder named Bobby Balcena. Twenty-five summers later I met with him and spent a pleasant evening reminiscing about that '55 season. Although he "was only in the major leagues for a cup of coffee with no cream or sugar," as he put it, Balcena was a genuine star to me in 1955 with his timely hitting and brilliant defensive play in the outfield.

By the end of the 1950s the major leagues had reached the west coast. Seattle was still in the Pacific Coast League but, with Leo Lassen retiring from the broadcast booth and the name of the team changed to Angels, things weren't quite the same. There would be another pennant in the mid-1960s; but I was off in the military service in the state of Texas, where I had the opportunity to view major league baseball in person for the first time. The expansion Astros were still struggling against names like Koufax, Mays, Banks, and Clemente. Shortly after my return to Seattle the American League expanded to my city. Only the retirement of Yankee star Mickey Mantle in spring training of that same 1969 season spoiled the excitement. Much more disturbing than not seeing Mantle in Seattle in 1969 was not having the Pilots there in 1970 as they shifted to Milwaukee after their first and only season in my home city. I contemplated ending a twenty-year love affair with the game. While looking to the future for a second chance at the big leagues, I also looked backward to my childhood heroes of the 1950s.

It was also at this time that I was captivated by Roger Kahn's book *The Boys of Summer,* which updated the lives of the Brooklyn Dodger stars of the 1950s. What had become of those other faces on the baseball cards I had collected during the 1950s? What had become of the members of the 1950 Phillies "Whiz Kids," the 1951 miracle Giants, the '54 Cleveland Indians who had temporarily stalled the Yankee Dynasty, or the '59 Go Go White Sox team which also interrupted a string of Yankee pennants? Where were all the members of the slugging Cincinnati Reds teams of the mid-1950s or the members of the National League champion Milwaukee Braves teams of 1957 and '58? What had become of all the other Boys of Summer?

TO THE READER:

Our aim in this book is to give you a general idea of what each player has been doing since the end of his playing career. Although we have attempted to report his current status, job, and area of residence, it's inevitable that some changes will have occurred since we collected the information for the manuscript. We have listed a player's residence only when his job location isn't mentioned.

If you can enlarge upon or refine any of the facts we cite in the book, we will be happy to hear from you. You may drop a letter to either of us, Rich Marazzi or Len Fiorito, in care of the publisher.

To qualify for inclusion in this book, a player had to have appeared in a major league box score during the years 1950 to 1959, the greatest decade in baseball history.

R.M.
L.F.

A

AARON, Henry "Hank"
Atlanta Braves Vice President and Director of Player Development

Among "Hammerin' Hank's" numerous impressive career totals, he has hit more home runs (755) and hit into more double plays (320) than any other player in baseball history. He combined with brother Tommy as the all-time leader in homers by a brother combination. Of course, Hank carried most of the load with 755 to Tommy's 13.

Aaron played in 24 All-Star Games, a record he shares with Stan Musial and Willie Mays. He is the only player who hit a home run in three consecutive playoff games, as he did in 1969 against the Mets. He was elected to the Hall of Fame in 1982.

Hank originally wore number 5 in his 1954 rookie season. He then changed to number 44 and on four occasions hit 44 home runs in a season. His historic 715th clout came off Al Downing, who also wore number 44. It also happened during the 4th month (April) in the 4th game during the 4th inning in a nationally televised contest. He once tied Willie McCovey, who also wore number 44, with 44 homers in a season.

In 1954 Aaron was due to be sent down to the minors until Bobby Thomson broke his ankle in spring training. Later that year when Thomson was in the lineup, Aaron pinch-ran for him and broke *his* ankle.   .305

ABER, Al "Lefty"
Salesman for a housewares distributor
Cleveland, OH

Al appeared in one game for the Indians in 1950. He returned to the big time in 1953 and said goodbye in 1957, spending time with Cleveland, Detroit, and Kansas City. "Lefty" finished 24-25.

1

ABERNATHIE, Bill
   Fyffe, AL

This right-handed chucker played in just one game for the 1952 Indians and was credited with a save in his only major league appearance.

ABERNATHY, Ted
   Lumber salesman, Gastonia, NC

If you were watching baseball in the late 1950s, you should remember Ted's sweeping underarm style. A relief specialist whose career spanned from 1955–72 with a bundle of teams, Abernathy was named *The Sporting News* "Fireman of the Year" in 1965 (Cubs) and in 1967 (Reds). This submarine-style hurler sunk permanently in '72 with the Royals and finished 63-69.

ABRAMS, Cal
   Employed by a plastics company and also involved with an Old Timers Speakers Platform, Hand Lake, Amagansett, NY

An outfielder for eight years (1949–56), Cal made his debut with the Dodgers. During the critical last game of the 1950 season, Cal was gunned down at the plate by Phillies' center fielder Richie Ashburn with the score tied in the ninth inning. The "Whiz Kids" went on to win on Dick Sisler's dramatic four-bagger.

Abrams split the '52 campaign between Brooklyn and Cincinnati. If you have a baseball bubble gum card of Abrams in a Reds uniform, it is worth about $45 today because of its rarity. He says, "One of my great thrills was putting on a Dodger uniform for the first time. I had one grand-slam home run in my career, and it was off Ruben Gomez of the Giants. I still have the bat." Before calling it quits, Cal made stops at Pittsburgh, Baltimore, and Chicago.   .269

ACKER, Tom
Mutuel clerk,
Meadowlands race track,
East Rutherford, NJ

A right-handed pitcher for four years (1956–59), all with
the Reds, Tom went 19-13 overall, including a 10-5 season
in 1957.

ADAIR, Jerry
Manual laborer, Sand Springs, OK

An outstanding fielding second baseman throughout the
1960s, Jerry broke in with Baltimore in 1958 after attending Oklahoma State University, where he played college basketball under legendary cage coach Hank Iba.
After college he played basketball with the Phillips 76ers,
one of the nation's top AAU teams.

Jerry's glove work around the keystone bag was especially brilliant from July 1964 until May '65 when he set a
major league mark of 89 straight games and 485 chances
without an error. He wound up the '64 season with a record fielding percentage of .994 and an all-time low of just
five errors.

Adair lost his job to Dave Johnson in '66 and missed out
on the Orioles' 1966 World Series team, but was part of the
Red Sox A.L. championship squad in '67 after spending
time with the White Sox. Jerry completed his career with
K.C. in 1972. He was the first-base coach for the World
Champion Oakland team in the early 1970s.   .254

ADAMS, Bobby
Chicago Cubs infield instructor

Although numerous father-son and brother combinations
have reached the majors, very few have had a brother and
a son make it to the biggies. Bobby's brother Dick played
briefly with the Philadelphia A's in 1947 and his son Mike
played with the Twins, Cubs, and A's in the '70s. Strange
but true, Bobby and his brother Dick each collected six hits
on the same night in the minors, in 1947.

Bobby's 14-year career (1946–59) was divided among the Reds, Cubs, White Sox, and Orioles. He spent most of his days with the Reds. Playing with Cincinnati on May 13, 1954, Adams led off the game with a home run off the Phillies' Robin Roberts. The wallop proved to be the sole Reds' hit that day as Roberts retired the next 27 batters in order, for an 8-1 victory.   .269

ADAMS, Herb
Post office employee, Wheaton, IL

Herb played in a total of 95 games—all with the White Sox as an outfielder from 1948–50—and finished with a .261 lifetime batting average.

ADCOCK, Joe
Raises thoroughbred horses
Coushatta, LA

Joe paced LSU to Southeastern Conference Basketball titles in both 1945 and 1946, then chose professional baseball over the infant NBA. Four of his career total 336 homers came on July 31, 1954, against the Dodgers at Ebbets Field. He also doubled in that contest for a still-standing major league mark of 18 total bases in a game. The following day he started off the month of August as he had left off on the last day in July (with a double), then was beaned by Clem Labine and carried off the field.

An amazing aspect of his single game display of awesome power was that he swung at just five pitches for his five extra base hits. However, his best-remembered home run is the one that was taken away in the Harvey Haddix masterpiece, when he passed Hank Aaron on the basepaths after Aaron left the field in the 13th inning. Haddix had hurled 12 perfect innings. It was the first and only hit for the Braves. Joe managed the Indians in 1967 to an 8th-place finish in a 10-team race.

Adcock joins Hank Aaron and Lou Brock as the only three players to homer into the distant center-field bleachers in the Polo Grounds during a regular-season game.
                                     .277

ADDIS, Bob
> Director of Athletics for the Euclid, OH public schools

Bob spent his four years in the majors as an outfielder with the Braves, Cubs, and Pirates (1950–53). His best campaign was in 1952 when he hit .295 in 93 games for the Cubs. A graduate of Kent State University, Bob finished with a lifetime average of .281.

AGGANIS, Harry "The Golden Greek"
> Died June 27, 1955, at the age of 25, in Cambridge, MA

After an outstanding all-around high school career in Lynn, Mass., Harry went on to Boston University, where he became an All-American backfield star in 1952. He was the outstanding performer in the 1952 Senior Bowl game at Mobile, Ala. Agganis was considered by Cleveland Browns' coach Paul Brown to be the successor to the legendary Otto Graham. However, Harry turned down a reported offer of $25,000 from the Browns, to play with the Red Sox. In 1954 he was the team's regular first baseman.
In May of 1955 he was stricken with pneumonia and spent ten days in the hospital. On June 4th he complained of chest pains in Kansas City and was sent back to Boston, where he died suddenly of a massive pulmonary embolism. Harry was hitting over .300 at the time his career came to this abrupt end. He had five hits in a doubleheader on May 15, 1955, before going out of action with the illness that led to his death.   .261

AGUIRRE, Hank
> Cable TV announcer for Detroit Tigers games; president of Mexican Industries
> Detroit, MI

With a lifetime batting average of .085 (33-388), Aguirre ranks in a class with Bob Buhl, Dean Chance, and others for batting futility. Unfortunately, his career ended before the designated-hitter rule. Fortunately he was a pitcher, and a pretty good one, with a lifetime 75-72 mark. He spent most of his days on the mound with the Tigers after

breaking in with Cleveland. Hank also made stops with
the Dodgers and Cubs. In 1962 he won 16 games with
Detroit and led the A.L. in ERA with 2.21.

Under Leo Durocher he became a Cubs coach with a
unique title—"Information and Services Coach"—he was
Leo's liaison man with the press. He became just another
coach in mid-season the following year when "The Lip"
was fired and replaced by Whitey Lockman.

ALBANESE, Joe
Architect
New Brunswick, NJ

Joe hopped up to the majors with the 1958 Senators, pitching six innings and six games with no record. The lanky
Senator, who stood 6'3", did a hop, skip, and a jump out of
the majors, never to return.

ALBRECHT, Ed
Died in 1979, at age 50, in Centerville, IL

He pitched in one game with the St. Louis Browns in 1949.
Ed doubled his appearance the following year and saw action in two games. He finished 1-1.

ALEXANDER, Bob
Salesman for Sperry and Hutchinson Company
Citrus Heights, CA

Bob went 1-0 for the Orioles in 1955. In 1957 the right-
hander reversed results, going 0-1 with the Indians. He
threw no-hitters in both the American Association and
PCL in the early fifties.   1-1

ALLIE, Gair
General manager
Lone Star Distributing Co.
Bexar County, San Antonio, TX

Gair had just one year in the majors—1954. Unfortunately, he made it into the record books when he banged

out just 83 base hits, compiling a .199 average. At the
time, the 83 hits established the all-time season low for a
player who had at least 400 at-bats.

ALLISON, Bob
    General manager
    Coca-Cola Bottling Midwest, Inc.
    Twin Cities Marketing Division
    St. Paul, MN

Bob played college football at the University of Kansas in
the mid-1950s. By 1959 he was the A.L. Rookie of the Year
as an outfielder with the Washington Senators. Bob was
an integral part of the power-packed Twins lineup in the
mid-1960s. On July 18, 1962, he teamed with Harmon
Killebrew to hit grand-slam home runs in the first inning
in a game against Cleveland. When he led the A.L. in runs
scored with 99 in 1963 it was the first time since 1918 that
the league leader had been under 100.
    Allison ranks among the all-time leaders in homers and
RBIs for the Senators-Twins franchise, but possibly he is
best remembered for his spectacular diving catch off the
Dodgers' Jim Lefebvre in the second game of the 1965
World Series.   .255

ALOMA, Luis
    Tavern owner
    Chicago, IL

This Cuban right-handed pitcher had a brief but successful
four-year stay (1950–53) with the White Sox as a relief
specialist. He was 18-3 in 116 appearances—all but one in
relief. His one start in the big leagues was a route-going
shutout in 1951.

ALOU, Felipe
    Montreal Expos coach

The oldest of the three brothers who played in the majors,
Felipe first appeared in 1958 with the San Francisco

Giants. On Sept. 15, 1963, Felipe started in right field for the Giants with Willie Mays in center and Willie McCovey in left. By the eighth inning the Giants were demolishing the Mets 13-4, when Giants' skipper Al Dark inserted Matty Alou in left, and brother Jesus in right, and moved Felipe to center to set up baseball's first all-family outfield.

The only time brothers finished one-two in a batting race was in 1966 when Felipe (.327) placed second behind Matty (.342). Not even the famed Waner duo of "Big Poison" and "Little Poison" managed to achieve that feat. Felipe, who hit a career-high 31 homers during '66, is the only player ever to hit lead-off home runs in consecutive games twice in his career.   .286

ALSTON, Tom
High Point, NC

Thomas Edison Alston, the first black to play for the Cardinals, was born in the year of the great inventor's death (1931), and was a first baseman for parts of four seasons (1954–57) with the Cardinals, compiling a .244 average in 91 games. If Tom could have invented a way to replace Stan Musial at first base, he might have been around for a longer period of time.

ALTMAN, George
Employed on the Board of Trade
Chicago, IL

George actually had two baseball careers. The first one, in the N.L., was spent mostly with the Cubs, where he twice hit over .300 in the early 1960s. He was in his mid-thirties by the late 1960s when he began his "second" career in Japan. Altman was earning close to $100,000 past his fortieth birthday after several years in Japan, where he had over 200 homers and a .300 career average.   .269

ALTOBELLI, Joe
Manager of 1983 World Champion Baltimore Orioles

Manager of the Year with the Giants in 1978, Joe achieved his greatest managerial success in his first year as Orioles' skipper in 1983. In between he coached third base for the Yankees and managed their Columbus (AAA) farm team. Joe came to the majors with the Cleveland Indians in 1955 and, after a stint in the minors, returned to them in 1957 to replace Vic Wertz. The first baseman-outfielder closed his career with the Minnesota Twins in 1961.   .210

ALUSIK, George
Woodbridge, NJ

George appeared in two games for the Tigers in '58. He reappeared for Detroit in 1961, and bowed out with the K.C. A's in '64. A .256 lifetime hitter, the flychaser batted .270 in 1962, splitting the season with the Tigers and A's.

ALVAREZ, Ossie
Pittsburgh Pirates scout in Latin America

Señor Alvarez played in a total of 95 games, 87 of which were with the Senators in '58. The remaining tilts were spent in a Tigers uniform the following season.   .212

AMALFITANO, Joey
Los Angeles Dodgers coach

Joe spent ten years as a utility infielder with the Giants, Astros, and Cubs spanning the years 1954–67. He has coached and managed for the Cubs, and has also coached for the Giants, Padres, and Reds. As a bonus player for the '54 Giants, he came to bat just five times all year, but still collected a full $10,000 World Series share. He is the first USC alumnus to manage in the majors.   .244

AMARO, Ruben
    Chicago Cubs coach

Primarily a shortstop for 11 years, Ruben came on stage
with the 1958 Cards, but played most of his career in the
City of Brotherly Love with the Phillies. Following three
years with the Yankees, he hung up his spikes after one
season with California. Amaro played in 940 big league
games.   .234

AMOR, Vincente
    Havana, Cuba

This 6'3" Cuban right-hander emerged on the scene in
1955 (Cubs) and 1957 (Reds). He appeared in 13 games,
gave up 13 walks, and had a 1-3 record.

AMOROS, Sandy
    Formerly employed with New York City Parks Dept.
    Lives in Miami, FL

October 4, 1955—"The Catch." Sandy's dramatic snare of
an apparent Yogi Berra home run in game seven of the '55
Fall Classic will never be forgotten. The Dodger outfielder
went 4-for-12 in the WS and parked a two-run homer in the
5-3 Dodgers' win in game five. When asked about his famous catch he replied, "I dunno, I just run like hell."
    Amoros was around for seven seasons, during six of
which he wore the Dodger blue. The last team he played
for was the Detroit Tigers in 1960.   .255

ANDERSON, Bob
    Gary, IN

This right-handed pitcher was around for seven years
(1957–63), and all but the final season were with the Cubs.
Bob had his best campaign in '59 with 12 wins, but only
won more games than he lost in his final big league fling
with the Tigers in 1963 when he was 3-1. He is a graduate
of West Chester State in Pennsylvania.   36-46

ANDERSON, Ferrell
　　Died March 12, 1978 at age 60 in Joplin, MO

An all-conference lineman for two years at the University
of Kansas, Ferrell shared the Dodgers' catching with
Bruce Edwards in 1946, playing in 70 games. He returned
to the majors seven years later to catch in 18 games for the
'53 Cardinals.　　　　　　　　　　　　　　　　　　.261

ANDERSON, Harry
　　Independent manufacturers' representative
　　Greenville, DE

1958 was the year Harry hit 23 homers and swatted a nifty
.301 average for the Phils. A left-handed hitting outfielder
and first baseman, Anderson spent five years in the N.L.
from 1957–61 with the Phils and the Reds. During his first
three seasons he was a regular in the Phillies' garden.

ANDERSON, John
　　Great Falls, MT

John spent parts of three seasons (1958, '60, '62) in the
majors. He failed to earn a decision in 24 games as a member of the Phils, Orioles, Cardinals, and Houston.

ANDERSON, George "Sparky"
　　Detroit Tigers manager

Sparky was a one-year major leaguer as the regular second
baseman on the 1959 Phillies. He became one of baseball's
best-known names of the 1970s as manager of Cincinnati's
"Big Red Machine."
　Sparky was originally a member of the Dodgers' organization. With the Phillies he hit .218 in 152 games. As manager of the St. Petersburg team in the Florida State
League in 1966, his team lost a 4-3 29-inning game, then a
professional baseball record.

ANDRE, John
      Died Nov. 25, 1976 at age 52 in Centerville, MA

Born and raised in Brockton, Mass., Andre was a boyhood friend of Rocky Marciano. A right-handed chucker,
John lost his only big league decision with the '55 Cubs.
In a game against the Dodgers, he once faced just one
batter (Roy Campanella), and got him to hit into a triple
play.

ANTONELLI, Johnny
      Tire business
      Rochester, NY

John went directly to the majors in 1948 at age 18 when he
signed a $65,000 bonus with the Boston Braves. After four
years with the Braves he was traded to the Giants prior to
the 1954 season. The stylish left-hander blossomed in the
Polo Grounds, helping the Giants to the World Championship with a 21-7 record and a league-leading 2.30 ERA. His
six shutouts also were best in the National League. En
route to a 126-110 mark, he had seasons of 20 and 19 wins
for the Giants before bowing out with the Indians and
Braves in 1961.
      In 1969 he was named to the all-time Giants team as one
of the four pitchers. He was in fast company, considering
that the other three were named Hubbell, Mathewson, and
Marichal.

ANTONELLO, Bill
      St. Paul, MN

In 40 games with the '53 Dodgers, Bill subbed in the garden with Don Thompson, George Shuba, Dick Williams,
and Carmen Mauro. He had 1 double, 1 triple, and 1 home
run, and struck out 11 times.   .163

APARICIO, Luis
> Owns an insurance business; does TV commentary in
> the Venezuelan baseball league.

The A.L. Rookie of the Year in 1956, Luis ranks with such
great shortstops as Reese and Rizzuto. Luis appeared in
2,599 games, all at shortstop, which places him as the
all-time leader in games played at that position.

"Little Luis" made his debut with the White Sox, a team
he split two terms with. He also played five years in Orioles' flannels and three with the Red Sox. Aparicio led the
A.L. in fielding from 1959–66; and was the top base-stealer
in the junior circuit 1956–64.

He was a major force in the 1959 A.L. champion "Go-
Go" White Sox, and the '66 World Champion Orioles.
When traded from Chicago to Baltimore following the '63
season, he remarked to Sox General Manager Ed Short that
"the White Sox won't win another pennant for 40 years,"
in reference to the 1919–59 span when the team went
without a pennant. Luis returned to the White Sox a few
years later and changed his story to "Now we win a pennant next year." His first prediction may hold up as it is
now 25 years since the White Sox won their last pennant.

Luis married the niece of teammate Jim Rivera in '56
when both were with the White Sox. He was elected to the
Hall of Fame in 1984, the first Venezuelan to make it to
Cooperstown.   .262

APPLING, Luke "Old Aches and Pains"
> Atlanta Braves hitting instructor

Appling was voted the White Sox greatest player of all
time. Luke saw his career (which began in 1930) come to a
close in 1950. He was already in his late thirties when he
missed the 1944 season and most of 1945 during World
War II. Despite his advanced age as a player, he still returned for four more .300 seasons.

His number 4 uniform was the first ever retired by the
White Sox. Not only was 1964 the year he was inducted at
Cooperstown, but it was also the year he became involved
in the first-ever trading of coaches following the trade of
manager Jimmy Dykes from Detroit to Cleveland for man-

ager Joe Gordon. A few days later he moved from the Tigers to the Indians, with JoJo White going the opposite way. The stories of his ability to foul off pitches are legendary. Dizzy Trout once became so upset after Appling had fouled off numerous pitches that he took off his glove and threw it toward home plate. A Comiskey Park fan once shipped off a foul ball hit into the stands off Appling's bat to Cooperstown, where Hall of Fame officials put it on display.

Once, while playing against the Senators in Washington, he purposely fouled off numerous pitches at the expense of the Washington team since he was unable to secure passes for friends from his home town of High Point, N.C., who had journeyed to see the game. Luke was nicknamed "Old Aches and Pains" by his teammates because of his frequent complaints of various ailments.

In the first ever Cracker Jack Baseball Classic for old-timers in 1982, Luke hit a 275-foot home run into the left field stands at RFK Stadium in Washington, D.C.—a remarkable feat for a 75-year-old man.   .310

ARFT, Hank "Bow Wow"
Mortician, Schrader Funeral Home
Ballwin, MO

"Bow Wow" was a first-sacker for the St. Louis Browns, 1948–52, closing with a .253 average.

ARIAS, Rudy
Coca-Cola driver
Miami, FL

This Cuban-born southpaw hurled and won his only two decisions as a member of the 1959 A.L. Championship White Sox, his only year in the biggies.

ARROYO, Luis
New York Yankees scout in Puerto Rico

This veteran journeyman pitcher came into his own as a relief specialist for the Yankees in 1961. "Fireman of the

Year" that season with 15 wins and a league-leading 29 saves, Arroyo also broke Joe Page's Yankee record of 60 appearances, with 65. Although he was 34 at the time and had spent the majority of his career in the minor leagues, Luis had had some previous success as a 27-year-old rookie in 1955 with the Cardinals, when he won 11 games and was a member of the N.L. All-Star team.

The year 1961 provided his one banner season, and just two years later he was out of the biggies. Many of his saves came for Hall of Famer Whitey Ford, who won a career high of 25. On the banquet circuit that winter, Ford was quoted as saying, "Luis can come along and finish up my speeches!"   40-32

ASHBURN, Richie "Putt-Putt," "Whitey"
    Philadelphia Phillies announcer and columnist for
    The Philadelphia Daily News

As a rookie with the 1948 Phils, Richie hit a cool .333. He led the league in stolen bases, and established an N.L. rookie record hitting in 23 consecutive games. Richie won a pair of batting championships in '55 and '58. Following his second batting title, his average dropped over 80 points, from .350 to .266, and established an unflattering record of just 20 RBIs, the all-time low for a player appearing in over 150 games. However, he managed to go out with a .306 season in 1962, the last player to retire following a .300-plus season. Never a power hitter, "Whitey" had over 2,000 career hits, only 29 of them four-baggers.

Ashburn, who attended Norfolk Junior College, was labeled "Putt-Putt" by Ted Williams, who said that " 'Putt-Putt' had twin motors in his pants," in regard to Ashburn's speed around the bases. Richie was the first member of the Mets to play in an All-Star Game when he appeared in the second 1962 mid-summer classic.

A key member of the 1950 Phillies' "Whiz Kids," his throw from centerfield in the ninth inning of the final game of the 1950 season against the Dodgers cut down Cal Abrams at the plate and paved the way for Dick Sisler's pennant-clinching home run. He also played with the Cubs in '60 and '61.   .308

ASPROMONTE, Bob
      Coors Beer distributorship in Houston, TX

Bob struck out as an 18-year-old pinch-hitter with the '56
Dodgers. He returned to the big arena in 1960 with the
transplanted Los Angeles Dodgers, and hung around until
1971. During that time he played with Houston, Atlanta,
and the Mets. "Aspro" played throughout most of the
1960s as the regular third baseman for the expansion
Houston Astros. He retired with a .252 career average.

ASPROMONTE, Ken
      Coors Beer distributorship in Houston, TX

The elder of the Brooklyn-born brothers, Ken broke in with
the Red Sox in 1957 after winning the PCL batting title, and
played with several different teams until 1963. He had his
best season when he hit .290 for the 1960 Indians, a team he
would later manage. Ironically, both Ken and Bob enjoyed
their best season when they were 29 years old.   .249

ASTROTH, Joe
      Salesman for copper and brass company
      Chalfont, PA

A ten-year catcher, Joe went directly from the University
of Illinois to spend his entire career with the Philadel-
phia/Kansas City Athletics from 1945 through the mid-
fifties. His career RBI total is 156, but a record total of six
of those came in one inning of a game during the 1950 season. That was a third of his season total of 18. His most active campaign was in 1952, when he caught 102 games and
was the personal catcher of that year's Most Valuable
Player, 24-game winner Bobby Shantz.   .254

ATKINS, Jim
      Real estate broker
      Birmingham, AL

Jim's batting average was better than his pitching average as he went 2-for-4 (.500) with the stick. On the mound

he lost his only decision in four games in brief stints with the Red Sox in 1950 and '52.

ATWELL, Maurice Dailey "Toby"
Special millwork
Leesburg, VA

Toby spent five seasons behind the dish in the N.L. (1952–56) with the Cubs, Pirates, and Braves. His most productive year at the plate was his rookie season when he hit .290 in 107 games for the Cubs.   .260

AVERILL, Earl
Marketing director for Radio Shack
Seattle, WA

Earl Douglas Averill is the son of Howard (Earl) Averill, star outfielder in the 1930s, and a member of the Hall of Fame, who died in 1983. The younger Earl was born in Cleveland late in the 1931 baseball season, when his father hit .333 for the Indians.

A catcher, outfielder, and third baseman, young Earl started his career with the Indians in 1956. His most productive of seven big league seasons was with the expansion Angels in 1961 when he hit 21 home runs. Earl is a graduate of the University of Oregon.   .242

AVILA, Bobby
Ex-owner of the Aguascalientes team in the Mexican League; former Mayor of Vera Cruz, Mexico. Current president of the Mexican League.

Mexican-born Bob Avila was the first Latin American to win a batting title when he hit .341 in 1954 for the A.L. pennant-winning Indians. He spent most of his eleven-year trek with the Tribe, the team he came up with in 1949. Bobby once set an A.L. mark of 19 assists in an extra-inning game. Going from one extreme to the other, he also set a record with just one assist in two games in a row the same year. Of his 80 career homers, the popular second baseman whacked 3 in one game in 1951. In June of '54 he was hitting around .390 and stated, "If I hit .400, they make me President of Mexico." He didn't hit .400, but they did make him a mayor.   .281

AVREA, James "Jay"
     Proprietor of Jay's Florists of Wynnewood
     Dallas, TX

Jay pitched in two games for Cincinnati in 1950, but failed to get a decision.

AYLWARD, Dick
     Beer truck driver for coast distributors
     Spring Valley, CA

Dick caught four games for the Cleveland Indians in 1953.

B

BABE, Loren
     Chicago White Sox Coach

Another "Babe" on the Yankee roster in the early fifties, "Bee Bee" saw brief action for the Bronx Bombers before moving over to Philadelphia where he became the regular third baseman for the Athletics in 1953.   .223

BACZEWSKI, Fred
     Died Nov. 14, 1976 at age 50 in Culver City, CA

A left-handed pitcher for the Cubs and Reds (1953–55), Fred was 11-4 in '53, and had an overall respectable 17-10 mark.

BAILEY, Ed
Public relations and sales with Peterbilt
Knoxville, TN

Ed spent most of his 1,212 games as a left-handed hitting catcher for the Reds, 1953–61. Early in the 1961 season, he was traded to the Giants and it seemed to be a bad break, as the Reds went on to win the pennant. However, it turned out to be a good move for Ed, since the Giants were the 1962 N.L. flag winners. In his first major league at-bat, Lonas Edgar ("You can call me Ed") Bailey singled off Bob Buhl.

Ed had some productive years, most notably his 28-homer season in '56. Two distinctions dot his career. He twice came up with an unassisted double play (a rarity for a catcher), and he also was part of a brother battery briefly, when brother Jim pitched with the Reds in 1959.
.256

BAILEY, Jim
College Park, GA

Brother of Ed, he lost his only decision in three appearances for the 1959 Reds.

BAKER, Floyd
Minnesota Twins scout

Primarily a third baseman, he also played at second base and shortstop, 1943–55, with several teams. He should not be confused with the legendary "Home Run" Baker of an earlier period. Floyd hit exactly one roundtripper in 2,280 at-bats.
.251

BAKER, Gene
Pirates special assignment scout

An eight-year N.L. infielder with the Cubs and Pirates (1953–61), Gene broke into the majors with Ernie Banks in 1953. The two combined to form one of the National League's best double-play combinations. Baker led N.L.

second basemen in putouts and assists in '55, and led in double plays in 1956. He was traded to the Pirates for his last 3 seasons.

BALCENA, Bob
    Longshoreman
    Seattle, WA

Bob is the only Filipino to ever reach the majors. He scored two runs in two official at-bats in seven games for the 1956 Reds.

BALDWIN, Frank
    Westchester, OH

A catcher, Frank played in 16 games for Cincinnati in 1953.   .100

BAMBERGER, George
    Ex-New York Mets manager (resigned during the 1983 season)

Six members of the famed '51 Giants' team went on to manage in the big show. The least remembered is George Bamberger. Bigger names like Westrum, Lockman, Rigney, Dark, and Stanky also piloted big league teams. Bamberger never won a game for the '51 Giants or for any other big league team, but he did win over 200 games in the minors—most of them at the Triple-A level.
    After several years as a successful pitching coach with Baltimore, George became the Brewers' manager. George celebrated Father's Day of 1951 by becoming a father and pitching a no-hitter for Ottawa in the International League.

BANKHEAD, Dan
    Died May 2, 1976 at age 56 in Houston, TX

Dan became the first black ever to pitch in the majors when he took the mound for the Dodgers on August 8,

1947. He also hit a home run in his first big league plate appearance. Dan returned in 1950 to win 9 games for Brooklyn, then dropped out of baseball after the '51 season.   9-5

BANKS, Ernie "Mr. Cub"
Public relations work for Chicago bank

Ernie was tabbed by Chicago sportswriter Jim Enright as "Mr. Cub." In a career spanning the 1953-71 period, he won fielding championships at both shortstop and first base. Ernie was the N.L. MVP in both 1958 and '59. He hit 5 grand slams in 1955. In '59 his 143 RBIs were 91 more than those of his closest teammate, Bobby Thomson—the widest margin in history by which a player dominated that important statistic on his team. Elected to the Hall of Fame in 1977, he had a brilliant career except that he never played in a World Series.

Ernie holds the single season (47) and career (293) home run records for a shortstop. He had a total of 512 roundtrippers. When the Cubs blew what seemed to be a sure pennant in 1969, Ernie drove to a lonely beach on the city's lakefront one evening and wept quietly. That was a marked contrast to his usual sunny disposition characterized by his cheerful words, "It's a beautiful day. Let's play two."

Jimmy Dykes once said, "Without Ernie Banks, the Cubs would finish in Albuquerque."   .274

BANTA, Jack
Employed with the Dillon Grocery chain
Hutchinson, KS

Jack won 14 games in his four-year stint with the Brooklyn Dodgers (1947-50). Ten of the wins came in the 1949 season when the Dodgers won the N.L. pennant. He came on in relief in three of the World Series games against the Yankees without a decision. Jack led the International League in strikeouts in 1947 and 1948.   14-12

BARCLAY, Curt
    Lumber business
    Missoula, MT

A right-handed pitcher, Curt was 10-9 overall in three
years (1957–59), all with the Giants. As a rookie in 1957,
the right-hander went 9-9 for the Giants in their last season in New York.

BARMES, Bruce "Squeaky"
    Welder for Martin-Marietta
    Charlotte, NC

The Korean conflict ended in 1953 and so did Bruce's
major league career, as "Squeaky" just squeaked in five
games in the outfield with the '53 Senators.   .200

BARNES, Frank
    Greenville, MS

Frank had a 15-game career with the Cardinals (1957, '58,
'60). The right-hander had no-hitters in the Texas League
('55) and American Association ('58).   1-3

BARNEY, Rex
    Public address announcer
    Baltimore Orioles

"If home plate had been high and outside, I'd be in the Hall
of Fame"—Rex Barney.
    Actually, Rex had one fine season in the N.L. in 1948,
when he won 15 for the Dodgers including a no-hitter over
the rival Giants. Overall he won just 35, winding up with
the Dodgers' minor league team at Fort Worth in the
Texas League, where he gave up 16 bases-on-balls in his
first start before calling it quits.   35-31

BARRETT, Frank
> Retired; owned a Phillips 66 service station
> Leesburg, FL

Frank came up with the Cards in 1939. He pitched with both Boston teams, the Red Sox and Braves, during the war and made it into five games with the '50 Pirates, from whence he made his exit.   15-17

BARTIROME, Tony
> Pittsburgh Pirates team trainer

Born in Pittsburgh, Tony was the Pirates' regular first baseman in 1952. With no homers and only 16 RBIs, he didn't give the team much power at the normal power hitting position. He was generally the team's starter, playing in over 120 games. He does have the distinction of never hitting into a double play over an entire season. But it was his one and only year in the majors.   .220

BASGALL, Monty
> L.A. Dodgers coach

A second baseman with the Pirates in 1948, '49, and '51, Romanus "Monty" Basgall appeared in exactly 200 big league games, hitting .215.

BATTEY, Earl
> Athletic supervisor at a residential treatment center in New York; Con Edison program for free admission for youngsters; junior college baseball coach in Florida

Earl appeared as a catcher in over 1,000 games. He spent the last half of the 1950s as a part-time receiver for the White Sox before moving on to the Twins, where he was the regular catcher until 1966. Earl was respected by enemy runners for his rifle-like arm.

Battey was an outstanding high school basketball player in Los Angeles. in 1953 he turned down an offer by

Abe Saperstein to join the Harlem Globetrotters in favor of
signing with the White Sox.   .270

BATTS, Matt
    Batts Printing Co.
    Baton Rouge, LA

A ten-year catcher (1947–56), Matt was generally used
as a part-time receiver (he played over 100 games just
once). His main claim to fame was that when he came
up to the plate, his name in itself told the whole story.
Matt attended Baylor University before going on to play
with the Red Sox, Browns, Tigers, White Sox, and
Reds.   .269

BAUER, Hank
    Retired liquor store owner; scouts A.L. teams for the
    Yankees
    Overland Park, KS

Hank Bauer, the man of the hour, could also have been
called "Mr. October." The ex-Marine hit in 17 consecutive
World Series games from 1956–58. He hit safely in all
seven games during the '56 and '57 autumn classics. In the
'58 World Series, in which the Yanks beat the Braves,
Bauer belted 4 home runs.

Hank's 14-year run (1948–61) was spent mostly in pinstripes. He led the Yanks in triples for three straight
years. Bauer was traded to Kansas City in a deal which
saw Roger Maris come to the Yankees. He completed his
career in K.C. and was named manager in June of 1961.
He later took over at Baltimore. His '66 Orioles took four
straight from the Dodgers in the "Fall Classic," making
him the only manager in history with an undefeated
World Series record (4-0).

The hard-nosed Bauer, who, someone once said, "had a
face like a clenched fist," was hired by Charlie Finley in
1969, and was again fired by the fickle owner.   .277

BAUERS, Russ
Retired; former millwright with Reynolds Co.
Westchester, IL

Russ's playing days spanned three decades (1936–50). A
right-hander, he was a 13-game winner for the Pirates in
1937 and 1938. Bauers remained with the Bucs until 1941,
then returned to the majors after the war years with the
Cubs in '46. Absent from the big league scene for another
four years, he became a fifties player when he pitched in
one game for the the 1950 St. Louis Browns.   31-30

BAUMANN, Frank
Baumann Brothers Welding Service
St. Louis, MO

What's in a number? This lefty hurler was with the Red
Sox 1955–59, winning a total of 13 games. Baumann, who
signed for a $90,000 bonus in 1952, was shipped to the
White Sox on November 3, 1959, in exchange for first
baseman Ron Jackson. He responded by winning 13 games
for "The Hose" in '60. But the following year he lost 13
games. In '62 he had 13 decisions, going 7-6. The stocky native of St. Louis, Missouri, finished at 45-38.

BAUMGARTNER, John
Vice-president, Tractor Trailer Co.
Birmingham, AL

John Baumgartner played seven games at third base for
the Tigers and hit .185 in 1953.

BAUMHOLTZ, Frankie
Vice president
Marquart Bros. Food Co.
Cleveland, OH

Frankie had a .290 average in a 10-year N.L. career as an
outfielder. A college basketball star in the early forties at

Ohio University, he was named All-American in 1941, and
selected MVP of the N.I.T.

He was in his late twenties when he reached the biggies
following World War II. He also played pro basketball in
the winter of 1946–47 with the Cleveland Rebels of the
Basketball Association of America (B.A.A.). In 1952 he hit
.325 for the Cubs, and was the runner-up to Stan Musial for
the N.L. batting title. Interestingly enough, he was the
only batter to ever face Musial, the "pitcher," in a big
league game that season. A left-handed hitter, he switched
to the right side and was safe on an infield error.

BAXES, Jim
    Sheet metal worker
    Garden Grove, CA

Dimitrios Baxes is the elder of two San Francisco-born
brothers who played as infielders in the majors in the late
fifties. Jim played with both the Dodgers and Indians in
1959, his only big league season. During his playing days
he married the sister of Clint Conaster, an outfielder with
the Boston Braves, 1948–49.   .246

BAXES, Mike
    Mill Valley, CA

Mike played in 73 games for the K.C. A's in 1956. He also
appeared in 73 games for the K.C. A's in 1958, and—would
you believe—had a lifetime total of 73 hits. As Casey
Stengel said, "You can look it up." In 1957 he was sent to
Buffalo, where he was named the MVP of the International League. In a single contest, he had 10 RBIs on two
grand slams, a double, and a single—a good night in any
league.   .217

BEAMON, Charlie
    Counselor for job opportunity center
    Palo Alto, CA

Charlie made his debut late in the 1956 season for the
Baltimore Orioles, and it was a sensational one as he shut

out the champion Yankees and Whitey Ford, 1-0. He would win just two more games in the big leagues before returning to the minors.

Twenty years later, the name Charlie Beamon returned, as his son made a few brief appearances for the expansion Seattle Mariners as a first baseman. Charlie was a high school classmate of former basketball great Bill Russell at McClymonds H.S. in Oakland.   3-3

BEARD, Ralph
     Security guard, Pratt and Whitney
     West Palm Beach, FL

In 1954 the U.S.S. *Nautilus,* the first atomic-powered submarine, was launched, while big Ralph (6'5", 200 lb.) sunk with the Cardinals, going 0-4.

BEARD, Ted
     Automobile dealership in Indianapolis, IN

This 5'8" "Teddy" Beard was an outfielder with the Pirates (1948–52), then again with the White Sox (1957–58). At Hollywood in the Pacific Coast League, he once hit four home runs in a game and also established a PCL record for consecutive hits with 12.   .198

BEARDEN, Gene
     Automobile dealership
     Helena, AR

Gene was a left-handed hurler who had one spectacular season as a 28-year-old rookie in 1948, when he won 20 games for Cleveland, including a 8-3 win over the Red Sox in a playoff for the A.L. pennant. His 2.43 ERA topped all A.L. chuckers. In the WS he shut out the Boston Braves, 2-0, in game three to put the Indians up two games to one, as he allowed just five hits. In game six he came on in relief to save a 4-3 win for Bob Lemon as Cleveland won the Series in six games. He even helped his team with the bat, picking up 23 hits for a .256 average on the season, and went 2-for-4 in the Series. It was pretty much downhill after the glorious '48 campaign as he never won as many as he lost, and he drifted around to several other A.L. teams until the end of the line in 1953. But he could still swing the bat pretty well, picking up another 23 hits in 1952 for the St. Louis Browns for a .354 average.

Gene pitched with an aluminum plate in his skull and knee from an operation after surviving the sinking of the U.S.S. *Helena* in World War II. It's ironic that he now works in a city named Helena.   45-38

BECQUER, Julio
  Department store employee
  Minneapolis, MN

This Cuban first baseman was with the Senators (1955–60), and the Angels and Twins in the early sixties. Julio twice led the A.L. in pinch-hits, including 1957, when he garnered 18 emergency hits coming off the bench. That same season he led the Senators with three stolen bases. Washington's 13 stolen bases was the lowest in major league history.   .244

BELARDI, Wayne
  Fruit business
  San Jose, CA

From 1950 to '56 Wayne was playing first base with the Dodgers and Tigers. Belardi swatted 11 homers in just 69 games in 1953 as backup to Gil Hodges on the N.L. champion Dodgers.   .242

BELL, Bill
  Died October 11, 1962, at age 28, in Durham, NC

As an 18-year-old pitcher in the Pirates' organization at Bristol in the Class D Appalachian League in 1952, Bill threw back-to-back no-hitters. Later that same year he hurled a third no-hitter. He then went all the way up to Pittsburgh where he lost his only decision. Three years

later, he pitched one scoreless inning, then bowed out of
the majors.

BELL, Gary
Sales representative for a sporting goods store in San
Antonio, TX

Gary had his finest season in his second year (in 1959)
when he won 16 games for Cleveland. He remained with
the Indians until early in 1967 when he was dealt to the
Red Sox, who he helped to the A.L. pennant by winning 12
games. He had a loss and a save in the World Series that
fall against the Cardinals. He started his final season in
1969 by shutting out the White Sox in the only home
opener for the expansion Seattle Pilots.   121-117

BELL, Gus
Manages Minutemen—a temporary employment services company in Cincinnati, OH

David Gus Bell was a power-hitting outfielder with the
Reds throughout most of the fifties. Originally a member
of the Pirates, he led the N.L. in triples with 12, and had 89
RBIs in 1951. Despite all this, Gus was back in the minors
the following year because of a dispute with the Pirates'
front office (mainly Branch Rickey), over wanting to have
his family travel with him. He did return to the Reds,
where he went on to have several productive years.
 On July 21, 1955, Gus parked three homers in the same
game. He hit for the cycle on May 29, 1956. Bell logged a
.281 lifetime average with 206 four-baggers. Reds' manager Birdie Tebbetts once said of Bell, "He's so remarkably steady, he sometimes goes unnoticed." In the twilight
of his career he was an original Met in 1962, and finished
with Milwaukee in '64, just eight years before his son
Buddy became a member of the Cleveland Indians. "Buddy," whose given name is David Gus Bell, was part of the
family that Gus wanted traveling with him back in that
spring of 1952.

BELLA, Zeke
   Mailman
   Greenwich, CT

Zeke was an outfielder who was in five games for the 1957 Yankees. He then spent a portion of the '59 season with the K.C. A's.   .196

BENSON, Vern
   St. Louis Cardinals' scout

Vern was a third baseman in parts of five seasons with the Philadelphia A's in the mid-forties, and from 1951–53 with the Cardinals. A lifetime .202 hitter in 55 games, he has remained in baseball as a manager in the minors, and for several seasons has been a big league coach for the Cards, Yankees, and Reds.

BENTON, Al
   Died April 14, 1968, at age 57, in Lynwood, CA

Al's career spanned the years 1934–52, or just long enough to have the distinction of facing both Babe Ruth and Mickey Mantle. His most effective seasons came in the early 1940s with Detroit. He led the A.L. in saves with 17 in 1940. The following season he was 15-6 with an ERA under 3.00. During the 1941 season, he became the only player in history to lay down two successful sacrifice bunts in the same inning.   98-88

BERARDINO, John
   Television actor in Hollywood

John had an eleven-year run as an infielder, 1939–52. He put in two separate stints with three different teams—the St. Louis Browns, Pittsburgh Pirates, and Cleveland Indians.

   For the past two decades, "Bernie" has had a leading role in the ABC TV afternoon soap opera "General Hospital," playing the role of Dr. Steve Hardy. He makes a reported $250,000 a year in that part, making him one of a handful of retired major leaguers from an earlier era whose present salary can match up well with that of today's major leaguers. Other acting credits include a role as an FBI agent on the TV series "I Led Three Lives," and a part in the Academy Award-winning movie *Marty*. When he turned to acting following his baseball career, John changed the spelling of his name to Beradino.   .249

BERBERET, Lou
    Division manager for liquor distributor
    Long Beach, CA

Lou was around in the 1954–60 period. His first two years were brief stints with the Yankees. The next two years he had identical .261 seasons while sharing the catching duties with Ed Fitzgerald and Clint Courtney of the Senators.
    Berberet, a football lineman at Santa Clara University, set a Senators' record in '57 by catching 77 games without an error. The chunky backstop also played with the Red Sox and Tigers, and closed with a .230 lifetime average.

BERNIER, Carlos
    Bayamon, PR

In 1953 Carlos appeared in 105 games as an outfielder for the Pirates and hit .213, and managed to get his name in the record books for hitting three triples in a game. Before coming to the biggies, the speedy Bernier starred for the Hollywood Stars in the PCL.

BERO, John
    Employed with the city of Gardenia, CA

An infielder with the Tigers briefly in 1948, John appeared in 65 games as a shortstop for the St. Louis Browns in 1951.   .213

BERRA, Lawrence Peter "Yogi"
  New York Yankees manager

Probably the most famous of the "Berraisms" is the one which goes, "I want to thank all the fans for making this day necessary." That day might have come in his native St. Louis had the Cardinals offered him more than a $250 bonus when he tried out with them in 1942. He rejected that offer for one of $500 by the Yankees. He was the A.L. MVP three times—1951, '54, and '55.

Yogi became the first man in big league history to hit a pinch-hit home run in a World Series game when he connected off Dodger pitcher Ralph Branca on October 2, 1947. Berra managed both the Yankees and Mets to pennants. He played in a record 75 World Series games, covering a total of 14 WS. All-Star games weren't necessarily Yogi's cup of tea, as he batted only .195 in fifteen All-Star contests.

Cartoon character "Yogi Bear" was named after the popular Yankee backstop. He received the name "Yogi" because he used to cross his legs while watching movies. A friend remarked that he looked like a "Yogi," in reference to a Hindu fakir.

In 2,120 games, he swatted 358 home runs, and he sports a lifetime .285 average. He played four games for the Mets in '65. Yogi was elected to the Hall of Fame in 1972.

BERRY, Nail
  Carpenter
  Kalamazoo, MI

This carpenter was a utility infielder, 1948–54, with the Tigers, Browns, White Sox, and Orioles. He managed to hammer out 265 hits and a .244 lifetime batting average.

BERTOIA, Reno
  Toronto Blue Jays scout
  High school teacher
  Windsor, ONT, Canada

A $25,000 Tiger bonus player out of the University of Michigan, Reno was born in St. Vito Udine, Italy. He had a

ten-year career (1953–62) mostly as a part-time third baseman for Detroit. He also played for the Senators, Twins
and K.C. A's before saying *arrivederci* in '62.   .244

BESANA, Fred
>Baseball coach
>American River College
>Sacramento, CA

Fred glided around with the Orioles briefly in '56. A left-
handed hurler, he won his only decision in seven games for
Baltimore. His son, Fred Besana, is a quarterback in the
United States Football League.

BESSENT, Don
>Mechanical engineer with Thompkins and Beckwith
>Co.
>Jacksonville, FL

Fred Donald Bessent was 8-1 for the World Champion
Dodgers as a rookie in 1955. In that Series he was not
scored on in three bullpen appearances. In the 1956 "Fall
Classic," he was the winning pitcher in a 13-8 slugfest
over the Yanks—the longest nine-inning game in Series
history. Overall, Don was 14-7, in a four-year career.

BEVAN, Hal
>Died Oct. 5, 1968, in New Orleans at age 37

Hal bounced around with various teams. A third baseman,
he had brief stays with the Red Sox and Philadelphia A's
(1952), K.C. A's ('55), and Reds ('61). With all that packing
and unpacking, Hal played in a total of 15 games and hit
.292.

BICKFORD, Vern
>Died May 8, 1960, at age 39 in Richmond, VA

Vern spent the first four years of his career at the Class-D
level. His persistence proved fruitful, as he was on the

pitching staff of the N.L. champion Boston Braves in 1948, a staff which made the slogan "Spahn and Sain and pray for rain" popular. He won 11 that year and added 16 in 1949. But 1950 was his big year, winning 19 and leading the N.L. in complete games and innings pitched. One of his victories was a no-hitter over the Dodgers.

Born on August 17, 1920 (the same date Cleveland's Ray Chapman died from a beaning for the only fatality in major league history), Bickford himself died at the early age of 39 in 1960.   66-57

BILKO, Steve
Died March 7, 1978, at age 49, in Wilkes-Barre, PA

At about the same time that Phil Silvers was starring as Sergeant Bilko, Steve Bilko was at the pinnacle of his popularity. One of the greatest minor league players in baseball history, Steve spent ten years in the majors during the fifties and sixties. The strapping first baseman hit 76 fourbaggers in 600 games. While playing for the Los Angeles Angels of the Pacific Coast League in 1956, he was named the Minor League Player of the Year, winning the league's triple crown with a .360 average, 55 homers, and 164 RBIs.
                                                        .249

BIRRER, "Babe"
School teacher and coach
Buffalo, NY

Werner "Babe" Birrer was a right-handed flipper who saw brief action with the Tigers, Orioles, and Dodgers in the 1950s. But he did have one memorable game on July 19, 1955, for the Tigers. Appearing in relief in the last four innings for Detroit that day, this Fourth of July baby hit a pair of three-run homers in his two appearances at the plate. Thus came the nickname "Babe," and with the reputation pitchers have for discussing their hitting feats, today he has one memorable day with the bat to boast to his students about. The two homers were the only ones he hit in the majors.   4-3

BISHOP, Charlie
> Adjustor, Brewer Adjustments
> Doraville, GA

Born on New Year's Day, Charlie was a right-handed hurler (1952–55) with the Philadelphia and K.C. A's. He shut out the Red Sox in his first start, but then lost 17 straight decisions en route to a 10-22 career mark.

BLACK, Bill
> Brick contracting business
> St. Louis, MO

Bill was a right-handed chucker in 10 games in parts of 1952, '55, and '56 with Detroit. His first major league victory in '55 was a shutout. He won just one more, the following year, and completed his day in the sun at 2-3.

BLACK, Joe
> Vice president for special markets
> Greyhound Corporation
> Phoenix, AZ

One of Roger Kahn's *Boys of Summer*, Joe had great success as a 28-year-old rookie in 1952, winning 15 games and saving another 15 in relief. He was named the N.L. Rookie of the Year and became the answer to the trivia question, "Who was the first black to win a World Series game?" when he defeated Allie Reynolds and the Yankees, 4-2, in the opening game of the '52 series. Commenting on that, he stated, "Warming up before the game, I looked on the third base side and saw that the Yankees were all white, and the Dodgers were integrated with Jackie [Robinson], 'Campy' [Campanella], and Sandy [Amoros]. I found myself saying, 'Thank God for the United States, where you have a chance to make your dream come true.' Ten years before that, scouts had told me they couldn't sign me because I was colored." Joe also spent time with the Reds and Senators, leaving in '57.   30-12

BLACKBURN, Jim
   Died Oct. 26, 1969, at age 45, in Cincinnati, OH

Jim was a right-handed pitcher in 18 games with the Reds
in 1948 and 1951. He was called "Bones" by the players
around him.   0-2

BLACKBURN, Ron
   Recreation director at a correctional center
   Morgantown, NC

Ron arrived the year of the Edsel (1958) with the Pirates,
and like the Edsel, quickly disappeared with a 3-2 career
mark in '59.

BLACKWELL, Ewell "The Whip"
   Security guard
   Connestee Falls, NC

For those who began following major league baseball in
the early 1950s, he was already somewhat of a legend for
his awesome pitching. As a member of a second division
1947 Reds pitching staff, Ewell won 22, including 16 in a
row at one point. He also led the N.L. in strikeouts and
came very close to duplicating teammate Johnny Vander
Meer's feat of back-to-back no-hitters in 1938. He no-hit
the Boston Braves, and then went into the ninth inning
the next outing before allowing two hits. Remarkably,
Vander Meer's back-to-back feat had also come against the
same two teams: the Braves and Dodgers.
   A kidney operation, appendectomy, and sore arm cut
short his career, which ended with Kansas City in 1955.
                                                              82-78

BLAKE, Ed
   Plumber
   East St. Louis, IL

This righty chucker was in a pale total of 8 games in parts
of four different seasons (1951–53, '57) with the Reds and

A's, and had no decisions during his seesaw career. Eddie was a busy man in '55, as he attended law school at St. Louis U. while playing pro ball.

BLANCHARD, John
    Salesman
    T.C. Johnson Company
    Minnetonka, MN

A reserve catcher for the Yankees in the early sixties, John played an important role in the team's success, most notably in 1961 when he hit 21 homers and drove in 54 runs despite playing in under 100 games. At one point in July he hit homers in four consecutive appearances over a three-game period.

As a Yankee catcher he set a World Series record as a pinch-hitter when he came to bat ten times off the bench. He finished with K.C. and the Milwaukee Braves, with a lifetime .239 average.

John arrived with the Yankees and played in one game in 1955 but wasn't around again until '59.

BLASINGAME, Don
    Fielding instructor
    St. Louis Cardinals organization

Although there has never been a father-son combination playing for the same major league team at the same time, Don Blasingame, known as the "Blazer," was a teammate of his father-in-law, Walker Cooper, in 1955. He was a rookie with St. Louis that year while Cooper was in his final season with the Cardinals as a catcher. Along with that distinction, Don also ruined no-hit bids by opposing pitchers four times in his career by picking up his team's only hit. He did it twice in a two-week period in 1963. Exceptionally tough to double up, he led his league four times in hitting into the fewest double plays, and hit into a total of just 43 in over 5,000 at-bats. He was also with the Giants, Reds, and Senators.

Following his playing in the U.S.A., he became the most

highly respected American in Japanese baseball as a
player, coach, and the first American manager.   .258

BLATNIK, John "Chief"
    Actuary,
    Gates-MacDonald and Company
    Lansing, MI

A regular in the Phillies' outfield in 1948 with Richie
Ashburn and Del Ennis, John appeared briefly with the
Phils in '49 and with the Cards in 1950, and departed from
the scene with a .253 average.

BLAYLOCK, Bob
    Motel manager
    Tulsa, OK

This 6'1", 185 lb. right-handed hurler was around for a
total of 17 games with the Cardinals in 1956 and '59. Although he was only 1-7 lifetime, he did whiff 42 batters in
50 innings. Bob is no kin to Gary Blaylock or Marv
Blaylock below, or they to each other.

BLAYLOCK, Gary
    Kansas City Royals coach

Like Bob Blaylock a right-handed pitcher, Gary split the
1959 season between the Cardinals and Yankees. While
with the Cards, he was a teammate of Bob Blaylock.   4-6

BLAYLOCK, Marv
    Salesman, Maguire Music Co.
    North Little Rock, AR

Thankfully, Marv wasn't a pitcher. He played one game
for the Giants in 1950. Marv later spent three years with
the Phillies, 1955–57, and was their regular first baseman
in 1956.   .235

BLOODWORTH, Jim
   Carpenter, St. Joe Paper Co.
   Apalachicola, FL

A second baseman in the A.L. with the Senators and Tigers during the late 1930s and early 1940s, Jim later spent time with the Pirates and Reds before joining the Phillies during the 1950 season as a 33-year-old "Whiz Kid," or maybe "Fizz Kid."
   Three times he hit exactly .245.   .248

BLYZKA, Mike
   Denver, CO

Along with the distinction of being born on Christmas Day, this "Kris Kringle" was a pitcher for the last St. Louis Browns team in 1953, and the first edition of the Baltimore Orioles in 1954. Those were the only two seasons he went dashing and prancing. He rode out at 3-11, no season to be jolly!

BOKELMANN, Dick
   Employed with an insurance company
   Arlington Heights, IL

Richard Werner Bokelmann was 3-4 as a member of the Cards from 1951–53. The right-handed moundsman won all of his games during the '51 campaign.

BOLGER, Jim
   Office manager for Minutemen
   Cincinnati, OH

An outfielder, Bolger played in two games each in 1950 and '51 as a teenager for his home town Reds. With the Cubs in 1957 he was the National League's top pinch-hitter, going 17-for-48. He closed with the Indians and Phillies in 1959.   .229

BOLLING, Frank
    Staff member, United Way Fund
    Mobile, AL

The better of the two infielding brothers, Frank played in
over 1,500 games, all at second base. He displayed good
power for a keystoner, rapping out 106 home runs from
1954–66. He spent the first portion of his career with the
Tigers before being traded to the Milwaukee Braves in
1961. He ended his career in the team's first year in Atlanta in 1966.   .254

BOLLING, Milt
    Red Sox scout
    Mobile, AL

A shortstop with the Red Sox, 1952–57, he journeyed to
Washington, then to Detroit in '58 where he played briefly
alongside brother Frank in a few games. The Red Sox had
high hopes for Milt when he first came up. However, a fractured elbow in '55 hampered his career. John Bolling, the
uncle of Frank and Milt Bolling, played first base with the
Phils in 1939, and the Dodgers in 1944.   .241

BOLLWEG, Don
    Board of Election Commission
    Wheaton, IL

A left-handed hitting first baseman, Don played sparingly
for the Cards in 1950 and '51. In 1953 he donned the Yankee pinstripes and shared first base duties with Joe Collins
for the World Champions, hitting .297 in 70 games. In
1954 he went to the Philadelphia Athletics, and made his
exit with K.C. in '55.   .243

BOONE, Ray "Ike"
    Boston Red Sox scout

The father of the current Angels' catcher, Bob Boone, Ray
Boone was most productive during the mid-1950s with
Detroit. Early in his career he had the pressure of replac-

ing his manager as the team's shortstop when he took over for Hall of Famer Lou Boudreau with Cleveland. He was traded to the Tigers and moved to third base to make room for rookie Harvey Kuenn at shortstop. Ray was the A.L. RBI leader in 1955 with 116.

Ray Boone set a then A.L. record with four grand slams in 1953, hitting a pair with Cleveland, and then two more for Detroit. In 1961 Jim Gentile of the Orioles connected for five grand slams. Ray also played with the White Sox, A's, Braves, and Red Sox, where he finished in 1960.   .275

BORKOWSKI, Bob
    Parts department,
    Harris-Siebold Printing Co.
    Dayton, OH

Bob was a six-year N.L. outfielder (1950–55) with the Cubs, Reds, and Dodgers. One season as a regular in 1952 with Cincinnati he hit .252, one point above his career mark.   .251

BOROS, Steve
    Oakland A's manager

Signed by the Tigers to a $25,000 bonus out of the University of Michigan, Steve broke in with the Tigers in 1957 and was the regular third baseman in the early 1960s. He culminated his playing career in the mid-sixties with the Cubs and Reds.   .245

BOROWY, Henry Ludwig "Hank"
    Insurance salesman
    Bloomfield, NJ

A right-handed pitcher, Hank's career closed in the early 1950s. He was involved in a bizarre waiver deal during the 1945 season. Borowy had been with the Yankees for three seasons, winning between 14 and 17, and helping them win two A.L. flags. In '45 he was halfway to a 20-game season when he was put on waivers. None of the other A.L.

teams went for him, so he was sold to the N.L. Cubs, where he won 11 more for an overall 21-7 season. He joined Pat Flaherty and "Iron Man" McGinnity as the only pitchers to win 20, split between two leagues. His contribution to the Cubs helped them to win what still remains their last N.L. pennant. He eventually completed his days with the Detroit Tigers. An unusual aspect of his career is that he doubled twice in the same inning on May 5, 1946, while playing for the Cubs.   108-82

BOUCHEE, Ed
    Des Plaines, IL

One of just a handful of Montana-born major leaguers, Ed had his finest campaign in 1957, his first full season in the biggies as the Phillies' first baseman, when he batted .293. Bouchee was traded to the Cubs along with Don Cardwell for Tony Taylor and Cal Neeman in 1960. Ed closed with the original Mets, backing up Marv Throneberry at first base. Bouchee, who had a lifetime .265 average, attended Washington State University.

BOUDREAU, Lou
    Chicago Cubs announcer

The youngest full-time manager in A.L. history at age 24 with the Cleveland Indians, Lou was somewhat back in the limelight in the late 1960s as the father-in-law of controversial 30-game winner Denny McLain. Two years later Boudreau was elected to the Hall of Fame. McLain never will be.

Lou is also the only man ever to play for and manage a major league baseball team and play for and coach a professional basketball team. He coached and played for the Hammond, Indiana, team of the N.B.L., 1938–39. One of his teammates was future UCLA coach John Wooden.

Although he had a solid career as the Indians' shortstop throughout the 1940s, he is best remembered for his great season in 1948 when he hit .355 and had career highs in homers with 18 and RBIs with 106. He's remembered even more for hitting in the one-game playoff against Boston for the A.L. pennant. For all that Yankee shortstop Bucky Dent would do to the Red Sox 30 years later, Lou did even more damage with 2 homers and 4 hits in an 8-3 pennant-winning game.

He broke away in the early fifties with Boston before managing the Red Sox and K.C. A's, and then after a strange shift back near his native Harvey, Illinois, he returned to manage the Cubs. He was working in the broadcast booth for the Cubs when he switched jobs with Charlie Grimm as the field manager.

Boudreau is the only shortstop to collect five extra-base hits in a game. His uniform number, 5, has been retired by the Indians. He was the last "full time" player-manager. As manager he played in a total of 1,207 games.   .295

BOWMAN, Bob
     Sales supervisor,
     Joseph George Liquor Distributors
     San Jose, CA

Bob was a flychaser with the Phillies his entire five years (1955–59) when white bucks and penny loafers were in vogue. Bowman, who had a career .249 average, pitched briefly for the Phils in '59, losing his only decision. He attended San Jose State College.

BOWMAN, Roger
     Upholstery shop owner
     Los Angeles, CA

In the early fifties he pitched two no-hitters in the PCL, including a perfect game in 1954 with Hollywood. Roger made his debut going 2-4 for the Giants in 1951. He was 0-7 for the Pirates in the mid-fifties and 2-11 overall.

BOWSFIELD, Edward O. "Ted"
     Stadium manager
     Seattle Kingdome

A southpaw chucker from 1958–64, Ted was originally with the Red Sox and won just four times in '58, but three of the wins were over the powerful Yankees, whose manager, Casey Stengel, referred to him as "That fella that throws them ground balls." Ted had his best season in 1961, winning 11 for the expansion L.A. Angels organization where he did public relations work before becoming the team's traveling secretary, and then the manager of the Anaheim stadium. He left that job for a similar position at the Seattle Kingdome.   37-39

BOYD, Bob
   Employed with Metro Transit
   Wichita, KS

Nicknamed "Rope" for his line-drive hitting, he played first base for the White Sox and Orioles from the early 1950s to the early '60s. A solid hitter, who four times hit over .300, Bob had a career high of .318 in 1957 for Baltimore, making him the first Oriole to bat .300 playing for an entire season.   .293

BOYER, Clete
   Oakland A's coach

Clete is one of the three brothers who played in the major leagues; two others also played in the minor leagues. Clete, originally a bonus player with the K.C. A's in the mid-fifties, was the Yankees' regular third baseman during the early 1960's. His play at the hot corner was often sensational. His bat was at times suspect. But he did have a power explosion in 1967 after being dealt to Atlanta where he hit 26 homers with 96 RBIs. Eventually he had a falling out with the team's general manager, Paul Richards, and was released. Clete then played at Hawaii in the PCL, where he had the distinction of being the first American professional player ever traded to a Japanese League team (he was dealt to the Tayio Whales for John Werhas).   .242

BOYER, Cloyd
   Toronto Blue Jays minor league pitching instructor

The oldest of the playing brothers was the non-third baseman with the least distinguished career. As a pitcher he
played for the Cardinals, 1949–52, and ended his five-year
jog with K.C. in '55.   20-23

BOYER, Ken
   Died September 7, 1982, at age 51, in St. Louis, MO

The Cardinals' third baseman, 1955–65, Ken actually
started out in organized ball as a pitcher during his first
two years in the minors. In his third year with the Cards in
1957, he was the team's center fielder in over 100 games.
He played a few more games in the outfield the following
season, but the rest of his days were exclusively spent at
third base except for several games played at first at the
end of his career. The arrival of Curt Flood in '58 paved the
way back to the hot corner for Ken. He whacked 282 career
home runs, hitting a total of 24 for four straight years
(1961–64). He was the N.L. MVP in '64.
   When both Ken and Clete homered in game seven of the
1964 World Series, it marked the first time that brothers
connected for home runs in the same World Series game.
                                                          .287

BRADFORD, Bill
   Real estate; also in charge of the irrigation system for
   the Fairfield Bay Golf and Country Club
   Fairfield Bay, AR

Bill waited until he was 32 to debut in the majors. He had
a 9.00 ERA in two innings with the K.C. A's in his first
and last game in 1956.   0-0

BRADSHAW, George
   Horse Shoe, NC

While the nation was caught up in the chlorophyll craze in
1952, George caught ten games for the Senators.   .217

BRADY, Jim
   Norfolk, VA

The Man with a Golden Arm, starring Frank Sinatra, was a box office hit in 1956. It's doubtful that the movie title relates to Jim Brady, who in six games as a 20-year-old for the Tigers, left the diamond with 28.42 ERA. Jim was signed out of Notre Dame by the Tigers.   0-0

BRANCA, Ralph
   Life insurance business
   White Plains, NY

Ralph joined a select company of such Hall of Famers as Lefty Gomez, Bob Feller, Babe Ruth, and Christy Mathewson, because he was a 21-game winner for the 1947 Dodgers at the age of 21. Four years later his name became infamous when he threw the pitch to Bobby Thomson that became "the shot heard 'round the world." Concerning the fatal pitch, Branca commented, "I was trying to waste a fastball, high and inside." With one swing of the bat, Thomson wasted the Flatbush nine and shocked the 34,320 fans at the Polo Grounds that autumn day.
   Ralph never fared well during playoff games, as he also lost a playoff game to the Cardinals in 1946.
   Branca pitched nine seasons for the Dodgers, and he also wore Tiger and Yankee uniforms before his retirement. A basketball star at New York University, he was nicknamed "Hawk" because of his good shooting eye. He is the father-in-law of recent major leaguer Bobby Valentine. Ralph married the daughter of James Mulvey, one of the Brooklyn Dodgers' owners at the time.   88-68

BRANDT, Jackie "Flakey"
   Papillion, NE

A steady, if unspectacular, outfielder from 1956–67, this nail-biting flychaser was given his nickname for a variety of eccentric ways off the field. He was reported to have once taken teammates on a long drive to an ice cream parlor which had many flavors, and had then ordered vanilla

for himself! He came close to hitting .300 as a rookie at
.298. In the early 1960's he was with the Orioles where he
hit .297 in 1961. When a teammate commented that
"things seem to flake off his mind and disappear," the
name "Flakey" was born. .262

BRAZLE, Al
Died October 24, 1973, at age 59, in Grand Junction,
CO

A ten-year member of the St. Louis Cardinals as a left-
handed pitcher, he joined the Cards in 1943 and was 8-2
with a 1.53 ERA, and helped them to the N.L. flag. In his
ten-year stint, which concluded in 1954, he only once lost
more than he won (6-7 in '53) in compiling a lifetime winning percentage of over .600 at 97-64. Al led the league in
saves in 1952 and 1953.

BRECHEEN, Harry "The Cat"
Retired—Former Orioles pitching coach
Ada, OK

He picked up his nickname because of his catlike movements in fielding his position. In a ten-year period with the
Cardinals, 1943–52, Harry had just one losing season. Although his best year was in 1948 when he was 20-7 and led
the N.L. in winning percentage, ERA, and strikeouts, he
has the distinction of being the first left-hander to win
three World Series games in the same series, when he beat
Boston in 1946. His 0.83 ERA in over 32 innings of World
Series work remains the best of all time. 132-92

BRESSOUD, Ed
Junior college physical education teacher and baseball coach in Los Altos, CA

A twelve-year shortstop, Ed came on stage with the Giants
in 1956. He was traded to the Red Sox in '62. The crafty
shortstop had his finest season in Beantown in '64 when he
hit .293. He also played for the Mets and Cardinals at the

end of his playing days. Bressoud was the first player
drafted in Houston Colt history, but never played for them.
Strange as it may seem, Hobie Landrith was the first
player drafted by the Mets, and Landrith and Bressoud are
neighbors today. A graduate of U.C.L.A., Ed closed the
door with a .252 lifetime average.

BREWER, Tom
    Tobacco producer
    Cheraw, SC

A right-handed pitcher, Tom spent all eight years (1954–
61) with the Boston Red Sox. His best season was in 1955
when he went 19-9. He had won 91 big league games for
Boston by the time he was thirty, but he never won or
pitched in another.   91-82

BRICKELL, Fritz
    Died at age 30 on October 15, 1965, in Wichita, KS

A shortstop, Fritz appeared with the Yankees in 1958. He
went to the expansion L.A. Angels in 1961. His father,
Fred Brickell, who died in 1961, was an outfielder in the
N.L. with the Pirates and Phillies, 1926–33.   .182

BRICKNER, Ralph
    Deals with finances for the Traffic and Criminal Divi-
    sions of Hamilton County, Cincinnati, OH

How many pitchers can say they finished with a 2.18
ERA? Ralph can, although he only showed up for 14 games
with a 3-1 log for the Red Sox in 1952.

BRIDEWESER, Jim
    High school teacher
    Hermosa Beach, CA

Jim was signed off the USC campus by the Yankees in the
early fifties, but saw most of his playing time with the Ori-

oles in 1954 and again in 1957. He also played for the Tigers and White Sox.   .252

BRIDGES, Everett "Rocky"
    Manager at Everett, Washington; in the Northwest League

Rocky was a utility infielder with several teams, mostly the Reds, throughout most of the 1950s and early '60s. For the past two decades he has alternated between major league coaching jobs and minor league managerial positions.

One of the more popular characters in all of baseball the past three decades, he's easily recognizable by his big chaw of tobacco. He retired as one of the original Los Angeles Angels.   .247

BRIDGES, Marshall
    Carpenter
    Jackson, MS

Known as a great storyteller who smoked $2.00 cigars, Marshall was used mainly out of the bullpen for the Cards and Reds (1959–61). He joined the Yankees in 1962 where he had his most successful season at 8-4, including 18 saves. He parted at 23-15 with the Senators in '65.

BRIGGS, Johnny
    Orangeville, CA

A right-handed flipper, Johnny began his baseball career, which spanned the years 1956–60, with the Cubs. He was also with the Indians and A's. He is not to be confused with John Briggs, who was an outfielder in the sixties with the Phillies.   9-11

BRIGHT, Harry
    Montreal Expos scout

A utility player who could play first base or third, Harry spent parts of eight seasons in the majors after finally making it to the Pirates in 1958 when he was near 30. In 1963, when he was with the Yankees, he came up as a pinch-hitter in his first World Series game and, as he stated, "The whole country was pulling for me to strike out." Sandy Koufax did strike him out to establish a new World Series mark of 15 strikeouts in a game.   .255

BRINKOPF, Leon
    School administrator
    Cape Girardeau, MO

Leon tiptoed onto the baseball scene in 1952 with the Cubs. He had a .182 batting average, all in nine games for the '52 Cubs.

BRISSIE, Leland Victor "Lou"
    Insurance business
    Mauldin, SC

During World War II with an infantry patrol, Lou was the only survivor in his unit, which was wiped out in a battle zone. However, he nearly lost a leg from injuries. Following several operations over the next couple of years, he was able to resume his career as a pitcher. By 1948 he was a 14-game winner for the Philadelphia Athletics, and won a career high of 16 the following year. He remained in the majors until 1953 with Cleveland. A courageous athlete, he became the National Director of the American Legion baseball program following his playing days.   44-48

BRITTIN, John
    Illinois Board of Education
    Springfield, IL

John qualifies as one of the more obscure "Whiz Kids." He pitched in 3 games in 1950, giving up 3 walks and collecting 3 strikeouts. The following year he appeared in 3 games, and once again collected 3 strikeouts. It would be nice to say that his career record was 3-3, but in all honesty, Jack failed to gain a decision in his brief big league stay.

BRODOWSKI, Dick
Package store employee
Lynn, MA

Dick's life span in the big time occurred between 1952–59 with the Red Sox, Senators, and Indians. The 6'1" right-hander was 9-11 overall.

BROGLIO, Ernie
Warehouseman for a liquor distributor
Sunnyvale, CA

Ernie made his living playing for the Cardinals and Cubs from 1959–1966. In 1964, the curveball ace was traded from the Cards to the Cubs along with Bobby Shantz and Doug Clemons for Lou Brock, Jack Spring, and Paul Toth. Brock went on to become a stolen-base champion, while Ernie just won 14 games with the Cubs before he retired. Broglio shunned the sophomore jinx by going 21-9 in his second season in the biggies.   77-74

BRONSTAD, Jim
Fort Worth, TX

The Rebel, starring Nick Adams, came on the tube in 1959, the same year this rebel from Texas entered the majors. Jim departed with a 1-7 lifetime record with the Yankees ('59) and Senators (1963–64). He was signed out of the University of Texas by the Yankees.

BROSNAN, Jim "Professor"
Free lance writer in Morton Grove, IL

Jim was the first of the diary-keeping relief pitchers in baseball (Jim Bouton and Sparky Lyle would come along later). His book, *The Long Season,* gained a great deal of attention, as did a followup, titled *Pennant Race.* On the

mound he was a respectable relief pitcher who first arrived
with the Cubs in 1954. In '61 he won 10 and saved 16 as a
mainstay out of the Reds' bullpen in their pennant-winning season. He was released by the White Sox in 1963 because his contract stipulated that no writing could be
published during the season. Instead, he signed on with
ABC Radio to do sports commentary; the man who signed
him for that job was a then-little-known Howard Cosell.
Because of his writing skills, and the fact that he sometimes wore a beret and smoked a pipe, the nickname "Professor" was a natural.   55-47

BROVIA, Joe
    Retired
    Santa Cruz, CA

After sixteen years in the minors Joe broke in as a 33-year-
old graybeard with the Reds in 1955. He appeared in 21
games, all as a pinch-hitter, and never played defensively.
It was his only stint in the majors. When he finally received his call to the big time, Joe remarked, "Maybe it's
only for a cup of coffee, but at least when my kids ask me if
I ever was in the big leagues, I'll be able to say, 'Sure.'"
Joe's baseball career was interrupted while serving in the
European theater in World War II. In 1946 he hit in 39
consecutive games playing for Salt Lake City in the Pioneer League. Always a battler, Joe is battling today to re-
cover full use of his legs due to back problems.

BROWN, Alton
    Virginia Beach, VA

A right-handed pitcher, Alton's total statistics read: seven
games, no decisions for the 1951 Senators.

BROWN, Bobby
    Heart surgeon; A.L. president
    Fort Worth, TX

Not many medical students were late starting classes in
the fall semester, but Bobby Brown was while a member of

the Yankees in the 1947 and '49 World Series. Still, he managed to earn his degree in medicine from Tulane in 1950. A third baseman who sometimes played shortstop and second base, he was extremely successful in the "Fall Classic." In '47 he had two doubles, a single, and a walk as a pinch-hitter. In '49 he went 6-for-12. In game one of the '50 Series, he drove home the winning run. Overall he was 18-for-41 for .439 in World Series play.

He was barely thirty when he retired from baseball for a career in medicine with four World Series rings.   .279

BROWN, Dick
Died April 12, 1970, at age 35, in Baltimore, MD

A catcher for the Indians, White Sox, Tigers, and Orioles from 1957–65, Dick had a .244 average. He was a high school catcher for Herb Score in Lake Worth, Fla. Dick developed a brain tumor in 1966, and was forced to retire at 30. Following seemingly successful surgery, he threw out the ceremonial first pitch for the Orioles in the 1966 World Series. The recurrence of the tumor led to his death in 1970 at the age of 35. His younger brother, Larry, was an infielder in the A.L., 1963–1974.

BROWN, Hal "Skinny"
Fuel oil business
Greensboro, NC

Hal began his 14-year tour in 1951. He enjoyed his best years in the late 1950s and early '60s with the Orioles. Hal still holds the team record of hurling 36 consecutive scoreless innings during the 1961 season. The right-hander had a winning career mark until spending his final two seasons with the expansion Astros in '63 and '64 and going 8-26.   85-92

BROWN, Tommy "Buckshot"
   Inspector for the Ford Motor Co.
   Nashville, TN

By his 26th birthday he had played parts of 9 years in the big leagues, but played none after that 1953 season with the Cubs. "Buckshot" was playing shortstop with the Dodgers in August of '44, a few months short of his 17th birthday. The following August of 1945 he became the youngest player to ever hit a home run in the major leagues, when he connected off Preacher Roe, then of the Pirates. Tommy continued playing for the Dodgers on a part-time basis until he was traded to the Phillies in 1951. He closed with the Cubs in 1953, at an age when many players are still hoping to make their first major league roster.

   Tommy once hit three consecutive home runs for the Dodgers. He was called "Buckshot" because as a 16-year-old Dodger shortstop in 1944, he had a strong but erratic arm that "sprayed buckshot" around the field.   .241

BRUCE, Bob
   President of a construction company in Detroit, MI

Right-handed pitcher Bob Bruce began his career in 1959 in his home town of Detroit. In '62 he became a regular in the starting rotation for the expansion Astros. He had fair success, most notably in '64 when he went 15-9, including 4 shutouts. He fell off to 9-18 the following year, and closed with the Braves in '67.   49-71

BRUNER, Jack
   Lincoln, NE

"Pappy," as Jack Bruner was called, was a southpaw chucker who was 2-4 with the White Sox and Browns in 1949 and '50.

BRUNET, George
   Pitching in Mexican League

This lefty chucker, who spent 15 years in the majors with
several teams in both leagues, began his career with the
Kansas City A's in the mid-fifties. His most successful
years were losing ones in the mid-sixties with the Angels.
He led the A.L. in losses in both 1967 and '68 despite posting impressive ERAs, and in '68 threw five shutouts.

He's still pitching, a quarter of a century later (at age
49), in his twelfth season in Mexico.   69-93

BRUTON, Bill
   Chrysler Corporation executive
   Pontiac, MI

Bill is the son-in-law of William "Judy" Johnson, former
great third baseman in the Negro Leagues, who was
elected to the Hall of Fame in 1975.

When Bruton was scouted by John Ogden in 1949, he
was already 28 years of age. Although Ogden felt that
Bruton could make the majors with his great speed and
ability to hit, he felt that no team would be interested in a
28-year-old. As the story goes, Ogden took ten years off
Bruton's life and listed him as 18. When he reached the big
time in 1953 with the Milwaukee Braves, he was listed as
a 24-year-old rookie. If he was truly 34, then it becomes
quite a feat for a man to lead the league in stolen bases his
first three years in the league while in his mid-thirties.

Whether he was 24 or 34 at the time, it was the start of
a fine career (which lasted 11 years) when his opening
day home run gave the Braves a victory in their home
opener in Milwaukee after the franchise was moved
from Boston.

Bruton is also one of just two players to ever hit a pair of
bases-loaded triples in one game. Bill's big day came on
August 2, 1959, in a Milwaukee Braves uniform. In the '58
World Series, he topped all batters, going 7-for-17.   .273

BUCHA, Johnny
    Mink farmer
    Danielsville, PA

Johnny was a catcher with the Cubs in 1948 and '50. He hooked on with the Tigers in '53. In 84 games he batted .205.

BUDDIN, Don
    Electronics salesman
    Fountain Inn, SC

Don was the Red Sox shortstop from 1956–61. On July 11, 1959, Buddin hit a grand-slam home run in the tenth inning to defeat the Yankees, 8-4. He was traded to the Houston Colts for Ed Bressoud on November 26, 1961.
                                                                    .241

BUHL, Bob
    Maintenance manager in a trailer camp
    Kissimmee, FL

A right-handed pitcher in the N.L. from 1953–67, Bob had enough fine seasons to win 166 games. However, two factors obstructed what was generally a successful job of pitching. First, his best seasons when he won 18 games two years in a row in the mid-fifties were overshadowed by the presence of his other teammates, Warren Spahn and Lew Burdette.

The other factor was his total futility with a bat in his hands. Buhl's career hitting record shows a .089 average, with the 1962 season a total loss at 0-for-70.   166-132

BULLARD, George
    Retired stationary engineer
    Danvers, MA

George Bullard, a shortstop, appeared in four games with the Detroit Tigers in 1954.   .000

BUNNING, Jim
Republican state senator in Kentucky; defeated in 1983 gubernatorial race; player agent

This former outstanding right-hander has won elections in politics, but as yet has not been elected to Cooperstown, despite some great credentials. He was a 20-game winner only once (1957 with Detroit in his first year as a regular starter), but on four occasions won 19. His intimidating sidearm motion helped Jim to 224 wins, including over 100 in each league. He led both circuits in strikeouts and threw a no-hitter in each league. One of his no-hitters was a perfect game against the Mets on June 21, 1964. It was the first complete perfect game in the N.L. in 84 years as the Phils blanked the Mets, 6-0, in the opener of a doubleheader.

Bunning struck out a total of 3,643 batters in organized baseball. He collected 2,855 K's in the majors and 788 in the minors. Jim's brilliant career was marred only by failure to participate on a pennant winner.

Bunning won the first game ever played at Veterans Stadium in Philadelphia on April 10, 1971, when the Phils beat the Expos, 4-1. Jim is a graduate of Xavier U. in Ohio.

224-184

BURBRINK, Nelson
Milwaukee Brewers scout

Nelson caught 58 games with the Cardinals and hit .276 in 1955, his only season in the big arena.

BURDETTE, Lew
Public relations specialist for a cable TV company in Athens, GA

Selva Lewis Burdette was around from 1950–67. When he defeated the Yankees three times in the 1957 World Series for Milwaukee, he did it against the team he had originally come up with. After just a brief stay with the Yankees, the right-hander was traded away for veteran hurler Johnny Sain. Although Sain helped the Yankees to a cou-

ple of pennants, the Braves never regretted the deal. Two
of his three World Series wins that fall were shutouts.
That's incredible when you consider the Yankees were
shut out only twice all year. He probably pitched the most
under-publicized 13-inning shutout in the history of baseball as he was the victim in the game in which Harvey
Haddix pitched 12 perfect innings. Burdette threw a no-
hitter of his own the following season, winning 1-0 over the
Phillies.

Burdette was widely accused of throwing the spitball
during his successful 203-144 career.

BURGESS, Forrest "Smoky"
Atlanta Braves hitting instructor

A catcher from 1949–67, "Smoky" became one of the
premier pinch-hitters ever. His career total of 145 successful pinch-hits was the all-time record until broken
by Manny Mota in 1979. He started in the N.L. with the
Cubs, then went to the Phillies, Reds, and Pirates. In '59
he helped Pittsburgh to the N.L. pennant, and hit .333
in the World Series. As a member of the White Sox in
1965 he was 20-for-65 off the bench. In '66 he was 21-for-66
in his role as a pinch-hitter.

He was noted for his talking to batters while catching.
Richie Ashburn once remarked, "Smoky's a .300 hitter,
but a .400 talker." Forrest Burgess was nicknamed after
his father, who was also called "Smoky."   .295

BURGESS, Tom
Manager of Oklahoma City in the American Association

This Canadian-born first baseman was in 17 games for the
Cardinals in 1954, struggling at a .048 pace (1-21). Tom
gave it another try eight years later, playing 87 games for
the expansion Los Angeles Angels. He upped his average
to .196 and said goodbye.   .177

BURK, Mack
   Salesman, Nunn Electrical Supplies
   Houston, TX

Mack was signed to a $45,000 bonus by the Phillies in 1955. As a 21-year-old catcher, he singled in his only plate appearance for the Phillies in 1956. Two years later he batted unsuccessfully one more time to compile a career .500 average, going one-for-two. A versatile athlete, Mack played basketball for the Texas Longhorns.

BURKE, Leo
   Liquor store owner
   Hagerstown, MD

Defensively, Leo could be called "Mr. Utility," as he played every position on the diamond except that of pitcher in parts of seven seasons (1958–65) with the Orioles, Angels, Cardinals, and Cubs. Offensively, Leo could be called "Mr. Futility" with a lifetime .239 average. Leo was a football player at VPI before shedding his shoulder pads for sliding pads.

BURNETTE, Wally
   Owns Burnette's Grocery and Sandwich Shop
   Blairs, VA

In 1956, K.C. A's fans had their eyes on Wally Burnette. But Wally was gone after 1958, pitching three seasons for K.C. with a 14-21 record.

BURNSIDE, Pete
   High school teacher and coach
   Wilmette, IL

Peter Willits Burnside has to rank as one of the more intellectual men in this legion of fifties players. A Dartmouth graduate, Pete was a lefty hurler from 1955–63 with the Giants, Tigers, Senators, and Orioles, finishing 19-36.

BURRIS, Paul
   Huntersville, NC

Paul caught for the Boston Braves in 1948, '50, and '52, and then briefly for the Milwaukee Braves in '53.   .219

BURTON, Ellis
   Bank manager
   Burbank, CA

Ellis was around from 1958–65 as a switch-hitting outfielder with the Cardinals, Indians, and Cubs. He once hit home runs from each side of the plate in the same inning in an International League game, a feat duplicated only once in professional baseball history.   .216

BURTSCHY, Ed "Moe"
   Sales representative for a trucking company
   Cincinnati, OH

In parts of five seasons (beginning in 1950), Moe was with the Philadelphia and K.C. Athletics. He racked up 10 wins against 6 losses, and made his last bus stop in '56.

BUSBY, Jim
   White Sox scout; orange grove owner, Yalaha, FL

A quarterback on the 1945 TCU Cotton Bowl team before turning to professional baseball, Jim was one of the game's outstanding defensive players in centerfield throughout the 1950s. For three straight years, from 1952–54, he led all A.L. outfielders in putouts. His best season at the plate was in 1953 while with the Senators, when he hit .312. But he did have a couple of pretty big days on July 5th and 6th of '56 with the Indians when he hit grand-slam home runs on consecutive days. Jim broke in with the White Sox and retired as an original Houston Colt 45.   .263

BUZHARDT, John
    Kodak Company foreman
    Prosperity, SC

John was an eleven-year moundsman whose best season
came in 1965 with the White Sox when he won 13 games.
In 1961 he struggled along with his teammates as a member of the inept Phillies. When he won a game for them on
July 28th it would be their last victory for over three
weeks (or 23 games)—a modern-day record for consecutive
losses by a major league club. Finally on August 20th the
Phillies beat Milwaukee, 7-4, with Buzhardt as the winning pitcher. 71-96

BYERLY, Bud
    Construction company foreman
    St. Louis, MO

Eldred "Bud" Byerly was primarily a relief pitcher for
eleven years in and out of the majors from 1943–60. He
was 22-22 overall with the Cardinals, Reds, Senators, Red
Sox, and Giants.

BYRD, Harry
    Mechanic
    Darlington, SC

Harry was selected A.L. Rookie of the Year for the Philadelphia Athletics in 1952. He epitomized the so-called
sophomore jinx the following year, going 11-20.

Harry went to the Yankees in '54 and was 9-7 for the
second-place Yanks. From 1955–57 he jumped around
with the Orioles, White Sox, and Tigers, where he completed a 46-54 career.

BYRNE, Tommy
　　Former mayor of Wake Forest, N.C.; owner of Wake
　　Forest Country Club
　　Wake Forest, NC

This southpaw chucker, in and out of the majors from 1943
to 1957, was able to overcome his wildness enough to have
a relatively good career. His wildness was at its peak in a
'51 game while pitching for the Browns, when he walked
16 in 13 innings. For five straight seasons (1948–52) he led
the A.L. in hitting batters. Three of those years he led the
league in walks. He still managed to win 15 games in both
1949 and 1950. After drifting around the league and making a trip to the minors, he returned in 1955 and had what
may have been his best season (at 16-5, with an ERA close
to 3.00) in helping the Yankees regain the A.L. championship. A good hitting pitcher, he twice hit grand-slam
homers.   85-69

C

CABALLERO, Ralph "Putsy"
　　Owner of a pest control company
　　New Orleans, LA

"Putsy" broke in as a 16-year-old rookie in 1944 with the
Phillies. He shows a .228 average for his eight years as a
utility infielder in the big top.

CAFFIE, Joe
　　Warren, OH

Joe Caffie had a "Cup of Caffie" in parts of two seasons
with the Indians in 1956 and '57. In 1957, while playing
for Buffalo of the International League, he won one thousand dollars for hitting a bottle cap on a Pepsi-Cola sign.
                                                           .291

CAIN, Bob "Sugar"
  Retired salesman for Kraft Food Co.
  Euclid, OH

"Sugar" was a southpaw chucker with the White Sox, Tigers, and Browns (1949–54). Several highlights dot his career, but the one that he is best remembered for is being the pitcher for the Tigers in 1951 when Bill Veeck sent Eddie Gaedel, a midget, up to the plate for the St. Louis Browns. Cain walked Gaedel on four pitches.

There were several other notable days for Bob. His first major league start was a most impressive one; a 15-0 shutout over the A.L. champions at Yankee Stadium. In a 1952 game in which he was hurling for the Browns, he beat the great Bob Feller, 1-0, in a battle of one-hitters. It was the first time since 1906 that pitchers had thrown one-hitters in the same game. A sweet victory for "Sugar" Cain.

37-44

CALDERONE, Sam
  Liquor salesman
  Beverly, NJ

Sam broke in with the Giants in 1950. A catcher who also saw action with the Milwaukee Braves in '54, Calderone batted .291 in 91 big league games.

CALLISON, Johnny
  Automobile salesman
  Glenside, PA

One of the youngest of those who played during the 1950s, Johnny broke in with the White Sox in the late fifties while still just 19 years of age. He was at his peak in the early '60s with the Phillies. Callison established a major league record by leading his league in assists as an outfielder for four straight years, from 1962–65. In 1968 he went the entire season without committing an error. He was the hero of the 1964 All-Star Game, winning it for the N.L. with a home run in the bottom of the ninth inning. Callison was awarded the first Arch Ward Memorial

Trophy as the Classic's Most Valuable Player. He played for the Cubs and Yankees in the early seventies and batted .264 in 1,886 games.

CALVERT, Paul
Sherbrooke, Quebec

A Canadian-born right-handed chucker, Paul led the A.L. in losses in 1949, going 6-17 for the Senators. He also pitched for the Indians and Tigers in a career which ended in 1951.   9-22

CAMPANELLA, Roy
Public relations for the L.A. Dodgers

The Brooklyn Dodgers' catcher from 1948–57, Roy once hit three homers in a game off Reds' lefty Ken Raffensberger in Cincinnati, with each homer hitting a sign on a clothing store across the street (which won him a new suit for each of the three blasts).

Roy's auto accident in January of 1958 came in a car he was borrowing. He still owns the liquor store he was heading home from the night of the accident. Roy's book, *It's Great to be Alive*, was made into a TV movie many years later. Despite only a 10-year career, his Hall of Fame credentials are obvious. Along with Stan Musial he was the only three-time N.L. MVP (1951, '53, '55), combining power at the plate (242 homers) with a rifle arm behind the plate.

When asked about his days in a Dodger uniform, Campy responded with a smile, "I enjoyed those days at Ebbets Field. I don't think there were any baseball fans like the ones we had there. My biggest thrill in baseball was just putting on a Dodger uniform. Playing the Giants was a little special, playing the Yankees was a little special-special."

Roy was elected to the Hall of Fame in 1969.   .276

CAMPBELL, Paul
> Cincinnati Reds scout
> Fairfield Glade, TN

A first baseman, Paul qualifies for this mention by appearing in three games for the Tigers in 1950. However, his career began in 1941 with the Red Sox, for whom he played in 1941, '42, and '46. He journeyed to the Motor City in '48.   .255

CAMPOS, Frank
> Manager, Avis Rent-A-Car
> Miami, FL

Frank came up in 1951 with the Senators. The Cuban-born flychaser came out of the gate strongly, but then fell off the next two seasons and disappeared.   .279

CANDINI, Milo
> Liquor store owner
> Manteca, CA

Milo went 11-7 as a rookie for the Senators in 1943. He remained in Washington until 1950 when he went to the Phillies (where he ended his playing days in '51), winning one game each year. As a member of the 1950 Phillies' "Whiz Kids," he recalled Dick Sisler's dramatic home run against the Dodgers on the final day of the season: "Sisler's home run was a bit painful. The dugouts in Ebbets Field were low. I jumped up when Dick hit that ball and conked myself on the head pretty good." Milo completed his trip, taking home a 26-21 log and an Excedrin 735!

CARDWELL, Don
> Fleet and leasing manager
> Parkway Ford
> Winston-Salem, NC

This big right-hander played from 1957–70, but only two of the 14 were winning seasons. One of the losing years was in 1960, at 9-16. However, he accomplished something that year that no other pitcher ever has. He threw a no-hitter for the Cubs just two days after being dealt to them from the Phillies. It's the only time in major league history that a pitcher has thrown a no-hitter in his first start for his new team. Don managed to last long enough to be a part of the 1969 "Miracle" Mets pitching staff, for whom he won 8 games.   102-138

CAREY, Andy
    Insurance business
    Newport Beach, CA

Andy signed for a $60,000 bonus out of St. Mary's College in California. In 1954 he had his best year, hitting .302 in 122 games as the Yankees' regular third baseman.

He married a movie actress named Lucy Marlowe during his baseball playing days. Like so many other Yankee infielders of the era (Gil McDougald, Bobby Brown, Bobby Richardson, and Tony Kubek), Carey retired from the game at a relatively young age (just 31 when he departed for a stock brokerage business in southern California in 1962) after also playing for the A's, White Sox, and Dodgers.   .260

CARLSEN, Don
    Vice-president-manager, Newhard, Cook and Co.
    Littleton, CO

Don was with the Cubs and Pirates in 1948, '51, and '52. The right-hander appeared in a slim total of 13 games, and was 2-4 lifetime.

CARMEL, Duke
    Salesman, Capitol Distributors
    Hauppauge, NY

John "Duke" Wayne rode around in *Rio Bravo* in 1959 while Leon "Duke" Carmel jumped around as a first baseman/outfielder with the Cards, Mets, and Yanks from

1959–65. "Duke" was .211 in 124 contests. No—Duke
Carmel wasn't a candy bar.

CARRASQUEL, Alfonso "Chico"

Distributor for sporting goods firm, and active in
youth baseball programs in his native Venezuela

He had the dubious distinction of having to replace the
White Sox' greatest shortstop of all time (Luke Appling),
when he took over the position in 1950. Chico did a credit-
able defensive job until replaced in 1956 by Luis Aparicio.
In 1951 he set a major league mark of 53 straight games
without an error.

The shortstop made his exit with Baltimore in 1959. Chico
made stops at Cleveland, K.C., and Baltimore before calling
it quits after 1,325 games and a .258 swatting average.

CARREON, Camilo

City parks and recreation department
Tucson, AZ

In 1959, Camilo came up with the White Sox as a catcher.
He also played for the Indians and Orioles in a career
which lasted until 1966.   .264

CARROLL, Tom

Career diplomat as a foreign service officer in Bra-
silia, Brazil

A highly paid bonus baby out of Notre Dame, Tom saw limited action as a shortstop with the Yankees in 1955–56. After military service he returned to the majors with the A's
in 1959 and wound up his brief 64-game career despite an
overall batting average of an even .300.

CARSWELL, Frank

Carmine, Tex.

Frank played the outfield in 16 games as a 33-year-old for the
1953 Tigers. This was his only act in the big show.   .267

CASALE, Jerry
    Owns an Italian restaurant called "Pinos" on 34th
    St., in Manhattan

Jerry opened the door in 1958, but pitched his first full season the following year with the Red Sox. Casale had the
distinction of defeating each rival team that year. He also
spent time with the Angels and Tigers in an abbreviated
career which lasted from 1958–62. Jerry's best year was in
'59 when he went 13-8.   17-24

CASH, Norm
    Broadcaster, Detroit Tigers
    Detroit, MI

The Detroit Tigers' first baseman throughout the 1960s, he
was a member of the 1959 "Go-Go" White Sox A.L. champions. An outstanding halfback at Sul Ross State University in
Texas, Norm was drafted by the Chicago Bears of the N.F.L.,
but chose a career in professional baseball.
    He was traded from the White Sox to the Tigers at the
end of spring training in 1960. The transaction was completely overshadowed by the trade of Harvey Kuenn and
Rocky Colavito a few days later. Another overlooked aspect of Cash's career was his awesome 1961 season. In the
year that Roger Maris broke Babe Ruth's home run record,
Cash led the A.L. in hitting at .361, while hitting 41
homers, and driving in 132 runs. The following season he
suffered a drop of 118 points to .243. Although he had a
fine career, he never did hit .300 again, nor drive in 100
runs in a season.   .271

CASTIGLIONE, Pete
    Postal employee
    Pompano Beach, FL

Pete was an infielder in the N.L. with the Pirates and Cardinals for eight campaigns from 1947–54. Used primarily
at third base, Castiglione also played other infield positions. In 1950 he made one error at first base, two errors at

second base, three errors at third base, and four at shortstop. .255

CASTLEMAN, Foster
Cincinnati, OH

Lassie made her TV debut in 1954, the same year Foster
made his with the Giants. A utility infielder with the
Giants from 1954–57, he ended his playing days plagued
by bad knees at Baltimore in '58. .205

CAUSEY, Wayne
Kansas City Royals scouting supervisor

James Wayne Causey had an eleven year cruise that
spanned the years 1955–68 with the Orioles, K.C. A's,
White Sox, Angels, and Atlanta Braves. The well-traveled
infielder had his best seasons in '63 and '64 as a full-time
shortstop for Kansas City, hitting .280 and .281 respectively. .252

CAVARETTA, Phil
N.Y. Mets hitting instructor

A Chicago Cubs first baseman for 20 years (1934–53), his
career is the only one to span the Babe Ruth-Hank Aaron
gap. He retired after the 1953 season with the Cubs with
1,953 at-bats. However he then played from 1954–55 with
the White Sox. He was just 19 when he played in the World
Series for the Cubs, the second youngest player to ever appear in the "Fall Classic." Fred Lindstrom was a few
months short of 19 when he played for the N.Y. Giants in
the 1924 World Series.

In his first game he hit a home run to give the Cubs a 1-0
win. In 1945 he was the N.L. batting champion and MVP
in the last Cubs pennant-winning season. In July 1951, he
replaced Frankie Frisch as the Cubs' manager. Just a
week later (in his new role as player-manager) he led the

Cubs to a win in the first game of a twin bill against the Phillies, with 3 RBIs. He then inserted himself as a pinch-hitter in the late innings of the nightcap and hit a grand slam to lead the Cubs to a come-from-behind win. Fired in spring training of 1954, he signed on as a player with the White Sox where he ended it all in 1955.

In the 1944 All-Star Game, Phil reached base safely five times on a triple, single, and three walks. Cavaretta completed his impressive career with a .293 average.

CECCARELLI, Art
    High school teacher
    Milford, Conn.

Art was a lefty hurler who had his day in the sun between 1955–60 with the K.C. A's, Orioles, and Cubs, finishing 9-18. Plagued by injuries throughout his career, he said, "My biggest thrill was shutting out the Dodgers at the Los Angeles Coliseum."

CEPEDA, Orlando "The Baby Bull"
    Runs a baseball school
    San Juan, PR

The N.L. Rookie of the Year in 1958 with the San Francisco Giants, his first major league home run was also the second ever hit in a big league game on the West Coast (in April of 1958). He won the N.L. home-run title with 46 in 1961. Traded to the Cardinals early in 1966, he was the N.L. MVP, leading the Cardinals to the N.L. flag in 1967. He had his post-playing-day problems in the 1970s, spending some time in prison for narcotics dealings.

Orlando's father was a baseball star in Puerto Rico, and was nicknamed "The Bull." When Cepeda gained fame as a ballplayer, he became known as the "Baby Bull." Teammates also called him "Perucho."   .297

CERV, Bob
    Baseball coach at Sioux-Empire College
    Hawarden, IA

A college basketball player at the University of Nebraska
in the late 1940s, Bob was one of several players who divided playing time between the Yankees and Kansas City
A's in the 1950s. Originally a Yankee (from 1951–56), he
had his most productive seasons in the late 1950s with
Kansas City; most notably in '58 with 38 homers and 104
RBIs. He returned to the Yankees during the 1960 season.
    Cerv again returned to the Yankees in '61 after playing
briefly for the expansion L.A. Angels. Bob packed his suitcase for good after playing briefly with Houston in 1962.
He must have been a favorite with the umpires in '58
when he suffered a broken jaw and had his mouth wired
shut for a month. The mute Cerv continued playing, wires
and all.   .276

CHAKALES, Bob
    President of Quality Golf, Inc.,
    Richmond, VA

From 1951–57, Bob was trying to get batters out in the
A.L., playing for the Indians, Orioles, White Sox, Senators, and Red Sox.   15-25

CHAMBERS, Cliff
    Library services company
    Boise, ID

A product of Washington State University, Cliff was a
southpaw flipper with the Cubs, Pirates, and Cardinals.
Pitching for the Pirates on May 6, 1951, he hurled a no-
hitter in the second game of a twin bill at Boston. The 3-0
victory was the first no-hitter by a Pirates' pitcher since
Nick Maddox in 1907. The win was also the last for Chambers in a Pirate uniform. Less than a month later he was
traded to St. Louis, where he finished a 48-53 career that
lasted from 1948–53.

CHAPMAN, Sam
   Bay Area Air Quality District—industrial inspector
   Tiburon, CA

A star football player at the University of California in
1938, Sam was the Philadelphia A's regular outfielder
from the late 1930s through the 1950 season. He missed
three full seasons and most of a fourth in the mid-forties
due to military service in World War II. His one outstanding season came in 1941 when he hit .322 with 25 homers,
and 106 RBIs. After 11 years of playing for Connie Mack,
he was traded to Cleveland, where he wound up his career
in 1951. He is not related to another better-remembered
outfielder named Ben Chapman, whose career in the
majors lasted from 1930–46.   .266

CHENEY, Tom
   Truck driver for Green's Propane
   Leesburg, GA

Tom won just 19 games in a career which lasted parts of
seasons from 1957–66. However, he had one spectacular
performance as a member of the expansion Washington
Senators in September 1962, when he struck out more batters in a major league game than any other pitcher in history. Pitching against the Baltimore Orioles, he had 12
strikeouts after 9 innings. He went the entire distance in
the game, which lasted 16 innings, and wound up striking
out 21. Tom won the game, 2-1, allowing 10 hits while
throwing 238 pitches.   19-29

CHESNES, Bob
   Died May 23, 1979, at age 58, in Everett, WA

Bob completed his 3-year career at 24-22, all with the Pirates. The chucker went 14-6 during his freshman year in
1948.

CHIPMAN, Bob
>Died November 8, 1973, in Huntington, NY, at age 55

A left-handed pitcher, Bob spent 12 seasons in the big time with the Dodgers, Cubs, and Braves (1941–52), logging a respectable 51-46.

CHITI, Harry
>Sheriff's Dept.
>Community Relations Bureau
>Memphis, TN

Harry appeared in the biggies from 1950–62. He was the youngest player in the N.L. in the '50 and '51 seasons when he made brief appearances for the Cubs at just 17 and 18 years of age. The journeyman catcher, who also played with the K.C. A's, Tigers, and Mets, holds the dubious distinction of being traded to the Mets by the Tigers for a player to be named later. At the end of the season the Mets fulfilled their part of the deal by sending Chiti back to Detroit as the player to be named later. In other words, Harry Chiti was traded for Harry Chiti.   .238

CHITTUM, Nelson
>Postal inspector
>Muncie, IN

Nelson's trip was short and sweet. A right-handed pitcher, he lost his only decision with the Cards in 1958, but in '59 he won all three decisions and posted an outstanding 1.19 ERA in 21 games for the Red Sox.   3-1

CHRISLEY, Barbra O'Neil "Neil"
>Senior account agent
>All-State Insurance Company
>Greenwood, SC

Certainly one of the stranger names of the fifties, Neil played in the garden with the Senators and Tigers in the late 1950s, and finished his tour of duty with the Milwaukee Braves in 1961. He came to the major leagues after leading the American Association with 40 home runs for Louisville in 1956.   .210

CHRISTOPHER, Joe
Runs a baseball school in the Virgin Islands

This speedy outfielder from the Virgin Islands broke in with the Pirates in 1959. He was a member of the original Mets in 1962, and had his best season with them in 1964 when he hit an even .300 in 154 games. Joe departed in 1966 as a member of the Red Sox. He is one of six players in major league history to appear in two perfect games. Joe played for Pittsburgh in the 1959 game in which the Pirates' Harvey Haddix pitched 12 perfect innings against the Milwaukee Braves, and he played for the Mets in the 1964 game in which Jim Bunning of the Phillies was perfect.   .260

CHURCH, Emory "Bubba"
Manufacturer's representative for medical-surgical supplies
Birmingham, AL

Bubba broke in with an 8-6 mark as one of the Phillies' "Whiz Kids." He enjoyed his best season the following year with 15 wins. Church went from the Phils to the Reds for Johnny Wyrostek and Kent Peterson in 1952. He also pitched for the Cubs before hanging up his spikes at 36-37.

CHURN, Clarence Nottingham "Chuck"
Farmer
Townsend, VA

From 1957–59 this right-hander was 3-2 overall with the Pirates, Indians, and champion Dodgers. He was the winning pitcher in the game that broke the long winning streak of Pirates relief ace Elroy Face who had won 17 consecutive games in '59 (in addition to 5 in a row at the end of the '58 season).

CIAFFONE, Larry
   Sales division, Pitney-Bowes Corp.
   Brooklyn, NY

In 1951 Larry Ciaffone played in five games with the Cardinals. The fledgling Cardinal was hitless in five attempts.

CICOTTE, Al
   Insurance agent in Westland, MI, at the time of his
   death on November 29, 1982, at the age of 52

The nephew of Eddie Cicotte (one of the top pitchers in the
A.L. early in the century), Al was a right-handed hurler
with several teams (1957–62), starting with the Yankees
in '57, and closing with the expansion Astros in '62. When
the lights went out he was 10-13.

CIMOLI, Gino
   United Parcel driver
   Tiburon, CA

A ten-year outfielder with several teams, Gino started
with the Dodgers in Brooklyn, in 1956. He lasted three
years with the "Bums" through their first season in L.A.
in '58. In 1960 he was a semi-regular in over 100 games
with the World Series champion Pirates. Gino moved over
to the A.L. where he was a regular member of the K.C. A's
outfield from 1962–63, leading the league in triples (15) in
1962. The handsome flychaser completed his playing days
in 1965 with the California Angels.   .265

CLARK, Allie
   Iron construction worker
   South Amboy, NJ

Allie spent 7 years as a part-time outfielder with four different A.L. teams (1947–53). In '47 he was with the World
Champion Yankees. Allie hit .373 in limited action in
pinstripes that year, and was 1-for-2 in the World Series.
The following year he had the distinction of playing for

two different teams which won World Series in his first two years in the majors as he hit over .300 in 80 games with the 1948 Indians.   .262

CLARK, Mel
Insurance and investment business
Point Pleasant, WV

A part-time outfielder for the Phillies, 1951–55, Mel hit for such averages as .323, .335, and .298 in his first three seasons, but was never able to win a regular starting job. His last year was spent with the Tigers in 1957 when he appeared in five games.   .227

CLARK, Mike
Bartender at The Pub
Pennsauken, NJ

In 1952 Mike made his first appearance with the Cardinals. He won his only three decisions with them between 1952 and '53.

CLARK, Phil
Assistant principal, Merry Acres High School
Albany, GA

While Dick Clark was spinning records on American Bandstand in the late fifties, Phil Clark lost his only two decisions with the Cards in 1958–59.

CLARKE, Vibert
Died June 14, 1970, at age 50, in Cristobal, Canal Zone

In 1955, Vibert saved two games for the Washington Senators, who could have used a few more as they finished last with a 53-101 mark.

CLARKSON, Jim
>   Retired, former glass plant employee
>   Jeanette, PA

"Buster" was an infielder in 14 games for the Boston Braves in 1952, going 5-25 for a .200 average. That shouldn't have been too difficult for the "Quiz Kids," who appeared on NBC, to figure.   .200

CLEMENTE, Roberto
>   Died December 31, 1972, at age 38 in a plane crash in
>   San Juan, PR

Roberto had a brilliant 18-year career with the Pittsburgh Pirates (1955–72). He was elected to the Hall of Fame in a special election in the spring of 1973.

Clemente might have been a member of the Dodgers organization had he not gone unprotected on their Montreal AAA roster following the 1954 season when he hit just .257 in the International League. Along with Hank Bauer, he was the only player to hit safely in all seven games of the World Series twice. He did it in 1960 and 1971. Among his distinctions, he once hit 3 triples in a game in 1958. His last hit of his major league career and the last of the 1972 season was number 3,000 of his career, coming against the Mets.

During the 1956 season he hit an inside-the-park grand-slam home run. Roberto wore number 21, the same number as Arky Vaughan, the great Pirates' shortstop who died in a boating accident in 1952, a few years after he retired from the majors.   .317

CLEVENGER, Truman "Tex"
>   Automobile dealership
>   Porterville, CA

How many guys can say they broke Billy Martin's jaw? Tex can—he hit the volatile Martin with a wild pitch. Tex was around from 1954–62 with the Red Sox, Senators, Angels, and Yankees. He led the league in appearances (55) in '58 with the Senators, and finished 36-37 overall.

In a game played on May 11, 1958, at Yankee Stadium, Clevenger, who was pitching for the Senators, was struck by a line drive hit by Elston Howard in the seventh inning. The ball caromed off his leg into foul territory near first base. First baseman Norm Zauchin fielded the ball and tossed it to Clevenger covering first base, giving "Tex" both an assist and a putout on the same play.

COAN, Gil
> Insurance business
> Brevard, NC

A fleet-footed outfielder from 1946–56, Gil had his two finest seasons in 1950 and '51, when he hit .303 each year for the Washington Senators. In a 1951 game he hit two triples in one inning, the last player in the big leagues to do so.

COATES, Jim
> Shipyard employee
> Newport News, VA

This tall right-handed pitcher played a key role as a spot starter and long reliever with the Yankee championship teams in 1960–61. He was 13-3 and 11-5 those two years, and overall had a fine 37-15 record from 1959–62 with the Yankees.

Coates also wore the uniforms of the Senators, Reds, and Angels, going out 43-22.

COHEN, Hy
> High school teacher and baseball coach at Birmingham High School, CA; also owner of a family business-home accessories store
> Encino, CA

Appearing in seven games on the mound for the Cubs in 1955, Hy failed to gain a decision, and walked away with a 7.94 ERA.

COKER, Jim
   Rancher
   Throckmorton, TX

Jim spent parts of nine seasons (1958–67) behind the dish with the Phils, Giants, and Reds. He compiled a .231 average. Coker played football and basketball at Furman University before signing a pro contract with the Phils.

COLAVITO, Rocco Domenico "Rocky"
   Released as Kansas City Royals hitting coach following the 1983 season

Voted in 1975 in a poll of Cleveland fans as the "Most Memorable Personality" in the team's history, Rocky's career is an interesting one. He hit 41 homers in 1958, then a league-leading 42 in 1959. Rocky was then involved in a controversial trade to Detroit for the A.L. batting champion, Harvey Kuenn. Indian fans were irate over the trade of their popular home-run hero. In his return to Cleveland (playing for the Tigers) he went 0-for-6, striking out 4 times, hitting into a double play, and popping out. But the fans were still upset that he had been traded. In '59 he won the A.L. home-run title, but was at the bottom of the list in triples (with none) in nearly 600 at-bats. Four of his homers in that '59 season came in one game against Baltimore. 1961 was his biggest power season with 45 homers and 140 RBIs. Colavito went through the entire 1965 season without committing an error in the outfield after returning to Cleveland after one season in K.C.

   Another "perfect" aspect of his career was as a pitcher. In five innings overall, he was 1-0, with an ERA of 0.00. The win came as a member of the Yankees, his final team in 1968. .266

COLE, Dave
   Operates a Mack Truck outlet
   Hagerstown, MD

Dave was on the mound from 1950–55 with the Braves, Cubs, and Phils. 6-18

COLE, Dick
>   Central Scouting Bureau
>   Huntington Beach, CA

This bespectacled infielder had a six-year N.L. career with
the Cards, Pirates, and Braves. He wound up his playing
days in 1957.   .249

COLEMAN, Gordy
>   Director of Speaker's Bureau for the Cincinnati Reds

A former football player at Duke University, Coleman was
the Reds' regular first baseman during the early 60s.
Gordy broke in with the Indians in 1959. His 26 homers
and 87 RBIs helped the Reds to the N.L. flag in 1961.   .273

COLEMAN, Jerry
>   San Diego Padres announcer

As was the case with Ted Williams, Jerry twice had his career interrupted by military duty. A Marine Corps bomber
pilot with over 100 missions to his credit in WW II and the
Korean conflict, Jerry was in the service in the second
World War before playing in the majors. Coleman was the
Yankee regular second baseman on three consecutive
world championship teams from 1949–51.

   A lifetime .263 hitter, Jerry saved his best hitting for
last, going 8-for-22 for a .364 average in the 1957 Series
against the Milwaukee Braves. He retired at age 33 following the World Series. Jerry managed the Padres in 1980.

COLEMAN, Joe
>   Assistant Director of Parks
>   Fort Myers, FL

When Joe Coleman, Jr., broke into the biggies in 1965
with a pair of impressive victories, he was just an 18-year-
old. It was a decade after his father had last pitched in the
A.L. Joe won 52 games from the late 1940s to the mid-50s
pitching mostly with second division teams in the A.L. His

most productive years were 1948–49 with 13 and 14 wins with the Philadelphia A's.

In his next to last season pitching for the Orioles in 1954, he lost a no-hitter against the Yankees on an eighth inning single, winning 1-0 on a one-hitter. Twenty years later in 1974, his son Joe had a no-hitter against the Yankees (also in the eighth inning) when he lost his bid and wound up with a 2-hit victory.

Along with Bob Turley, Joe Sr. chalked up 100 K's in the Orioles' first season in Baltimore. His son won over 100 games during his big league stay, making the Colemans and the Bagbys (Jim Sr. and Jim Jr.) the only two father-son pitching combinations winning over 50 games. 52-76

COLEMAN, Ray
    Tobacco and soybean farmer
    Mayfield, KY

Ray was a semi-regular outfielder with the Browns, A's, and White Sox from 1947–52. In 1951, Coleman hit .280, splitting time between the Browns and White Sox. .258

COLEMAN, Rip
    Insurance salesman; manufactures fishing tackle
    Troy, NY

Michael Anthony gave away a million dollars to someone every week on *The Millionaire* from 1955–60 when Rip was struggling through a 7-25 pitching career with the Yankees, K.C. A's, and Orioles. Speaking of Michael Anthony, he was played by an actor named Marvin Miller—sound familiar?

COLES, Chuck
    Millwright
    Jefferson, PA

The Everly Brothers sang "All I Have to Do Is Dream" in 1958. That's about all Chuck Coles did as he played the outfield in only five games for the Reds that year. .182

COLLINS, Joe
    Executive for the People's Express Trucking Co.
    Union, NJ

Born Joseph Edward Kollonige, he was a steady if unspectacular first baseman for the Yankees in the early 1950s.
Used mainly against right-handed pitching in Casey
Stengel's platoon system, he played in 36 World Series
games with his biggest moment coming in the opener of
the '55 Series when he homered twice to lead the Yankees
to a 6-5 win over the Dodgers. His entire ten years was
spent with the Yankees, participating in seven World
Series.
    For several years, Casey Stengel referred to Collins as
"my meal ticket."   .256

COLLUM, Jackie
    Gas station owner
    Grinnell, IA

Jack broke in with the Cardinals in 1951 and pitched with
several teams until 1962. His most productive years were
in the mid-fifties with the Reds.   32-28

COMBS, Merrill
    Died July 8, 1981, at age 62 in Riverside, CA

Remember Merrill Combs? He was an infielder with the
Red Sox, Senators, and Indians from 1947-1952. At the
time of his death, he was a scout for the Cleveland Indians.
                                                              .202

COMMAND, Jim
    Detroit Tigers scout

Jim walked in with the 1954 Phillies and walked out with
the Phils in '55. As a Phillies' third baseman, he collected
his first major league hit, a grand-slam home run off Carl
Erskine, in the eighth inning of an 8-7 loss at Brooklyn.
                                                              .174

CONLEY, Bob
Roanoke, VA

Bob took the mound twice for the Phillies in '58 and departed 0-0.

CONLEY, Donald Eugene "Gene"
Foxboro Paper Company
Foxboro, MA

Although the 6'8" right-handed pitcher was not the first athlete to play more than one professional sport, he was the first to ever play for more than one in the same city. Gene signed out of Washington State where he played both basketball and baseball. The towering chucker played in the early '60s for the Boston Red Sox after having played for the Celtics in the NBA (mainly as a backup for center Bill Russell). His career high in wins came in his next to last campaign in the majors with the Red Sox in 1962, when he won 15. Along with being a member of an NBA championship team, he was also a 9-game winner on the 1957 Milwaukee Braves World Series Championship team.   91-96

CONNELLY, Bill
Died Nov. 27, 1980, at age 55 in Richmond, VA

After arriving with the Philadelphia Athletics in 1945, Bill didn't make a return trip to the majors until 1950, when he split time with the White Sox and Tigers. In 1952, Bill enjoyed his finest year when he went 5-0 for the Giants. After one more campaign, "Wild Bill" made his exit at 6-2.

CONNORS, Kevin Joseph "Chuck"
TV-movie actor
Hollywood, CA

As a member of the Boston Celtics of the NBA, Chuck once broke the glass backboard in a pre-game warmup, and this was in 1946, long before Darryl Dawkins was even born. Connors didn't distinguish himself particularly in basketball, and switched to pro baseball. Three years later he played in one game for the Dodgers in his home town of Brooklyn. In 1951 he hit .239 in 66 games as a lefty-hitting first baseman after being traded to the Chicago Cubs. Chuck hit two career homers for the Cubs, both coming off Giants' pitchers, Dave Koslo and Sal Maglie. That was the extent of his play in the majors.

Chuck eventually entered the film world and became better known in his TV role of *The Rifleman*. He has acted in several movies and television series, including a role in the classic, *Roots*.   .238

CONSOLO, Billy
      Detroit Tigers coach

A utility infielder 1953–62, Billy came up with the Red Sox, the team he spent most of his career with before making stops with the Senators, Twins, Phillies, Angels, and K.C. Before getting back into baseball as a coach, Billy was a hairstylist in California. He also played in the same high school infield with Sparky Anderson.   .221

CONSTABLE, Jim
      Former inventory control analyst with Magnavox; teacher
      Jonesboro, TN

A lefty chucker with the Giants, Indians, Senators, and Braves (1956–63), he was 3-4 overall, including a shutout win in his only complete game in the majors for the Milwaukee Braves in 1962.

CONSUEGRA, Sandy
      Miami, FL

Sandy was one of the many Cubans who was signed to the Senators' organization by scout Joe Cambria. His tenure lasted from 1950–57. He was 6-0 for the '52 Senators, but enjoyed his finest season in '54 with the White Sox at 16-3 and a league-leading .842 winning percentage.   51-32

CONYERS, Herb
     Died September 16, 1964, in Cleveland, OH, at age 43

Herb had a relatively simple career, playing in seven games for the 1950 Indians. His "cup of coffee' was a tasty one as he went 3-for-9, including a home run. The 6'5" first sacker led four different minor leagues in hitting.   .333

COOGAN, Dale
     San Jacinto, CA

Dale was a 19-year-old rookie first baseman during 1950 with the Pirates, his only season in the big leagues. He batted .240 in 53 games.

COOK, Cliff
     Manager
     Oshman's Sporting Goods Store
     Fort Worth, TX

Cliff was one of the early third basemen in a long line of third sackers in Mets history. Although winding up with a sluggish .201 average, Cliff came out of the gate strongly, going 8-for-21 with the 1959 Reds.

COOPER, Walker
     Owns a trucking firm
     Buckner, MO

A hard-hitting catcher for 18 years in the National League, Walker Cooper teamed with his late brother, Mort, to form an outstanding brother battery for the St. Louis Cardinals' championship teams of 1942, '43, and '44. He hit .318 and .317 for the '43 and '44 seasons, but his most productive year came in 1947 for the New York Giants—a career-high 35 homers and 122 RBIs to go with a .305 average.

During the early 1950s he was with the Reds, Braves, Pirates, and Cubs before closing out his career back in St. Louis in 1956 and '57. He finished with a .285 average and hit an even .300 in the 16 World Series games he played in for the Cards in '42, '43, and '44.

CORWIN, Al
President and general manager
Grohe America, Inc.
Geneva, IL

From 1951–55 it was enjoyable to watch right-hander Al Corwin, who racked up 18 wins against 10 losses with the New York Giants. Al went 5-1 for the N.L. pennant winners in '51.

COTTIER, Chuck
Seattle Mariners coach

Chuck broke in at the keystone position with the Milwaukee Braves in 1959, but spent most of his time in the A.L. during the sixties with the Tigers, Senators, and Angels as a .220 hitter.

Playing for the Senators on Aug. 6, 1963, he clipped Whitey Ford for two homers and four RBIs. At the time, it was Ford's only loss in 13 decisions against the expansion Senators.

COURTNEY, Clint "Old Scrap Iron"
Died June 16, 1975, at age 48 in Rochester, NY

"He's the meanest man I ever met. I'm glad he's on my side." That's what Satchel Paige said about Clint Courtney. Clint is the answer to the popular trivia question, "Who was the first catcher to wear glasses?" Courtney was also the first backstop to wear the oversized catcher's mitt to help catch the knuckleball. Clint played for seven teams in his eleven-year stint.

He came up with the Yankees in '51 and played one game for them before being traded to the St. Louis Browns.

As a member of the Orioles in '54, he hit the first home run in modern-day Baltimore Orioles history. Also that season, Clint set a team record which still stands of striking out just seven times in over 400 at-bats for the Orioles. "Old Scrap Iron" was voted *The Sporting News* Rookie of the Year in 1952 when he hit .286 for the Browns in 119 games. At the time of his death Courtney was the manager of Richmond in the International League.   .268

COVINGTON, Wes
    Sportswriter
    Edmonton, Canada

Wes was a solid hitting outfielder for eleven years from 1956–66. Although he wasn't considered a good fielder, he made a pair of sensational catches during the 1957 World Series. Knee injuries cut down his playing time during his career. In 1958 he helped the Braves to their second straight N.L. flag by hitting .330. That year he had 24 homers and 74 RBIs despite playing in just 90 games. He became a regular in the Phillies outfield during the early 1960s, just missing out on another World Series with the '64 Phils. However he did make it back to the "Fall Classic" and saw his last major league action as a pinch-hitter in the 1966 World Series for the L.A. Dodgers.

During the course of the 1961 season he wore the uniforms of two teams in each league: the Braves and Phillies in the N.L., and the White Sox and Kansas City A's in the A.L. In reference to Covington's performance in the 1957 World Series, Casey Stengel barked, "He beat me with his glove, his arm, and his bat."   .279

COX, Billy
    Died March 30, 1978, at age 58 in Harrisburg, PA

Billy was the Dodgers' classy-fielding third baseman from 1948–54. Before being converted to third base by Brooklyn in 1948, he spent the previous two seasons as the regular shortstop of the Pittsburgh Pirates. Although best remembered for his great glove work around the hot corner, he could hold his own with the bat, hitting .291 in

1953. In three World Series he played in 15 games and hit .302.

When Billy was traded by the Pirates to the Dodgers after the '47 season, and again when he was traded by Brooklyn to Baltimore following the '54 season, pitcher Preacher Roe was included in both deals. Cox played for the Orioles in '55, at which time the team was bringing along another of the all-time fielding greats (Brooks Robinson).   .262

COX, Glenn
Carpet store owner
Los Molinos, CA

Not as well known as Billy Cox, or for that matter Wally Cox (who played *Mr. Peepers* in the early fifties), Glenn was a right-handed pitcher who was 1-4 overall in 17 games in parts of four seasons with the K.C. A's from 1955–58.

CRADDOCK, Walt
Died July 6, 1980 in Parma Heights, OH, at age 48

Signed by the A's out of Syracuse University, this luckless southpaw was winless in seven decisions for the K.C. A's from 1955 to 1958.

CRAIG, Roger
Detroit Tigers pitching coach

As a starter for the expansion Mets in the early 1960s, Roger became baseball's losingest pitcher. However, he had some success prior to and after his stay with the Mets. As a member of the Dodgers, he helped them to three N.L. flags: two in Brooklyn ('55–56), and then in L.A. in '59. Unfortunately, he is best remembered as the pitcher who dropped 46 games in a two-year stint with the Mets. In 1963 he lost 18 in a row at one stretch. During that period the Mets were shut out eight times behind him, and four of the losses were by 1-0 scores.

In 1964 he was back in the World Series with the St. Louis Cardinals. He spent the 1970s with another expansion team, the San Diego Padres, as pitching coach, and in 1979 as the manager. 74-98

CRANDALL, Del
Seattle Mariners manager

The greatest catcher in Braves' history, Del broke in with the Boston Braves in 1949. During his sixteen-year stay he played a major role with the pennant-winning Milwaukee Braves in 1957 and '58.

From 1953–60 Crandall always caught in well over 100 games. He was on the receiving end of three no-hitters (Jim Wilson, Lew Burdette, and Warren Spahn). .254

CRAWFORD, Jake
Fort Worth, TX

Rufus "Jake" Crawford played in seven games for the St. Louis Browns in 1952, and made his exit with a .182 average.

CRIMIAN, Jack
Auto body work
Claymont, DE

A right-handed pitcher with the Cardinals briefly in the early fifties, Jack was in 54 of his 74 major league games in 1956 with the K.C. A's. In 1955 he was International League MVP with a 19-6 record. 5-9

CRISTANTE, Leo
Died August 24, 1977, at age 50 in Dearborn, MI

Leo Dante Cristante appeared in 1951 with the Phillies, and with the Tigers in '55. 1-2

CRONE, Ray
Baltimore Orioles scout

Ray had a 30-30 lifetime record with the Braves and
Giants between 1954–58. Unfortunately, Ray was transferred from Milwaukee in '57, the year the Braves won the
pennant.

CROWE, George
Lives a Robinson Crusoe-style existence in the Catskills, upstate New York

Although he was never able to win a regular starting job
during his nine-year career as a first baseman in the N.L.,
he was a very dangerous and effective pinch-hit specialist.
In his career, which spanned the 1952–61 years, he played
behind such people as Joe Adcock with the Braves, Ted
Kluszewski at Cincinnati, and finally, Stan Musial in St.
Louis. His most active season was in 1957 with the Reds,
when Kluszewski had an ailing back. Big George responded with 31 homers and 92 RBIs, playing in over 130
games.
   In '59 he collected four pinch-hit homers, and tied his
own record the following season. In all he had a career
total of 76 pinch-hits. One of those was a blast in 1955 in
the ninth inning, which ruined a no-hit bid by the Cubs'
Warren Hacker.   .270

CUELLAR, Charles
Interior designer and builder
Tampa, FL

In 1950 Charlie pitched in one inning for the White Sox as
a 32-year-old rookie. He had an ignoble debut (giving up
five runs), and never returned to the biggies.

CUELLAR, Mike
Pitching coach at Peninsula in the Carolina League

Although not a significant name in baseball in the 1950s,
he did make two appearances for the Cincinnati Reds

in 1959. Mike did not return to the majors until the mid-1960s when he became a starter for Houston. His greatest success came even later as a regular in the Baltimore Orioles' pitching rotation during most of the 1970s where he would post some outstanding records like 24-8, 23-11, and 20-9.   185-129

CUNNINGHAM, Joe
St. Louis Cardinals director of sales

A solid contact hitter, who had some fine seasons as a first baseman-outfielder with the Cardinals in the late 1950s, Joe hit for averages like .318, .312, and .345 from 1957–59. His .345 in '59 placed him second to Hank Aaron for the N.L. batting title. When he first joined the Cardinals in 1954, he had 3 homers and 9 RBIs after his first two games in a St. Louis uniform. Among his teammates he had the reputation as somewhat of a flake.

He tied a major league record by picking up two hits in an inning in a game in 1957 in which he appeared as a pinch-hitter. Joe moved over to the A.L. in the early 1960s with the White Sox and Senators. He suffered a broken collarbone in '63, and was never the same. Cunningham returned to St. Louis in an executive position with the Cards after his playing days. He worked in promotions, before taking his current post as director of sales.   .291

CURRIE, Bill
Farm owner
Arlington, GA

Bill pitched in three games without a decision for the 1955 Senators.

CUSICK, John
Demarest, NJ

John was in 114 games, split between the Cubs ('51) and Braves ('52). He had 2 doubles, 2 homers, 2 stolen bases, and 22 RBIs playing shortstop and third base.   .174

D

DAGRES, Angelo
  Restaurant owner
  Rowley, MA

In 1955 Angelo went 4-for-15 in eight games for the Orioles. The flychaser hit .267.

DAHLKE, Jerry
  Gas-pipe fitter
  Memphis, TN

In 1956 the Chicago White Sox had a pitching staff with names like Pierce, Harshman, Donovan, and Staley. Another flipper by the name of Dahlke pitched in five games with no decisions that year.

DALEY, Leavitt Leo "Bud"
  Upholstery and lawn sprinkler business
  Lander, WY

A left-handed pitcher, "Bud" came up with Cleveland in 1955. In '59 and '60 he was the ace of the Kansas City staff, winning 16 games each season. That earned him a "promotion" to the Yankees during the '61 season (as it did for so many of the A's who performed well during that period). He concluded his 10-year cruise with the Yankees in 1964.
60-64

DALEY, Pete
  Toiletries salesman
  Grass Valley, CA

Pete caught with the Red Sox, A's, and Senators from 1955–61. He departed with a .239 average.

DANIEL, Charles
    Retail sales representative
    International Harvester Co.
    Memphis, TN

Charlie appeared in one game on the mound for the 1957
Tigers. During his brief jaunt he failed to gain a decision.

DANIELS, Bennie
    Community program director for a Los Angeles hospital

Bennie spent nine seasons divided between the Pirates in
the late 1950s, and the Senators in the early '60s. He enjoyed his best season (12-11) with the Senators in '61.
Bennie also played briefly in the outfield with the Senators. He goes down in history as the first Senator pitcher to
win a game at DC Stadium (now RFK Stadium), on April
9, 1962, with President John F. Kennedy in attendance.
                                                    45-76

DANIELS, Harold "Jack"
    Operates Lea Foods, Inc. (caterers)
    Evansville, IN

It would be appropriate if "Jack" Daniels was a liquor distributor today! Also known as "Sour Mash," Daniels was a
one-year outfielder, playing in 106 games for the '52 Boston Braves when he batted .187.

DARK, Alvin "Blackie"
    Board of Directors of Baseball Chapel, Inc.
    Leucadia, Calif.

One of the better all-around athletes in the game, Al was a
three sport star at L.S.U. Along with being the high scorer
on the basketball team, he was a backfield star on the football team, and was drafted by the N.F.L. Philadelphia
Eagles. He chose baseball, and in 1948 was the Rookie of
the Year in helping the Boston Braves to the pennant.

Dark was traded to the N.Y. Giants after one more season with the Braves, and in 1951 was the key figure in the Giants' pennant when he hit .303 and led the N.L. in doubles (with 41).

He hit .417 in the World Series against the Yankees. Alvin continued to hit around the .300 mark for the next three years, and in the Giants' four-game sweep over Cleveland in the '54 World Series he went 7-for-17. He began drifting around the N.L. in 1956, playing for the Cardinals and Phillies, and then ended his career with the Braves (the team he began with), though now in Milwaukee.

The ex-shortstop managed the Giants to the 1962 N.L. pennant and then, following managerial jobs in Kansas City and Cleveland, he piloted Oakland to the A.L. championship and World Series win over the Dodgers in 1974. Alvin is the only man to manage both the A.L. and N.L. in the All-Star Game. His last managerial position was with the San Diego Padres. He was fired during spring training in 1978.   .289

DARNELL, Bob
    Springdale, AZ

Bob pitched in seven games without a decision in parts of 1954 and '56 with the Brooklyn Dodgers.

DAUGHERTY, Harold
    Teacher/football coach at Bedford High School
    Bedford, OH

Born in Paris—Paris, Pennsylvania—"Doc" came to bat in one game for the '51 Tigers.   .000

DAVALILLO, Pompeyo
    Angels scout and baseball coach at Caracas University in Venezuela

"Yo Yo" is the older brother of Vic Davalillo. He played shortstop in 19 games for the '53 Senators.   .293

DAVENPORT, Jim
San Francisco Giants scout

Jim quarterbacked Mississippi Southern University in two Sun Bowls (1953–54), but then went into professional baseball. He spent his 13 years as the Giants' regular third baseman, beginning in 1958. His best year was in 1962 when he hit .297 to help lead the Giants to the N.L. pennant. He also set a league record at the hot corner by going 64 consecutive games without committing an error. Although not as dramatic as Bobby Thomson's home run eleven years earlier, he drew a base-on-balls which forced in the winning run in the third and final playoff game with the Dodgers for the N.L. pennant. Except for stints as manager at Phoenix in the Pacific Coast League, and as a coach for San Diego, he has remained in a Giants uniform as a coach.   .258

DAVIE, Jerry
Southgate, MI

Jerry became a one-season big leaguer, pitching in 11 games for the Tigers in '59 with a 2-2 mark; he was 4-for-10 with the stick.

DAVIS, Jim
San Mateo, CA

A left-handed pitcher in the N.L. in the mid-fifties, Jim struck out four batters in an inning on May 27, 1956, for the Cubs. This marked the first time in 40 years that this feat had been accomplished. His best season was with the Cubs in 1954 when he was 11-7. He completed his career in '57 with the N.Y. Giants, where he joined his uncle, Marv Grissom, in the team's bullpen. While with the Cubs in '54, Jim didn't show Uncle Marv too much respect, as he beat the Giants in a game in which Uncle Marv was the losing pitcher.   24-26

DAVIS, Robert B. "Bob," "Brandy"
    Chicago Cubs scout

Bob played 38 games as an outfielder with Pittsburgh in
1952–53. He attended Duke University before his professional baseball days.   .187

DAVIS, Robert E. "Bob"
    New York, NY

Bob lost all four of his decisions with the Kansas City A's
in 1958. A Yale graduate, this "Bulldog" didn't bark too
loud.

DAVIS, Thomas Oscar "Tod"
    Died December 31, 1978, at age 53, in West Covina,
    CA

Tod was an infielder who saw brief action with the Phillies
in 1949 and 1951. Tod danced away with a .233 average.

DAVIS, Tommy
    Ex-Seattle Mariners coach

An outfielder who played throughout the 1960s and into
the late 1970s with ten different teams, Tommy played in
one game and struck out as a pinch-hitter in '59. In 1962
he racked up 153 RBIs to go with his 27 four-baggers. Tom
played at least 100 games with six different clubs. After 21
seasons with 1,999 games, Tommy retired with a .294 average. He batted over .300 six different times, with a season high of .346 in 1962.

DEAL, Ellis "Cot"
    Houston Astros coach

"Cot" was a right-handed chucker with the Red Sox in the
late forties, and the Cardinals in the early fifties. He finished at 3-4 and has coached for several major league
teams.

DELIS, Juan
    Havana, Cuba

Juan hit .189 in 54 games with the 1955 Senators at second base, third base and in the outfield.

DEL GRECO, Bobby "The Greek"
    Pittsburgh Press employee; also throws batting practice for the Pirates

Bobby had a lengthy career as an outfielder spanning the years 1952–65. He broke in with his home town Pirates, but didn't return until '56. He also played with the Cards, Cubs, Phils, A's, and Yankees, and said goodbye with a .229 average.

DELOCK, Ivan Martin "Ike"
    Manufacturer's representative
    Needham, MA

Ike was a fixture on the Red Sox pitching staff from 1952–63. A spot starter and a reliever, he had his most success out of the bullpen, going 34-15, as compared to 50-60 as a starter. In 1956 he started off 10-0 and wound up 13-7. His most wins came in '58, with 14. Noted for his hot temper, Ike was the only Red Sox pitcher to pitch eleven seasons for the Beantowners, the longest of any Bosox hurler.

84-75

DELSING, Jim
    Advertising salesman for *The St. Louis Review*
    St. Louis, MO

Jim was the only player in major league history to ever pinch-run for a midget. A ten-year outfielder, he started with the White Sox in 1948. Traded to the Yankees, he hit well (7-for-20, .350) in '49, and at a .400 clip in just a dozen games in 1950 before being swapped to the lowly Browns. It was a bad break (going from a top team to a bottom team), but it allowed him to become part of the legendary story when Bill Veeck sent Eddie Gaedel, a midget, up to the plate as a pinch-hitter in a 1951 game. Delsing, a regular for the Browns, was inserted as the pinch-runner for Gaedel after he walked. Jim was traded to Detroit the following season, and had his finest of five years for the Tigers in '53, hitting .288 in 138 games.   .255

DeMAESTRI, Joe "Oats"
     Beer distributorship
     Novato, CA

Joe was a smooth-fielding but not a very strong-hitting shortstop in the A.L. from 1951–61. He was with the White Sox in 1951 and the Browns in '52 before moving over to the A's, where he spent the bulk of his career. He ended his playing days in 1960 and '61 as a member of the Yankees, being used as a utility infielder. DeMaestri was 1-for-2 in brief action in the '60 series.

     Mike Garcia won't forget Joe. Two times in just a three-week period during the '54 season, DeMaestri picked up the only hit off Garcia in one-hitters pitched by "The Bear" in games against the Athletics. In '55 Joe once went 6-for-6 in a game for the K.C. A's.   .236

DEMARS, Billy
     Montreal Expos coach

Billy played in a total of 80 games with the Athletics ('48) and Browns (1950–51). The snappy shortstop had a lifetime .237 average.

DEMERIT, John
     Recreation director
     Port Washington, WI

A gifted athlete, John was a basketball player at the University of Wisconsin before his big league days, which ran between 1957–62 for the Milwaukee Braves and New York Mets. Signed by the Braves during his junior year out of the U. of W. for an estimated $100,000, John had a career average of .174.

DEMETER, Don
> Minister; owner of a swimming pool company
> Oklahoma City, OK

A tall outfielder who played from 1956–67, Don broke in
with the Brooklyn Dodgers in '56, and was a key figure on
the '59 N.L. and World Series teams, as he finished with
18 homers and 70 RBIs. He was traded to the Phillies in
'61 and had his finest season for them the following year,
with 29 homers, 107 RBIs, and a .307 average. On Sept. 12,
1961, Don had a single and three home runs in a game
against the Dodgers. From September 1962 until July
1965 he went through 266 straight games and 229 chances
without committing an error—an all-time major league
record. His son was the Yankees' first selection in the 1979
free-agent draft. Many fans remember Don as the man
who replaced Duke Snider.   .265

DEMETER, Steve
> Minor league instructor for the Pittsburgh Pirates

Steve had a quiet 15-game career as a third baseman with
the Tigers ('59) and Indians ('60). He was born in Homer
City, Pa., but never "homered" in the majors.   .087

DEMPSEY, Con
> Teacher and baseball coach at Giannini High School
> San Francisco, CA

In 1951 Con lost his only two decisions in three games for
the Pirates—the extent of his time in the big show. He is a
graduate of the University of San Francisco.

DENTE, Sam "Blackie"
> Vice-president, Merit Mailers, Inc.
> Elizabethport, NJ

"Boston Blackie" was an early TV detective. This "Blackie" spent nine years as a utility infielder in the big
leagues. Primarily a shortstop, he was with the Red Sox

and Browns for a season each, before taking over as a regular for the Senators in 1949. Sam later spent two seasons each with the White Sox and Indians.   .252

DERRINGTON, Jim
     Produce company manager
     Anaheim, CA

Despite being only in his early forties, he last pitched in a big league game almost a quarter of a century ago. At the age of 16 years and 10 months he started and lost a game for the Chicago White Sox, making him the youngest pitcher to ever start a game in major league history. The following season he appeared in 20 more games for the White Sox, and before he reached his 18th birthday, he had pitched for the last time in the big leagues. In that one game in '56, he did pick up a base hit to become the youngest ever to do so in A.L. history.   0-2

DICKSON, Murry
     Carpenter
     Leavenworth, KS

A durable little right-handed pitcher, Murry just missed spanning four decades, the 30s, 40s, 50s, and 60s, as did the careers of Mickey Vernon, Ted Williams, and Early Wynn. He first appeared for the Cardinals in 1939. Following military duty in World War II, he was a key member of the St. Louis pitching staff, going 15-6 to help them to the N.L. flag. Murry started the memorable seventh game of the 1946 World Series against Boston. Although not involved in the decision, he had a clutch hit during the rally that led to the Cards' win.

He was traded to the cellar-dwelling Pirates in '49, and despite their seventh place finish in '51, he was a 20-game winner. However, the next two seasons he lost 21 and 19 games, the most in the N.L. in each of those years. In '54 he was with the Phillies, and for a third straight season led the N.L. in losses, with 20.

After almost two decades in the senior circuit, he was in the A.L. in '58 and was 9-5 with the K.C. A's at age 42.

Down the stretch, he was picked up by the Yankees as they won another A.L. flag. He also pitched in two World Series games that fall. Dickson departed with K.C. in '59 at age 43, just missing by one year his fourth decade.   172-181

DIERING, Chuck
   Automobile dealership
   St. Louis, MO

Chuck spent five seasons with his home town Cardinals. In 1952 with the Giants he was used mainly as a late-inning defensive replacement by manager Leo Durocher, and completed his career with the Orioles from 1954–56 at .249.

DIETZEL, Roy
   Sales representative, insurance company
   Charlotte, NC

In 1954 Roy Dietzel came up as a Senators' infielder. He was 5-for-21 and departed with a .238 average.

DILLARD, Don
   Owns a sporting goods store and marina called Dillard's in Waterloo, SC

Don appeared in box scores between 1959 and 1965 with the Indians and Milwaukee Braves. The flychaser hit .244.

DILLINGER, Bob
   Canyon County, CA

Already in his late twenties in 1946 when he joined the St. Louis Browns, Bob went on to lead the A.L. in stolen bases for three straight years from 1947–49 with 34, 28, and 20, respectively. In '48 he hit .321 and led the A.L. in base hits with 207. The following year he hit .324. Traded to the Philadelphia A's before the 1950 season, he was hitting over .300 again when he was strangely waived out of the A.L. He finished the season with the Pirates, and again

was over .300. The following year, 1951, was to be the last
for this third baseman, at age 33. Bob was dealt to the
White Sox where he hit .301, culminating a six-year
swing.   .306

DiMAGGIO, Dominic "Little Professor"
    President, Latex Fibre Co. (retired)
    Lawrence, MA

Les Brown's band had a song with the lyrics, "He's better
than his brother Joe—Dominic DiMaggio." He wasn't, but
was quite an outfielder himself. He spent his entire career
from 1940-53 with the Red Sox. Dom was in the military
during World War II and missed three seasons.

The "Little Professor" hit .316 in '46, helping Boston to
the A.L. flag. In '49 he made a run at his brother's consecu-
tive-game hitting streak with 34. His last chance at ex-
tending the streak to 35 was on a line drive to Joe in
centerfield. In 1950 he hit .328 and led the A.L. in stolen
bases with 15, triples with 11, and runs scored with 131.
His career average was .298. No Hall of Famer, not better
than his brother Joe, but an outstanding player—Dominic
DiMaggio.

DiMAGGIO, Joe "The Yankee Clipper," "Joltin' Joe"
    Baltimore Orioles Board of Directors; TV commercials

Voted the greatest living player in 1969, Joe played on ten
Yankee championship clubs. He collected two singles and
a triple in his first big league game. Between Joe, Dom,
and Vince (who all have the same middle name, Paul),
they received 1,952 walks, the most walks received by a
brother combination.

Possibly the most amazing thing about his 56-game
hitting streak in 1941 is that he went on to hit in 17 more
consecutive games after being stopped. During the 56-
game streak, he collected 56 singles, and scored 56 runs.
The longest streak in professional baseball belongs to another "Joe"—Joe Wilhoit of Wichita, who hit in 69 straight
games in the Western League in 1920.

Nicknamed "The Yankee Clipper" after a speedy Bos-

ton-to-New York train, a song was written in his honor, titled "Joltin' Joe DiMaggio." Elected to the Hall of Fame in
1955, Joe finished with 361 home runs and a .325 average.

DiPIETRO, Bob
    Advertising agency
    Yakima, WA

In 1951, Bob was listening to Les Paul and Mary Ford's big
hit, "How High the Moon." It wasn't too high for Bob that
year, as he only played in four games for the Red Sox.
.091

DITMAR, Art
    Recreation director
    Brook Park, OH

Art was around from 1954–62. His first win came on the
final day of the '54 season as a member of the Philadelphia
A's. He defeated the Yankees in a game in which Yogi
Berra was at third base and Mickey Mantle at shortstop.
That may have been an unimportant game, but after leading the A.L. in losses with 22 in 1956 while still with the
A's (who were now in Kansas City), Art was ready for his
"promotion" to New York. The right-hander was with
three Yankee pennant winners in four seasons. Art had
his best year in 1960 when he won 15 (which was the most
on the Yankee staff). During the '61 season he returned to
the A's where he took his last lap the following year.
72-77

DITTMER, Jack
    President of his own motor company
    Elkrader, IA

Jack was in the giant arena primarily with the Braves
from 1952–57. A second baseman with a .232 lifetime average, he played his last season with the Tigers.

DIXON, John "Sonny"
    Charlotte, NC

A right-handed pitcher, "Sonny" had an 11-18 mark divided among the Senators, Athletics, and Yankees from 1953–56.

DOBBEK, Dan
    Laundry company employee
    Portland, OR

A graduate of Western Michigan University, Dan was an outfielder with the Senators and Twins (1959–61). He carried a .208 average.

DOBSON, Joe
    Retired, Tombstone, AZ

Joe spent most of his fourteen years with the Red Sox. In 1946 he helped Boston to the A.L. pennant with a 13-7 record. The 6'2" right-hander, who was often called "Burrhead," won a career high of 18 in 1947, then averaged 15 wins a year for the next three years. On April 30, 1950, Joe shut out the A's, 19-0, while pitching for the Red Sox.

In '51 he was sent to the White Sox along with Dick Littlefield and Al Zarilla for chuckers Ray Scarborough and Bill Wight. He was back in Boston in 1954, where he completed an impressive 137-103 mark.

DOBY, Larry
    Director of community relations
    New Jersey Nets of the NBA

An A.L. outfielder from 1947–59, Larry was Jackie Robinson's counterpart as the American League's first black player when he joined the Indians during the 1947 season. He once struck out 5 times in a game in '48, but his .301 average helped Cleveland to the A.L. pennant. Doby twice led the junior circuit in homers, with 32 in both 1952 and

1954. In the pennant-winning '54 campaign he was the league leader in RBIs with 126.

He managed the Chicago White Sox during the 1978 season, only the second black to ever pilot a big league team.

Doby, who attended Long Island University, had 253 home runs. He also played with the White Sox and Tigers, and finished with a .283 average.

DOERR, Bobby
Ex-Toronto Blue Jays hitting coach; retired in Agness, Oregon

Born in 1918 during World War I, his middle name of Pershing was taken after the U.S. war hero, General John Pershing. He had a fourteen-year career (all as a second baseman) for the Boston Red Sox from 1937–51. Bobby never played in another defensive position in over 1,800 games. Twice in his career (1938 and 1946) he had second-inning singles off Bob Feller for the only hit Feller allowed in both games. He set an A.L. record by not committing an error in over 400 chances for a three-month period in the 1948 season.

In 1946 his 116 RBIs aided Boston to the A.L. flag. He hit well in the Series that fall, going 9-for-22 for a .409 average. His most productive season offensively came in 1950 when he collected 27 homers, and 120 RBIs. Other highlights include hitting for the cycle twice ('44 and '47) and leading A.L. second basemen in double plays five different years.

In 1969 Bobby was voted by the fans as the Red Sox all-time second baseman.   .288

DONNELLY, Ed
Service manager, Exxon Car Center
Houston, TX

In 1959 Ed Donnelly had a dream come true by hurling in 9 big league games for the Chicago Cubs. When he awoke he was 1-1.

DONNELLY, Sylvester "Blix"
   Died June 20, 1976, at age 62, in Olivia, MN

"Blix" pitched in the N.L. for eight seasons (1944–51) with the Cards, Phils, and Boston Braves. In 1950 he won a pair of games during the season as a 36-year-old member of the Phillies' "Whiz Kids," one of the wins coming in the last week of the hectic season. Because of their age, it was common to refer to Donnelly and Ken Heintzelman as the "Fizz Kids" who helped the "Whiz Kids."

   Following his playing days, he operated an anhydrous ammonia business.   27-36

DONOSO, Lino
   Havana, Cuba

During the years 1955 and '56, Lino Donoso went 4-6 with the Pirates.

DONOVAN, Dick
   Owner, real estate and insurance firm
   Quincy, MA

Dick spent his 15-year trip with five different teams. After making brief appearances in the early 1950s with the Braves and Tigers, the right-hander came into his own with the White Sox in 1955 when he won 15 games. He was 16-6 in 1957 for the highest winning percentage in the A.L. He also led the league in complete games that year with 16. Dick moved on to the expansion Washington Senators in 1961 and, despite a mediocre 10-10 record, had the best ERA (2.40) in the A.L. He had his big season in 1962 as a 20-game winner for Cleveland, the team he ended with in 1965. Twice in that '62 season he hit two home runs in a game.   122-99

DORISH, Harry
   Minor league pitching instructor for the Reds

"Fritz" spent his 10-year run mainly as a relief pitcher from 1947–56. He is the last hurler in the American

League to ever steal home, having done so in 1950. In a 1951 game with the White Sox, he was pitching in relief in the late innings of a close game when manager Paul Richards switched him to third base as Billy Pierce was called in to pitch to Ted Williams. Dorish then returned to the mound and was the winning pitcher.

His best seasons were with Chicago in 1952 when he was 8-4 (with a league-leading 11 saves) and in '53 when he logged a 10-6 mark (with an additional 18 saves). He has remained in the game as a scout, pitching coach, and instructor in the past two decades.   45-43

DOTTERER, "Dutch"
New York Yankees scout

Signed off the campus of Syracuse University, Henry "Dutch" Dotterer compiled a .248 average with the Reds (1957-60) and Senators ('61). He was called the new Moe Berg as he held a master's degree from Syracuse U. in Latin American public relations, and could speak Spanish and Portuguese fluently. Dutch once caught a baseball dropped from a helicopter at 575 feet at Crosley Field.

.248

DOUGLAS, Charles "Whammy"
Location unknown

"Whammy" was 3-3 in 11 games for the Pirates in 1957. "Whammy" was a one-eyed pitcher who had an artificial right eye.

DRABOWSKY, Moe
Sales representative for the Garden City Envelope Co. Chicago, IL

Moe had a seventeen-year tenure which lasted from 1956-72. Born in Ozanna, Poland, Drabowsky broke in with the Cubs, then had short stints with the Braves and Reds, before transferring to the A.L. where he spent the bulk of his career with K.C. and Baltimore, followed by short stays with the Cards and White Sox.

In the 1966 WS, Moe had one of the more brilliant performances in Series annals as a member of the Orioles staff in game one against the Dodgers. Entering the game in the third inning, he set L.A. down on just one hit the rest of the game. He had 11 strikeouts, including a record six in a row at one point. The nifty WS performance has allowed him to be remembered in a positive way, not just as the pitcher who gave up Stan Musial's 3,000th base hit, or as the losing pitcher when Early Wynn won his 300th game.

One of baseball's most notorious pranksters, Moe used to love to visit Fenway Park. He revealed that "Fenway Park had that hand-operated scoreboard against the Green Monster which indicated scores such as K.C. at Detroit, Cleveland at Chicago, etc. I'd always get out there during batting practice and rearrange the signs. I'd have an A.L. team playing against a N.L. team. When the announcer ran down the scores he might say, 'Houston 2, Minnesota 1; Detroit 4, Cincinnati 3.' Then he would say 'What in the world is going on?' I just like to throw a monkey wrench into the system once in a while."   88-105

DRAKE, Solly
    Los Angeles, CA

Solly was involved in a shuttle service between the majors and minors from 1956–59. In 141 games (Cubs, Dodgers, Phillies) he had a .232 average. His younger brother Sammy was an infielder with the Cubs and Mets in the early sixties. Solly and Sammy were the first black brothers since 1900 to play in the majors. Moses and Welday Walker played before the turn of the century.

DREWS, Karl
    Died August 15, 1963, at age 43 when struck by an intoxicated driver in Dania, Florida.

Karl spent eight years in the majors (1947–54), starting out in the Yankees organization. He was 6-6 for the '47 A.L. champions, with two appearances out of the bullpen in the WS. The righty flipper was traded to the Browns and later the Phillies where he had his best season in 1952 when he won 14 games, including 5 shutouts.   44-53

DROPO, Walt "Moose"
    Imports fireworks from China
    Boston, MA

Walt's nickname "Moose" could originate in size (6'5" and 225 lbs), but it actually derives from the name of his home town, Moosup, Connecticut.

A star football player at the University of Connecticut, he was drafted by the NFL Chicago Bears. He chose professional baseball and in 1950 was the A.L. Rookie of the Year with an outstanding season, hitting .322, with 34 homers and 144 RBIs. Although he never repeated that season, Walt did set a major league record in 1952 (which still stands) by hitting safely in 12 consecutive appearances at bat. This came just a few weeks after he had been traded to the Tigers from Boston. The streak tied a record set by "Pinky" Higgins, but his streak had been interrupted twice by bases-on-balls. Dropo's came with 12 hits in 12 at-bats.

Walt also played with the White Sox, Reds, and Orioles before calling it a day in 1961. As a member of the White Sox, he startled the baseball world by hitting two pinch-hit grand-slam home runs within a month. Walt, who finished with a .270 average and 152 home runs, says, "The excitement of fireworks is like hitting a game-winning home run." He also claims to be the only baseball player ever to hit a home run over the Great Wall of China.

DROTT, Dick
    Chicago, IL

Dick came in like a lion and went out like a lamb. He won 15 games as a Cubs' rookie in '57 but had trouble finding the plate, issuing a league-leading 129 walks. On May 26, 1957, he fanned 15 Braves, including Hank Aaron three times. The hard-throwing right-hander broke his arm dur-

ing the '59 campaign. He was dealt to Houston after the
'61 season and retired there a couple of years later.   27-46

DRYSDALE, Don "Big D"
Chicago White Sox announcer

This big handsome right-hander was in the big show for
fourteen years—all with the Dodgers. In 1968 Don pitched
58⅔ consecutive scoreless innings, breaking Walter Johnson's 45-year record. Among his many distinctions, he
holds the mark for the longest career in the majors,
playing for just one manager—Walter Alston.

"Big D" wasn't afraid to shave a hitter or two, and holds
the lifetime record with 154 nicks. He was generous to
Hank Aaron, giving up 17 roundtrippers to the home-run
champion. On April 17, 1965, he had a four-strikeout inning.

Don carried a big stick to the plate, leading big league
hurlers in home runs in four different seasons. In 1961 he
hit a grand slam off Don Nottebart, and once banged out
two home runs in the same game in 1958. His 208th (and
next to last of his career 209 wins) came against the Padres
by a score of 19-0. Don also had the reputation of throwing
a pretty good "spitter." "Big D" was elected to the Hall of
Fame in 1984.   209-266

DUBIEL, Walt "Monk"
Died October 25, 1969, at age 50
Hartford, CT

"Monk" broke in as a 13-game winner for the Yankees in
1944. In the late forties and early fifties he did his throwing for the Phillies and Cubs. After 7 years of work he was
45-53.

DULIBA, Bob "Ach"
School teacher and coach
Exeter, PA

Bob was a right-handed reliever who worked 176 games for
the Cards, Angels, Red Sox, and A'a. Duliba had his best

season in '64, when he won 6 and saved 9 for the Angels.
While pitching for Peoria in '54, his manager Whitey
Kurowski gave him the handle "Ach," after the German
song title "Ach, Du Lieber Augustine."   17-12

DUNLAP, Grant
> Athletic director and baseball coach at Occidental College
> Los Angeles, CA

Grant Dunlap, who went 6-for-17 (.353) for the Cardinals
(including a home run), came up in 1953 and disappeared
in '53.

DUNN, Jim
> Division superintendent at Goodyear
> Gadsden, AL

Jim emerged with the 1952 Pirates when he made three
appearances with no decisions.

DUREN, Rinold "Ryne"
> Rehabilitation director at community hospital
> Stoughton, WI

Over a decade after his last appearance in 1965, he was
back in the public eye with his autobiography, *The Comeback*, which told of his victory over alcoholism. Wild and
hard throwing, the story goes that he once hit Billy Hunter
with a pitch in a Texas League game while Hunter was in
the on-deck circle.

His most successful pitching came as a Yankee bullpen
ace in the late 1950s. In 1958 he had a league-leading 20
saves. In 1961, with the expansion California Angels, he
struck out four batters in an inning. An unusual enough
accomplishment, but his extra strikeout cost him the game
as the man he struck out reached first base when the ball
evaded the catcher, and he eventually came around to
score the winning run.

An intimidating fastball hurler, Ryne averaged better

than one strikeout-per-inning during his ten-year trip.

27-44

DURHAM, Joe
Salesman for a liquor distributor; pitches batting
practice for the Orioles
Randallstown, MD

This flychaser used to like to call himself Joe Van Durham. He did his shagging with the Orioles (1954 and '57) and Cardinals, briefly, in '59. In 93 games he hit .188.

DURNBAUGH, Bob
Construction worker and sells insurance
Dayton, OH

Jimmy Dorsey had a big hit with "So Rare" in 1957, the year Bob had no hits in two rare games as a Reds' shortstop.

DUSAK, Erv
Insurance salesman
Lombard, IL

Erv was a Cardinal outfielder throughout most of the forties and also played the infield and did some pitching. His best season was in 1947 when he batted .284. His playing days ended in Pittsburgh in '52. As a pitcher Erv was 0-3; as a batter he finished at .243.

DUSER, Carl
Sales assistant, Bethlehem Steel Co.
Bethlehem, PA

Carl arrived in 1956, departed in '57, and returned in '58. However, after two brief stints (which totaled three games) with the K.C. A's, all Carl could take home was a 1-1 record.

DYCK, Jim
 Bowling alley owner
 Cheney, WA

Jim glided around from 1951–56, mostly with the Browns and Orioles. A career .246 average, he also made brief stops in Cleveland and Cincinnati.

E

EADDY, Don
 Burger King business
 Boston, MA

Don, a graduate of the University of Michigan, played in 15 games with the Cubs. The third baseman was an All-American selection on the 1952 University of Michigan NCAA baseball championship team. He also made the All-Big-Ten basketball team as a guard, and played on the gridiron.   .000

EASTER, Luke
 Shot to death on May 29, 1979, in Cleveland, OH

When Luke Easter was tragically shot to death in Cleveland in May of 1979 there was much doubt as to his true age. Listed as age 58 at his death by various baseball encyclopedias, he may have been in his mid-sixties. In 1952 his 31 homers were second in the A.L. to teammate Larry Doby. Easter most likely would have won the league's home run title had he not spent a portion of the season in the minor leagues. A left-handed hitting first baseman, Easter hit a lifetime .274 in the majors, but continued to play at the AAA level until the mid-1960s when he was close to 50 years of age.

Luke once hit 75 home runs in a season during his days in the Negro leagues. In tribute to Luke, the Luke Easter

Scholarship Fund has been established at Cleveland State University.   .274

EASTON, John
    Division manager
    Public Service Electric and Gas
    New Brunswick, NJ

This Princeton graduate made one pinch-hit appearance for the Phillies in 1955. Four years later John made three pinch-hit appearances for the Phillies. Before turning pro, Easton captained the Princeton baseball team.   .000

EDELMAN, John
    School teacher
    Haverford, PA

If you combed the sports pages closely in 1955 you would have come across the name of John Edelman, a 19-year-old chucker who pitched in five games without a decision for the '55 Braves.

EDWARDS, Charles "Bruce"
    Died April 25, 1975, at age 51
    Sacramento, CA

Bruce was the Dodgers' regular catcher before Roy Campanella. In 1947 he hit .295 for the N.L. pennant winners. He shared the catching chores with Campanella the following year, and then was his backup before being traded to the Cubs in 1951. Edwards completed his ten-year career with the Reds in 1956.   .256

EDWARDS, Hank
    Driver/messenger for Armored Transport Co.
    Los Angeles, CA

No relation to Bruce, Hank was an outfielder for the Indians during the 1940s. He had his best season in 1946 (following a two-year absence because of military service)

when he hit .301 and led the A.L. in triples with 16.
Edwards did hit .364 on a part-time basis with the Cubs in
1950. Hank finished his 11-year career as a member of the
last St. Louis Browns' team in 1953.   .280

ELLIOT, Harry
Teacher, and baseball and soccer coach at El Cajon
Valley High School
El Cajon, CA

A punter on some strong University of Minnesota football
teams in the late forties, Harry played in a total of 92
games for the Cardinals, split in the years 1953 and '55.
                                                        .256

ELLIOTT, Bob
Died May 4, 1966, at age 49
San Diego, CA

A fifteen-year player from 1939 to '53, Bob came up as an
outfielder with the Pirates, but was moved to third base after a few seasons. He was traded to the Boston Braves following the 1946 season, and in 1947 was voted the MVP in
the N.L. with a .317 average and 113 RBIs. The following
year Bob helped the Braves to the N.L. pennant with 100
RBIs. Elliott last appeared with the White Sox in 1953 with
2,061 hits and a .289 career average. He was the manager
of the Kansas City A's in 1960.   .289

ELLSWORTH, Dick
Real estate salesman
Fresno, CA

Dick is one of the few major leaguers ever born in the state
of Wyoming. He moved to Fresno as a youngster, and was
a high school teammate with another future major leaguer—Jim Maloney.
  Signed to a big bonus by the Cubs in 1958, Ellsworth im-

mediately threw a four-hit shutout over the cross-town White Sox in an exhibition game. He made just one appearance in '58 and didn't return until 1960.

In 1962 Dick was 9-20, but turned that around to 22-10 the following year. In 1966, his final year with the Cubs, the lefty throwing Ellsworth was a 22-game loser. He parted in 1971 with Milwaukee. 115-137

ELSTON, Don
Sales representative
Danly Machine Co.
Chicago, IL

With the exception of appearing for the 1957 Dodgers, the right-hander spent the remainder of his 450-game career in a Cubs' uniform. In the late 1950s and early '60s he was the ace of the Cubs' bullpen, leading the NL in appearances in both the '58 and '59 seasons. He finished 49-54, plus 63 saves.

ENNIS, Del
Operates a bowling alley
Jenkintown, PA

A home-town product, Del was a fixture in the Phillies' outfield for most of his fourteen-year stay. From 1946–56 he played 1,610 games in the garden for the Phils. He was the *Sporting News* Rookie of the Year in '46.

Ennis, who led the league in RBIs (126) for the '50 "Whiz Kids," was traded to the Cardinals for outfielder Rip Repulski and infielder Bobby Morgan in 1956. He also made brief stops with the Reds and White Sox before it all ended in '59.

A lifetime .284 hitter, with 288 home runs, Del also broke up three no-hitters during his career. Until Mike Schmidt surpassed him in 1980, Del was the all-time Phillies' home-run hitter.

EPPERLY, Al
Scott County, Iowa, sheriff's office
Davenport, IA

Experiencing one of the more unusual careers in big
league history, Al won his only two decisions for the
Chicago Cubs in nine appearances in 1938. Remarkably, he reappeared on the big league scene a dozen
years later in 1950 at the age of 32 when he took the
mound five times without a decision for the Brooklyn
Dodgers.   2-0

ERAUTT, Eddie
La Mesa, CA

Eddie was a right-handed chucker with the Reds from
1947–51. He split the '53 season with Cincinnati and the
Cardinals, and made his exit at 15-23.

ERAUTT, Joe
Died Oct. 6, 1976, at age 55 in Portland, OR

The catching half of the Erautt family, he was with the
White Sox for 16 games in each of the 1950 and '51 seasons.   .186

ERICKSON, Don
Insurance agent with the city of Springfield, IL

In 1958, 9's were wild for Don Erickson, who pitched in 9
games for the Phillies, giving up 9 walks and striking out
9 batters. The right-hander finished 0-1.
    For several years running, Don was the Illinois state
horseshoe pitching champion.

ERICKSON, Hal
>   A. C. Nielson Co.
>   Venice, FL

For Hal Erickson, life was no picnic in the majors as a
33-year-old rookie who was 0-1 in 18 games for the '53 Tigers.

ERNAGA, Frank
>   Building contractor
>   Susanville, CA

Frank came in roaring with the '57 Cubs as he homered off
Warren Spahn in his first major league at-bat. This gave
Ernaga the distinction of being the first Cub to ever homer
in his first major league at-bat. As an encore, he tripled in
his second trip to the plate. In his first eight at-bats the
sizzling rookie had five extra-base hits. In 20 games he hit
.314, including a pair of homers. The UCLA product appeared in 9 games for the '58 Cubs and was never seen
again.   .279

ERSKINE, Carl
>   Executive Vice President and Director of the First Na-
>   tional Bank of Madison County; also Kennedy Foun-
>   dation Special Olympics Committee
>   Anderson, IN

"Oisk" spent his entire 12 years (1948–59) with the Dodgers. His highlights include a pair of no-hitters, one in 1952,
and the other in '56. The first one came close to being a perfect game, as only a base-on-balls against pitcher Willard
Ramsdell in the third inning kept the performance against
the Cubs from being "perfect."

Carl's outstanding year came in 1953 when he was 20-6.
In the World Series he set a single-game record with 14
strikeouts against the Yankees. Among Erskine's victims
was Mickey Mantle, who fanned four times.

He was the winning pitcher in the Dodgers' first game in
the Los Angeles Coliseum on April 18, 1958, when the
Dodgers beat the Giants. Carl has the dubious distinction

of giving up Dale Long's eighth consecutive game blast at Forbes Field on May 28, 1956.   122-78

ESCALERA, Nino
   New York Mets scout

In 1954 Nino struggled as a first baseman-outfielder with the Reds, hitting .159 in 73 games—his only big league season. He was the first black to play for the Reds.

ESPOSITO, Sam
   Head baseball coach at North Carolina State University

A ten-year utility infielder with the A.L., Sam spent all but his final season with the White Sox, where manager Al Lopez platooned him against left-handers. A basketball player at Indiana University, he ended his career in 1963 with the K.C. A's.   .207

ESSEGIAN, Chuck
   Attorney
   Encino, CA

Chuck was an outfielder for six seasons with six teams from 1958–63. In 1952, as a member of the Stanford football team, he was on the losing end of a 40-6 score to the University of Illinois in the Rose Bowl.

   "Twilight Zone" was first telecast on October 2, 1959. Chuck was in a "Twilight Zone" of his own that day, as his pinch-hit homer led the L.A. Dodgers to a come-from-behind victory over the White Sox in game two of the World Series, tieing the series at 1-1. Chuck pinch-hit a second homer in the '59 Series when he pinch-hit for Duke Snider. This gave Essegian the distinction of being the first player to hit two pinch-hit four-baggers in a WS. The feat was duplicated by Bernie Carbo (Red Sox) in the '75 "Fall Classic."

   Chuck picked up where he left off the next spring, when on opening day he hit another pinch-homer to give the Dodgers a victory over the Cubs.   .255

ESTOCK, George
Retired; formerly in employee relations with DuPont Co.
Claymont, DE

George pitched in 37 games for the 1951 Boston Braves—the extent of his big league visit. In his one and only starting assignment he pitched creditably, giving up just 3 runs in eight innings. Unfortunately, that was the day Cliff Chambers of the Pirates no-hit Estock and the Braves. The no-hit loss was, oddly enough, his only major league decision.

EVANS, Al
Died April 6, 1979, at age 62, in Wilson, NC

A twelve-year A.L. catcher, Al spent all but his final season with the Senators from 1939–50. He closed out with the Red Sox in '51.
Al has an oddball record for most consecutive seasons hitting 2 home runs per year (6) (1945–50). He carried a .250 average in 704 games.

EVANS, Bill
Airport limousine driver
Grand Junction, CO

A Bill Evans won two games for the Pirates in 1916. This Bill Evans lost his only decision in four games with the White Sox in 1949. He tried again with the '51 Red Sox and came up 0-0.   0-1

EVERS, Walter "Hoot"
Detroit Tigers director of player development

He received his nickname as the result of being a great fan of western movie star "Hoot" Gibson. An all-around athlete at the University of Illinois in the late 1930s, Evers made an appearance in just one game for the Tigers in 1941 before entering the military in World War II.

Returning to Detroit in '46, he was a regular in the Tigers outfield until traded to the Red Sox in 1952. "Hoot" hit over .300 three straight seasons (1948–50) with the '50 campaign his best (at .323, with 21 homers, and 103 RBIs). Unfortunately, in 1951 his average dipped almost an exact .100 points to .224.   .278

F

FACE, Elroy
   State of Pennsylvania civil service commission; carpenter at Mayview State Hospital

Roy was the relief ace of the Pirates for most of his sixteen years (1953–69). Elroy started just 27 times in 848 appearances, and 23 of them came in his first two seasons. His 802 games with the Pirates ties Walter Johnson for the most games pitched for one team. Roy's banner year was 1959 when he went 18-1 for a .947 percentage, an all-time record for a season for pitchers with at least 15 decisions. That year Pittsburgh was just barely a .500 team. The following year Face was 10-8, but his 24 saves were a big factor in the team's winning the N.L. pennant. He appeared in four of the seven World Series games against the Yankees, picking up 3 saves. From May of 1958 until late in the '59 season, he won 22 consecutive games. Over the stretch, Roy appeared in 92 games without a loss.

Face finished with the expansion Montreal Expos in 1969.   104-95

FAHR, Gerald
   Industrial engineer for Emerson Electric
   Paragould, AR

Gerry had his fling when he pitched five games with no decisions for the 1951 Indians.

FAIN, Ferris "Burrhead"
   Retired; former building contractor
   Georgetown, CA

Ferris was a left-handed hitting first baseman from
1947–55. His father, Oscar Fain, was a jockey who was on
the horse which finished second in the 1912 Kentucky
Derby. In his first four years in the majors, Ferris never
hit .300. Then in 1951 and 1952 he won back-to-back batting titles, hitting .344 and .327. Fain was then traded by
the Philadelphia A's to the White Sox. He tailed off to .256,
and two years later, at age 34, he was gone from the big
league scene.
   Ferris participated in a record 194 double plays for the
'49 Athletics.   .290

FAIRLY, Ron
   California Angels hitting instructor and broadcaster

Signed out of USC, Ron spent the 1959 season with the
L.A. Dodgers. He never hit for the big average, but was a
clutch performer who played a big part in the Dodgers'
N.L. pennants in 1959, '63, '65, and '66. He did average
.300 in those World Series, including hitting safely in all
seven games against the Minnesota Twins in 1965. In '69
he joined the expansion Montreal Expos. Fairly later
played for Toronto, the other Canadian franchise, and finished in 1978 back in southern California with the Angels.
   In the '65 World Series, the lefty hitting first baseman-
outfielder was 11-for-29 (.379). He had 2 homers and 3 doubles among his 11 hits. He also scored 7 runs and had 6
RBIs. Ron is the only player to represent both Canadian
major league teams in the All-Star Game.   .266

FANNIN, Cliff
   Died December 11, 1966, at age 42 in Sandusky, OH

Cliff spent his entire career in a St. Louis Browns' uniform
(1945–52), going 34-51.

FANNING, Jim
> Montreal Expos Vice President of Player Development and Scouting

Jim almost quit baseball to become a school teacher and coach. But he stayed on to catch in 64 games for the Cubs between 1954 and '57. He has remained in baseball.   .170

FANOVICH, Frank
> New York City police dept.
> Suffern, NY

1949 and 1953 weren't too good for Frank, who went 0-2 for the Reds, and 0-3 for the Athletics.   0-5

FARRELL, Dick "Turk"
> Died in auto accident at age 43, June 11, 1977 in Great Yarmouth, England

Death came just eight years after he completed a fourteen-year stint as a right-handed relief specialist. Starting with the Phillies in 1956, he appeared in over 200 games over the next four seasons—all in relief.

After spending one year with the L.A. Dodgers in '61, Dick joined the expansion Astros and became a starter. He was a 20-game loser in '62 despite an ERA near 3.00. He pitched .500 ball the next few seasons in Houston, then wound up where he started in the Phillies' bullpen in the 1968–69 seasons, pitching in an even 100 games (all in relief).   106-111

FASZHOLZ, John
> Pastor of a Lutheran church
> St. Louis, MO

The "G.E. Theater," with Ronald Reagan as its host, appeared in 1953, the same year John hurled in four games with no decisions for his home town Cardinals. Faszholz studied to become a minister while playing pro ball.

FEAR, Vern
    Died Sept. 6, 1976, at age 52 in Spencer, IA

In 1952 Vern was trying to establish himself as a major
league pitcher, appearing in four games for the Cubs.   0-0

FEDEROFF, Al
    Lincoln Park, MI

A second baseman for the Tigers in 1951 and '52, Al played
in 76 games. He spent many seasons as a minor league
manager following his playing days. His players coined
the phrase, "You're better off with Federoff."   .238

FELLER, Bob "Rapid Robert"
    Commentator for Cleveland Indians on cable TV

Bob's entire professional career from age 17 to 38 ended in
1956 (with time out for military duty between the years
1942–46).
    The fireball ace originally signed with the Indians for
$1.00 and an autographed baseball. No salary was stipu-
lated, although he soon received a $10,000 bonus.
    On opening day, April 16, 1940, he no-hit the White Sox.
Forty years later the somewhat tricky trivia question
asks, "What team had every player finish with the same
exact batting average as when the game started?"
    Feller no-hit the Tigers on July 1, 1951, and 11 days
later was a 1-0 loser, as Allie Reynolds of the Yankees no-
hit the Indians. Along with three no-hitters, Feller also
hurled 12 one-hitters. His only frustration was being unable to win a World Series game. Bob lost a one-hitter to
the Browns in 1952. That day, opposing pitcher Bob Cain
also hurled a one-hitter to win, 1-0.
    Finishing with 266 career wins, Feller would have eas-
ily topped the 300 mark had he not missed four seasons
during World War II. With over 2,500 strikeouts, he also
would have surpassed Walter Johnson's career strikeout
record.
    He is currently involved in plans to travel around the

country with Hall of Fame displays. Bob was elected to the coveted Hall in 1962.   266-162

FELLER, Jack
    Onstead, MI

This Feller's career wasn't quite as long as the one above, as he caught in one major league game for the 1958 Tigers. No relation to Bob, he was given Bob's No. 19 with the Tigers.   .000

FERNANDEZ, Chico
    Dodgers infield instructor
    Detroit, MI

Humberto "Chico" Fernandez arrived as a shortstop with the Dodgers in 1956 but spent most of his eight year run with the Phillies and Tigers in the late fifties and early sixties. He finished with the Mets in '63.   .240

FERNANDEZ, "Nanny"
    Marine clerk for I.L.W.U. (Longshoreman's Union)
    Lomita, CA

Frolian "Nanny" Fernandez was an infielder-outfielder with the Braves and Pirates (1942, '46, '47, '50), closing out at .248.

FERRARESE, Don
    Owner, Ferrarese's Family Deli
    Victorville, CA

A little left-handed pitcher with several teams from 1955–62, his overall mark was just 19-36. Don only appeared briefly for the Orioles in 1955, but in '56 he struck out 13 Indians in his first start, only to lose the game. Soon after that, his first major league victory in May of '56 was a two-hit shutout over the Yankees at Yankee Stadium. He had a no-hitter going until a leadoff single in the ninth inning spoiled his bid.

FERRICK, Tom
   Kansas City Royals scout

A big right-handed pitcher, Tom was with all the second-division teams in the A.L. in the 1940s, but finally got his chance with a contender when he joined the Yankees early in the 1950 campaign. With Joe Page not having much success out of the bullpen, Tom became a key factor in the Yankees' A.L. pennant, with 8 wins and 9 saves. Early the following season he returned to Washington where he culminated a 9-year career at 40-40.

FERRIS, Dave "Boo"
   Baseball coach at Delta State College
   Cleveland, MS

As a rookie in 1945, he was 21-10 for the Red Sox with an ERA under 3.00. The following season he led the A.L. in winning percentage with an outstanding 25-6 mark (.806). Dave also shut out the Cardinals in game three of the World Series. Though 46-16 after two years in the majors at age 24, this was the extent of his success. He was 12-11 and 7-3 the next two seasons, and had no decisions in either 1949 or '50 in brief appearances. "Boo" actually pitched in just one inning in 1950, his last in the big top at age 28.
   He made his debut with a pair of shutouts (April 29 and May 6) in 1945 and was not scored on until the fifth inning of his third start. Dave picked up his ninth win of the '45 season by defeating the Senators, giving him the distinction of having beaten every team in the A.L. the first time he faced them.
   When he attended Mississippi State College, he played first base left-handed and pitched right-handed.   65-30

FINE, Tom
   Retail sales work, Mobil Oil Corp.
   Burbank, CA

Tom was with the Red Sox in 1947 and the Browns in '50, compiling a 1-3 record while living out of his suitcase. In

1952 with Scranton of the Eastern League he won a league-record 17 consecutive games.

FINIGAN, Jim
Died May 16, 1981, at age 53 in Quincy, IL

As a rookie in 1954, he broke in with the Philadelphia A's. The team's regular third baseman, he hit a solid .302 and was the last regular to ever hit over .300 for the A's in Philly. He tailed off the next two seasons with the A's in Kansas City. After stays with the Tigers and Giants, Jim joined the Baltimore Orioles in 1959, where he lost his job in mid-season to Brooks Robinson. Jim attended Quincy College and St. Ambrose. Before his death he was a printing salesman in Quincy, Ill. and coached the baseball team at Quincy College.   .264

FISCHER, Bill
Kansas City Royals minor league pitching coach

Bill had a nine-year run with five A.L. teams, 1956–64. Although he wasn't too successful, with an overall 45-58 mark (mostly as a reliever), Bill did establish a major league record in 1962 which still stands today. Pitching for the Kansas City A's, he went just 4-12, but for the most part he was throwing strikes. From August 3 to September 30 in 84⅓ consecutive innings, Bill never issued a base-on-balls. This surpassed the former record of 68 innings held by Hall of Famer Christy Mathewson. Overall, he walked just 8 in 128 innings that summer. Fischer bowed out in 1964 with Minnesota. After scouting for the Kansas City Royals during most of the 1970s he joined the Cincinnati Reds as their pitching coach.

In the early fifties he was a drill instructor in the Marines.

FISHER, Eddie
     Bank manager
     Altus, OK

This Eddie Fisher made a living with his arm, not his vocal cords. Of the two pitchers named Fisher who first appeared in the majors in 1959, Eddie was the more successful—his career lasted into the 1970s (for 15 seasons). Fisher's best effort was with the White Sox in 1965 (when he won 15 and saved 24), and was voted the "Fireman of the Year." The following season he was traded to Baltimore, and his work out of the bullpen for the Orioles helped them to the A.L. flag. The former relief ace is a graduate of UCLA.   85-70

FISHER, Harry
     Died September 20, 1981, at age 55 in Waterloo,
     Ontario, Canada

In 1952, Harry didn't have much to laugh about, going 1-2 in eight games for the Pirates, the chucker's only season.

FISHER, Jack
     Pitching coach for St. John's University; also coaches
     in college summer leagues
     Long Island, N.Y.

Jack was around from 1959–69, and was on the losing end more often than not. However, his first major league victory late in the '59 season for the Orioles was a three-hit shutout over the A.L. champion White Sox. In 1960 Fisher was 12-11 for his only winning season in the majors. On September 28th he gave up the dramatic home run to Ted Williams at Fenway Park in his final at-bat in the bigs. Almost one year later to the day, on September 26, 1961, he surrendered Roger Maris' 60th home run of the season. Jack was with the Mets during the mid-1960s, suffering through league leading 24, and 18 defeat seasons.   86-139

FISHER, Maury
Senior tool designer
Fisher Body division, General Motors
Mansfield, OH

Of all the Fisher-men who played in the big leagues, Maury took home the smallest catch as a one-game pitcher for the '55 Reds.   0-0

FITZGERALD, Ed
Janitorial service company
Sacramento, CA

While Uncle Milty (Milton Berle) was entertaining TV audiences with his slapstick comedy from 1948–59, Ed was a backstop in a career that spanned 807 games (mostly with the Pirates and Senators). "Fitzy," who walked away from the Indians and a .260 average, was one of the seven brothers who barnstormed as The Traveling Fitzgerald Basketball Team. Playing with the Senators on opening day in 1959, he hit into a triple play, making him the first player in major league history to hit into a triple play on opening day.

FITZGERALD, John
Location unknown

John pitched in one big league game for the San Francisco Giants in 1958.   0-0

FLANIGAN, Tom
Independence, KY

Del Flanigan was a big boxing name in the fifties. Tom Flanigan was a right-handed pitcher who came up with goose eggs in '54 (White Sox) and '58 (Cardinals).   0-0

FLETCHER, Van
  Contractor and tobacco farmer
  Yadkinville, NC

Van had no decisions in 9 games with the '55 Tigers.

FLOOD, Curt
  Oakland A's announcer in 1978; Oakland, CA, parks
  dept.

The St. Louis Cardinals centerfielder from 1958–69, Curt
was originally in the Reds' organization and made a brief
appearance for them in 1957 where he picked up his first
major league hit, a home run off Moe Drabowsky. Curt's
best seasons were with the Cardinals, and at times he was
considered the best centerfielder in the game during the
sixties when he helped the Cardinals to three N.L. pennants.
  Unfortunately, Flood is best remembered for unsuccessful-
ly challenging baseball's reserve clause when the Cardinals
traded him to the Phillies following the 1969 season. Curt
made a futile comeback with the Washington Senators in
1971. His controversial book, *The Way It Is*, followed.
  Flood was back in the game briefly in 1978 as an announcer for the A's in his native Oakland. Six times he
was over .300, including a career high of .335 in 1967,
compiling a lifetime .293 mark.

FLORES, Jesse
  Minnesota Twins scout

This Mexican right-hander was 44-59 in 176 games, most
of them with the Philadelphia Athletics in the forties. His
last season was in 1950 with the Cleveland Indians.

FLOWERS, Ben
  Sales manager, Industrial Electric
  Rocky Mount, NC

From 1951–56, Ben was with the Red Sox, Tigers, Cardinals, and Phillies. Ben holds the A.L. mark for appearing

in most consecutive games as a relief pitcher, with eight.
3-7

FODGE, Gene
Employed with Al's Butcher Block
South Bend, IN

In 1958 Gene went 1-1 in 16 games for the Cubs.

FOILES, Hank
Insurance agent
Virginia Beach, VA

Hank caught in 608 games with nine different teams, including two stops each with the Reds and Indians, from 1953–64. The traveling backstop swung for a .243 average. He was originally signed by the Yankees out of the University of Virginia.

Foiles was the first catcher (and possibly the first major leaguer) to wear contact lenses.

FONDY, Dee
Milwaukee Brewers special assistant to the general manager

Dee was a first baseman in the N.L. from 1951–58. As the regular first baseman for the Cubs, he hit an even .300 in '52, and .309 in '53. He was traded to Pittsburgh during the '57 campaign and enjoyed another .300-plus season. In 1958 Fondy fell off to .218 playing for the Reds in his final dash in the big leagues.

Dee attended San Bernardino Valley College, and closed out his career with exactly 1,000 hits. He was traded from the Pirates to the Reds in 1957 for Ted Kluszewski. .286

FORD, Whitey, "The Chairman of the Board"
   Spring training coach for the Yankees, and runs a baseball camp

The all-time Yankee leader with 236 wins, Whitey was 25-4 in 1961, and 24-7 in 1963. In his first major league appearance, after being recalled from the minors in 1950, he came on in relief against the Red Sox, and was roughed up for 5 runs and 7 hits in a few short innings. Ford was rarely hit that hard again. At age 21, he was 9-1 (his rookie year), and was the winner in the final game of a four-game sweep over the Phillies in the '50 WS. Whitey hurled consecutive one-hitters in 1955. In a '56 game against the Athletics he fanned six consecutive batters.

The Cy Young Award winner in 1961, Whitey holds several World Series records, including total games pitched, games won, and strike-outs.

With a total career mark of 236-106, his .690 winning percentage is the second best in major league history. He was elected to the Hall of Fame in 1974.

FORNIELES, Mike
   Automobile salesman
   Brighton, MA

A Cuban-born chucker, Mike spent 12 years with five teams in the A.L. from 1952–63. As a 20-year-old in his first big league game, he threw a one-hitter for the Washington Senators. Used mostly as a reliever, his best season came in 1960 with the Red Sox when he appeared in a league-leading 70 games and was voted the "Fireman of the Year."   63-64

FOWLER, Art
   Released as Yankees pitching coach in 1983

Billy Martin's buddy, Art pitched for the Reds as a starter from 1954–56. He was already in his mid-thirties at the time, after spending a decade in the minors. Well past his 40th birthday, he did some outstanding work out of the Los Angeles Angels' bullpen in 1963. Although he was in the big top for just one more season, Art was still pitching at close to 50 years of age at Denver in the American Association in 1970. He has been Martin's pitching coach with the Tigers, Rangers, Yankees, and A's. Like many pitchers, Fowler never cared for running, and was once quoted as saying, "If you pitched with your legs, Jesse Owens would have won 30." 54-51

FOWLER, Dick
Died May 22, 1972, at age 51 in Oneonta, NY

Dick was a ten-year hurler (all with the Philadelphia A's) from 1941–52. Late in the 1945 season he rejoined the A's after spending two years and most of '45 in military service. His only win in three decisions late in that '45 campaign was a 1-0 no-hitter over the St. Louis Browns. It was the first no-hitter in the majors since Bob Feller's on opening day of the 1940 season. The game also marked the only time in modern big league history that a pitcher recorded a no-hitter for his only victory of the season. It was the first no-hitter in the majors ever thrown by a Canadian (Fowler was born in Toronto). 66-79

FOX, Howie
Died October 9, 1955, at age 34 in San Antonio, TX, in a tavern he owned, from knife wounds received while breaking up a fight

A righty flipper with the Reds in the forties, Howie closed out a 43-72 record with the Orioles in 1954, after a brief visit with the Phils two years earlier. Howie was 9-14 for the Reds in '51, but four of his victories were shutouts.

FOX, Nellie
Died December 1, 1975, at age 47 in Baltimore, MD

The premier A.L. second baseman in the 1950s, Nellie was the Wee Willie Keeler of his time, leading the league a record seven straight years from 1954–60 in singles. He started out in 1947 with the A's, and following the 1949 season was dealt away to the White Sox for catcher Joe Tipton. That first year he hit .247, but from then on was always near or over the .300 mark for the duration of the decade. Four times he led the league in base hits. Extremely hard to strike out, during the 1958 season he went a record 98 consecutive games without a whiff. The most times he ever struck out in a season was 18, while coming to bat no fewer than 600 times, 1951–62. Whitey Ford once said, "Nellie was the toughest out for me. In twelve years I struck him out once, and I think the umpire blew the call."

Nellie was the A.L. MVP in 1959 when he spearheaded the White Sox to their first pennant in 40 years, hitting .306 (the only member of the White Sox to hit over .300). He was the last second baseman to win the MVP award prior to Joe Morgan, who copped the coveted award in 1975 and 1976. An All-Star selection 10 times, Nellie holds the A.L. mark for best career fielding percentage by a second baseman. The "mighty atom" had 2,663 hits, of which 2,262 were singles.

Born on Christmas Day, he met his wife on Christmas Day, and had a daughter born on Christmas. His number two has been retired by the White Sox.   .288

FOYTACK, Paul
    Salesman for industrial rubber/plastics firm
    West Bloomfield, MI

Paul spent ten of his eleven seasons with the Detroit Tigers from 1953–63 before parting in 1964 with the Angels. From 1956–59 he won 14 and 15 games twice for Detroit. Paul gave up the first of Roger Maris' 61 home runs in 1961. By 1963 he was with the Angels. On July 31st of that year, he gave up four consecutive home runs to the Cleveland Indians. Woodie Held, pitcher Pedro Ramos, Tito Francona, and Larry Brown all connected. It is a dubious feat, most likely to stand for a while.   86-87

FRANCONA, Tito
Beaver County recreation director
New Brighton, PA

John Patsy Tito Francona was a fifteen-year outfielder from 1956–70 with six different A.L. teams, and three N.L. clubs. With Cleveland in 1959 he hit .363 (which was well above his lifetime .272 mark). However, he had only 399 official at-bats, and was not eligible for the batting title which went to Harvey Kuenn (.353). Tito's son Terry is currently with the Montreal Expos.

FRAZIER, Joe
Manager at Louisville in American Association during 1982

Joe first appeared with Cleveland in 1947. After an absence of seven years, he returned in 1954 with the St. Louis Cardinals. That season he was an outstanding pinch-hitter, going 20-for-62 (leading the league in both categories). Two years later he was again out of the majors, and after two decades he returned to manage the NY Mets in the late 1970s.   .241

FREEMAN, Hershell
Superintendent at delinquent children's home
Orlando, FL

A right-handed pitcher for six years (1952–58), Hershell had one very good year in 1956 as the bullpen ace for the Cincinnati Reds, when he won 14 games and saved 18 more. One he did not win was a combination no-hitter that he, Johnny Klippstein, and Joe Black threw at the Braves in May of '56. The Braves were held hitless through the first nine innings, but eventually won the game, 2-1, in extra innings. Freeman was not involved in the decision. He finished with the Cubs in '58. Hershell attended the University of Alabama.   30-16

FREEMAN, Mark
Mutual funds salesman in Denver, CO

While Hershell last appeared in the majors in '58, Mark (no relation) arrived with brief appearances in 1959 with both the Yankees and Kansas City A's. In 1960 he was with the Cubs and had a record of 3-3, which proved to be his lifetime mark. Freeman is a product of Louisiana State University.

FREESE, Gene
Owns Third Base Inc. (cocktail lounge)
New Orleans, LA

This third baseman was seen in baseball backyards from 1955–66. When he came up with the Pirates as a 21-year-old rookie in '55, he competed for the third-base position with his older brother, George. Gene shared the third-base job with his brother and also played in over 50 games at second base. George, who was eight years older, returned to the minors while Gene remained in Pittsburgh for several additional seasons. He drifted around the majors for a few more seasons until 1961, when he became the regular third baseman for the N.L. champion Cincinnati Reds. He played a key role in the Reds' march with 26 homers, and 87 RBIs. He eventually returned to the Pirates, and then made a second stop with the White Sox before closing with the Astros in 1966.   .254

FREESE, George
Sporting goods manager for department store
Portland, OR

George, the brother of Gene Freese, played in 61 big league games with the Tigers ('53), Pirates ('55), and Cubs ('61). "Bud" hit .257 while on tour.

FRICANO, Marion
     Died May 18, 1976, at age 52 in Tijuana, Mexico

A right-handed flipper with the Philadelphia and Kansas City Athletics, he was 15-23 in 88 games from 1952–55.
     Marion was a school teacher in upstate New York when he died, while vacationing, in Mexico.

FRIDLEY, Jim
     Supervisor for Duriron Company
     Dayton, OH

An outfielder, who didn't reach the big time until he was 27 years old in 1952, he took advantage of the opportunity, hitting a home run for his first major league hit (and providing the Indians with an opening day, 1-0 win over the White Sox). Later that same season he became the first rookie in baseball history to go 6-for-6 in a game. He was later sold to the St. Louis Browns, and returned to the majors in '54, at which time the team became the Baltimore Orioles. Jim was a part-time outfielder for them in '54, and then appeared briefly for the Reds in 1958.   .248

FRIEND, Bob "Warrior"
     Insurance business
     Fox Chapel, PA

Bob spent 16 years, 1951–66, in the big arena. Except for the final season (which he spent with both the New York Yankees and Mets), Friend made his living with the Pirates. His first seven years were spent with a Pittsburgh team which either finished last, or next to last, in the N.L. Friend's record suffered, except in 1955 when he was 14-9, and became the first pitcher in big league history to ever lead a league in ERA (2.83) while pitching for a cellar team. His best season was in 1958, when he won 22 to lead the N.L. in wins.

With an overall mark of 197-230, Bob just missed joining Bobo Newsom and Jake Powell as the only pitchers to win over 200, and suffer a larger amount of defeats. Bob was the starting and winning pitcher for the Pirates in the last game the Giants played in the Polo Grounds in 1957. He also collected three hits that day.

FRIEND, Owen
    Wichita, KS

Owen played in 208 games as a utility infielder with the Browns, Tigers, Indians, Red Sox, and Cubs from 1949–56. He owns a .227 average. Friend was a minor league manager for several years following his playing days.

FROATS, Bill
    Location unknown

In 1955 "Captain Kangaroo" leaped into the living rooms of many, while Billy Froats leaped out of the majors after pitching in one game with the Detroit Tigers. Froats pitched at Notre Dame before his brief big league stay.

                                                                0-0

FURILLO, Carl "Skoonj"
    Former county sheriff
    Stony Creek Hills, PA

A fifteen-year outfielder (1946–60), all with the Dodgers, Carl was a solid hitter, as he hit over .300 four times, and over the .290 mark an additional six times, in compiling a lifetime .299 mark with over 6,000 at-bats. An additional 15 hits, or just one a season over his 15-year career, kept him from a career .300 average. His 106 RBIs and .322 average helped lead Brooklyn to the 1949 pennant. Carl's only off season was in 1952 when he fell to .247. However, the following season he had his best year (winning the N.L. batting title) by increasing his average nearly 100 points over the previous season with a .344 mark. He missed the last few weeks of that campaign as he suffered a broken finger during a brawl with Giants' manager Leo Durocher, after being hit by a pitch thrown by Ruben Gomez. He returned in time for the World Series, and went 8-for-24 against the Yankees.

Furillo continued to hit well for the next several years and remained as the starting right fielder for the Dodgers through their first season in L.A. in 1958. By '59 he was relegated to part-time duty, but in the third game of the World Series he had a pinch-hit single with the bases loaded late in the game, to give L.A. a 3-1 win (and a 2-1 lead in the Series they eventually won from the White Sox in six games). It was his last big hit as the following year he was released early in the season. His career ended on a sour note when he sued the team for releasing him without pay. He won the lawsuit. Carl operated a delicatessen and did construction work before being elected to the office of County Sheriff.

Carl was nicknamed "Skoonj" (from the Italian word for snail) because of his slowness while running the bases. Because of his strong throwing arm, he was also called "The Reading Rifle" (he played minor league ball at Reading, Pennsylvania). According to some accounts, Carl threw six runners out at first from his rightfield position.

FUSSELMAN, Les
Died May 21, 1970, at age 49 in Cleveland, OH

Les was catching baseball games for the Cardinals from 1952–53. In 43 games he hit .169.

G

GABLER, Bill
Mercury Welding Service
St. Louis, MO

Bill struck out in each of his three pinch-hitting appearances in three games for the Cubs in 1958. Bill was on top of the world one night in '54 while playing for Fort Worth in the Texas League. He drove in 10 runs in three successive innings with a bases-loaded double, a three-run homer, and a grand slam.

GABLER, John
Nursery owner
Overland Park, KS

John went 7-12 in 53 games split between the Yankees and Senators between 1959 and 1961. A nice guy, but not too much to gab about.

GAEDEL, Eddie
Died June 18, 1961, at age 36 in Chicago, IL

The most talked about publicity stunt ever conceived in the history of baseball took place in 1951 at Sportsman's Park in St. Louis, when Eddie Gaedel, a midget, appeared in a game for the inept St. Louis Browns. Gaedel, who was 3'7" and weighed 65 pounds, emerged from a large birthday cake between games of a doubleheader with the Tigers. The celebration which commemorated the fiftieth anniversary of the Falstaff Brewing Company (the Browns' radio sponsor), was put together by promotion czar Bill Veeck.

To the surprise of the 18,369 fans, Gaedel stepped out of the cake wearing elves' shoes and number ⅛ on his

Browns' uniform. As the midget strolled to the plate in the bottom of the first inning as a pinch-hitter for Frank Saucier, Tiger skipper Red Rolfe protested Gaedel's presence on the field. However, Zack Taylor, the Browns' manager, produced a legitimate contract that had been filed with the A.L. office and cleared by umpire Ed Hurley.

Detroit pitcher Bob Cain walked the diminutive Gaedel on four straight pitches. As the miniature Brownie waddled down to first base, the crowd roared with excitement, realizing the spectacle they had just witnessed. Jim Delsing then ran for Eddie. Manager Taylor said, "The little fellow was so scared I had to help him tie his shoelaces."

American League prexy Will Harridge was furious with Veeck's burlesque and wanted Gaedel's name forever stricken from the record book. Veeck justifiably argued that the major leagues had no maximum height restriction, so why have a minimum height restriction?

A few years later Gaedel returned to a major league game (but not as a player) when he and three other midgets came out of a helicopter that landed behind second base at a White Sox game. Dressed as Martians, they captured Luis Aparicio and Nellie Fox of the White Sox.

Gaedel, who received one hundred dollars for his pinch-hitting appearance, died ten years later, the result of injuries suffered in a speakeasy skirmish. And Bob Cain, the pitcher who walked Gaedel, traveled from Cleveland to Chicago to attend the midget's funeral!　　　　　　.000

GARAGIOLA, Joe
　　NBC-TV baseball announcer

The odds would have to be heavily against two youngsters' growing up in the same neighborhood and both becoming major league catchers. However, both Joe and Yogi Berra made it. Joe's career was not as illustrious, but he is as well known today as Yogi.

Garagiola's best-selling book of 1960, *Baseball Is a Funny Game*, helped set the tone for his jokes about his own shortcomings as a player. He did play in the majors from 1946–1954. In '46, as a rookie, Joe hit .316 in the

World Series, helping the St. Louis Cardinals defeat the
Red Sox. He had a four-hit game in that Series. Joe was
traded to the anemic Pirates in the early 1950s, but did hit
a respectable .273 in 1952 for the cellar-finishing team.

He jokingly claims that the manager would give him the
take sign on the 3-and-2 count. Garagiola went out with
a winner as he finished with the world champion N.Y.
Giants in 1954.   .257

GARBER, Bob
Sales specialist
S. C. Johnson and Son Wax Co.
Redwood City, CA

In 1956 Johnny Cash sang "I Walk the Line" while Bob
Garber was walking three batters in four innings of pitching, in two games for the Pirates.   0-0

GARBOWSKI, Alex
Yonkers, NY

Alex was released after appearing in two games for the '52
Tigers as a pinch-runner.

GARCIA, Mike "The Big Bear"
Dry cleaning business
Fairview Park, OH

"The Big Bear" spent twelve of his fourteen years (1948–61)
as a member of the Cleveland Indians. Mike was 20-13 in
'51, then had his best season in 1952, winning 22, including a league-leading 6 shutouts. His 2.64 ERA topped the
A.L. in the Indians' pennant-winning season of 1954. He
again led the league in shutouts that year, with five.
                                                  142-97

GARCIA, Vinicio "Chico"
Managing in the Mexican League

"Chico" hit a pale .113 in 39 games for the 1954 Orioles in
his only big league season. The second baseman continued

in professional baseball well into his forties in the Mexican
League.

GARDELLA, Danny "Tarzan"
Warehouseman in Queens, NY

A muscular outfielder, Danny played his last game with
one pinch-hitting appearance for the St. Louis Cardinals
in 1950. However, his name is one that was forerunner to
Curt Flood, Andy Messersmith, or any others, in suing
major league baseball over the reserve clause. In the late
1940s the case was set for the Supreme Court, but was settled out of court.

His legal fight gave him much publicity at the time. He
had been one of the players who jumped to the Mexican
outlaw league in 1946. In 1945 he was a N.Y. Giants regular in the outfield, and hit 18 home runs for a .272 average.
A brother, Al, also appeared briefly for the Giants that season as a first baseman. Following the out-of-court settle-
ment in which he was reported to have received $60,000,
he signed a contract with the Cardinals. But he made just
that one appearance as a pinch-hitter in 1950 before being
sent to the minors.   .267

GARDNER, Billy
Minnesota Twins manager

A ten-year performer, Billy was a utility infielder for
the world champion N.Y. Giants in his rookie season of
1954. He was sold to Baltimore after the 1955 season
and was the Orioles' regular second baseman for the
next four years. In 1957 he led the A.L. in doubles with
36. In 1961 he was a part-time player in a utility role for
the Yankees.

Billy, who has managed in the minors since his playing
days have ended, also had a reputation as a top-notch pool
player.   .237

GARVER, Ned
Public relations work for a food company (retired)
Ney, OH

Born 12-25-25, he had his one outstanding season at age 25
(in 1951) when he became the first pitcher in major league
history to win 20 games for a team which lost 100 games.
He was 20-12 for the last place St. Louis Browns that season. In his fourteen year stay (1948–61), he never pitched
for a first division team.

In his banner year in 1951 he also led the A.L. in complete games with 24. Garver also helped himself with the
bat as he hit .305, going 29-for-95. Ned was with Detroit
during the mid-50s and the best they finished during that
period was fifth. He was effective in '54 with 14 wins and
an ERA under 3.00.

The last few years of the decade were spent with another
second division club, the Kansas City A's. He was with the
expansion L.A. Angels in his final season in '61.

His overall mark of 129-157 is not all that bad considering the teams he pitched for.

GASTALL, Tom
Died at age 24 on September 20, 1956 in Chesapeake
Bay, MD

In June of 1955 Tom signed with the Baltimore Orioles for
a large bonus out of Boston University. Due to the rule at
the time that a player signing for a bonus of over $4,000
must remain with the big league team for two seasons, he
remained with the Orioles as a part-time catcher throughout the 1955 campaign and until late in the '56 season. He
died at a very young age when the small plane he was pi-
loting crashed into Chesapeake Bay.   .181

GEIGER, Gary
Building superintendent at a private school
Tulsa, OK

A twelve-year outfielder from 1958–70, Gary broke in with
Cleveland in 1958. From 1959 to 1965 he was with the Red

Sox, playing regularly in 1961 and '62. He made his last
stop with the Houston Astros in 1970. In 1961 he had 18
homers and 16 stolen bases; in '62 he had 16 homers and
18 stolen bases. .246

GENOVESE, George
    San Francisco Giants scout

In 1950 George Genovese appeared in three games as a
pinch-hitter for the Senators. .000

GENTILE, Jim "Diamond Jim"
    Manager of automotive center
    Mesa, AZ

This big left-handed hitting first baseman spent several
years in the Dodgers' organization in the minors. He did
have brief trials with the Dodgers in their last season in
Brooklyn in '57, and their first year in L.A. in '58. Jim was
purchased by the Orioles from the Dodgers American Association team, and in 1960 had a fine season playing full
time in the A.L., hitting .292, with 21 homers, and 98
RBIs.
    But 1961 was his sensational season, though it was over-
shadowed by the assault on Babe Ruth's home-run mark
from the Yankees' Roger Maris and Mickey Mantle. Jim
hit .302 with 46 homers and 141 RBIs. He trailed Maris by
one for the RBI title. Gentile finished third in the MVP
vote behind the M & M boys. His five grand slams that
year tied a major league record. Gentile hit two of them on
May 9th in successive times at-bat (the first time it was
ever accomplished in major league history). Traded to
Kansas City in '64, Jim closed in '66 in Cleveland. .260

GENTRY, Harvey
    General foreman, Raytheon Co.
    Bristol, TN

In 1954 Harvey went 1-for-4 as a pinch-swatter for the
New York Giants. .250

GEORGE, Alex
    Kansas City, MO

Prez Prado played "Cherry Pink and Apple Blossom
White" in '55 while a pink-cheeked 17-year-old named
Alex George went 1-for-10 for his home town K.C. A's.
                                                    .100

GERNERT, Dick
    Texas Rangers scout

A first baseman, Dick played eleven seasons from 1952–63.
As a rookie with the Red Sox he hit 19 homers in 1952. He
remained with Boston and was a part-time player for the
Red Sox through the 1959 season. Near the end of his career, Dick hit .302 in 40 games for Cincinnati to help the
Reds' drive for the N.L. pennant (in 1961).
    Gernert is the nephew of Dom Dallessandro, who played
for the Red Sox (1937) and Cubs (1940–47). Gernert attended Temple University.   .254

GETTEL, Al
    Heavy equipment operator
    Virginia Beach, VA

Al was a right-handed pitcher for the Yankees, Indians,
White Sox, and Senators from 1945–49, and with the
Giants in '51 and '55.   38-45

GIALLOMBARDO, Bob
    Brooklyn, N.Y.

Mr. Giallombardo snuck into six games for the L.A. Dodgers in 1958 as a 19-year-old chucker, never to return.   1-1

GIBSON, Bob
    Atlanta Braves pitching coach

Bob played college basketball at Creighton University in
the mid-fifties and averaged over 20 points per game. He

then played a season for the Harlem Globetrotters before turning to professional baseball.

"Gibby" did not have his first full year in the majors until 1961, but he did spend some time with the Cardinals in both 1959 and '60. His credentials include 251 wins, 3,117 strikeouts, and a career 2.91 ERA. Bob had an all-time low ERA of 1.12 in 1968. A two-time Cy Young award winner, he was the N.L. MVP in 1968.

Gibson was especially tough at World Series time with a record 17-strikeout game and a Series record 35 strikeouts against Detroit in 1968. He has an overall World Series mark of 7-2 and a 1.89 ERA. His 92 strikeouts in World Series action is just two under record-holder Whitey Ford. It took Ford 22 games for his 94 while Gibson had his 92 in just 9 games.

A good hitting pitcher, Bob homered in the seventh and decisive game of the '67 Series over the Red Sox, and then again in game four of the '68 classic, becoming the first hurler to ever hit two home runs in Series play.   251-174

GIEL, Paul
    Athletic director at University of Minnesota

One of the top backfield stars in college football for the Golden Gophers of Minnesota, Paul was selected as the Back of the Year by AP and Player of the Year by UPI. Paul wasn't the Heisman Award winner, but he was drafted by the NFL Chicago Bears. He was also an outstanding pitcher in baseball, and chose to sign with the N.Y. Giants for a large bonus. Giel made a strong showing out of the bullpen by striking out the side in his first appearance. One of his strikeout victims that day was Vic Janowicz, who himself had been an outstanding college football player at Ohio State and a Heisman Trophy winner.

He had no decisions that season in a few brief appearances and was just 4-4 the following year before entering the military. Giel returned in 1958 to the Giants, who were now in San Francisco. Paul moved over to the

Pittsburgh Pirates after that season, and won his only two decisions in 1960 for the N.L. champions.

Giel finished with the Twins and A's with a total record of 11-9.

GIGGIE, Bob
   Supervisor for a computer drafting firm
   Milton, MA

Between 1959–62, Bob went 3-1 in 30 games with the Milwaukee Braves and Kansas City A's.

GILBERT, Drew
   Knoxville, TN

"Buddy" had a 7-game stint with the Reds in '59. He was 3-for-20 at the plate. Two of his hits were home runs.   .150

GILBERT, Harold "Tookie"
   Died June 23, 1967, at age 38 in New Orleans, LA

His father, Larry Gilbert, was a member of the 1914 "Miracle" Boston Braves as a part-time outfielder. As a first baseman for the N.Y. Giants in 1950, "Tookie" hit .220 in over 100 games. He was not with the Giants again until 1953 when he played in 70 games for the extent of his major league career. A brother, Charlie, was an outfielder in the N.L. for six seasons during the 1940s.   .203

GILE, Don
   Investment banker
   Citrus Heights, CA

Between 1959–62, Don played first base and caught with the Red Sox in a total of 58 games. He was signed by the Red Sox out of the University of Arizona.   .150

GILLESPIE, Bob
Press room supervisor for *Journal* and *Sentinel*
Winston-Salem, NC

Like Don Gile, Bob Gillespie appeared in 58 games. His
run came in the forties with the Tigers and White Sox, and
in one game with the Red Sox in 1950.   5-13

GILLIAM, Jim "Junior"
Died October 8, 1978, at age 49 in Inglewood, CA

"Junior" replaced Jackie Robinson at second base in his
rookie season in 1953, with Robinson moving to third base.
Jim led the league in triples with 17 that rookie season,
and was voted the N.L. "Rookie-of-the-Year." His playing
career lasted until 1966 with the last two as a player-
coach. Gilliam was still a coach in 1978 when he died (after
being in a Dodger uniform for a quarter of a century).
   In the World Series after his rookie year in '53, he tied
an all-time record for extra-base hits in a six game series
with three doubles, and two home runs. A valuable, versatile player, "Junior" played in over 1,000 games at second
base, another 700-plus at third, and over 200 in the outfield. He had excellent bat control and was a big factor in
Maury Wills' stolen base records by hitting behind Wills
in the lineup.
   Jim is the only player in major league history to appear
in both a regular season perfect game and a World Series
perfect game. He played in Sandy Koufax's gem in 1965
and in Don Larsen's Series classic in 1956.
   He was called "Junior" because he was only 17 years old
when he joined the Baltimore Elite Giants of the old National Negro League. The city of Los Angeles has titled a
baseball playing field in his name.   .265

GINSBERG, Myron "Joe"
Sales rep for Jack Daniel's Distributing
Northfield, MI

Joe played for most A.L. teams except for the one from
his native N.Y. He did play in several games at the end

of his career with the Mets in 1962. A thirteen-year career man as a catcher, starting in 1948, Ginsberg played for the Tigers, Indians, Athletics, Orioles, White Sox, and Red Sox.

Joe was well known around the league as a clubhouse comedian.   .241

GIORDANO, Tom
   Baltimore Orioles director of scouting

As a second baseman, Tommy played in 11 games for the '53 Philadelphia Athletics.   .175

GLAVIANO, Tommy
   State department of motor vehicles
   Sacramento, CA

Sometimes called "Rabbit," Tommy played third base most of his career with the Cardinals, and then briefly with the Phillies from 1949–53. He sports a lifetime .257 average, with his best season coming in 1950 as the regular third baseman with the Cardinals.

Tom would like to forget May 18, 1950, when he made errors on three consecutive plays in the ninth inning, aiding a four-run Brooklyn rally that gave the Dodgers a 9-8 victory.

GLYNN, Bill
   Supervisor, Alta Dena Dairy
   San Diego, CA

A first baseman, Bill came up with the Phillies in '49, then played with the Indians from 1952–54. He batted .251 in 111 games for the A.L. Champion Indians in '54. In one game he collected three homers and seven RBIs, and barely missed a grand slam by inches.   .249

GOLDSBERRY, Gordon
> Head of minor league and scouting departments for the Cubs

Gordon's career as a first baseman spanned 1949-52 with the White Sox and Browns. He was the top pinch-hitter in the A.L. in 1950, going 12-for-39. Goldsberry attended UCLA. .241

GOLIAT, Mike
> Trucking business
> Seven Hills, OH

He had just one full season under the big top (1950) as the regular second baseman for the Phillies. Mike hit just .234, but he did provide some punch in the batting order with 13 homers and 64 RBIs. His only other years in the biggies were as a part-time player for the Phillies in 1949, and a few brief appearances for the St. Louis Browns in 1951 and 1952, after the Phillies sent him to the minor leagues early in '51.

His name is the only one which generally stumps trivia buffs in naming the starting lineup and key players for the "Whiz Kids." .225

GOMEZ, Ruben
> Rio Piedras, PR

Ruben spent ten years in the limelight, starting as a 13-game winner for the N.Y. Giants in 1953. He was a key member of the Giants' starting rotation in 1954, when he went 17-9, and had a fine 2.88 ERA.

He fell off the next two years, but did come back to win 15 games in 1957. After one year with the Giants, in San Francisco, Gomez was dealt to the Phillies, and parted in 1967 at 76-86 overall.

The right-hander had an excellent screwball. Ruben was the winning pitcher in the first major league game in Seals Stadium on April 15, 1958, when the Giants beat the Dodgers, 8-0.

GONZALEZ, Vince
    Died March 11, 1981, in Campeche, Mexico

Gonzalez, a left-handed chucker, had only one chance to
view the game 60'6" from the catcher, as a one-gamer for
the Washington Senators in 1955.   0-0

GOODMAN, Billy
    Real estate business
    Sarasota, FL

Billy was one of the most versatile players in baseball history, playing in over 1,600 games between 1947–62. He did
everything but pitch and catch.

    Goodman spent the first ten years with the Red Sox
where he hit .310 as a rookie in 1948. Two years later he
was the A.L. batting champion with a .354 mark while
used primarily as a utility man at five different positions.
Billy didn't move into the starting lineup on a full-time
basis until after mid-season when he stepped into left field
to replace Ted Williams, who had injured his elbow in the
All-Star Game. From 1951–57, when he was traded to
Baltimore in mid-season, Goodman was generally over
.300, or close to it, every year.

    In 1958 he was a member of the A.L. champion White
Sox as a part-time starter at third base.

    Billy made his exit with a lifetime batting average of
.300.

GORBOUS, Glenn
    Oil company employee
    Calgary, Canada

This rifle-armed Canadian-born outfielder, who played
from 1955–57 with the Reds and Phillies, had a .238 average in 277 games.

GORDON, Joe "Flash"
Died April 14, 1978, at age 63 in Sacramento, CA

During his 11-year journey as a second baseman from 1938–50, "Flash" hit 253 homers, and had a lifetime .268 average. As a rookie in 1938, he helped the Yankees to a four-game sweep over the Cubs in the World Series, going 6-for-15, including a home run. Gordon hit for a .500 mark (7-14) as the Yankees beat the Dodgers in five games in the 1941 series. In 1942 he hit for a personal high .322, and was elected the A.L. MVP.

Following the '46 season, in which he fell off to an anemic .210 mark after two years of military service, he was traded to Cleveland for pitcher Allie Reynolds. It turned out to be one of those trades that aided both clubs. Reynolds was a mainstay of the Yankees' pitching staff for the next few seasons. In '48 Gordon had his most productive power season with 32 homers and 124 RBIs, in helping the Indians to the A.L. pennant, and a World Series win over the Boston Braves. During the 1960 season Joe was traded from K.C. to Detroit for Jimmy Dykes (in a trade for managers).

In 1961 he managed the Kansas City A's, and then in '69 returned to Kansas City to manage the expansion Royals. A top-flight gymnast, he used to return to Eugene, Oregon, to perform at halftimes of University of Oregon basketball games during his playing days.

GORDON, Sid
Died June 17, 1975, at age 57 in New York

Sid was a long-ball-hitting outfielder for 13 years (1941–55) with two seasons out for military service in 1944–45. He hit 30 homers with 107 RBIs in 1948 for the N.Y. Giants. On July 31, 1949, he hit two home runs in one inning. Following that season he was traded to the Boston Braves. Sid had over 100 RBIs for the next two years, and stayed with the Braves through their first season in Milwaukee in 1953. In 1955 he finished with the Pirates and Giants with 202 homers and a .283 lifetime average.

GORIN, Charles
    Dean of boys at Reagan High School
    Austin, TX

In 1954 Charlie came up with the Milwaukee Braves and
went down the following year. In two brief seasons the
chucker was 0-1 in seven games.

GORMAN, Herb
    Died April 5, 1953, in San Diego, at age 27

Herb pinch-hit for the Cardinals in 1952 in his only big
league at-bat. Gorman's death in 1953 was the first death
of any of the players who appeared in the fifties. Gorman
died at his left field position when a blood clot reached his
heart while he was playing with San Diego in the PCL in
'53. It was the first game of a Sunday doubleheader. The
tragedy caused the cancellation of the nightcap. Prior to
his death, he doubled in both of his trips to the plate.

GORMAN, Tom
    Specialty sales representative
    Kronenbourg Beer Co.
    New York City

Tom worked out of the Yankees' bullpen on A.L. and
World Series winning teams in 1952–53. He made brief appearances in the World Series both years, but was not involved in any decisions.
    Gorman spent the rest of his career with the Kansas
City A's from 1955–59. Tom was a fixture in the A's
bullpen in 1955 with 7 wins and 18 saves.   36-36

GORYL, John
    Cleveland Indians coach

A six-year utility infielder with the Cubs (1957–59) and
Twins (1962–64), John carried a .225 average in 276
games.

GRABER, Rod
 Dispatcher, Coca-Cola Co.
 San Diego, CA

An outfielder, Rod played in four games with the Indians.
He departed with a .125 average.

GRAFF, Milt
 Pittsburgh Pirates Director of Scouting

Milt, who attended Penn State, played 61 games at the
keystone position with the K.C. A's in 1957–58, and batted
21 points above his playing weight of 158.   .179

GRAMMAS, Alex
 Detroit Tigers coach

A N.L. shortstop from 1954–63 with St. Louis, Cincinnati,
and Chicago, Alex hit .264 his rookie year as the Cards'
regular shortstop.
 Following his playing days he became a coach for the Pirates. Late in the 1969 season when manager Larry
Shephard was fired, he managed the team in the last five
games and won four of them. He was considered to be the
leading candidate for the manager's job, which went instead to Danny Murtaugh. Grammas then joined Sparky
Anderson as a coach for the Reds. He managed Milwaukee
in 1977 for his only year in the A.L. since coming to the
majors over a quarter of a century before. After being fired
as the Brewers' manager, he rejoined the Reds as a coach.
Alex attended Mississippi State.   .247

GRANT, Jim "Mudcat"
 Public relations for Budweiser beer distributorship
 Cleveland, OH

A twin at birth, he would have his big season at age 30 in
1965, pitching for the Twins. Jim spent his first six seasons in the biggies (beginning in 1958) with the Indians.
His best campaign in Cleveland was in 1961 when he went

15-9. In 1965 he was the mound ace of the Twins' A.L. championship team, leading the league with 21 wins, a winning percentage of .750, and shutouts (with six). In the World Series he beat the Dodgers, 8-2, in the opener. He lost as the starter in game four, but was the winner in game six by a 5-1 score with his three-run homer providing the key hit.

His 21 wins in '65 made him the first black pitcher ever to reach the 20-win figure in the A.L. In his final two seasons ('70–'71) in the big show, the current entertainer became a relief ace for both the Oakland A's and the Pittsburgh Pirates. In '70 he won six and saved 24 for the A's, before being sold to Pittsburgh late in the season. He then won a pair of key games over the Mets to help the Pirates to the N.L. East title.　　　　　145-119

GRASSO, Mickey
　　　Died October 15, 1975, at age 55, in Miami, FL

Newton "Mickey" Grasso was nicknamed "Mickey" because of his resemblance to Hall of Fame catcher Mickey Cochrane. Grasso first arrived on the scene with the Giants in 1946. From 1950–53 he did his catching in the nation's capital with the Senators, where he had his finest year in 1950, batting .287 in 75 games. His seven-year blast ended where it had begun, with the New York Giants in 1955.

While serving in the infantry from 1942–45, Mickey was taken prisoner in North Africa during World War II.　.226

GRAY, Dick
　　　School teacher
　　　Anaheim, CA

From the time the Dodgers first moved to the west coast in 1958, until Ron Cey took over on a permanent basis in 1973, the Dodgers tried over three dozen players at third base. Dick Gray was the Dodgers' starting third baseman at the start of the 1958 season. After hitting .249 with 9 homers that year, he was dealt to the Cardinals during the

'59 campaign, and made his last appearance with them the
following season.   .239

GRAY, John
Apartment building manager
Miami, FL

John arrived in 1954. He struggled to a 3-12 mark for the
Philadelphia Athletics in their last season in the "City of
Brotherly Love" before the move to Kansas City. He was
with the A's in K.C. in '55, then returned to the majors in
'57 with Cleveland, where his one victory (and last in the
majors) was a shutout. His final season was back in Philadelphia, this time with the Phillies in 1958.   4-18

GRAY, Ted
Sales representative for auto parts company
Clarkston, MI

A southpaw flipper (1946-1954) with the Detroit Tigers,
Ted played with a record four teams his last year in 1955.
During that busy '55 season, he was in two games each for
the White Sox and Indians. Ted pitched in one game for
the Yankees, and then in nine more for the Orioles.   59-74

GRBA, Eli
Ex-minor league pitching instructor for Milwaukee
Brewers

Eli was with the Yankees (1959 and '60), and L.A. Angels
during their first three years in the A.L. (1961-63).
   On opening day of the 1961 season, the right-hander
won the first game ever played by the expansion Angels,
by defeating Baltimore. He won 11 games in that first-ever
season for the franchise.   28-33

GREASON, Bill
Minister in Birmingham, AL

In 1954 Bill pitched in three games for the Cardinals, losing his only decision.

GREEN, Elijah "Pumpsie"
    Dean of Boys and assistant baseball coach at a high
    school
    Berkeley, CA

When he broke in as a rookie second baseman with the
Boston Red Sox in 1959, "Pumpsie" became the Red Sox'
first black player. Boston was the last team in the majors
to have a black player in their lineup, a dozen years after
Jackie Robinson broke in with the Dodgers.
    He remained with them through 1962 and departed af-
ter one year for the New York Mets.
    His brother, Cornell Green, was an All-American bas-
ketball player at Utah State, who went on to become an
All-Pro cornerback with the Dallas Cowboys in the NFL.
                                                    .246

GREEN, Fred
    Insurance business
    Pittsburgh area

Fred was with the Pirates for parts of the 1959 and '61 seasons, and again in his final year in 1964. But during the
pennant-winning campaign in 1960, the southpaw was
8-4, with another three saves in 45 appearances. Fred still
pitches batting practice for the Pirates.   9-7

GREEN, Gene
    Died May 23, 1981, at age 47, in St. Louis, MO

A good opposite field hitter, Gene divided his playing
time between the outfield and catching from 1957–
1963. In his first full season in 1958, he hit .281 for the
Cardinals. In his only other season playing in at least
100 games Gene hit .280 with 18 homers (for the expansion Washington Senators in 1961). Prior to his death,
he was the manager of Mr. Frank's Cocktail Lounge in
St. Louis.   .267

GREEN, Lenny
 Security officer for Ford Motor Co.
 Detroit, MI

Lenny played for six teams in twelve years (1957–1968), all in the A.L. In May of 1959 he was with the Orioles when he was traded to the team they were in the middle of a series with the Washington Senators. Lenny remained with them through their first three seasons in Minnesota.

 The outfielder returned to the Orioles late in 1964 when, for the second time in his career, he was traded away to a club that his current team was playing. The Orioles were in L.A. when Lenny was told to switch to the Angels' dressing room. Following the first game of that series, he was swapped back to the Orioles. Green concluded his career after stints with both the Red Sox and Tigers in 1968, with a career .267 average.

GREENGRASS, Jim
 Deputy sheriff
 Marietta, GA

Jim was on center stage from 1952–56. He had fairly productive seasons as a regular outfielder for the Reds in 1953 and '54. In '53 he had 20 homers, and 100 RBIs. The following season he banged out 27 roundtrippers and collected 95 RBIs. Jim was traded to the Phillies the following year, where he spent just one more season in the majors.   .269

GREENWOOD, Bob
 Golf pro and instructor at the Skywest Golf Club
 Hayward, CA

Bob had a "tall cup of coffee," appearing on the mound in a total 13 games for the Phillies in '54 and '55. He departed at 1-2. Bob signed his contract out of St. Mary's in California.

GREGG, Hal "Skeets"
  Bullhead City, AZ

Hal spent parts of nine seasons in the big arena from 1943–52. He won just 40 games but nearly half of those came when he won 18 for the Brooklyn Dodgers in 1945. In 1947 he was just 4-5 with a very high ERA (just under 6.00) for the pennant-winning Dodgers. But in game four of the World Series, while the Yankees' Bill Bevens was working on a no-hitter, Gregg kept the Yankees in check for seven innings of strong relief work.

He later pitched for the Pirates and N.Y. Giants, wrapping it up in 1952.   40-48

GRIGGS, Hal
  Pompano Beach, FL

Hal was working as a 21-year-old bellhop in a Miami hotel when he met the owner of a minor league team at Deland, Florida. He had never played baseball anywhere (not high school, Little League, etc.). When asked by the owner if he wanted to try out for the team, Hal jumped at the opportunity. Hal was 8-21, including 18 consecutive losses, but he finally made it to the biggies.

Griggs entered the majors in 1956 and lasted four years with the Senators, going 6-26 off the mound.

He was married on the pitcher's mound while in the Carolina League.

GRIM, Bob
  Ex-liquor salesman
  Overland Park, KS

In 1954 the Yankees went to spring training seeking a sixth straight A.L. pennant and World Series championship. However, ace pitchers Raschi, Lopat, and Reynolds were now past their prime. Out of nowhere came a 24-year-old right-hander who was not even on the team's spring training roster, after spending the previous two years in the military. The Yankees didn't win the 1954 pennant, but Grim went 20-6 and was selected the A.L. "Rookie-of-

the-Year." He made his exit with the Kansas City A's in
1962.   61-41

GRIMSLEY, Ross II
    Maintenance employee, E.I. Dupont Co.
    Memphis, TN

Most recently, Ross Grimsley III pitched in the biggies
with the Orioles in 1982. His father was also a major
leaguer, although not as well remembered as the fathers of
other big leaguers like Buddy Bell and Bump Wills. Ross II
appeared in just 7 games for the 1951 White Sox without a
decision. Like his son, he was a left-hander.

GRISSOM, Marv
    Oakland A's pitching coach

A right-handed pitcher whose brother, Lee, was a pitcher
in the N.L. from 1934–41, Marv first appeared for the N.Y.
Giants in 1946. After some years in the minors and stints
with three A.L. teams in the late 1940s and early 1950s, he
returned to the Giants and was a key factor in their '54
N.L. pennant, with 10 wins and 19 saves out of the
bullpen. Marv was the winner in relief in the opening
game of the World Series when Dusty Rhodes' pinch-hit
homer beat Cleveland.   47-45

GROAT, Dick
    Operates Champion Lakes, an 18-hole golf course in
    Ligonier, Pennsylvania with former teammate Jerry
    Lynch. Also a manufacturer's representative for four
    Pittsburgh area firms and the expert analyst for Uni-
    versity of Pittsburgh basketball broadcasts.

Although the Pirates were not a strong team in the early
fifties they may have been able to compete favorably in the
NBA with the likes of the O'Brien twins and Groat on
their roster. Dick was an All-American selection in both
his junior and senior seasons at Duke (in 1951 and '52)
averaging over 23 points per game.

A spray hitter who used all fields, he hit .284 as a rookie in '52 with the Pirates. He then played in the NBA for the Fort Wayne Pistons. Following two years in the army, Groat became the regular Pittsburgh shortstop for the next eight years, starting in 1955. He hit over .300 three of those years, including 1960, when he won the N.L. batting title at .325 and was named the N.L. MVP, as the Pirates won the pennant and the World Series.

Traded to St. Louis after the 1962 season, he helped the Cardinals to the N.L. flag in 1964, and was part of another world championship.

Dick completed his fourteen year run in 1967 with 2,138 hits, and a career .286 average.

GROB, Connie
   Tavern owner, Connie's Home Plate
   Middleton, WI

Connie might have been a guest at Elvis Presley's "Heartbreak Hotel" in 1956, as the right-handed hurler was 4-5 with a 7.83 ERA for the Senators in his only big league fling. One consolation is that Connie swung a pretty good stick, going 6-for-18.

GROMEK, Steve
   Insurance salesman
   Birmingham, MI

A long-time righty hurler in the A.L. from 1941 to 1957, Steve's high was in 1945, when he won 19 for the Indians. In 1948 he was 9-3 as a spot starter and reliever for the A.L. champions. During that 1945 season he once beat the Yankees, 4-2, in a complete game effort without the benefit of a single assist by his defense. The 27 outs came as the result of 15 fly balls to the outfield, four popups to the infield, four strikeouts, a pair of pop-ups to the catcher, and two ground balls to the first baseman, handled unassisted.

In 1953 Steve was traded to the Tigers, and in his first start gave up nine runs to the Red Sox (in the inning they scored the record-shattering 17). Just four days later he returned to the mound and shut out the Philadelphia A's. In '54 Gromek had another fine season, winning 18 for Detroit. He said goodbye in 1957 at 123-108 and with a very respectable 3.41 ERA.

Steve pitched an 18-inning scoreless tie that was called by rain in 1943 against Rochester. That same year he led the International League in strikeouts.

GROSS, Don
Mount Pleasant, MI

Don did his chucking for the Reds and Pirates between 1955–60. When he took his last walk to the dugout, he was 20-22 in 145 games.

GROSSMAN, Harley
Retired; former manager of Thomson-McKinnon Securities, Inc.
Evansville, IN

Johnny Ray was singing "Cry" in 1952 when Harley was crying for more playing time. He pitched in just one inning of a game for the Senators.

GROTH, Johnny
Atlanta Braves scout

A fifteen-year outfielder for five different teams, Johnny enjoyed his best season as a Detroit regular in the early fifties. In 1950 he had his best year with a .306 average, and career highs in all offensive statistics, including 12 homers and 85 RBIs. In the mid-fifties Groth was with the Browns, White Sox, Senators, and A's, before finishing in Detroit from 1958 to 1960.

An outstanding defensive outfielder, his .987 career fielding average ranks among the top ten of all time for major league outfielders.   .279

GRUNWALD, Al
    Pressman, *Daily News*
    Van Nuys, CA

Al made two brief stops with the Pirates (1955) and
K.C. A's (1959). He finished with a 0-1 record in 11
games.

GUERRA, Mike
    Havana, Cuba

A Cuban-born catcher, Mike was in one game with the
Senators in 1937. He returned to the biggies with Washington in 1944 and remained in the A.L. until 1951, also
playing for the Philadelphia Athletics and Red Sox before
taking his last bow with the Senators in '51. In 565 games,
Señor Guerra batted .242.

GUINTINI, Ben
    Roseville, CA

This Italian "dish" played in two games for the Pirates in
1946, and three more with the '50 Athletics. Ben's career
wasn't too spicy, as he went hitless in seven tries.

GUMBERT, Harry "Gunboat"
    Retired
    Houston, TX

Harry pitched for four different clubs in the N.L. in a
fifteen-year career dating from 1935. He was a member
of the N.Y. Giants' starting rotation from 1936 to 1940.
In '36, his 11-3 mark helped the Giants to the N.L. pennant. Traded to the Cardinals during the 1941 season,
Gumbert posted 9-5 and 10-5 records in each of the next
two years as a member of the pennant-winning St. Louis
team.
    Hoping that his presence would help them to a N.L. flag,

the Reds dealt for him during the 1944 season. Although Harry contributed 10 victories a season three times for them, the Reds never made it to the "Fall Classic" during his stay.

"Gunboat" ended in 1950 with just one appearance for the Pirates.   143-113

GUMPERT, Randy
   Scouting supervisor for the Major League Scouting Bureau

About the time when Harry Gumbert was becoming a fixture with the N.Y. Giants' pitching staff, Randy Gumpert was struggling to become a member of the Philadelphia A's mound staff. He was out of the majors from 1939 until after World War II. But in 1946 he returned to post a fine 11-3 record, with an ERA of 2.31, for the New York Yankees. He was 4-1 for them in 1947, and from there was dealt to the White Sox, for whom he pitched through the 1951 season, or just long enough to serve up Mickey Mantle's first major league home.

He closed the door the next season with Washington. Randy worked in the Yankees' organization for several years as a coach and scout before joining the Scouting Bureau.   51-59

GUSTINE, Frank
   Restaurant owner
   Pittsburgh, PA

A twelve-year versatile infielder from 1939–50, he spent most of his time with the Pirates until his final two seasons in 1949 and '50 when he was a member of the Cubs and St. Louis Browns.

A career .265 hitter, his best year was in 1947 when he hit .297 while playing in 156 games, all at third base, for the Pirates.

_H_

HAAS, Bert
Retired; former wholesale liquor store employee
Tampa, FL

A first baseman-third baseman-outfielder for nine years,
Bert broke in with Brooklyn in 1937. He was with the Reds
in the mid-forties, then walked out with the White Sox in
1951. Haas scored and drove home the same total of runs,
263.   .264

HAAS, Eddie
Manager of Richmond in the International League

From 1957–60 Eddie played 55 games in the outfield with
the Cubs and Braves.   .243

HABENICHT, Bob
Died December 24, 1980, at age 54, in Richmond, VA

This St. Louis-born thrower pitched in three games with
the Cardinals in 1951 and one game for the Browns in
1953, giving him the distinction of wearing the uniform of
two major league teams in his home town. He was an attorney at the time of his death.   0-0

HACKER, Warren
San Diego Padres pitching instructor

Warren spent most of his dozen seasons with the Chicago
Cubs. He was on the losing end for the most part, including
a league-leading 19 losses in 1953. Hacker did have a fine
season in 1952 when he won 15 games, including five shut-

outs and a glossy ERA of 2.58. The right-hander was with
the Cubs from 1948–56. After spending 1957 and '58 with
the Reds and Phils, Warren was out of the majors for two
years before working out of the Chicago White Sox bullpen
in 1961.   62-89

HADDIX, Harvey "Kitten"
Pittsburgh Pirates pitching coach

May 26, 1959—36 up and 36 down. The 12 perfect innings
are what he's best remembered for, but Haddix was also
the winning pitcher in relief in the seventh game of the
1960 World Series, when Bill Mazeroski's homer gave the
Pirates their dramatic win. It was his second victory of the
Series, having started and won the fifth game over the
Yankees, 5-2.

In his first full season in 1953, he was a 20-game winner
for St. Louis. He also led the league in shutouts with six.
His resemblance to former Cardinal pitcher Harry "The
Cat" Brecheen resulted in his nickname of the "Kitten."
Harvey was an 18-game winner in 1954. After another
campaign in St. Louis, he spent a year each with the
Phillies and Reds, before joining the Pirates in '59. Inter-
estingly, his record that season was 12-12.

Haddix took his final walk to the mound in the mid-
sixties as a member of the Orioles.   136-113

HADLEY, Kent
Insurance business
Pocatello, ID

Kent came to the Yankees from K.C. with Roger Maris
and Joe DeMaestri for Dan Larsen, Marv Throneberry,
Hank Bauer and Norm Siebern. Hadley, a left-handed batter, played in 171 games at first base for the A's and Yanks
from 1958–60. He graduated from USC.   .242

HAEFNER, Mickey
    Former construction worker
    New Athens, IL

Mickey was one of the knuckleballing hurlers on a Senators' pitching staff that included Roger Wolff and Dutch Leonard in the mid-forties. His 16 wins in 1945 was his career high. The southpaw finished with the White Sox and Braves in 1950.
             78-91

HAHN, Fred
    Public works dept. (highway division)
    Orangetown, NY

Fred pitched two scoreless innings for the 1952 Cardinals.
             0-0

HAIRSTON, Sam
    Chicago White Sox scout

In 1951 Sam made it into four games as a catcher for the Chicago White Sox—the extent of his big league life. When his son John played in just three games for the Cubs in 1969—the extent of his major league playing time—it marked the first time in major league history that the son of a black former major leaguer made it to the big show. Another son, Jerry, currently plays for the White Sox. Sam, who was the first black ever signed by the White Sox organization, went 2-for-5 for a .400 average.

HALE, Bob
    High school principal
    Park Ridge, IL

Bob came up to the Orioles midway through the '55 season to hit .357 in 67 games. At the time, the first baseman had been playing deep in the Baltimore farm system in the Piedmont League. When he led his team to an "upset" of the parent Orioles with three hits in an exhibition game, he was called all the way up to the big club. He shuttled back and forth between the Orioles and the farm team, then was with the Indians in 1960 when he was the leading pinch-hitter in the A.L. with 19 pinch-hits. He made his exit with the Yankees in 1961.

His post-playing career saw him earn his master's degree at DePaul University. He then went on to Northwestern University, where, along with coaching the baseball team, he earned his doctorate. .273

HALL, Bill
Farmer
Hartsfield, GA

Bill was a catcher with Pittsburgh briefly in both 1954 and '56. In 1958 Bill hit .284 in 51 games. .262

HALL, Bob
Died March 12, 1983, at age 59, when a drunk driver struck him while he was working as a construction company's traffic director

Bob pitched for the Boston Braves in 1949 and '50. His only other season was in a Pirate uniform in 1953, when he was 3-12. 9-18

HALL, Dick
Certified public accountant
Baltimore, MD

A 6′6″ right-handed pitcher, Dick was very effective in relief for the Orioles during the mid-sixties, and then again in 1969 and '70, after two years with the Phillies. He was originally with the Pirates as an outfielder and third baseman in 1952, and played as one of the tallest second baseman in major league history in a few games in 1953. In '54 he hit .239 in over 100 games in the Pirates' outfield. He switched to the mound in '55. Dick struggled, going 0-7 in '56, but hit for a .345 average. He stayed with pitching, however, and became a durable reliever for four different Oriole pennant winners.

Dick had excellent control and, remarkably, threw only one wild pitch in over 1,200 innings of pitching covering 16 seasons.

He was 41 when he retired after the '71 season at 93-75.

HAMILTON, Tom
Died November 29, 1973, at age 50 in Tyler, TX

Tom, a first baseman-outfielder, played in 67 games for the Philadelphia Athletics in 1952–53.   .197

HAMLIN, Ken
Operates baseball camp
Climax, MI

Not to be confused with Luke "Hot Potato" Hamlin, Ken's career encompassed the years 1957–66, with time missing in between. An infielder with a .241 lifetime average, he saw action with the Pirates, K.C. Athletics, L.A. Angels, and Washington. Ken spent his collegiate days at Western Michigan University.

HAMNER, Granville "Granny"
Infield instructor for the Philadelphia Phillies minor league system
Clearwater, FL

"Granny" was elected the Phillies' all-time best shortstop in 1969. He was just 17 in 1944 when he first came up. In 1945 his brother Wes was a member of the Phillies as a second baseman and shortstop in his only big league season.

Hamner switched over to second base in '48, but was the starting shortstop in a then-record 157 games for the 1950 "Whiz Kids." Although the Phillies were stopped cold in the World Series by the Yankees, losing four straight, he led the team in hitting, going 6-for-14 for a .429 average. "Granny" continued playing in over 150 games per season for the next four years, with his best mark coming in 1954 when he hit .299 while returning as a second baseman.

He was traded to the Cleveland Indians during the 1959

campaign, after picking up over 1,500 hits in over 1,500
games in a Phillies' uniform. Hamner retired following the
'59 season, only to make an abbreviated comeback as a
knuckleball-throwing hurler in 1962 for the Kansas City A's
where he lost his only decision in three games as a pitcher.
"Granny" also lost a game on the mound for the '56 Phils. His
tenure of sixteen seasons in a Phillies' uniform is the most of
any player in the club's history. He had a .262 average.   0-2

HAMRIC, Bert
      Shipper for P. H. Glatpelter
      West Carrollton, OH

Bert was plucked by the Orioles in '58 after appearing in
two games for the Dodgers in '55. Bert went 1-for-9 at the
plate in 10 games as a pinch-hitter.   .111

HANEBRINK, Harry
      Real estate business
      St. Louis, MO

Harry was an infielder-outfielder with the Milwaukee
Braves (1953, '57, and '58). He completed his four-year
tour with the Phillies in 1959 after 177 games and a .224
average.

HANSEN, Andy
      Atlantis, FL

Baseball fans often associate the '44 season as the year of the
"Trolley Series," when the Cardinals and Browns clashed.
For Andy, that was the year he broke into the biggies. He
hung around until 1953, and with 270 games under his belt
split between the Phillies and Giants, he went 23-30.

HANSEN, Doug
      Hacienda Heights, CA

Doug saw limited action as a pinch-hitter in three games
with the Indians in 1951.   .000

HANSEN, Ron
Manager at Paintsville in the Appalachian League

A rangy shortstop, Ron was the 1960 A.L. Rookie-of-the-Year for the Baltimore Orioles, when he collected 22 homers and 85 RBIs. He previously made some brief appearances with Baltimore in 1958 and '59.

Hansen was with the Orioles through '62, and then was the White Sox shortstop from 1963–67. As a member of the Washington Senators in 1968 he pulled off the last unassisted triple play in the majors. Shortly after the spectacular play, he was swapped back to the White Sox. Ron later played with the Yankees and A's before retiring in 1972.   .234

HARDIN, Bill "Bud"
Northridge, CA

Hank Williams' "Your Cheatin' Heart" was a juke box hit in 1952. A more appropriate title might have been "Your Cheatin' Hardin," as Bill played in a total of just three games for the Cubs in '52.   .143

HARDY, Carroll
Assistant general manager of the Denver Broncos of the N.F.L.

A University of Colorado football star in the mid-fifties, Carroll was drafted by the San Francisco 49ers of the N.F.L. Hardy instead chose a career in professional baseball. He signed with the Cleveland Indians, where he made his living in '58 and '59. Carroll hit just one home run his first two years, but it was slammed while pinch-hitting for then-Indian outfielder Roger Maris.

During the 1960 season he was traded to the Red Sox where he made an even more memorable pinch-hitting appearance (though it resulted in his hitting into a double play). He became the first and only player ever to hit for Ted Williams when Williams fouled a pitch off his instep and was forced to leave the game. In 1961 he pinch-hit for Carl Yastrzemski.

Hardy was with the Astros (1963 and '64) and Twins (1967). How many players can say they pinch-hit for Ted Williams, Roger Maris, and Carl Yastrzemski? He played briefly with the 49ers as a defensive back.   .225

HARDY, Francis "Red"
  Jewelry business
  Phoenix, AZ

"Red" pitched in two games for the New York Giants in 1951, and walked away without a decision.

HARMON, Chuck
  Baseball promotions manager for MacGregor Sporting Goods

A member of the University of Toledo basketball team which made it to the N.I.T. finals in 1942, Chuck was a third baseman-outfielder with the Reds, Cardinals, and Phillies from 1954–57.   .238

HARRELL, Billy
  Placement and counseling for New York State Youth Division in Albany County
  Troy, NY

The Indians thought they had a gift when Billy went 8-for-19 as a utility infielder in 1955. He was also with the Tribe in '57 and '58 before calling it quits in Boston three years later.   .231

HARRINGTON, Bill
  Security police for state of North Carolina; also farmer
  Garner, NC

Bill broke in with the Philadelphia Athletics in 1953. He also logged some time in K.C. (1955–56) before he laid his flipper to rest with a 5-5 mark in 58 games.

HARRIS, Bill
    Manages a restaurant
    Kennewick, WA

Bill's finest hour came in the early fifties when he pitched
a perfect game for Mobile in the Southern Association. His
big league jaunt consisted of two games, both with the
Dodgers ('57 and '59)—but miles apart—in Brooklyn and
Los Angeles.   0-1

HARRIS, Charles "Bubba"
    Lake Worth, FL

"Bubba" was a lanky 6'4" right-handed relief pitcher who
divided his time (1948, '49, '51) between the Athletics and
Indians.   6-3

HARRIS, Gail
    Nationwide regional insurance representative
    Manassas, VA

A lifetime .240 swatter, Gail was with the Giants (1955–57)
and Tigers (1958–60). The best year for this left-handed
hitter was in '58 as the regular Detroit first baseman,
when he hit .273 with 20 homers. He was the last player to
homer for the New York Giants when he walloped two
roundtrippers in the second game of a doubleheader on
Sept. 21, 1957.

HARRIS, Maurice "Mickey"
    Died April 15, 1971, at age 54 in Farmington, MI

Hailed as the second coming of Lefty Gomez, Mickey was
with the Red Sox in 1940 and '41, and was a major factor in
their 1946 A.L. pennant as a 17-game winner (after missing the four previous seasons during World War II).
    Harris was traded to Washington in 1949. The following
year he had 15 saves in 53 games, with both figures top-
ping the A.L. He parted, winning all three of his decisions
in 1952, with the Cleveland Indians.   59-71

HARRISON, Bob
  President, Indiana Lumbermen's Insurance Co.
  Indianapolis, IN

Bob pitched in one game in '55 and one in '56 with the Orioles.   0-0

HARRIST, Earl "Irish"
  Deputy sheriff in Lincoln Parish
  Ruston, LA

Earl had a split career that spanned the years 1945–53, pitching in such cities as Cincinnati, Chicago (White Sox), Washington, St. Louis (Browns), and Detroit. After 132 games, "Irish" was 12-28.

HARSHMAN, Jack
  State Welfare Dept.
  Warehouse, CT

Jack was a power-hitting first baseman in the minors before switching to the mound. In 1951 he led the Southern Association with 47 homers and 141 RBIs, but switched to pitching the next season. In '52 he made it to the big top and lost his only two decisions with the New York Giants.

   Jack had his best years with the Chicago White Sox from 1954–57. In 1954 he won 14 games, including a 16-inning shutout, 1-0, over the Tigers. Harshman also had a club record 16-strikeout performance against the Red Sox at Fenway Park that year. He won a career high 15 games in 1956. Jack was later with the Orioles, Red Sox, and Indians before wrapping it up in 1960. He showed occasional power at the plate, hitting a career total 21 home runs, including six each in 1956 and '58.
                                                                    69-65

HARTMAN, Bob
    Sports director for a Christian youth center
    Kenosha, WI

Bob gave it a shot with the Braves (1959) and Indians (1962). He lost his only decision in 11 games, but you can't blame a guy for trying.

HARTSFIELD, Roy
    Manager of Indianapolis in the American Association

Roy had a three-year stint as a second baseman for the Boston Braves from 1950–52. Hartsfield started a managerial career in the minors in the late fifties, and from the early seventies was a major league coach with both the Dodgers and the Braves before becoming the first manager of the Toronto Blue Jays in 1977. Recently Hartsfield was quoted as saying, "Baseball survived the loss of Ty Cobb, Babe Ruth, and Stan Musial. It will survive the loss of Roy Hartsfield."   .273

HARTUNG, Cling "The Hondo Hurricane"
    Foreman for Marathon Oil
    Sinton, TX

Because of his speed and power and the fact that he came from Hondo, Texas, he was labeled "The Hondo Hurricane." Clint was hailed as another Babe Ruth in a big buildup over his pitching and hitting feats while playing for military teams. Although another nickname was "Floppy" because of his large ears, it could have been used to describe his overall major league career.

As a pitcher he was 9-7 in 1947, and he hit for a .309 average. But overall, in a career that was spent with the New York Giants until 1952, he was 29-29 on the mound and .238 with the bat.

HATFIELD, Fred
   Detroit Tigers coach

Hatfield did not arrive until 1950 with the Red Sox. A direct descendant of the legendary Hatfield clan, notorious for their feud with the McCoys, Fred was with the Tigers, White Sox, Indians, and Reds, in a career which lasted until 1959.   .242

HATTEN, Joe
   Postal worker
   Redding, CA

This southpaw chucker first arrived as a 29-year-old rookie for the Brooklyn Dodgers in 1946. He won 14 games that year with a very good ERA of 2.84. In '47 he was a key factor in the Dodgers' N.L. pennant as a 17-game winner. In 1949 he won 12 to help the Dodgers to another pennant.

   Joe was traded to the Cubs during the 1951 season, and departed the following year with a lifetime 65-49 mark.

HATTON, Grady
   Houston Astros scout

A Cincinnati Reds' third baseman from 1946 to 1953, Grady had his best season in 1947 with career highs: 16 homers, 77 RBIs, and a .281 average. He moved around during the mid-fifties playing with the White Sox, Red Sox, Cardinals, and Orioles. Grady was out of the biggies the last three years of the decade, but returned in 1960 with the Cubs, hitting .342 in 28 games in his final big league swing.

   Hatton managed the Houston Astros from 1966–68, then moved up to the front office for the team as vice-president. In 1973 he returned to the field as a coach for Houston under Leo Durocher.

   Grady attended the University of Texas from 1939–43.
                                                    .254

HAUGSTAD, Phil
    Logging and trucking business
    Black River Falls, WI

Phil made his debut in 1947. A right-hander, he had a
broken career between the years 1947–52, spending 28 of
his 37 games with the Dodgers, and the remaining with
the Reds.   1-1

HAWES, Roy
    Owns the Mountain Chemical Co.
    Ringgold, GA

The Senators gave Roy his pink slip after he played in
three games for them in 1951.   .167

HAYDEN, Gene
    Vacaville, CA

In 1958, Gene was in and out, pitching just three games for
the Reds that summer.   0-0

HAYNES, Joe
    Died January 6, 1967, at age 49 in Hopkins, MN

Joe was with us from 1939–52 as a member of the
Washington Senators and Chicago White Sox. Originally with Washington, he was traded to Chicago after
the 1940 season, and remained with them through 1948.
His best year came in '47 when he was 14-6, with a fine
2.42 ERA.
    Haynes had been married to the daughter of Senators'
owner Clark Griffith in 1941. He returned to pitch for his
father-in-law's team his final four years. From 1953–55 he
was a coach with the Senators; then, following the death of
Griffith in '55, he became a vice-president of the team. He
remained in that capacity through the team's franchise
shift to Minnesota until his death in 1967.   76-82

HAZLE, Bob "Hurricane"
>   Salesman for the Ben Arnold Co.—wines and spirits
>   distributor for the state of South Carolina
>   Columbia, SC

The 1957 season has oftentimes been referred to as the
"Summer of Hurricane Hazel." A left-handed hitting outfielder who had previously seen brief playing time for the
Cincinnati Reds in 1955, Bob was recalled to the Milwaukee Braves in July of 1957 when regular Billy Bruton had
to be placed on the disabled list. He immediately had a
four hit game, and followed that with a three hit, three
RBI show. Bob continued to consistently pick up two and
three hits a game, and after a month was hitting around
the .500 mark. The Braves went on to win the N.L. pennant and "Hurricane" finished at a .403 pace in 41 games
in the Braves stretch run.

However, he was slowed down by Yankee pitching in the
World Series, hitting just .154. Twenty games into the following season, he was struggling at just .179 when he was
sold to Detroit, where he eventually went out to sea. Because he started like a storm, he was given the name
"Hurricane."   .310

HEARD, Jehosie
>   Location unknown

This southpaw hurled in only two games for the Orioles in
1954, and was never heard from again.   0-0

HEARN, Jim
>   Owner of a golf center
>   Atlanta, GA

Jim had a 13 year cruise from 1947–59. As a rookie with
the Cardinals, he was a 12-game winner. But by 1949 he
returned to the minors and was placed on waivers. The
Giants claimed him, and he immediately turned it all
around to go 11-3 and post a league-leading 2.49 ERA.

In 1951 he played a key role in the Giants' N.L. pennant
as he won 17 games. Jim remained with New York until

his last three seasons when he wore a Phillies' uniform. Hearn closed at 109-89, with the 89th loss coming some two months after he retired, as he was the loser of a suspended game that was completed after he had left the team.

HEGAN, Jim
New York Yankees scout in New England

A light-hitting but excellent defensive catcher, Jim spent the majority of his seventeen years (1941–60) with the Cleveland Indians. He handled more 20-game winners than any other receiver in major league history. Among them were Hall of Famers Bob Lemon (7 times), Early Wynn, and Bob Feller (4 times each).

With his son Mike, they form the only father-son combination to each play in two World Series. Jim was the catcher for both the 1948 and 1954 Indians. Mike appeared as a pinch-hitter for the Yankees in the 1964 classic, and played first base for the Oakland A's in 1972.

Jim had a career batting average of .228 in 1,600 major league games.

HEINTZELMAN, Ken
McDonnell Douglas Aircraft employee
St. Louis, MO

Ken was a 35-year-old veteran with the 1950 Phillies. He was born in 1915, the day after the Phillies had last appeared in a World Series.

The southpaw originally broke in with Pittsburgh in 1937. He joined the Phillies in '47, and had his first and only season with a record above the .500 mark in 1949, when he was 17-10. He wasn't that effective the following year when Philadelphia won the N.L. pennant, as he was just 3-9. He finished in 1952 at 77-98. Ken won't forget August 7, 1951. Pitching for the Phillies, he out-dueled Warren Spahn and the Braves, 1-0, in fifteen innings.

His son Tom was in the N.L. as an infielder during the seventies with both St. Louis and the Giants.

HEISE, Jim
   Assistant principal at Colonial High School
   Orlando, FL

1957—Elvis was "All Shook Up"; and Jim Heise was "All Washed Up" after losing all three of his decisions in 8 games with the Senators.

HELD, Mel
   Hardware store owner
   Edon, OH

Mel slid out of the biggies after pitching in four games without a decision for the Orioles in 1956.

HELD, Woodie
   Construction worker; "jack-of-all-trades"
   Dubois, WY

In the late 1940s Woodie was a batboy for the Sacramento team in the Pacific Coast League. Held played briefly with the Yankees in 1954, but was traded to Kansas City where he hit 20 homers in his first full season in 1957. He spent his best years with Cleveland from 1959–64, hitting a career-high 29 homers in '59.   .240

HEMUS, Solly
   Gas and oil leasing business
   Houston, TX

This N.L. infielder was with the Cardinals and Phillies (1949–1959). From 1951–53 Hemus was the full-time shortstop for St. Louis. In 1954 he hit .304 playing in 124 games. He was traded to the Phillies in 1956. Three times Hemus led the league in being hit by pitches, including 20 plunks in 1952.

   Solly finished back in St. Louis in 1959, the same year he became their manager. After finishing seventh, he led them to third place in 1960, but was fired from his first and last managing position midway through the following campaign. He was last seen in uniform as a coach for the Mets (1962–63) and Indians (1964–65). Nicknamed "Mighty Mouse," he was known as a "wheeler-dealer" among his teammates.   .273

HENLEY, Gail
Managed the Lethbridge Dodgers of the Pioneer League in 1983

Along with Jim Brideweser, Gail was a member of the 1948 USC NCAA champion baseball team. As an outfielder he played in a mere 14 games with the Pirates in '54. His "cup of coffee" was a sweet one as he batted .300, going 9-for-30.

HENRICH, Bob
Insurance business
La Habra, CA

Bob was in the unemployment line before he could shave, as he played in only 48 games with the Reds (1957–59), all before his 21st birthday.   .125

HENRICH, Tommy "Old Reliable"
Retired
Prescott, AZ

During the mid-thirties, Tommy was in the minors in the Cleveland Indians organization. The Indians were charged with covering him up, as he was not advanced to a major league team despite some outstanding hitting marks. In the spring of 1937 Commissioner Landis declared him a free agent, and Tommy was signed by the Yankees. He hit .320 for the pinstripers in his first of 11 big seasons.

Henrich missed three years (1943–45) while in military service in World War II. In 1947 he had ten hits in the World Series to help lead New York past the Dodgers. Three of "Old Reliable's" hits were game-winning shots.

His ninth inning home run in the opening game of the '49 World Series broke up a scoreless duel between Allie

Reynolds and Don Newcombe. Although he was sometimes called "The Great Debater," his popular nom de
plate of "Old Reliable" was created by long-time Yankee
broadcaster Mel Allen, after a train called "Old Reliable."

Tom departed in 1950 with a lifetime .282 average and
182 homers.

HENRY, Bill
Former Astros scout in Houston, TX

Bill was used almost exclusively in relief after his first
four seasons with the Red Sox. He started 42 times for Boston in those four years, but would start only two more
times in another dozen years in the big leagues.

While with the Cubs in 1959, the southpaw led all N.L.
chuckers in appearances with 65. Bill had 16 saves in 1961
to help the Reds to the N.L. pennant. He was also with the
Pirates and Astros in his long career (1952–69). Bill left
46-50, registering 90 saves.

HERBERT, Ray
Department store manager
Livonia, MI

Ray did his thing from 1950–66 with the Tigers, Kansas
City A's, White Sox, and Phillies. The right-hander had
his big year in 1962 when he was 20-9 for the White Sox.
The following season he was 13-10, but seven of those wins
were shutouts, tops in the league. He said goodnight with
the Phils in 1966.   104-107

HERMANSKI, Gene
Sales representative, Tose Inc.
Fairview, N.J.

A nine-year flychaser (1943–53), with two years out for
military service, Gene broke in with the Dodgers in 1943,
hitting an even .300. Back from the service in '46, his average was an anemic .200 in 64 games. But he was a part-
time starter in the Brooklyn outfield the next few seasons,

and three times was over the .290 mark. He was a member
of the Brooklyn pennant teams in 1947 and '49, then was
traded to the Cubs in '51, and finished with the lowly Pirates in 1953, with a lifetime average of .272. He once connected for three consecutive home runs while playing for
the Dodgers.

One year, during spring training with the Dodgers,
teammate Bobby Morgan almost drowned in a strong un-
dertow until Gene came to the rescue and saved Bobby's
life.

HERNANDEZ, Gregorio Evelio
    Baseball coach at Loyola high school
    Miami, FL

Evelio's career consisted of a total of 18 games with the
Senators. He came up in '56 and went down in '57 with a
1-1 record.

HERRERA, Juan "Pancho"
    Manager in Mexican League

"Pancho" played first base for the Phillies from 1958–60.
He hit .281 in 1960, but entertained opposing pitchers,
striking out 136 times (setting a then National League
mark for most strikeouts in 150 games or more). However,
it doesn't compare to Bobby Bonds and his 189 whiffs in
1970 as a member of the Giants. Juan said "Buenas
noches" after 300 games and a .271 career average.

HERRERA, Tito
    Laredo, TX

President Truman relieved Gen. MacArthur of his duty in
1951. After Tito pitched in 3 games and compiled a 27.00
ERA in two innings of work, the St. Louis Browns relieved
him of his duty.   0-0

HERRIAGE, Troy
>Design engineer
>Modesto, CA

After struggling through a nightmarish 1-13 campaign with the K.C. A's in 1956, Troy sunk like the *Andrea Doria* and was never seen again.

HERRIN, Tom
>San Jose, CA

Tom was in 14 games with the Red Sox in 1954. He went 1-2.

HERSH, Earl
>Supervisor of physical education and athletics for the Carroll County Board of Education
>Westminster, MD

Baseball fans had to search for Earl after the '56 season, his only campaign in the big arena, when he saw action in seven games as a flychaser for the Milwaukee Braves.
>.231

HERTWECK, Neal
>Engineering supervisor at Western Electric
>Winston-Salem, NC

Neal appeared in only two games at first base for the Cardinals in 1952.
>.000

HERZOG, Dorrel Norman Elvert "Whitey"
>Manager of the St. Louis Cardinals

An A.L. outfielder (1956–63) with the Senators, A's, Orioles, and Tigers, Whitey's best season came in '61 with Baltimore when he hit .291. The previous year, as a member of the A's, he hit into the first, and most likely the last, all-Cuban triple play (against the Senators), with pitcher

Camilio Pascual, first baseman Julio Becquer, and short-stop Jose Valdivielso pulling off the triple killing.

Following his playing days he coached for the A's, and Mets, then worked as the Mets Director of Player Development from 1967–71. Herzog then managed the Texas Rangers where he replaced Ted Williams before being replaced by Billy Martin.

Whitey managed the Kansas City Royals to three Western Division titles in the late 1970s before leading the Cardinals to a World Championship in 1982.   .257

HETKI, John
>   Traffic foreman for Simkins Industries, Inc.
>   Cleveland, OH

From 1945–54 John jumped around with such teams as the Reds, Browns, and Pirates. A right-handed thrower, John finished at 18-26.

HICKS, Clarence "Buddy"
>   Manager for Automotive Warehouse Distributors
>   Bell, CA

After playing in only 26 games for the Detroit Tigers in 1956, "Buddy" departed from the biggies.   .213

HICKS, Joe
>   Charlottesville, VA

Joe was in the garden for 212 games with the White Sox, Senators, and Mets from 1956–63, and skipped away with a .221 average. Joe's campus days were spent at the University of Virginia.

HIGBE, Kirby
>   Manages a retail shopping center
>   Columbia, SC

Kirby pitched in the N.L. from 1937–50. He had his best seasons with the Dodgers in the early forties, especially in

'41 when he led the N.L. in games won with 22, as Brooklyn captured the N.L. pennant.

For three straight years (1939–41) Higbe led the N.L. in bases-on-balls; he also led in strikeouts, with a relatively low figure of 137 in 1940. Before his peak years with the Dodgers, he was with the Cubs and Phils. In 1950, Kirby finished with the Pirates and N.Y. Giants.

118-101

HILL, Dave
Evanston, IL

A left-handed hurler, Dave pitched in two games as a 19-year-old for the K.C. A's in 1957—the extent of his big league career. The first batter he faced was Tony Kubek, once his high school classmate. Dave pitched Northwestern to the Big Ten title, and signed after his sophomore year.

0-0

HILLER, Frank "Dutch"
National director of Group Field Management for Massachusetts Mutual Life Insurance Co.
Berwyn, PA

"Dutch" showed up in the late forties and made his exit in 1953. A right-handed pitcher, Frank did his flinging for the Yankees, Cubs, Reds, and Giants.

30-32

HILLMAN, Dave
Clothing salesman for Fuller and Hillman
Kingsport, TN

Darius Dutton "Dave" Hillman was 21-37, spending parts of eight years (1955–62) with the Cubs, Red Sox, Reds, and Mets.

HINRICHS, Paul
    Minister of the Trinity Lutheran Church
    Manchester, MO

In 1951 Paul pitched in four games without a decision for the Red Sox. The son of a minister, Paul was studying for the ministry while playing baseball.

HISNER, Harley
    Monroeville, IN

If you think Mr. Hinrichs had a short ride, you should have been with Harley, who zoomed out of Boston after starting and losing his only major league game with the Red Sox in 1951.

HITCHCOCK, Billy
    Retired in 1980 as President of Class AA Southern
    League

Billy was a running back for three years at Auburn University before signing with the Yankees' organization. An older brother, Jim, had been an All-American football player at the same school a few years earlier, and had also gone on to play pro baseball, though briefly, as an infielder for the Red Sox in 1938. Billy had a much longer ride (1942–53). An infielder, he was in over 200 games as a third baseman and second baseman, and another 100-plus at shortstop.

Originally with Detroit where he hit .211 in '42, he later was with the Senators, Browns, Red Sox, and A's (for whom he had his best year)—.306 in 1951. In a strange twist, this Hitchcock ending came as it started, hitting .211 again back in Detroit.

He has remained in the game for over the past quarter of a century since his playing career ended, as coach, scout, and manager. Billy was at the helm of the Orioles in 1962–63, and with the Braves in '66. He held his past position as President of the Southern League for ten years.
                                                        .243

HITTLE, Lloyd
    Telephone repairman for the Pacific Telephone Co.
    Lodi, CA

In '49, '50 Lloyd went 7-11, including a pair of shutouts
with the Senators.

HOAK, Don "Tiger"
    Died October 9, 1969, at age 41 in Pittsburgh

Death came at an early age for this hard-nosed player, at a
time when the N.Y. Mets were about to pull off their miracle World Series win over the Orioles in 1969. Don had
been involved in a pair of recent World Series surprise
champions himself, as third baseman on the 1955 Dodgers.
He was also the starting third baseman for the 1960 Pirates' team that beat the Yanks in the Series.
    A Marine and a professional boxer prior to his baseball
career, Hoak was in his share of fights on the diamond. As
a boxer he was knocked out in his last seven fights, which,
he stated, "contributed to ending my ring career." Nicknamed "Tiger" because of his penchant for fighting, he
once hosted a Pittsburgh television show called "Tiger by
the Tail."
    After leaving the Dodgers, he was with the Cubs and
Reds before going to the Pirates in 1959. He shuffled out in
1964 with the Phils. Don once hit against Fidel Castro
while playing winter baseball in Cuba. He was married to
singer Jill Corey, once a regular on the TV show "Your Hit
Parade."
    On May 2, 1956, as a member of the Cubs, he struck out
a record six times in the team's 17-inning loss to the
Giants at the Polo Grounds. Exactly one year later (May 2,
1957), playing with the Reds against the Giants at the Polo
Grounds, he went 4-for-5 and had 5 RBIs, including a
game-winning hit in the ninth inning. What a difference a
year makes!   .265

HOBBIE, Glenn
Plant superintendent at a roller skate company
Hillsboro, IL

Glenn did his chucking from 1957–64, all with the Cubs
except for a brief and final stop with the Cardinals in 1964.
He was a 16-game winner in both 1959 and '60 for the
Cubs. However, in '60 he also lost a league-leading 20
games. Hobbie won only twenty more in the next four
years and skated away at 62-81 at age 28.

HODERLEIN, Mel
Employed with Cincinnati Millicron Purchasing
Dept.
Cincinnati, OH

Mel Hoderlein wasn't quite a household name, but he did
hit .252 in 118 games for the Red Sox (1951) and Senators
(1952–54).

HODGES, Gil
Died April 2, 1972, at age 47 in West Palm Beach, FL

Gil had many career highlights with the Dodgers. His ini-
tial exposure was as a third baseman in just one game in
1943. After World War II, he was the third string catcher
for Brooklyn behind Bruce Edwards and Bobby Bragan.
He moved to first base the following year, and was the regular first-sacker for the Dodgers through their first four
seasons in L.A.

He hit four homers in a game, giving him the distinction
of being the first player to homer four times in a night
game. He only led the N.L. in one category in an otherwise
distinguished career, and that was in striking out—99
times in 1951. But from 1949–55, a seven-year stretch, he
had over 100 RBIs every season.

His 0-for-21 slump in the '52 World Series was more
than made up for in his subsequent Series appearances. He
was 8-for-22 (.364) in the '53 classic. In game four of the '59
Series, his homer gave L.A. a 5-4 win, to put them up
three-games-to-one.

Statistically, his best overall season was in '54 with a .304 average, 42 homers, and 130 RBIs, all career highs. He was an All-Star first baseman from 1949–57. Hodges was with the Mets in his final two seasons as a player, and on April 11, 1962, he hit the first home run in Mets' history. Gil managed the Senators in the early sixties before taking over as the Mets' miracle worker in '68. Career homers: 370.   .273

HOEFT, Billy
Sales representative for Compugraphic
Southfield, MI

A southpaw chucker, Billy had a fifteen-year run from 1952–66. In '56 Hoeft became the only Detroit left-hander between Hal Newhouser (1945) and Mickey Lolich (1971) to win 20 games. Billy went to the Red Sox for a brief time, then spent three seasons with the Orioles before pitching with the Giants, Braves and Cubs.   97-101

HOFMAN, Bobby
Director of scouting
N.Y. Yankees

A utility infielder, Bobby also did some catching with the N.Y. Giants, starting in 1949, and then from 1953–57. He has coached for several A.L. teams in recent years, including the Oakland A's, where under budget-minded Charlie Finley, he served in the unique dual capacity as a combination coach and traveling secretary.

Hofman had an uncle, Art "Circus Solly" Hofman, who was in the majors from 1903–16.   .248

HOGUE, Bobby
Newspaper circulation manager in Miami, FL

As a 27-year-old rookie in 1948, Bobby was a key member of the N.L. champion Boston Braves bullpen as he went 8-2 in 40 appearances. Bob was with the Braves until early in 1951 when he went to the St. Louis Browns. Late that season, he joined the Yankees and won his only decision in 7 games for the A.L. champions. The Yankees then sent him back to the Browns where he ended in 1952.   18-16

HOGUE, Cal
   Steam and pipe fitter, S and D Mechanical
   Dayton, OH

No relation to Bobby, Cal was 2-10 with the second-division Pirates during his short stay (1952–54).

HOLCOMBE, Ken
   Supervisor for Beacon Manufacturing
   Asheville, NC

Ken spent parts of six seasons with the Yankees, White Sox, Browns, and Red Sox. A right-handed chucker who arrived in 1945, Ken departed in '53 at 18-32.

HOLLMIG, Stan
   Houston Astros scout until his death, Dec. 4, 1981, at
   age 55, in San Antonio, TX

"Hopalong Cassidy" rode Topper from 1949–51. Stan Hollmig galloped along in the Phillies' organization during that period harnessing a .253 average in 94 games.

HOLLOMAN, Alva Lee "BoBo"
   Advertising business
   Athens, GA

On May 7, 1953, "BoBo" no-hit the Philadelphia A's in his first major league start, 6-0, before a "crowd" of some 2,000 in St. Louis. Although it was his first official start, he had started two games earlier that season for the Browns, but both were washed away by rain. In his no-hitter, "BoBo" collected 2 hits and 3 RBIs.

Although he vanished just two months after his no-hitter, never to return, he did win two more games that season in fairly impressive fashion.   3-7

HOLMES, Tommy
    N.Y. Mets director of community relations

Originally in the Yankees' minor league system, Tommy
arrived with the Boston Braves in 1942, and was a regular
in their outfield until 1950. He was highly successful in
1945 when he was named the *Sporting News* MVP in the
N.L. with a .352 average, and league-leading totals in hits
(224), doubles (47), and homers (28). His career home run
total was just 88, or an average of eight per season, but in
'45 he showed his power. He struck out just 9 times, the
only time in major league history the home run champion
was also the hardest to strike out.

    Tommy also established a new N.L. consecutive-game
hitting streak in '45 at 37 games, breaking the mark of 33
set by Rogers Hornsby. He was 66-for-156 for a .423 pace
during the torrid streak. Although that was his finest
year, he did hit over .300 three more times, including a
.325 clip in 1948, helping the Braves to the N.L. flag.

    Holmes became the Braves' player-manager in June of
1951, but lost the job the following year. He parted with
the Dodgers after making one appearance in the '52 World
Series. Tommy later managed several minor league teams
and did some scouting before taking over his current position with the Mets. A quarter of a century after retiring,
he was back in the news in 1978 as Pete Rose challenged
and broke his 33-year-old record of hitting in 37 consecutive games.

    Tommy remembers "The Jury Box," a section of seats in
the old Braves' field. He said, "No one in the history of the
game was loved any more than the people in the 'Jury Box'
loved me. I had 1,100 people behind me all the way." .302

HOOK, Jay
    Group vice president with MASCO, a conglomerate in
    Detroit, MI

Jay spent eight years (1957–64) on the mound with the
Reds and expansion Mets, for whom he struggled to 8-19
and 4-14 seasons. He attended Northwestern U. and was

signed by the Reds after his sophomore year to a $65,000
bonus.   29-62

HOOPER, Bob
Died March 17, 1980, at age 57 in Somerset, NJ,
where he had been a high school teacher

This Canadian-born right-hander was a 15-game winner
as a 28-year-old rookie for the Philadelphia Athletics in
1950. He also pitched for the Indians and Reds in a stint
that ended in 1955 at 40-41.

HOOVER, Dick
Died at age 55 on April 12, 1981, in an auto accident in
Lake Placid, FL

Dick vanished after pitching in two games with the Boston
Braves in 1952. In one of those games, on April 23, he gave
up a home run to Hoyt Wilhelm in Wilhelm's first big
league at-bat. Wilhelm never hit another homer in his entire career.
    Pitching for Columbus in the International League in
1955, Dick hurled a no-hitter. Four days later he was on
the losing end, as Ken Lehman threw a perfect game
against him and his Columbus teammates. He had been a
retired police sergeant in Columbus, OH.

HOPP, John "Hippity"
Public relations for insurance company
Hastings, NE

A fourteen-year first baseman-outfielder (1939–52),
Johnny was a member of the Cardinals (1942–44) N.L.
champions. He hit just .224 in 1943, but in '44 he swatted a
cool .336, an increase of over 100 points. Later he was with
the Boston Braves, and had a .333 mark in 1946. However,
Hopp went to Pittsburgh in 1948 and was not a part of the
Braves '48 pennant. He was hitting at a .340 pace in 1950
when the Yankees maneuvered to purchase him through

waivers. "Hippity" hit over .300 down the stretch to help
them capture the A.L. flag.

He departed with the Tigers in 1952.   .296

HOSKINS, Dave
Died April 2, 1970, at age 45 in Flint, MI

In 1953 Dave went 9-3 with the Indians as a 28-year-old
rookie. After losing his only decision the following year
with the Tribe, Dave tiptoed away and never returned.
Dave has the distinction of being the first black ever to
play in the Texas League.   9-4

HOST, Gene
Machine setup man
Ford Motor Co. glass plant
Nashville, TN

A 27-game winner with 315 strikeouts in the minors in
1952, Gene reported to the Tigers in spring training of '56.
Everyone in the Detroit organization was saying, "Host is
the Most"—that he had both the best fast ball and sharpest
curve in camp. That season he went 0-0 in one game with a
7.71 ERA for the Bengals.

The following year he joined the seventh place K.C. A's
and went 0-2 in 11 games. After that "Host was a Ghost,"
never to return.

HOUK, Ralph "Major"
Boston Red Sox manager

Houk's nickname comes from his rank in the military during World War II. As a catcher with the Yankees, he saw
extremely limited playing time from 1947–54. In 1949 he
came to the plate just 7 times, but had 4 hits. Overall,
Ralph was in just 91 games with a .272 mark.

Ralph is the only man to have World Series Champions
in his first two seasons as a major league manager when
he led the Yankees in 1961 and 1962. After becoming General Manager, he returned to managing and was at the

helm when the Yankees finished an uncharacteristic
tenth in the A.L. Ralph managed the Tigers from 1974–78
and, after a short two-year "retirement," became the Red
Sox skipper.

HOUSE, Frank "Pig"
Insurance company
Birmingham, AL

Frank signed as a bonus player with Detroit in the late
1940s for a reported $70,000. He appeared briefly in 1950
and '51, then from 1954–57 averaging over 100 games per
season as a catcher for the Tigers. Career highs include 15
homers and a .259 average. House was with Kansas City
(1958–59), then concluded a ten-year trip with the Reds
and Tigers (1961). The chunky Alabaman once lamented,
"All I ever read while I was in Detroit was that the Tigers
needed help in the catching department."   .248

HOUTTEMAN, Art
Paragon Steel Company executive
Detroit, MI

Art first pitched for the Detroit Tigers in 1945, just out of
high school in that city. Early in his career he survived a
near fatal auto crash. In 1950 he had his finest season at
19-12 with a league-leading 4 shutouts. After a year in the
military, Art was back with the Tigers in 1952, and at 8-20
led the A.L. in losses. Traded to the Indians the following
season, he joined the great pitching staff headed by Lemon, Wynn, Garcia, and Feller. Houtteman went 15-7 in
making an important contribution to their 1954 A.L. pennant.   87-91

HOWARD, Elston
Died December 14, 1980, at age 51 in New York City

Howard was the first black player to ever wear the Yankee

uniform. This was in 1955 when he hit .290, mostly as an outfielder. He hit a home run in his first World Series at-bat off the Dodgers' Don Newcombe. Ellie went on to play in ten World Series including one with the Red Sox in 1967. The 1963 MVP in the A.L., he was traded to Boston during the '67 season. Nearing the end of his trail, Elston hit just .147, but his experience, leadership, and handling of Red Sox pitchers was an important factor in the team's first A.L. pennant in over 20 years.

In 1969 he became a coach for the Yankees and the first black to ever coach in the A.L. He invented the weighted donut which batters use when they are in the on-deck circle.   .274

HOWARD, Frank "Hondo"
   New York Mets coach

A big name in the 1960s, "Hondo" first came on the scene in a handful of games in both the 1958 and '59 seasons for the L.A. Dodgers. The big 6'7" first baseman-outfielder had been an All-Big-Ten Conference basketball player at Ohio State. Drafted by the NBA, he instead signed a $100,000-plus bonus with the Dodgers, and in 1960 was the N.L. Rookie of the Year. In his only World Series he was 3-for-10, including a home run, in the Dodgers' four game sweep over the Yankees in 1963. Traded for pitcher Claude Osteen after the '64 season, Frank became one of the premier long-ball hitting sluggers in the game. From 1967 to 1970 he hit 172 homers, including a league leading 44 twice, and a career high of 48 in 1969. He also became the first player to ever hit a ball into the upper deck of Washington's Griffith Stadium, something he did twice.

Although "Hondo" didn't break Dale Long's 1965 record of 8 homers in 8 straight games, he went on an even more impressive streak in May of 1968. It was the hottest home run streak in major league history as he hit 10 homers in 20 at-bats over a six-game period. He left with 382 homers, and a .273 average.

HOWE, Cal
    Maintenance work for public schools
    Grand Rapids, MI

In 1952 Cal was with the Chicago Cubs, where he pitched
two hitless and scoreless innings, never to return.   0-0

HOWELL, Millard Fillmore "Dixie"
    Died March 18, 1960, at age 40 in Hollywood, FL, in
    spring training for Indianapolis

A right-handed pitcher who first appeared in three
games for the Indians in 1940, he did not return to the
big leagues until nine years later when he lost his only
decision in five games for the Reds. Then, six years later
at age 35, Howell returned with the White Sox where he
had 8 wins and 9 saves working out of their bullpen in
1955. He last pitched for "The Hose" in '58 just two
years before his death.
    On June 16, 1957, Dixie blasted two home runs while
pitching for the White Sox. The oddity about this story is
that he hurled less than four innings that memorable day.
                                                    19-15

HOWELL, Homer Elliot "Dixie"
    Member of Board of Realtors
    Louisville, KY

This Dixie Howell was a catcher who appeared in 76
games for the Pirates (1947), Reds (1949–52), and Dodgers
(1953, '55–'56).
    He caught in over 60 games for Cincinnati in that '49
season while Millard Fillmore "Dixie" Howell was on the
mound five times for the Reds. This raises the possibility
that on at least one occasion, the Reds' battery would have
read: Dixie Howell and Dixie Howell.   .246

HOWERTON, Bill
    Truck driver for Moore Business Forms
    Hayward, CA

From 1949–52 Bill played 247 games in the outfield with
the Cardinals, Pirates, and Giants for a .274 average.

HOYLE, Roland "Tex"
    Retired; former guard at Fairview State Hospital
    Carbondale, PA

"Tex" pitched in three games with the 1952 Philadelphia
Athletics and failed to record a decision.

HUDSON, Hal "Bud"
    Location unknown

Hal broke in with the Browns in 1952 and broke away
with the White Sox in '53. He shows no record in a six-
game pitching career.

HUDSON, Sid
    Texas Rangers pitching coach

Sid had a 12-year hitch (1940–1954) with three years out
for military service during World War II. In April of 1947,
on Babe Ruth Day at Yankee Stadium, Sid shut out the
Yankees, 1-0, before a crowd of over 58,000. He was with
the Senators until 1952 when he was traded to Boston
where he finished up his career in 1954. After scouting for
the Red Sox for a few years, Hudson rejoined Washington
as a pitching coach and instructor, and is still with them
today in Texas.   104-152

HUGHES, Jim
    Toronto Blue Jays scout

This "Fireman" was with the Brooklyn Dodgers (1952–56)
then was dealt to the Cubs early in '56. Jim closed with the
White Sox in 1957. His best year was in 1954 when he was

8-4 and led the N.L. in appearances with 60, and saves
with 24. Hughes is a natural born "Fireman," as his father
and several uncles and a brother were with the Chicago
Fire Department.

Another Jim Hughes was a 28-game winner for Brooklyn during the 1899 season.   15-13

HUGHES, Tom
  Houston, TX

There have been four pitchers named Tom Hughes who
have pitched in the big leagues dating back to "Long Tom"
Hughes, a 20-game winner for the Red Sox in 1903. This
Tom Hughes was defeated in both his major league starts
for the Cardinals in 1959.

HUNT, Ken
  Bartender
  Gardenia, CA

An outfielder (1959–64), Ken broke in with the Yankees,
going 4-for-12. He then spent the remainder of his playing
time with the expansion Angels, and Senators in the early
1960s. Most of his statistics were accumulated in '61 as a
regular flychaser with the Angels, when he had 25 of his
career total 33 homers.   .226

HUNTER, Billy
  Baseball coach at Towson State College in Maryland

Originally Dodger property, Billy was sold to the St. Louis
Browns for $95,000, and later moved to the Yanks and A's
in multi-player deals. Billy enjoyed a six-year ride (1953–58),
breaking in as the last regular shortstop for the St. Louis
Browns, hitting .219 and playing in all 154 games. As a
member of the Browns, he once pulled a ruse on Jimmy
Piersall that the "Waterbury Wizard" will never forget.
Billy asked Piersall to adjust the second base bag. Com-
plying with Hunter's request, Piersall did so, and to his

embarrassment was tagged out by Hunter who had the ball concealed in his glove.

Hunter and Satchel Paige were the last two players to represent the St. Louis Browns in an All-Star Game when they were chosen for the mid-summer classic in '53. Billy was the last player to homer for the Browns when he parked one on Sept. 26, 1953.

Billy moved to Baltimore in 1954 when the franchise shifted. For the next two seasons he was a utility infielder with the Yankees. However, a broken leg kept him out of the lineup most of the '56 season. Hunter, who attended Indiana State Teachers College, finished with the Indians in '58. After several minor league managing jobs, he became the third base coach for the Orioles in the mid-sixties through four A.L. pennants, before taking over as the Texas Rangers manager.   .219

HURD, Tom
Machine shop foreman for Hawkeye Steel Products until his death on Sept. 5, 1982, at age 58, in Waterloo, IA

Tom relieved in 99 games for the Red Sox, closing at 13-10 from 1954–56.

Hurd spent several years in the White Sox organization in the minors before being purchased by the Red Sox. Then, late in '54 as a 30-year-old rookie, he won his first game over guess who?—the White Sox.

HUTCHINSON, Fred "The Big Bear"
Died November 12, 1964, at age 45 in Bradenton, FL

Everything came at a young age for "Hutch" as he was in the majors at 19, a big league manager at just 32, and died of cancer at age 45. A Cancer Research Center in his name is located in his birthplace of Seattle. It is headed by his brother, Dr. Bill Hutchinson.

Fred spent his entire pitching career with the Tigers. He made his debut in relief on May 2, 1939, in Detroit in a game won by the Yankees, 22-2. That was the day Lou Gehrig's consecutive game streak of 2,130 ended. After pitching in a few more games that season and the next, Hutchinson returned to the minors, then served four years in the Navy during the war.

He was a regular in the Tigers' pitching rotation from 1946–1951. He won a career high of 18 in 1947. A good hitting pitcher, he also hit .302 that season, one of four years in which he hit over .300. He had a 95-71 lifetime mark on the mound and a respectful .263 batting average. Fred became the Tigers' manager in mid-season of 1952, and stayed through the '54 campaign. He later managed the Cardinals and then the Reds. His Cincinnati team won the N.L. pennant in 1961.

HYDE, Dick
Garage attendant with Illinois Power
Champaign, IL

A submarine-style pitcher, Dick was around from 1955–1961, all but one year as a relief pitcher with the Washington Senators. He never won or saved more than four games in a season nor had an ERA under 4.00, except in 1958, when he was absolutely brilliant with a 10-3 mark, 18 saves, and a sparkling 1.75 ERA. The following year, Hyde had his "Jekyll" year, going 2-5 with a 4.97 ERA. His last stop was in 1961 with the Orioles.   17-14

IRVIN, Monford "Monte"
Public relations work in Baseball Commissioner's office

Normally, a player who hits for a lifetime mark of .293 in just eight big league seasons would not be inducted into the coveted Hall, but Monte was already past 30 when he joined the N.Y. Giants in 1949. One of the early black players, he had been a strong hitter in the Negro Leagues both before and after military duty during the war. His election to Cooperstown in 1973 was by a special committee on the Negro Leagues.

He was a key member in the '51 Giants miracle finish and N.L. pennant, as he led the N.L. in RBIs with 121. In the World Series opener against the Yankees he equalled a record with four hits, and also stole home to spark the Giants' win. Although the Yankees eventually won the Series in six games, Irvin went 11-for-24. He suffered a broken ankle in spring training the following year which limited his playing time, but came back to hit .329 in 1953. He stayed with the Giants through the 1955 season, and ended with the Cubs in '56.

J

JABLONSKI, Ray
Construction work
Chicago, IL

As a rookie third baseman for the St. Louis Cardinals, Ray had a good year playing in 157 games, hitting 21 homers and driving in 112 RBIs. The following year in 1954 he upped his batting average from .268 to .296, and again had over 100 RBIs.

After that it was mediocrity until the end of his career in 1960. Traded to Cincinnati after that '54 season, he tailed off to .240 and actually spent some of the season in the minors. Jablonski then drifted to the Giants, back to the Cards, and then to the A.L. with Kansas City.   .268

JACKSON, Al
New York Mets minor league pitching coach

Al is best remembered for losing games with the expansion Mets in the early 1960s despite occasionally pitching quite effectively. He was 8-20 in both the 1962 and 1965 seasons.

He had originally been with the Pirates in 1959, and was
again in 1961.

Traded from the Mets to St. Louis, Jackson was very effective in 1966 despite a losing 13-15 mark, as he had an
excellent 2.51 ERA. The southpaw helped the Cards to the
'67 pennant with a 9-4 record. Back to the fledgling Mets
in 1968, Al was with them until early in '69 when he went
to Cincinnati. A tough luck pitcher, Jackson saw his career come to an end that season.   67-99

JACKSON, Larry
     Vice-president, Capital Planning Services
     Boise, ID

The most successful of the five Jacksons during the decade
was this right-handed chucker, who was around from
1955-1968. Larry was a very consistent pitcher with the
St. Louis Cards from 1957-1962 when he won between 13
and 18 every year, and was always around the 3.50 ERA
mark. In 1960, the year he won 18, he was the busiest
pitcher in the N.L., working in 282 innings with a league-
leading 38 starts.

Traded to the Cubs in 1963, he had his best season as a
24-game winner in 1964, leading the league in wins.
Jackson then lost 21 the following year. After a pair of
13-win seasons with the Phillies, he retired after being
placed in the expansion pool and being selected by the
Montreal Expos.

Back in his native state of Idaho, he worked as a
sportswriter, and also served in the state congress. He was
an unsuccessful candidate for governor of the state.
                                                      194-183

JACKSON, Lou
     Died May 27, 1969, at age 33 in Tokyo, Japan

Lou was a flychaser who was with the Cubs in 1958-59,
and five years later, briefly with the Orioles. He then
transferred his skills to "The Land of the Rising Sun"
where he passed away.   .213

JACKSON, Ransom "Randy"
International Life (insurance firm)
Athens, GA

Randy was a ten-year third baseman whose career spanned the entire decade (1950–59). From 1951 to '55 he was the regular third sacker for the Cubs, averaging 20 homers and 70 RBIs per season from 1953–55. In 1956 Randy was in over 100 games as a part-time starter for the Dodgers. He was the last player to hit a home run for the Brooklyn Dodgers, unloading on Sept. 28, 1957. He remained with the Dodgers when they moved to L.A., then departed with the Cubs in 1959.

During his college football career he was a member of the 1944 TCU team, and played in the 1945 Cotton Bowl for the Horned Frogs along with Jim Busby. He then transferred to the University of Texas and played for the Longhorns in '45. In the '46 Cotton Bowl, he completed a 50-yard pass on a Statue of Liberty play, taking the ball from a QB named Bobby Layne.   .261

JACKSON, Ron
Insurance agent
Kalamazoo, MI

This big first baseman, who measured 6'7", spent portions of seven seasons in the A.L. (1954–60), all but the final one with the White Sox. He concluded his .245 career with the Red Sox. As a bonus baby, Ron occupied the White Sox bench for the better part of two seasons. He spent his undergraduate days at Western Michigan, where he played basketball.

JACOBS, Forrest "Spook"
Owner of donut shop
Milford, DE

As a 29-year-old rookie in 1954 for the Philadelphia A's, "Spook" was the regular second baseman and hit .258. His debut was a good one as he had four hits. He remained with the A's organization and played in Kansas City (1955

and '56) before going out to sea with the Pirates in '56.
                                                              .247

JACOBS, Tony
Died December 21, 1980, at age 55 in Nashville, TN

Tony pitched in a total of two games in two different decades—split seven years apart. The right-hander was on the hill in one game for the '48 Cubs, and returned in '55 to pitch another one for the Cardinals.   0-0

JAMES, John
Real estate and shopping center property management
Scottsdale, AZ

John pitched in one game for the '58 Yankees. After a year in the minors, he returned in 1960 to post a 5-1 mark for the Yanks. John went out with the Angels in '61.   5-3

JANOWICZ, Vic
Salesman, Samuel Strapping Company
Columbus, OH

Vic was the Heisman Trophy winner as the nation's outstanding college football player in 1950. He helped Ohio State to a Rose Bowl win over another future major leaguer, Jackie Jensen, and the University of California in 1950.

Janowicz was a number-one draft pick by the Washington Redskins, but chose instead a professional baseball career, by signing a bonus with the Pirates. He was a catcher and third baseman for Pittsburgh (1953–54), hitting just .214 in limited playing time.

He then moved to pro football and was with the Redskins from 1954–55. In 1956 his athletic career came to an end when he was seriously injured in an automobile accident.

JANSEN, Larry
    Real estate salesman
    Forest Grove, OR

A thirty-game winner for San Francisco in the Pacific
Coast League in 1946, Larry was 21-5, for a league-leading
winning percentage of .808 as a 27-year-old rookie for the
N.Y. Giants in 1947. He was a steady winner the next
three years, winning between 15 and 19 games per season.

In 1951 Jansen was a key factor in the Giants' pennant
drive as he won a league-leading 23 games. Although
Ralph Branca is well remembered as the losing pitcher
and victim of Bobby Thomson's dramatic homer in the
playoffs, Jansen was the winning pitcher in a relief role
that memorable day. Larry remained with the Giants until 1954, and then reappeared briefly for Cincinnati in
1956 where he finished at 122-89. He was later the Giants'
pitching coach for eleven years, and then spent a couple of
seasons in the same capacity for the Cubs.

JAY, Joey
    Owns oil wells, taxicab companies, limousines, and a
    carpet cleaning company in WV

Joey was the first graduate of the Little League baseball
program to reach the biggies. He had been the subject of a
petition attempting to bar him from the Little League because of his advanced size when he was 12 years old. Later,
as an established major leaguer, he wrote an article titled
"Don't Trap Your Son in Little League Madness."

As a teenager in 1953, he hurled a shutout for the
Milwaukee Braves for his first major league win. All
totaled, he won 24 games for the Braves from 1953 to 1960.
Jay was traded to Cincinnati, and in 1961 nearly equalled
that total with a league leading 21 wins as he was a main
factor in the Reds' N.L. pennant. In the World Series he
won game two, 6-2, for the Reds (their only win over the
Yankees).

Joey again won 21 in 1962 but had much less success in
the next three years before returning to the Braves, who
were now in Atlanta, for his final big league fling in 1966.
99-91

JEFFCOAT, Hal
    Continental Can Company
    Tampa, FL

A twelve-year performer, Hal made a successful switch
from the outfield to pitching in mid-career. From 1949–53
he was a part-time player for the Cubs, with his best season in 1951 when he hit .273 in over 100 games. He
switched to pitching the next season, primarily as a reliever. In 1955 he was 8-6 with a fine ERA of 2.95 in 50
games. Jeffcoat was traded to the Reds, and was 8-2 and
12-13 the following two seasons. He finished with the Cardinals in 1959. Overall, he had a .248 batting average and
was 39-37 as a pitcher.

    An older brother, George, was a pitcher for the Dodgers
in the late thirties, and the Boston Braves in 1943.

JENNINGS, Bill
    Route salesman for a dairy in St. Louis, MO

A shortstop for the St. Louis Browns in 1951, Bill hit .179
in his only swing in the big top.

JENSEN, Jackie
    Died July 14, 1982, at age 55, in Charlottesville, VA,
    where he owned a Christmas tree farm and a baseball
    camp

There are many highlights and distinctions for this eleven
year A.L. outfielder who was the "Golden Boy," All-
American backfield star at the University of California before turning to professional baseball. Jensen is the only
All-American to ever win major league MVP honors. As a
football player, Jackie also played in the Rose Bowl and
the East-West Shrine Game. He was a pitcher on the 1947
NCAA Champion California team.

    After playing with the Yankees and Senators in the
early fifties, he was part of a strong Red Sox outfield for
the remainder of the decade which also featured Jimmy
Piersall and Ted Williams. In 1954 he was the A.L. stolen
base champion with 22, but that same season he set the du-

bious mark of grounding into 32 double plays. His MVP year was 1958, when he hit 35 homers and had a league-leading 122 RBIs. Jackie led the A.L. in that department for a third time in '59, with 112.

At age 32 he announced he was retiring to be with his family. He had been married to Olympic diving champion Zoe Ann Olsen. The marriage didn't last, and neither did the retirement. Jensen returned for one last season in 1961. Career totals: .279 average. He missed the 200-home-run club by just one. Although not the author of the best-seller *Fear of Flying*, he had a definite aversion to airplane flights.

JESTER, Virgil
Solar heating business in Westminster, CO

Virgil pitched with the Braves in 1952 and '53. Plagued by a sore arm, he left baseball and went to work for a meat packing company before attempting a comeback with Denver in the American Association.   3-5

JETHROE, Sam "Jet"
Owns Jethroe's Restaurant in Erie, PA

Sam was the first black player to ever wear a Boston uniform in the majors. As a 28-year-old rookie in 1950 with the Braves, he led the league in stolen bases with 35, and was selected the N.L. Rookie-of-the-Year. He again had 35 steals in '51, and then 28 in '52. Sam also had identical home run totals in 1950 and '51, with 18 each season.

Sam, who terminated his career playing two games for the '54 Pirates, was sometimes called "Larceny Legs" for obvious reasons.   .261

JOHNSON, Benjamin Franklin
Foreman, Monsanto Textile Co.
Greenwood, SC

Ben Franklin Johnson tried to invent ways of disposing of enemy hitters. In summary, Ben was 2-1 in 21 games for the Cubs in 1959–60.

JOHNSON, Billy "Bull"
   Overseer of shipping for Sibley Division of the Gran-
   iteville Mills Co. (retired)
   Augusta, GA

Billy was the Yankee third baseman in a good part of the
forties until 1951, when he was traded to the Cardinals for
Don Bollweg and $15,000. The "Bull," who had a rifle
arm, hit .280 as a rookie in 1943, and helped the Yanks to
a World Series win over the Cards by going 6-for-20 in the
Series. In the '47 WS when the Bronx Bombers defeated
the Dodgers, Billy scored 8 runs and had a record three
triples. He ended his playing days wearing a Cardinal uniform in 1953.   .271

JOHNSON, Connie
   Ford Motor Company
   Kansas City, KS

This lanky 6'4" right-hander broke in with the White Sox
in '53. Traded to the Orioles in '56, he combined with
George Zuverink to throw a one-hitter against the White
Sox, only to lose, 1-0, to Jack Harshman, who also hurled a
one-hitter.   40-39

JOHNSON, Darrell
   Texas Rangers scout

Darrell's travels spanned the years 1952–62 with several
teams. A catcher who was with the Browns and White Sox,
he worked mainly out of the Yankees' bullpen, playing behind Yogi Berra and Elston Howard on the 1957 and '58
A.L. championship teams. He went over to the N.L. in the
early 1960s and hit .315 down the stretch in 1961 after
joining the Reds, to help them to the N.L. flag.
   Johnson was the Red Sox manager in their dramatic
1975 World Series against the Reds. Darrell was released
as the Seattle Mariners' manager during the 1980 season.
                                                        .234

JOHNSON, Don
>   Taxi cab driver
>   Portland, OR

As a 20-year-old, he was 4-3 for the 1947 A.L. champion Yankees. This taxi-driving chucker was in and out of the big time throughout most of the fifties, "hacking" around with such teams as the Browns, Senators, White Sox, Orioles, and in '58 (his last year) with the S.F. Giants.   27-38

JOHNSON, Earl
>   Northwest scout for Red Sox
>   Seattle, WA

This southpaw flipper spent most of his time with the Red Sox, and was last seen with Detroit in 1951. In 1946 he was 5-4 for the Bosox and was the winning pitcher in relief over the Cardinals in the opening game of the World Series. The next two years were his best, going 12-11 and 10-4. Overall, 40-32.

His brother Chet also pitched in the majors, for the St. Louis Browns in 1946.

JOHNSON, Ernie
>   Atlanta Braves radio/TV announcer

A right-handed relief specialist, Ernie made his mark throughout the 1950s with the Boston and Milwaukee Braves, except for his final season in '59, when he was with the Orioles.

He won 7 games during the Braves' 1957 pennant season. But in the World Series he was charged with the defeat in game six in relief. He made two other appearances out of the bullpen against the Yankees and was very effective, giving up just 2 hits and 2 runs in 7 innings of work.

He's been a Brave through all the franchise shifts as a pitcher in Boston and Milwaukee, and since 1962 as an announcer in Milwaukee, and now in Atlanta.   40-23

JOHNSON, Dick
    Scottsdale, AZ

A pinch-hitter with the Cubs, Dick played in 8 games and strolled out of the biggies hitless in 1958.

JOHNSON, Ken C.
    Vice-president
    Harris-Burns Insurance Co.
    Wichita, KS

A lefty chucker, Ken C. was with the Cards from 1947–50. Dealt to the Phils early in 1950, he was 4-1 for the "Whiz Kids." His last stop was Detroit in '52.   12-14

JOHNSON, Ken T.
    Director of Development; baseball coach
    Louisiana College
    Pineville, LA

Ken T. was around for 13 seasons (1958–70). After pitching for the A's and Reds in the late 1950s and early '60s, he was a starter in the regular rotation for the expansion Houston Astros from 1962 until traded to the Braves in 1965. Just 11-17 in '63, he was a hard-luck pitcher, as evidenced by his excellent 2.65 ERA. In April of '64 tough luck peaked as he lost to the Reds, 1-0, despite throwing a no-hitter. His own throwing error put the eventual game-winning run on base.

In 1969 Ken started the season with the Braves. The right-hander was traded to the Yankees, and then went to the Cubs late in '69 as they were blowing the N.L. East to the Mets. Johnson drove away with the Montreal Expos the following season.   91-106

JOK, Stan
    Died March 6, 1972, at age 45 in Buffalo, NY

Of the more than 1,500 "jocks" who appeared in baseball bastions throughout the fifties, Stan is the only real "Jok."

A third baseman, Stan played in 12 games with the Phillies (1954–55).

While playing with Toronto on Sept. 6, 1957, he hit an apparent ninth-inning, bases-loaded home run to defeat Rochester, 6-2. However, thirty minutes after the game ended, umpire Walter Vanderhoof decided Jok's game winning hit, which hit the scoreboard, had not left the park and was therefore only a single, making the final score 3-2. In retrospect, it's safe to say that this Jok's career did not have a silver lining.   .158

JOLLY, Dave
Died May 27, 1963, at age 39 in Statesville, NC

"Ann Sothern—Private Secretary" was taking notes on TV from 1953 to '57. Dave Jolly, a right-handed chucker with the Milwaukee Braves, was taking notes on opposing hitters. A good hitting pitcher, he owns a .292 batting average.   16-14

JONES, Gordon
N.Y. Yankees scout
Pasadena, CA

Gordon was used primarily as a reliever in his eleven year pilgrimage, starting with the St. Louis Cardinals in 1954. His most wins (4) in a season came during his rookie year when he also collected his only two shutouts. Gordon then pitched with the Giants, Orioles, A's, and Astros.   15-18

JONES, Sam—"Toothpick," "Sad Sam"
Died November 5, 1971, at age 45 in Morgantown, WV

Although not as distinguished as the original "Sad Sam" Jones (1914–35), he had an interesting career himself from 1951-64. Sam became a starter for the Cubs in 1955 and went 14-20, leading the N.L. in losses. He also led the league in both strikeouts and walks that year, and again the following season. While with the Cardinals in 1958, he was the league leader in both departments for a third time.

His best season came with the S.F. Giants in 1959 when he
won 21 and had an ERA of 2.83, the best in the N.L., thus
becoming the first S.F. Giants' pitcher to win 20 games.

In '55 he had the distinction of giving up more bases-on-
balls (185) than he did base hits (175). Probably the prime
example of how he accomplished this came on May 12,
1955, when he became the first black pitcher to ever throw
a no-hitter in the majors. With a no-hitter in progress, he
walked the first three batters in the ninth inning and was
almost removed from the game. Sam struck out three
pretty good hitters (Dick Groat, Roberto Clemente, and
Frank Thomas) in succession to nail down the no-hitter.
He went to the full count on all six batters. Because of that
no-hitter, he was awarded a gold toothpick. This and the
fact that he pitched with a toothpick in his mouth, led to
the name "Toothpick."   102-101

JONES, Sheldon "Available"
   Greensboro, NC

Sheldon was with us for eight seasons (1946–1953), all but
the final two with the N.Y. Giants. In his best years
(1948–'49), he won 16 and 15 games respectively.

The right-hander was used mainly as a reliever for the
'51 N.L. champs. He also made two appearances in the
World Series against the Yankees, and was credited with a
save in game three. Lifetime mark: 54-57.

Born on 2-2-22, in 1947 his won-loss mark was 2-2.

JONES, Vernal "Nippy"
   Public relations for insurance company
   Sacramento, CA

A N.L. first baseman for seven seasons (1946–52), Nippy
was back in the majors after a five-year absence as a
back-up first baseman and pinch-hitter for the 1957 N.L.
champion Milwaukee Braves. It was his final appearance
that he'll always be remembered for as he came up as a
pinch-hitter in game four of the WS against the Yankees.
What transpired has gone down as the "shoe polish" incident. A low inside pitch by the Yankees' Tommy Byrne

was called a ball by umpire Augie Donatelli. Jones claimed he was hit on the foot by the pitch and showed the umpire the shoe polish on the ball to prove it. Donatelli then changed his call and awarded Jones first base. The Braves rallied that inning to even the series, as Johnny Logan doubled, and Eddie Mathews homered.

Earlier in his career he was with the Cardinals from 1946–51, and had his best season in 1949 when he hit an even .300 in 110 games. In '52 he was with the Phillies.
.267

JONES, Willie "Puddin' Head"
Retired from oil company when he died on October 18, 1983, at age 58, in Cincinnati, OH

A third baseman for 15 seasons (1947–61), Willie spent most of his time with the Phillies. In 1969 he was voted that team's all-time third baseman. Willie was a regular from 1949 until midway through the 1959 season. In April of '49 he tied a major league mark with four consecutive doubles. He played in a then-record 157 games for the 1950 "Whiz Kids." His 25 homers helped the Phils to the N.L. flag. Although most of the Phils were stopped cold by Yankee pitching, "Puddin' Head" went 4-for-14. Considered to be the National League's top fielding third baseman in the early '50s, he had the best fielding percentage every season from 1952–56 for all N.L. third basemen. When Jones retired he ranked among the top ten in several lifetime statistics for the Phillies. Also, his .963 fielding average ranked among the top ten in major league history for third sackers.
.258

JOOST, Eddie
Sales representative for sporting goods company
Zephyr Cove, NV

Eddie had a long stay as a shortstop with the Reds, Boston Braves, Philadelphia A's, and Red Sox (1936–1955). He didn't hit much early in his career and in 1943 set the dubious mark of the all-time low batting average in major league history for a player with 400 or more at-bats, when he hit just .185. But a few years later he established a home-run record of sorts when he hit six leadoff home runs for the A's in the '48 season.

Eddie received 100 or more walks in six consecutive years from 1947–52.

In 1942 Paul Waner was looking for career hit number 3,000 as he neared the end of his career. Only half a dozen players had reached the figure at the time. Waner hit a shot past Joost at shortstop. He got his glove on it, but couldn't handle it. It was ruled a hit, which would have been No. 3,000 for Waner. But Waner waved to the press box to rule it an error as he wanted his 3,000th to be a clean one. The official scorer changed the ruling, charging Joost with an error. Waner eventually got his 3,000th hit, but Joost was charged with a league-leading 45 errors.

Eddie was the last manager of the A's in Philadelphia in 1954, and returned as a player in '55, in his final season.
                                                                        .239

JORDAN, Milt
    Lansing, NY

"From Here To Eternity" was viewed by millions in 1953. As for Milt, he was here with the Tigers pitching in eight games. He then vanished for eternity at 0-1.

JORDAN, Niles
    Foreman, lumber company
    Sedro-Woolley, WA

In '52, Niles did a cha-cha out of the biggies with a 2-4 career mark, split between the Phils ('51) and Reds ('52). He hurled a 2-0 shutout victory over the Reds in his first big league start with the Phillies.   2-4

JORGENSEN, John "Spider"
    Philadelphia Phillies scout

A third baseman with the Dodgers and Giants (1947–51), his only season as a regular was his first as Brooklyn's third baseman in 129 games, when he hit .274. "Spider" did hit for an even .300 playing on a part-time basis the following year. In 1950 he went to the Giants where he crawled away in '51. .266

JUDSON, Howie
 Shipping and receiving clerk
 Stulper Co.
 Walworth, WI

Howie galloped into the big arena in 1948. He went 17-37 overall with the White Sox (1948–52) and Reds (1953–54). In 1949, Judson had an ignoble record of 1-14. Spending part of the '53 season in the Texas League, he went 11-0.

K

KAAT, Jim
 Retired from baseball during the 1983 season as a St. Louis Cardinals pitcher

Jim's appearance against the Texas Rangers in a relief role in April, 1980, placed him in an exclusive group of major leaguers to participate as an active player in four decades.

Kaat lost his only two decisions with the Washington Senators in 1959. But over the next 20-plus years he won 263 games to rank among the top 25 of all time. In the 1965 World Series he was 1-2 against the Dodgers, but he did set a World Series mark with five putouts in a game. A top fielding pitcher, he was the Gold Glove winner for the outstanding fielder at his position 16 times.

Jim's best season came in 1966 when he was a 25-game winner for the Twins. Thought to be past his peak, he was waived by Minnesota in 1973 when he was 35. The next two years he was a 21- and 20-game winner for the White Sox, the team that claimed him on waivers.

The outstanding left-hander retired with an overall 283-237 mark. During Jim's long career, he pitched to seven father-son combinations: Ray and Bob Boone, Gus and Buddy Bell, Maury and Bump Wills, Yogi and Dale Berra, Tito and Terry Francona, Jim and Mike Hegan, and Marty and Matt Keough.

KAISER, Don
   Deputy sheriff
   Ada, OK

"The Honeymooners," with Jackie Gleason and Art Carney, was first shown in 1955, the year Clyde Donald Kaiser broke in with the Cubs' mound staff. Don's honeymoon lasted from 1955–57, finishing 6-15. Kaiser was a $50,000 bonus player signed by the Cubs out of high school in Oklahoma where he was 49-1, including several no-hitters.

KALINE, Al
   Detroit Tigers' announcer

Elected to the Hall of Fame in 1980, Al is the youngest to ever win a major league batting title (by one day over Ty Cobb). Kaline was just 20 when he won the '55 title, not turning 21 until December 19th. Cobb was also 20 when he won the title in 1907, and turned 21 on December 18th. Ironically, both were baby Bengals. A Tiger all the way, he never played in the minors, nor ever wore the uniform of another major league team.

In April of '55 he hit two homers in one inning to become the first player to do so since Joe DiMaggio in 1936. Al never won another batting title nor had another 200-hit season, but he did hit over .300 another eight times, including 399 homers among his 3,007 hits. Kaline hit three homers in games that were washed out by rain. If credited, he would join Carl Yastrzemski as the only two A.L. players to collect 3,000 hits and 400 home runs. The only other time this crack right fielder led the league in an offensive statistic was in 1961, when he had 41 doubles.

He took full advantage of his only chance in the World

Series in 1968, hitting .379, with 2 homers and 8 RBIs as the Tigers took the Cardinals in 7 games. Al batted a sweet .324 in 16 All-Star Games, and handled 22 chances without an error. His uniform No. 6 was retired by the Tigers on August 17, 1980, in ceremonies honoring the celebrated Hall of Famer. Concerning his number, Kaline remarked, "When I first came up, I wore No. 25. But when I was a kid I thought the best ballplayers wore low numbers. I wanted to become a good player so I wanted a low number. Ted Williams wore No. 9, and Stan Musial wore No. 6, so I wanted 9 or 6."   .297

KASKO, Eddie
    Boston Red Sox director of scouting

A ten-year infielder, Eddie played in over 500 games as a shortstop and another 400-plus at third base. Originally with the Cardinals in 1957 and '58, he had his finest years with Cincinnati. Kasko was an important member of the Reds' 1961 N.L. pennant winner, hitting .271.
    He managed the Boston Red Sox in the early 1970s.
                                                            .264

KATT, Ray
    Assistant professor, athletic director, head baseball coach, and assistant football coach at Texas Lutheran College
    Seguin, TX

Ray was an eight-year catcher (1952–59) with the N.Y. Giants and St. Louis Cardinals. In 1954 he once was charged with four passed balls in a single inning on the receiving end of Hoyt Wilhelm's knuckleballs. He was the Giants' starting catcher the next season, but hit for just a .215 average. His final two years (1958 and '59) were with St. Louis. He coached for the Cardinals and the Indians in the sixties.   .232

KAZAK, Eddie
  (born Edward Tkoczuk)
  Post office employee in Austin, TX

Kazak spelled backward spells Kazak. A five-year career average of .273, including his best season of .304 in 92 games in 1949, Eddie was 2-for-2 in the '49 All-Star Game—his only All-Star tilt.

KAZANSKI, Ted
  Insurance business
  Rochester, MI

An $80,000 bonus player with the Phillies out of the University of Detroit, Ted never really lived up to the high hopes the Phillies had for him as a shortstop replacement for Granny Hamner. He hit .217 as a 19-year-old who was handed the regular shortstop job in 1953 when Hamner moved to second base. In 1956 he hit even less (.211) while playing second base, and Hamner moved back to shortstop. His best season was 1957 when he hit .265 in 62 games, most of which he played at third base.

   His career ended after just five seasons at age 24.   .217

KEEGAN, Bob
  Purchasing agent for an optical company
  Rochester, NY

Bob had a six-year stint (1953–58), all with the Chicago White Sox. As a 32-year-old rookie in '53, he was 7-5, with an excellent 2.74 ERA. His best year was in '54 when he won 16. On August 20, 1957, at age 37, he threw a no-hitter at the Washington Senators, a 6-0 win at Comiskey Park. It was the first no-hitter in the majors since Don Larsen's perfect game, and the only no-hitter thrown in the majors that season. Keegan spent several years in the Yankee farm system, after originally signing out of Bucknell University.   40-36

KEEGAN, Ed
    Franklinville, NJ

Not related to Bob, this chucker limped in with the
Phillies in 1959, going 0-3. He also worked for the Kansas
City A's ('61) and the Phillies ('62). After he pitched his
last game, he was still 0-3.

KELL, Everett "Skeeter"
    Sporting goods business and sales representative for
    class rings
    Pine Bluff, AR

"Skeeter," brother of the more famous George Kell, played
in 75 games as a second baseman for the Philadelphia Athletics in 1952.
    "Skeeter" finished his short jaunt with a .221 average.

KELL, George
    Detroit Tigers announcer

George's impressive numbers, which include a lifetime
mark of .306 and over 2,000 hits from 1943–57, gained him
entry into the Hall of Fame in 1983.
    Kell once went 0-for-10 in an extra-inning game early in
his career with the Philadelphia A's, but recovered to have
many productive days. He was the outstanding third baseman in the A.L. from the late 1940s through the mid-
fifties. He was the A.L. batting champion by a fraction
over Ted Williams in 1949—.3429 to .3427. Williams won
the home run and RBI titles that year, and was barely deprived of the Triple Crown. George was the first third
sacker to ever win an A.L. batting title, and the last until
George Brett, almost 30 years later.
    Kell was a .300 hitter 9 times, including eight years in a
row from 1946–53, most of those seasons with Detroit. In
1969 he was voted the Tigers' all-time third baseman. He
later played with the Red Sox, White Sox, and Orioles, for
whom he still hit .297 in his final year in '57, retiring at
age 35 to make way for another outstanding third sacker
named Brooks Robinson.   .306

KELLER, Charlie "King Kong"
    Owns horse ranch "Yankee Land"
    Frederick, MD

Charlie was not as big as the current "Kong" named
Kingman, but he was possibly as strong. A 14-year outfielder (1939–52), all but two were with the Yankees. He
also wore Tiger threads for a couple of years.

Keller hit .334 as a rookie in 1939, and in the Yankees'
first ever World Series appearance (without either Ruth or
Gehrig on the team), he picked up the slack with three
homers, a triple, and a double for six RBIs, as the Yankees
swept the Reds in four straight. He had his most productive season in '41 with 33 homers and 122 ribby's.

A career average of .286, with 189 homers, Charlie was
especially tough in October, as he hit over .300 in four
Series. "King Kong" collected 18 RBIs and five homers in
19 WS contests. He coached with the Yankees in the late
1950s before turning to raising horses full time. Charlie
Keller Jr. was a first baseman in the Yankee organization
in the early 1960s, but never made it to the big leagues.

"King Kong" graduated with a B.S. degree from the
University of Maryland, where he established a scholarship for young athletes.

KELLER, Hal
    Seattle Mariners General Manager

Compared to his brother "King Kong," Hal's career was
more along the lines of one of the Marquis chimps, who
were frequent guests on the Ed Sullivan show. The younger of the Keller clan, Hal caught in 25 games in parts of
three seasons with the Senators (1949–50–52).   .204

KELLERT, Frank
    Died November 19, 1976, at age 52 in Oklahoma City,
    OK

In the mid-fifties, hula hoops and Davy Crockett caps were
fads. Frank was more than a fad as he hung around from

1953–56 as a first baseman with the Browns, Orioles, Dodgers, and Cubs.

Kellert, a graduate of Oklahoma A&M, was involved in some controversy a few weeks after the 1955 WS. He was the batter when Jackie Robinson stole home in the first game. Upon being traded by the Dodgers to the Cubs following the Series, he stated that umpire Bill Summers had missed the call and that his then-teammate, Jackie Robinson, should have been called out.   .231

KELLNER, Alex
    Sundt Construction Co.
    Tucson, AZ

Alex was a 20-game winner in 1949 as a rookie for the Philadelphia A's. The following season he lost 20 to lead the A.L. in losses. He remained with the A's through their franchise shift to Kansas City before going to the N.L. with the Reds (1958) and Cardinals (1959).

Kellner had the unique hobby of hunting fish with a bow and arrow. During the off season he hunted and captured mountain lions for zoos and circuses in his native Arizona.
                                                      101-112

KELLNER, Walt
    Sundt Construction Co.
    Tucson, AZ

Walt was a teammate of his brother Alex when he pitched in three games with the A's in 1952 and '53 with no decisions.

KELLY, Bob
    Senior personnel rep., Electric Boat Division, General
    Dynamics
    Groton, CT

A career mark of 12-18 in 123 games, Bob did his hurling with the Cubs (1951–52) and Reds ('53). He returned in '58 with the Reds and Indians.

KELTNER, Ken
    Salesman
    Colonial Refining and Chemical Co.
    Milwaukee, WI

One of the top third basemen in the A.L. during the forties
with the Cleveland Indians, Ken made his exit with the
Red Sox in 1950. He was selected as the Indians' all-time
third baseman in 1969. Keltner hit a career high .325 in
1939. In 1948 he helped the Indians to the A.L. pennant
with 31 homers and 119 RBIs.

His .965 fielding average is the sixth highest of all time
in the major leagues. He is best remembered for stopping
Joe DiMaggio's 56-game hitting streak with a pair of sensational plays at third base in 1941.   .276

KEMMERER, Russ
    English teacher, high school football coach
    North Vernon, IN

Pitching for the Red Sox in his first start on July 18,
1954, Russ hurled a one-hitter against the Orioles. After 302 games between 1954–63, Kemmerer was 43-59
with the Red Sox, Senators, White Sox, and Astros. A
talented artist, he did sketches of players during his
playing days.

KENNEDY, Bill
    Bartender at time of death, April 19, 1983, at age 62
    in Seattle, WA

Bill was pitching with the Indians, Browns, White Sox,
Red Sox, and Reds from 1948–57. In 1952 he led the A.L. in
appearances (47) for the White Sox.

In 1946, Bill struck out 456 in the Western Carolinas
League, the all-time professional baseball record.   15-28

KENNEDY, Bob
Houston Astros Vice President for Baseball Operations

Bob was a third baseman-outfielder from 1939–57, in a career twice interrupted by military service. A Marine pilot, he missed three years during World War II, and also most of the 1952 season in the Korean War. Traded from the White Sox to the Indians in mid-season in 1948, he helped them to the A.L. flag, hitting .301 in the second half of the season. Bob later played with the Orioles, Tigers, and Dodgers in their final season in Brooklyn in 1957.

He was the Cubs' skipper in 1963–64 and managed the A's in 1968. Bob scored 514 runs, matching his RBI total. His son Terry is a power-hitting catcher for the San Diego Padres. .254

KENNEDY, John I.
Location unknown

One year after John F. Kennedy debated Estes Kefauver at the Democratic National Convention, John I. Kennedy played in five games with the '57 Phillies. The first black to play for the Phillies, John came directly from the Kansas City Monarchs of the Negro League. .000

KENNEDY, Monte
Retired policeman
Richmond, VA

Monte spent his entire big league life (1946–53) with the New York Giants, going 42-55. The left-hander won't forget 1949, the year he won 12 games and hit a grand-slam home run against the Dodgers.

KEOUGH, Marty
St. Louis Cardinals scout

There has been a member of the Keough family in the majors almost continually since Marty first broke in as an outfielder for the Red Sox in 1956. He remained with Boston until 1960, and later played with Washington, Cincinnati, Atlanta, and the Cubs, departing in 1966 with a .242 average.

His younger brother, Joe, was an outfielder with the A's, Royals and White Sox, from 1968 through 1973. Four seasons later, in 1977, Marty's son Matt reached the big show as a pitcher for the Oakland A's. Marty signed an estimated $75,000 bonus in '52 with the Red Sox out of Pomona High School in California, where he was considered the best athlete to come out of that school since the legendary "Mr. Outside," Glenn Davis.

KERIAZAKOS, Gus
Sales manager for Essex Chemical Co.
Clifton, NJ

Constantine "Gus" Keriazakos should have received pay raises for just signing his autograph. Gus was around in parts of three seasons (1950, '54, '55) with the White Sox, Senators, and K.C. A's.   2-5

KERR, John "Buddy"
N.Y. Mets scout

A N.L. shortstop for nine seasons (1943–51), Kerr played all but the final two with the N.Y. Giants. He had his best campaign in 1947 when he hit .287. Defensively, Buddy played errorless ball the final 52 games of the 1946 season and into the first 16 games of the '47 campaign, a string of 68 games, in which he handled 384 consecutive chances without an error. He closed with the Boston Braves his last two years.   .249

KIELY, Leo, "Black Cat"
Retired; formerly employed with an automobile dealership
North Arlington, NJ

Leo spent most of the fifties with the Red Sox and the K.C.

A's in 1960. Primarily a reliever, the southpaw was 26-27, plus an additional 29 saves.

While a member of the Red Sox pitching staff, Leo had the habit of carrying a toy black cat to the bullpen every day. In 1956, after a long drought where he was starved for a victory, he finally won a game, and continued to bring the cat to the Fenway Park bullpen daily. Leo was a 20-game winner for San Francisco in the PCL in 1957, with all 20 wins coming in relief.

KILLEBREW, Harmon "Killer"
Part-owner of an insurance and securities company in Boise, ID

Harmon ranks fifth on the all-time home run list, but tied for last in sacrifice bunts (with none in over 8,000 major league at-bats). Killebrew reached the majors at age 17 in 1954. After a trip to the minors, he became a full-time player for the Senators in 1959, leading the A.L. in homers with 42. This slugger hit over 40 homers on eight occasions, including a high of 49 in both 1964 and '69. Six of those years he was the league leader.

His final year was in 1975 with the Kansas City Royals. His 573 homers, all in the A.L., is second to Babe Ruth in the league lifetime. Harmon was originally signed by the Senators on the advice of Senator Herman Welker (of his home state of Idaho) to Washington owner Clark Griffith. Harmon was elected to the Hall of Fame in 1984.   .256

KILLEEN, Evans
Elmont, NY

In 1959 Evans came up with the K.C. A's, pitching in 4 games without a decision.

KINDALL, Jerry
University of Arizona baseball coach

An infielder for ten years (1956–65), Jerry was a part-time player for the Cubs from 1956–61, then played in 154

games for the Indians in 1962. Traded to the Twins in
1964, he was the second baseman in 125 games for the A.L.
champions in '65, his last year.

An All-American college player at the University of
Minnesota, Jerry was a member of the 1956 NCAA baseball championship team. He later became the only former
player on an NCAA title team to coach a school to the national championship, when his Arizona Wildcats took the
title.   .213

KINDER, Ellis "Old Folks"
   Died October 16, 1968, at age 54 in Jackson, TN

Ellis was a part of our national pastime from 1946–57. He
was already 32 when he finally reached the big arena with
the Browns in '46. Kinder had his greatest success with
the Red Sox as both a starter and a reliever. In 1949 he was
23-6 with a league leading six shutouts and best winning
percentage (at .793).

The game he might have won which would have given
him a 24th victory, would have taken the pennant from
the Yankees. It wasn't his fault however. It was the last
weekend of the '49 season, and the Red Sox needed to win
one of the final two games in a head-on clash with the Yankees for the A.L. pennant. He trailed, 1-0, in the eighth
inning, having given up just two hits. However, the right-
hander was lifted for a pinch-hitter. The Yankees then
added four insurance runs. Boston rallied for three runs in
the ninth, which most likely would have been enough the
way Kinder was pitching. He did win 13 in a row at one
point during his great '49 season.

In both the 1951 and '53 seasons, "Old Folks" was the
premier relief pitcher in the A.L. Ellis pitched for the Cardinals and White Sox in 1956 and '57. He should have been
labeled the White Sox Killer, as he defeated "The Hose"
17 times in a row from 1948–53.

"Old Folks" finished at 102-71. Along with his 102 career wins, he had 102 career saves.

KINER, Ralph
New York Mets announcer

In 1942 Ralph led the Eastern League in home runs with the relatively low total of 14. In his first season he led the N.L. in roundtrippers with 23. But there was nothing but big numbers in the home run department for the Pirates outfielder the next several years.

The fences were brought in for veteran Hank Greenberg, and thus resulted "Greenberg's Gardens." Hank was in his final season with the Pirates in 1947 and did hit 25. However Kiner led the league with 51, and went on to hit 40, 54, 47, 42 and 37 in the next few years, to lead or tie for the league lead every year from 1946–52.

Traded to the Cubs in a multi-player deal in 1953, Ralph was with the Wrigley gang the following season. The slugger finished his ten-year march with the Indians in '55. A back ailment shortened his career as he was not yet 33 when he retired with 369 four-baggers.

Kiner once went on a homer tear. He recalled, "I once had a string of seven home runs in three games. The next day I faced Red Barrett of the Braves at Forbes Field. Barrett predicted that I wouldn't hit one off him. I did, which made it eight homers in four games. That I'll never forget."

Kiner has been credited with coining the expression "Home run hitters drive Cadillacs and singles hitters drive Fords." However he said that former pitcher Fritz Ostermueller invented the popular slogan. Ralph was elected to the Hall of Fame in 1975.   .279

KING, Charlie
Owns the Metal Culvert Co.
Paris, Tenn.

An outfielder from 1954–59 with the Tigers, Cubs, and Cardinals, Charlie batted .237.

KING, Clyde
New York Yankees manager in 1982 before returning to front-office position

Clyde pitched in 1944–45 and 1947–48 with the Dodgers,

going 13-11. In 1951 he was the mainstay out of the Dodgers' bullpen, compiling a 14-7 mark, with 13 of those wins
coming in relief. He bowed out in '53 with the Reds and a
lifetime mark of 32-25.

The right-hander managed the S.F. Giants in 1969, then
in '73 became the Braves' manager.   32-25

KING, Jim
Telephone Co. employee in Elkins, AR

An outfielder for eleven years, Jim started with the Cubs
in 1955–56. After stops with the Cardinals and Giants, he
was a regular for the expansion Washington Senators for
six seasons. Jim had a career average of .240 with 117
home runs, including a high of 24 in 1963 for Washington.

KING, Nelson
Sports information director at Duquesne University
Pittsburgh, PA

The King and I was a motion picture hit in 1956, during
which time this not too powerful king reigned in the
majors. King Nelson, or should we say Nelson King, was
7-5 in parts of four seasons as a relief chucker for the Pirates from 1954–57. For several seasons he teamed with
Bob Prince in the Pirates' broadcasting booth.

KIPP, Fred
Owner/operator of underground utility company
Overland Park, KS

One has to wonder how often Fred said, "Let's win this one
for the Kipp!" A lefty hurler with the Dodgers in the late
fifties and the Yankees in 1960, his L.A. Dodger teammates won six for the Kipp in '58 when he went 6-6 with
O'Malley's transplants. The Yankees never won one for
the Kipp as he left at 6-7.

In '58, 5s were wild for Fred. During his 5-5 season, his
5th win came in a game he entered in relief with the score
tied, 5-5. Kipp is a graduate of Kansas State Teachers' College, where he was All-Conference in basketball.

KIPPER, Thornton
    Public relations firm
    Kipper Associates
    Scottsdale, AZ

Between 1953–55 Thornton went 3-4. Signed by the Phillies out of the University of Wisconsin, he became the 1,000th player to wear a Philadelphia (N.L.) uniform since 1883. How about one for this "Kipper"!   3-4

KIRKLAND, Willie
    Detroit, MI

A nine-year outfielder, starting with the Giants in their first season in San Francisco (1958), Willie had 22 and 21 home runs for the Giants in '59 and '60 before being traded to Cleveland. In '61 with the Indians he had his most productive season with 27 homers and 95 RBIs.

Willie was later with the Orioles and Senators before leaving in 1966 with a .240 lifetime average and 148 home runs. He played for several seasons in Japan following his major league career.

KIRRENE, Joe
    Manager of AAA Automobile Club
    San Jose, CA

Joe entered in 1950 as a fuzzy-cheeked 18-year-old. He went 1-for-4 for the White Sox. Joe didn't return until 1954 when he played in 9 games. A ten-game story, Joe hit .296.

KITSOS, Chris
    Superintendent of Parks for Mobile, AL

In 1954, Chris got into his one and only big league game as a shortstop for the Cubs.   .000

KLAUS, Billy
> Paint store and real estate
> Sarasota, FL

After brief tours with the Red Sox in 1952 and the Milwaukee Braves in '53, Billy became the Red Sox starting shortstop in 1955, and hit a career high .283 in his first full season in the big top. He played mostly at third base for the Red Sox in '56 before moving back to shortstop the following season. Billy also spent two years each with the Orioles, Senators, and Phillies before his eleven-year trek came to an end in 1963.

Klaus played for a season in Japan and then managed in the minors for several years. His younger brother, Bobby, arrived on the scene in 1964, the year after Billy's exit.
                                                          .249

KLEIN, Lou
> Died June 21,1976, at age 58,
> Metairie, LA

Lou arrived in 1943 and hit .287, playing in all 154 games as a second baseman and shortstop for the N.L. champion St. Louis Cardinals. However, the rest of his career was limited to part-time action with the Cardinals in 1945, '46 and '49, before ending with the Indians and A's in 1951.

Lou managed the Cubs in 1961 and '62, and then again in '65. In '61 he was part of owner Phil Wrigley's innovative Board of Coaches. Klein was in charge of the final 12 games, in which the Cubs were 5-7 during that stretch. Under him in '62 they were 12-18 in 30 games. He was a full-time manager for most of the '65 season replacing Bob Kennedy.   .259

KLIEMAN, Ed
> Died November 15, 1979, at age 61,
> Homosassa, FL

Ed spent eight years (1943–50) with the Indians, Senators, White Sox, and Athletics. While with the Indians in '48, the right-hander led the league in appearances (58) and saves (17).   26-28

KLIMCHOCK, Lou
   Sales manager,
   Coors Distributing Co.
   Tempe, AZ

A utility player, Lou was in and out of the majors from 1958–70 with the Kansas City A's, Milwaukee Braves, Senators, Mets, and Indians.   .232

KLINE, John "Bobby"
   Lawn and pest control company
   St. Petersburg, FL

After 77 games, during which time he played in the outfield and pitched in one game (giving up 3 runs in one inning), Bobby departed with a .221 average. His brief stint was with the '55 Senators.

KLINE, Ron
   Automobile agency manager
   Callery, PA

As a 20-year-old for the Pirates in 1952, Ron lost all seven of his decisions.

In the early 1960s he was with the Cardinals, Dodgers, and Tigers, before joining the Senators in 1963. For the next few seasons he was one of the top relief specialists. His ERA was under 3.00 for four straight seasons, and in 1965 he led the league in saves with 29.

In 1968, Kline found himself back where he started 16 years earlier. Now a veteran at 36, he had a 12-5 record and a very impressive 1.86 ERA for the Bucs. He then was with the Giants, Red Sox, and his tenth and final club, the Atlanta Braves, in 1970. When it was over he had played for 15 different managers.

Overall he was 114-144, but 53-47 in relief (with 108 saves). With 736 major league games pitched, he ranked tenth on the all-time list at the time of his retirement.

KLIPPSTEIN, Johnny
    Vice-president of sales for a corrugated box company
    Palatine, IL

An eighteen-year stint from 1950–67, Johnny was with
the Cubs from 1950–54, and then with the Reds from '55
until traded to the L.A. Dodgers in '58. Klippstein was
with a different team every season in the early 1960s, but
finally settled in at Minnesota in 1965, and played an important role in the Twins' A.L. pennant, going 9-3 with a
fine 2.24 ERA.

    Johnny is married to the niece of the old knuckleballer
Dutch Leonard. His lifetime mark is 101-118 with 66 saves
in relief.

KLUSZEWSKI, Ted "Big Klu"
    Cincinnati Reds coach; also Reds minor-league hitting
    instructor

An end on the 1945 University of Indiana Big Ten championship football team, Ted is best remembered for his bulky
muscular arms and sleeveless uniform. But more than just
a power-hitting first baseman, he was a fine fielding first
sacker, leading the N.L. in fielding percentage at the position for five straight years (1951–55).

    Unlike most of the big home-run hitters, "Klu" was not
a free swinger who was just as likely to go down swinging
as knocking one into the upper deck. In his two big home-
run seasons of 1954 and '55, he actually struck out fewer
times than he homered. In '54 he had 49 homers and
fanned just 35 times. In '55 he walloped 47 four-baggers
and whiffed just 40 times. Overall, Kluszewski hit 279
homers and struck out 365 times.

    The muscular first sacker was bulging with success in
1954, with 49 homers, 141 RBIs, and a .326 average: all
three career highs.

    He was with the Pirates in 1958 until joining the White
Sox down the stretch in 1959. He gave the "Go-Go" A.L.
champions a touch of power that carried over into the
World Series against the Dodgers. Chicago lost the Series
in six games, but he hit .391, with 3 homers and a six-game
Series record of 10 RBIs.

"Klu" ended up with the expansion Los Angeles Angels in 1961 where he whacked two home runs in the Angels' very first league game against the Orioles, leading the team to a 7-2 victory. .298

KLUTTZ, Clyde
    Died May 12, 1979, at age 61
    Salisbury, NC

Clyde was a nine-year catcher, starting with the Boston Braves in 1942. He later played for the Giants, Cards, and Pirates in the N.L. Kluttz hit .302 in 1947 for Pittsburgh. In 1951, with the St. Louis Browns and Senators, he hit for a career high .313. His final season was with Washington in 1952. Lifetime average—.268.

Over 20 years later his name was in the news again as he was scouting in the Yankees organization, and was a key factor in their signing fellow North Carolina native "Catfish" Hunter as a free agent. He was in the Orioles' organization as a Director of Player Development when he died.

KOBACK, Nick
    Employed with Udolf's Big and Tall Men's Store in Hartford, CT; golf pro at the Bel Campo Golf Club in Avon, CT

Between 1953–55 Nicholas Nicholia Koback caught a total of 16 games for the Pirates. .121

KOKOS, Dick
    Toolmaker
    Chicago, IL

Dick spent his entire five years with the Browns (1948, '49, '50, '53) and Orioles ('54). Born Richard Kokoszka, Dick hit .298 as a 20-year-old rookie in '48. The next two years he had back-to-back seasons of unusual consistency, playing in 143 games, and hitting .261 both years. His lifetime mark was .263.

Playing with the Browns on September 5, 1953, Dick hit a twelfth-inning home run to give the Browns a 1-0 win. It was the first time in A.L. history that a 1-0 extra-inning game was ever won on a home run.

KOLLOWAY, Don
Restaurant employee
Chicago, IL

Don spent twelve years as a first baseman and second baseman in the A.L. Kolloway began in 1940 and was with the White Sox throughout most of the forties until traded to Detroit in 1949 when Nellie Fox became the Chicago second baseman. In 1942 Don led the A.L. in doubles with 40. His best seasons were with the Tigers in 1949 and '50, when he hit for .292 and .289 averages. He finished his career playing in two games for the Philadelphia A's in 1953. Kolloway had a total of 76 stolen bases, and on June 28, 1941, he stole his way around the bases pilfering second, third and home.   .271

KONIKOWSKI, Al
Plumber
Seymour, CT

A card game might have affected this pitcher's career. The year Al came up (1948) with the Giants, he beat manager Leo Durocher in a game of gin rummy on a train from New York to Boston. Al says, "I don't think Leo ever forgave me for that." "Whitey" hurled with the Giants in 1951 and '54. Al was gone, holding his deck of cards, after 35 games and a 2-3 record.

KONSTANTY, Casimer James "Jim"
Died June 11, 1976, at age 61
Oneonta, NY

Jim had brief stints in the mid-forties with the Reds and Braves, but the 1950 season was a banner year as he was 16-7 with 22 saves in (a then-record) 74 appearances. Jim never started a game that year, but was called upon to do so in the first game of the World Series. He pitched very well, allowing just 4 hits, but lost, 1-0, to Vic Raschi and the Yankees.

Konstanty had two more fine years. In 1953 he won 14 games as a spot starter and reliever for the Phillies. With the Yankees in 1955, he helped them to the A.L. pennant with fine work out of the bullpen, going 7-2 with 11 saves. Jim's lifetime mark stands at 66-48 with 74 saves. He was the N.L. MVP in his great 1950 season.

A four-letter winner at Syracuse University in 1939 (baseball, basketball, boxing, and wrestling), he was the last to do that there, until Jim Brown accomplished the feat several years later.

KOPPE, Joe (born Joe Kopchia)
    Painter
    Westland, MI

At Shreveport in the Texas League in 1953, Joe hit .194 and committed 57 errors at shortstop. Yet five years later he made it to the majors and lasted eight seasons. Koppe was the Phillies' regular shortstop, with Sparky Anderson at second base in 1959. From early in the 1961 season until 1965 he was with the Los Angeles and later California Angels.   .236

KORCHEK, Steve
    Academic dean, Manatee Junior College
    Bradenton, FL

Steve caught in four seasons with the Senators, 1954–55, and again in 1958–59. A graduate of George Washington University, he was a star center on the school's football team, and was a third-round draft pick of the S.F. 49ers. His brother Mike, who was with the Dodgers' organization, died at age 24 in 1954 of uremic poisoning.   .159

KOSHOREK, Clem
  Sales engineer for the John W. Gillette Co.
  Ferndale, MI

Up in 1952 and down in '53, Clem played 99 games in the
Pirates infield.   .260

KOSKI, Bill
  Planning technician, county planning commission
  Modesto, CA

Bill lost his only decision in 13 games as a 19-year-old with
the Pittsburgh Pirates in 1951.

KOSLO, Dave
  Died December 1, 1975, at age 54 in Menasha, WI

Born George Bernard Koslowski, this southpaw chucker
spent most of his twelve years, starting in 1941, with the
New York Giants.
  His 19 losses in 1946 were the most in the N.L. He won a
career high of 15 in '47. In 1949, despite a losing record of
11-14, he had the best ERA in the N.L. at 2.50. He accomplished this without a shutout, the only time in big league
history that a pitcher led his league in that statistic without throwing a shutout. Koslo was 10-9 for the 1951
Giants, and was the starter and winner in the first game of
the World Series, when he beat the Yankees, 5-1, in a complete game effort. He also started in game six, losing 4-3.
Koslo was gone after stints with the Orioles and Braves in
1954 and '55.   92-107

KOUFAX, Sanford "Sandy"
  L.A. Dodgers pitching instructor

No pitcher in major league history was ever as dominating
and overpowering as this Brooklyn native was during a
five-year period in the mid-sixties. He broke in with the
Dodgers in his home town in 1955. Sandy won just two
games in each of the '55 and '56 seasons, and did not ap-

pear in either World Series. That first year in '55 he struck
out in all 12 of his trips to the plate. His hitting eventually
improved slightly, his pitching improved significantly. In
1959 Koufax was 8-6 for the Dodgers, now in L.A. He was
the starter and loser in game five to the White Sox, 1-0, before a record crowd of over 92,000 at the L.A. Coliseum.

Sandy posted a 27-9 log in his last year in baseball, thus
becoming the only pitcher in modern baseball to retire
with 25 or more wins in his final season.

Koufax is the only athlete in history to win two Hickock
Belts as the professional athlete of the year. With the Los
Angeles Dodgers, he led the N.L. in victories three times,
in strikeouts four times, and in ERA five times. In four
World Series, he owns a 4-3 record with a 0.95 ERA—
fourth best on the all-time list.

Koufax authored four no-hitters, one being a perfect
game against the Cubs in 1965. Following a star-studded
career that saw him go 165-87, Sandy married the daughter of actor Richard Widmark. He also worked as an announcer for NBC-TV baseball telecasts. Sandy was the
youngest player ever elected to the Hall of Fame at age 36.

KOZAR, Al
Expediter with Pratt and Whitney Aircraft Co.
West Palm Beach, FL

Al was the Washington Senators' regular second baseman
in 1948, appearing in 150 games as a rookie. He played
just two more seasons in the biggies before his last hurrah
with the White Sox in 1950.   .254

KRALICK, Jack
Unit operator for the city of Soldotna, AK

This lefty chucker first arrived with the Washington Senators in 1959. In '61 he was a 13-game winner for the
Minnesota Twins. Jack won 12 in '62, including the first
no-hitter for the franchise on August 26th when he beat
the Kansas City A's, 1-0.

Traded to Cleveland, he won 14 and 12 games for the Indians in 1963 and '64, finishing up at 67-65. Jack was the

Recreation Director for the Alaskan pipeline in recent years.

KRALY, Steve
Employed with IBM Corp.
Binghamton, NY

In 1953 Steve lost his only two decisions in five games with the Yankees. Luck changed for him late in the decade; while back in the minors he won two straight games in relief (in games in which he faced just one batter on each occasion).

KRAMER, Jack
New Orleans, LA

Not to be confused with the great tennis player of the era, this Jack Kramer was a pitcher from 1939–51. The right-hander was with the St. Louis Browns for his first nine years and was a key member, winning 17 games in 1944 when they won their one and only A.L. pennant. In the World Series against the Cardinals, Jack hurled a 6-2 complete-game victory in game three. He also pitched in relief later in the Series, and overall was very effective with 12 strikeouts in 11 innings of work, allowing no earned runs (for a perfect 0.00 ERA). In 1948 Kramer was 18-5 for the Red Sox for the best winning percentage in the A.L. at .783. His career ended in 1951, pitching for the two teams that faced each other in the World Series: the N.Y. Giants and Yankees. Jack accused the Red Sox of railroading him out of the A.L. in '51 because of differences with Manager Joe McCarthy.   95-103

KRAVITZ, Danny
Employed with G.T.E. Sylvania
Dushore, PA

Danny was a backstop with the Bucs until he was traded to the K.C. Athletics early in 1960 where he finished.   .236

KRESS, Charlie
Rush Lake Resort
Ottertail, MN

Charlie was a first baseman with the Reds ('47), White Sox
(1949–50), and then in his final season with both the Tigers and Dodgers, briefly, in 1954. .249

KRETLOW, Lou
Oil business; golf pro
Enid, OK

Lou spent parts of eleven seasons in the A.L. (1946–56)
with the Tigers, Browns, White Sox, Orioles, and K.C. A's.
Lou once qualified for the U.S. Open. He holds the world
record for the longest hole-in-one, a 427-yard shot. 27-47

KRIEGER, Kurt
Died August 16, 1970, at age 43
St. Louis, MO

Born in Triesen, Austria, this right-hander appeared in
one game in 1949, and two more in '51 with the Cardinals.
0-0

KRSNICH, Rocky
Wichita, KS

Rocky punched his way into the biggies with the White
Sox in 1949. He wasn't seen again until 1952 and '53 when
he closed with the White Sox and a .215 average. His
brother Mike was an infielder-outfielder for the Milwaukee Braves in 1960 and '62. .215

KRYHOSKI, Dick
Branch manager for engineering company
Cleveland, OH

Dick hit .294 as a rookie in 54 games with the 1949 World
Champion Yankees. He spent the rest of his seven-year ca-

reer with the Tigers, Browns, Orioles, and A's, batting
.265. Once, while playing for the Orioles, he made a putout
in the ninth inning that he thought ended the game. Not
realizing it was only the second out of the inning, he threw
his glove into the air victoriously and started to trot to the
dugout. Color me red!

KUBEK, Tony
NBC TV baseball announcer and Toronto Blue Jays
TV announcer

Tony spent nine years, all with the Yankees, playing in
seven World Series from 1957–65. Although many remember
him for being hit in the Adam's apple (the result of a
bad hop in the 1960 WS), he deserves better. Kubek was
selected by *The Sporting News* as the A.L. "Rookie-of-
the-Year" in 1957, hitting .297 in 127 games playing
shortstop, left field, and third base for the A.L. pennant
winners. In the World Series, back in his native Milwaukee, against the N.L. champion Braves, he hit two homers
and had 3 RBIs in leading the Yanks to a 12-3 win in the
third game.

His father, Tony Sr., never played in the majors, but did
hit .350 as an outfielder with the Milwaukee Brewers in
the American Association many years ago.   .266

KUCAB, John
Died May 26, 1977, at age 57 in Youngstown, OH

Between 1950–52 Johnny went 5-5 in 59 games with the
Philadelphia Athletics.

KUCKS, Johnny
Employed with Sealand Service Steamship Co. in the
World Trade Center, New York, NY

Johnny was 8-7 as a rookie in 1955 for the Yankees, and
made several appearances in relief in the World Series.
The following season was his banner year. Going 18-9, he

won a third of his career total 54 wins. In the World Series he again was limited to relief roles in both games one and two. In game seven he was the starter and shut out Brooklyn, 9-0, on just 3 hits, as the Yankees regained the championship. He rates that performance as "The thing that stands out most in my mind."

Kucks had just eight victories in each of the next two seasons before being traded to the K.C. A's, where he won just four in 1960, parting at age 27.   54-56

KUENN, Harvey
    Managed Milwaukee Brewers to American League
    pennant in 1982; fired after 1983 season

Harvey enjoyed a fifteen-year stay from 1952-66. He was the Detroit shortstop early in his career before switching to the outfield in the late fifties. In 1952 he joined the Tigers after a brief period in the minors after leaving the University of Wisconsin, where he also played college basketball.

In '53 Kuenn was the A.L. Rookie-of-the-Year, hitting .308 with a league-leading 209 hits. Harvey hit over the .300 mark eight times, including a career and league high of .353 in 1959. Prior to the 1960 season, he went to Cleveland for home-run champion Rocky Colavito in a controversial trade. Kuenn spent just one season with the Indians before transferring to the San Francisco Giants from 1961–65. He hit .304 for the '62 N.L. champion Giants. He finished with the Cubs and Phillies in 1965 and '66, with a lifetime mark of .303.

Harvey made baseball history in a dubious kind of way by making the last out in two of Sandy Koufax' no-hitters. On May 11, 1963, he grounded out playing for the Giants, and on September 9, 1965, he struck out as a member of the Cubs when Koufax hurled a perfect game.

Before taking over as Brewers' manager midway through the '82 season, Harvey had served the club as a coach and batting instructor. Early in 1980 he had his right leg amputated due to a blood clot.

KUHN, Ken
   Location unknown

A three-year career (1955–57), Ken played in the infield
with the Cleveland Indians, and hit .210 in 70 games. At
age 20 it was curtains for Ken.   .210

KUME, John
   Shipper and receiver, Trumbull Bronze Co.
   Warren, OH

John lost his only two decisions in six games with the K.C.
A's in 1955.   0-2

KUTYNA, Marty
   Night supervisor for John Wanamaker Stores
   Philadelphia, PA

This right-handed hurler was on the scene from 1959–62
with the Kansas City A's and the Washington Senators,
compiling a 14-16 mark. On opening day of the 1962 campaign, he caught the first ball of the season, thrown out by
President John F. Kennedy. The chief executive auto-
graphed the ball and later sent Kutyna the picture showing him autographing the baseball. The Hall of Fame has
asked for the baseball, but Marty plans on keeping it.

KUZAVA, Bob "Sarge"
   Salesman for beverage company
   Wyandotte, MI

Bob did his chucking from 1946–57. He was with the
White Sox, Indians, and Senators before joining the Yanks
midway through the '51 season. He won eight games down
the stretch, and then in the World Series, came in to stop a
Giant rally late in game six, as the Yankees won the
Series. In '52 he was 8-8, then waited until the seventh and
final game of the "Fall Classic" against the Dodgers to
again be on the scene for a dramatic moment. Brooklyn
had the bases loaded with dangerous Jackie Robinson at

the plate. Kuzava coaxed him into hitting an infield popup that Billy Martin caught with a last second lunge. The rally was choked off, and he then set the Dodgers down in order in both the eighth and ninth innings, as the Yankees again prevailed as World Champions.

In 1953 Bob was 6-5, and in one rare start just missed a no-hitter against the White Sox—not allowing a hit until there was one out in the ninth inning.

Pitching for the White Sox on August 26, 1949, he once fanned six consecutive Red Sox batters in the first two innings of a game at Chicago. He was with the Orioles, Phillies, Pirates, and Cardinals, 1954–57, going 49-44 lifetime.

LABINE, Clem
Manager, sports apparel company
Woonsocket, RI

The Dodgers' bullpen ace from 1952–57, Clem was primarily a reliever during his tenure (1950–1962). Labine had two shutouts, both in 1951. One was in game two of the playoff against the Giants. However, the following day, Bobby Thomson's homer took away the glimmer. He also shut out the Yankees in a ten-inning effort the day following Larsen's perfect game in the '56 World Series.

In 1955 Clem was 13-5 for the World Champs with a league-leading 60 appearances. He also was credited with a win in game four in the Series, and a save in game five, as Brooklyn took all the marbles for the first time. In '55 he went 3-for-31 with the bat. Strange but true, his three hits were all home runs.

In both the 1956 and '57 seasons, Labine led the league in saves with 19 and 17 respectively. In his later years he was also with the World Champion L.A. Dodgers ('59) and Pirates ('60). Clem wrapped up his career with the Mets in 1962. Lifetime: 77-56 and 96 saves.

LADE, Doyle
    Gas/oil delivery man
    Geneva, NE

At a time when the country was recovering from the effects of the giant world war, Doyle pitched with the Cubs (1946–50). This oil man went 25-29 before he ran out of fuel.

LAKE, Eddie
    San Leandro, CA

Eddie played shortstop with the Cards, Red Sox, and Tigers in an eleven-year stint which began in 1939 and ended in 1950. During the '44 season he pitched in six games for the Red Sox. By the time he took his final swim, he batted .231.

LAKEMAN, Al
    Died May 25, 1976, at age 57 in Spartanburg, SC

A catcher during the forties with the Reds, Phils, and Braves, Al was gone for five years until he reappeared in five games for the Tigers in 1954. Al was a Red Sox coach from 1963–69.   .203

LANDENBERGER, Ken
    Died July 28, 1960 in Cleveland, OH the day before
    his 32nd birthday

"Victory at Sea" showed up on TV in 1952, the year Ken played first base in two games for the White Sox and sank.   .200

LANDIS, Jim
    Designs safety signs for industrial workers
    Napa, CA

Jim is considered to be one of the best defensive center fielders in big league history. His .989 career fielding average is second only to Jimmy Piersall as best of all time. Landis' tour lasted from 1954–67.

Landis' best year with the bat was in 1961 when he had career highs of 22 homers, 85 RBIs, and a .283 average.

Traded from the White Sox to Kansas City following the '64 season, he also played for the Indians, Astros, Tigers, and Red Sox before hanging up his spikes in 1967 with a lifetime average of .247.

LANDRITH, Hobie
> Directs the sales activities of several Volkswagen dealers in northern California

Hobie was a fourteen-year catcher (1950–63) with the Reds, Cubs, Cards, S.F. Giants, Mets, Orioles, and Senators. He was the first player selected in the expansion draft by the N.Y. Mets, making him the "Original Met." However, in mid-season of their first year, the Mets traded Hobie to the Orioles for the player who became the most memorable of all Mets—"Marvelous" Marv Throneberry.

Playing for the Cubs, Landrith once busted up a Bob Friend no-hitter with a single.

Hobie and six of his brothers had a dynasty as the catchers for an entire decade at their high school in Detroit. The string of Landriths was broken just once, by a backstop named Harry Chiti. Landrith and Chiti were later teammates with the Cubs. Hobie, who attended Michigan State, batted .233 lifetime.

LANDRUM, Don
> Pittsburg, CA

Don walked into the biggies in 1957. An outfielder until 1966, Don was with the Phils, Cardinals, Cubs, and S.F. Giants. He hit .234 during his long journey home.

LANDRUM, Joe
    Real estate salesman
    Columbia, SC

Joe broke in with the Dodgers in 1950. A right-handed chucker, Joe was 1-3 in 16 games with the Brooklyn Dodgers in 1950 and '52.

LANE, Jerry
    Owns and operates apartment buildings
    Chattanooga, TN

From 1953–55 Jerry was 2-6 in 31 games with the Senators and Reds.

LANIER, Max
    Retired
    Rio Vista, FL

Hubert Max Lanier had his best seasons with the Cardinals in 1943 and '44 as a 15 and 17 game winner. In '46 he came out of the gate strong, winning and completing his first six starts. He then jumped to the "outlaw" Mexican League. Max returned to St. Louis in '49, and parted in '53 with the St. Louis Browns. In the 1944 World Series, Lanier was the starting and winning pitcher, 3-1, in the sixth and final game for the Cardinals over the cross-town opponent Browns.

    His son Hal was an infielder with the S.F. Giants in the 1960s. When Hal signed in 1961, Max was given a contract to scout for the Giants.   108-82

LaPALME, Paul
    Manager of an engraving company
    Leominster, MA

This manager of an engraving company etched a 24-45 mark in a career which lasted from 1951–57 with the Pirates, Cardinals, Reds, and White Sox. He came in like a lion by shutting out the Boston Braves in his first major league start.

LARKER, Norm
Export business
Torrance, CA

Plagued by ulcers, Norm was a first baseman from 1958–63. He was a member of the L.A. Dodgers' 1959 N.L. and World Series champions, sharing first base with Gil Hodges. In 1960 he had his finest year hitting .323. He rode out at .275.

LARSEN, Don
Blake, Moffet, and Towne Paper Co. salesman
San Jose, CA

"Would You Say That's the Best Game You Ever Pitched?"
Endorsements from Don's perfect game were generally modest, mainly because he never cared for making commercials, personal appearances, etc. "It disrupted my routine," he was quoted as saying. When he was eventually traded from the Yankees to Kansas City, Roger Maris came to New York. Larsen's social activities on the eve of his perfect game have been greatly exaggerated. Don recalled, "I just took it easy and had a few beers with a friend. I couldn't have been in all those places people said I was." In 1953 he set a record for pitchers with seven consecutive hits as a member of the St. Louis Browns. In '54 he was 3-21 with the Orioles. In 1962 he won a Series game in relief for the Giants over his former team.

In retrospect, 1956 was an unforgettable year for Don. Not only did he hurl his perfect gem, but he also connected for a grand slam against Frank Sullivan of the Red Sox. During spring training that year he was in an early morning accident in St. Petersburg, Florida, which prompted manager Casey Stengel to remark, "He was either out pretty late or up pretty early." In reference to a fine, Stengel added, "Anybody who can find something to do in St. Petersburg at five in the morning deserves a medal, not a fine!" Larsen had such nicknames as "Gooney Bird,"

"Perfect Game," and "The Ghoul," the latter because of his penchant for reading morbid comic books.

October 8, 1956, a day to remember!   81-91

LARY, Al
      Carpet cleaning business
      Northport, AL

The brother of famous Tiger hurler Frank Lary, Al was much more tame. A right-handed pitcher, he appeared in one game with the '54 Cubs. He tried again eight years later and lost his only decision in 15 games. Al was an All-Southeastern Conference end at the University of Alabama in 1950.

LARY, Frank
      Carpet cleaning business
      Northport, AL

"The Yankee Killer" will always be remembered for his success against the great Yankee teams of the era, more than for his overall career. This is justified, as he was 28-13 against the Bronx Bombers, and under .500 against the rest of the league, compiling a 128-116 lifetime mark. A prime example was in 1958 when he went 7-1 opposite the Yankees and just 9-14 against the rest of the league. Frank had his biggest years in 1956 and 1961 when he was a 21 and 23 game winner.

A member of a baseball-playing family, there were seven baseball brothers, all of whom played at the University of Alabama; and all but one were pitchers.

LASORDA, Tom
      Los Angeles Dodgers manager

Tom was with the Brooklyn Dodgers in four games each in 1954 and '55 with no decisions. In '55 the southpaw was sent to the minors to make room for a guy named Koufax.

The rest of his spotty playing life was spent in 1956 as a member of the Kansas City A's, when he lost all four of his decisions. Except for that season, he has been a Dodger all the way. Since his playing days, he has scouted, managed in the minors, and coached third base under Walter Alston prior to becoming their skipper. As he said, "I bleed Dodger blue."

LASSETTER, Don
Electric utility company employee
Perry, GA

Elvis sang "One Night" in '57, which was a bit shorter than Don's four-game career as an outfielder with the St. Louis Cardinals. A quarterback at the University of Georgia, Don batted .154.

LATMAN, Barry
Location unknown

Arnold Barry Latman (1957–67) was 8-5 for the 1959 White Sox A.L. champs, but did not appear in the WS. Barry enjoyed his finest season in '61, going 13-5 with the Indians. He also hurled for the Angels and Astros.

As a teenager, he sang with a professional boys choir in Hollywood, CA. Barry married into the Schwab family, owners of the Schwab drugstore chain on the West Coast.
59-68

LAU, Charlie
Chicago White Sox batting coach

A catcher from 1956–67, Charlie was behind the plate for Warren Spahn's 1960 no-hitter for the Braves. In 1962 Lau hit four doubles in a game to tie a major league record. In '64 he tied another big league mark with two hits in an inning as a pinch-hitter. He has a mediocre lifetime batting average of .255, but has become one of the most respected hitting coaches in the majors. His theory on hitting is widely accepted among big leaguers today. He has served as the hitting coach for the Oakland A's and Kansas City Royals before joining the Yankees in 1979. His book, *The Art of Hitting .300*, was published in 1980.

LAW, Vernon
    Manager of Denver (American Association)

Vernon spent his days (1950–67) with the Pittsburgh Pirates. 1960 was his premier season, when he won 20 games for the N.L. champions, and was selected as the "Cy Young Award" winner. He also won two games over the Yankees in the World Series. Plagued by a sore arm the next four years, Law was the comeback player of the year in 1965 when he won 17 games.

Vernon's son Vance is an infielder with the Chicago White Sox at this writing. A twin brother was a catcher in the Pirates' organization, but never made it to the majors. In 1947, Idaho Senator Herman Welker recommended Law to Bing Crosby, who was part owner of the Pirates. Welker and Crosby had been classmates at Gonzaga University in Spokane, WA.   162-147

LAWRENCE, Brooks "Bull"
    Employed by firm which recycles X-rays and photographic papers to recover silver
    Cincinnati, OH

Ulysses Brooks Lawrence won 15 games as a 29-year-old rookie for the Cardinals in 1954. The right-hander was a 19-game winner in 1956, and won another 16 in '57 despite a relatively high ERA, as he benefited from the hitting of his teammates on the hard slugging Cincinnati Reds of that period.

While a high school student in Springfield, Ohio, Brooks was a football teammate of comedian Jonathan Winters. Lawrence went by his middle name because his friends kiddingly called him "Useless," not Ulysses. He attended Miami University of Ohio where he played baseball, football, and basketball.   69-62

LEE, Don
    Boston Red Sox scout

Don was 40-44 from 1957–66. His father, Thornton Lee, was a left-handed chucker from 1933–48. This is as close as

any father-son combination came to both playing in the
majors in the 1950s. Ted Williams managed a home run off
both father and son. Don had his best years in the early
1960s with the expansion Los Angeles/California Angels
from 1962–64. Don attended the University of Arizona.

LEEK, Gene
San Diego, CA

Gene broke in with the Cleveland Indians in 1959. The
third baseman also played with the expansion Angels in
'61 and '62. Gene was a football player at the University of
Arizona.   .221

LEHMAN, Ken
Semi-retired; school bus driver
Sedro Woolley, WA

Ken was a southpaw chucker with the Dodgers in 1952
and '56 until he was sold to the Orioles early in the '56 season. During the 1955 campaign he hurled a perfect game
for Montreal in the International League. His best season
was in '57 at 8-3, working out of the Orioles' bullpen. Ken
concluded with the Phillies in 1961. He later coached baseball at the University of Washington.   14-10

LEHNER, Paul "Gulliver"
Died December 27, 1967, at age 47 in Birmingham,
AL

A seven-year A.L. outfielder (1946–52), Paul was with the
St. Louis Browns from 1946 to '49, before joining the Philadelphia Athletics in Connie Mack's last season as manager in 1950. Paul was on top of his game that year, hitting
.309. The nickname "Gulliver" must have been given him
in 1951 when he wore the uniforms of the Athletics, White
Sox, Browns, and Indians. In '52 he concluded his jaunt
with yet another team, the Red Sox. "Gulliver" batted
.257 during his travels.

LEJA, Frank
    Insurance business
    Nahant, MA

At a time when wash and wear clothes and Polaroid cameras became parts of American households, Frank Leja was a highly touted teenage Yankee in 1954 and '55. He was the Yankees' first big bonus player when he signed out of high school in '53. Experts raved that he would be the next Lou Gehrig. Playing in only 19 games, he was sent back to the minors and didn't return until 1962 when he played in seven games for the Angels. A 26-game career man, Frank batted .043.

LEMBO, Steve
    Works for Abraham and Straus
    New York, NY

Steve arrived in 1950 as a catcher with his home town Brooklyn Dodgers. Appearing in only five games, Steve was missing the following year, but returned to play in two games for the '52 Dodgers.   .182

LEMON, Bob
    New York Yankees scout

The Cleveland Indians' star right-handed pitcher in the late 1940s through the mid-1950s, Bob returned to prominence twenty years later when he was elected to the Hall of Fame in 1976.

Originally a third baseman, he once hit three homers and a triple in a game in the minors in 1942. On April 30, 1946, he was playing center field when Bob Feller hurled a no-hitter. He threw one no-hitter of his own in 1948, the first-ever night game no-hitter in the A.L. Bob won 20 games for the first of seven times that year and exactly half of those 20 wins were shutouts. He also won twice in the World Series over the Boston Braves. Lemon's career high in victories was 23 both in the 1950 and '54 seasons.

His lifetime total of 207 wins is remarkable since he started pitching after several years as an infielder and outfielder. Bob's career total of 37 homers ranks second only to the 38 hit by Wes Ferrell as most-ever by a pitcher. He managed in the Pacific Coast League, coached for the Indians, Phillies, Angels, and Royals before becoming a Royals, White Sox, and Yankee manager. Overall 207-128 and .232 as a batter.

LEMON, Jim
Minnesota Twins coach

Like Bob Lemon (no relation), Jim was originally with the Indians as an outfielder in 1950 and '53. However, his best seasons came after being traded to the Washington Senators. In 1956 he led the A.L. in striking out—138 times, but also led the league in triples with 11. He had a three home-run game that year on August 31st. The three came in succession, the first player to ever do so in Washington's spacious Griffith Stadium. The four-baggers were hit off Yankee great Whitey Ford with President Eisenhower in the stands.

In 1959 he hit 33 homers with 100 RBIs. In one inning on September 5th, he hit two homers and drove in a record 6 runs. Jim walloped 38 homers and again garnered an even 100 RBIs in 1960. He left with a career total of 164 homers and a .262 average.

He coached with the Twins from 1965–67 and managed the Senators in 1968 to a tenth-place finish.

LENHARDT, Don
Boston Red Sox scout

Don had a well-traveled five-year run as an outfielder in the A.L. from 1950–54.

He hit 22 homers as a rookie in 1950 for the St. Louis Browns, then was traded to the White Sox during the '51 season. In '52 he was with the Red Sox, Tigers, and back with the Browns. Lenhardt broke away in '54 with the Red Sox. Don has remained with them for the past quarter-century as a scout, except for a four-year period from 1970 to 1973 when he was back in uniform as a Red Sox coach.

.271

LENNON, Bob
> Ironworker
> Dix Hills, N.Y.

Bob had a brief and undistinguished career as an outfielder for the Giants and Cubs in the mid-fifties. But in
1954, playing for Nashville in the Southern Association,
he hit 64 home runs, one of the highest totals ever for a
season in professional baseball. He was the triple crown
winner in the league that year, hitting .345 and driving in
161 runs.   .165

LEONARD, Emil "Dutch"
> Retired from job with Illinois State Youth Commis-
> sion when he died on April 17, 1983, at age 74, in
> Springfield, IL

The original "Dutch" Leonard made headlines from
1913–25. This knuckleball-throwing Leonard arrived in
1933 and lasted until age 44 in 1953. He is the only pitcher
to ever lead both leagues in losses, losing 19 for the Senators in 1940, and then a N.L. leading total of 17 losses for
the Phillies in 1948. But, his overall mark is a winning one
at 191-181, which includes two significant victories. He
was the winning pitcher over the Yankees on Lou Gehrig
Day at Yankee Stadium in 1941. Even more significantly,
he defeated 27-game winner Dizzy Trout and the Tigers on
the final day of the 1944 season for Washington that
handed the St. Louis Browns their only A.L. pennant in
history. He was a special guest at the Browns' victory
party after that win.

Leonard had one 20-victory season in 1939 for the Senators. Even while in his 40s, he was an effective relief
pitcher for the Cubs, winning 10 games in 1951, and saving 11 in 1952 at age 43.

LEPCIO, Ted
>   General sales manager for Northeast District
>   St. Johnsbury Trucking Co.
>   Dedham, MA

A ten-year infielder from 1952–61, Ted spent most of those years with the Red Sox, later playing for several other teams in his final seasons.
  He is out of Seton Hall in New Jersey.   .245

LEPPERT, Don E.
>   General manager for a baking company
>   Memphis, TN

Don hit just .114 in 40 games as a second baseman for the Orioles in 1955, the extent of his career. (Don G. Leppert caught in the majors in the early sixties.)

LERCHEN, George
>   Employed with Burton Brothers Construction
>   Garden City, MI

George put his act in gear with the Tigers in '52 and Reds in '53. In 36 games he hit .204. His father, "Dutch" Lerchen, played briefly with the Red Sox in 1910.

LEVAN, Jesse
>   Salesman, Berks Packing Co.
>   Reading, PA

Jesse came up with the seventh-place Phillies in 1947. He was among the missing until 1954 when he reappeared with the Senators. Gone after '55, he hit .286 in a total of 25 games.

LEWANDOWSKI, Dan
>   Buffalo, NY

"A Streetcar Named Desire" with Marlon Brando and Vivien Leigh was a motion picture success in 1951, the year a pitcher loaded with desire (named Lewandowski) lost his only decision in two games for the Cardinals.

LIDDLE, Don
Department supervisor
Snap-On Tool Corp.
Mount Carmel, IL

Don was a lefty flipper for four seasons starting in 1953 with the Milwaukee Braves. In '54 he was 9-4 for the N.L. champion N.Y. Giants, and was on the mound in relief in game one of the World Series against the Indians when Willie Mays made the famous catch off the bat of Vic Wertz. In game four, Don was the starter and winner for the Giants as they completed their four-game sweep. He won 10 games in '55 and departed in 1956 with a lifetime 28-18 mark, a World Series win, and a great view from the pitcher's mound of one of baseball's most famous plays.

LILLIS, Bob
Houston Astros manager

A ten-year N.L. infielder, Bob was used mostly as a short-stop from 1958–67, starting with the Dodgers in '58. He was the regular shortstop for the expansion Astros for their first several years. Bob became a coach for the team following his playing days. Lillis, who attended the University of Southern California, hit for a lifetime .236 average.

LIMMER, Lou
Air conditioning/refrigeration work
Bronx, NY

Lou broke in with the Philadelphia Athletics in 1951. Absent the next two years, Lou returned to the A's in 1954. The first baseman batted .202 lifetime.

Lou was the last player to homer for the Philadelphia Athletics. It came on Sept. 25, 1954, and was the last of his 19 career four-baggers.

LINDELL, Johnny
   Employee of Hollywood Park Race Track
   Laguna Beach, CA

An interesting career for this pitcher-turned-outfielder-turned-pitcher again. Johnny started out in the Yankees organization in the mid-1930s as a pitcher and worked his way up to the Newark team in the International League, where he was a 23-game winner in 1941. Lindell then joined the Yankees, but switched to the outfield. He remained with the pinstripers throughout the 1940s and had some fine years, including 1944 when he hit an even .300 with over 100 RBIs, and led the A.L. in triples with 16.

In the 1947 World Series he led New York past Brooklyn, going 9-for-18. He hit a career high .317 the following season. Sold to the Cardinals in 1950, Lindell was back in the minors at Hollywood in the PCL in '52. He was a 24-game winner on the mound that year, and often hit in the cleanup spot. Back to the big leagues in '53, this time as a pitcher, he was just 5-16 for the Phillies. Overall .273, 8-18 on the mound.

He was in the California Angels Speakers Bureau from 1961–72.

LINDEN, Walt
   Manager with Ernst and Whinney CPA firm
   Western Springs, IL

In 1950 Walt went 2-for-5 in three games for the Boston Braves.   .400

LINDSTROM, Chuck
   Baseball Coach at Lincoln College and President of
   Diamond Dry Unlimited
   Lincoln, IL

The son of Hall of Fame third baseman Fred Lindstrom, Chuck had just one at-bat in one big league game as a catcher with the White Sox in 1958. And would you believe he had a base hit for a 1.000 average!

LINHART, Carl
   Bricklayer foreman for National Steel
   Granite City, IL

In 1952 Carl Linhart, who was born in Czechoslovakia, appeared in three big league games as a pinch-hitter for the
Tigers.   .000

LINT, Royce
   Milwaukie, OR

In '54 Royce was on the mound as a 33-year-old rookie with
the St. Louis Cardinals. His only year in the big show, he
was 2-3 in 30 games.

LIPETRI, Michael Angelo
   Court officer of the County Court of Nassau County in
   Mineola, NY

Not quite as artistic as his namesake, Mike pitched in a
total ten games for the Phillies in '56 and '58 without a decision.

LIPON, Johnny
   Manager of Alexandria in the Carolina League

Johnny has been in baseball in one capacity or another for
some 40 years. A shortstop for the Tigers in the early forties, he became the regular at the position for them in
1948, and had his best season in 1950 when he hit .293 in
147 games. His playing days were over in 1954 with a .259
average. All but one game was played in the A.L. His only
appearance in the N.L. was in his final big league game for
the Reds in 1954.
   Lipon has mainly been a minor league manager from
the lowest to the highest levels for the past 25 years. He
did coach for the Indians in 1969–70 and managed the
team for the balance of the '71 season when Alvin Dark
was fired.

LITTLEFIELD, Dick
  Tool and die worker
  Southfield, MI

Dick played for a record ten teams from 1950–58.

The Red Sox, White Sox, home town Tigers, and the Browns were his first stops. After the '53 season, the Browns moved to Baltimore and Dick was traded from the Orioles to the Pirates, where he was 10-11. He then began a journey around the N.L. to the Cardinals and N.Y. Giants. Following the '56 season, he was traded to the Dodgers for Jackie Robinson, but when Robinson retired, the trade was nullified. Littlefield was traded anyway to the Cubs, and completed his travels in '58 with the Milwaukee Braves. He has stayed put in his native Detroit area for the past several years.   33-54

LITTRELL, Jack
  Employed with Louisville-Nashville Railroad
  Crestwood, KY

Jack played shortstop (1952–57) with the Philadelphia and K.C. Athletics. In 111 games he batted .204.

LITWHILER, Danny
  Baseball coach at Michigan State University (retired, 1982); instructor for Cincinnati Reds

An outfielder (1940–51), Danny hit for a career average of .281. He broke in with the Phillies where he hit .305 in 1941. From late in that '41 season until early in 1943, he played in a record 187 consecutive games without committing an error. Litwhiler was fortunate enough to be traded from the lowly Phillies to the Cardinals, and was a member of the 1943 and '44 N.L. championship St. Louis teams. He hit a home run in the fifth game of the all-St. Louis '44 "Trolley Series" as the Cards won, 2-0.

Danny wasn't so lucky being traded from the Cards to the Boston Braves in 1946, or from the Braves to the Reds in '48. Both the '46 Cardinals and the '48 Braves won the N.L. pennant. Danny closed as a player and coach for the Reds in 1951.

LIVINGSTON, Thompson Orville "Mickey"
　　Retired from Bethlehem Steel at time of death on
　　April 3, 1983, at age 69, in Houston, TX

A catcher throughout most of the forties with four clubs
(Phillies, Cubs, Giants, and Braves), Mickey hit for a lifetime average of .238. He made appearances in two games
in the 1930s and the 1950s with some success. In 1938 he
picked up three hits in four at-bats with the Senators. After a pair of games for Brooklyn in 1951 when he collected
two hits in five at-bats, Mickey said goodnight.

LOCKE, Bobby
　　Dunbar, PA

Lawrence Donald (Bobby) Locke arrived with the Indians
in 1959. During his nine-year trip, the chucker also saw action with the Cardinals, Phillies, Reds, and Angels.　16-15

LOCKE, Charlie
　　Fire loss investigator for insurance company
　　Poplar Bluff, MO

The Chordettes sang "Mr. Sandman" in 1955. Charlie
Locke was sound asleep after pitching three hitless-
scoreless innings in two games for the '55 Orioles.　　0-0

LOCKLIN, Stu
　　Junior high school counselor; youth baseball program
　　supervisor
　　Appleton, WI

A Wisconsin graduate, Stu hit .167 in 25 games as an outfielder for the Indians in 1955 and '56. While at Wisconsin,
Stu played basketball and football.

LOCKMAN, Carroll "Whitey"
　　Montreal Expos scout

Whitey had a sixteen-year career as a first baseman-
outfielder (1945–60) with his best seasons coming as a

member of the Giants. He homered in his first at-bat as an
18-year-old in 1945. Originally an outfielder, he moved to
first base during the Giants' memorable '51 season. Somewhat of a forgotten hero for his role in the dramatic ninth-
inning rally of the third playoff game that fall, he doubled
to knock Don Newcombe out of the game. Ralph Branca replaced Newcombe to face Bobby Thomson, and the rest is
history.

Traded to St. Louis in 1956, Whitey was back in a
Giants' uniform in their final season in New York in 1957,
and then for the first season in San Francisco in 1958. He
concluded after stints with the Orioles and Reds.

Following his playing days, Whitey has remained in
baseball as a coach in the minors and majors, a big league
manager, vice-president, and for the past few seasons as a
scout.   .279

LOES, Billy
    Former youth counselor
    Jackson Heights, NY

A colorful and somewhat eccentric right-handed pitcher,
Billy was once quoted as saying, "If you win 20, they want
you to do it every year." He never did win 20, but won as
many as 14, and was 50-25 overall in a four-year period for
Brooklyn from 1952–55.

Along with claiming to lose Vic Raschi's ground ball in
the sun ('52 WS), he was reported to have picked the Yankees to win the Series over his team, the Dodgers. In the
'53 "Fall Classic," he beat the Yankees and Whitey Ford
7-3 in game four.

Since 1950, five players have walloped four home runs
in a game. Billy has the one-in-a-thousand distinction of
being in uniform at the park on four occasions. In '50 and
'54 Billy was in Dodger threads when Gil Hodges and Joe
Adcock banged out four roundtrippers in a game. Loes was
in Baltimore flannels in '59 when Rocky Colavito sent four
over the wall. As a member of the S.F. Giants, the right-
hander was the winning pitcher when Willie Mays had his
four-homer day in 1961.

In a recent quote Billy said, "They got guys playing now

with earrings in their ears. If I was pitching, I'd stick one in their earring." He is also reported to have remarked that Sandy Amoros' famous catch in the '55 World Series was an accident. Par for Billy Loes!   80-63

LOGAN, Johnny "Yachta"
   Sells advertising novelties (semi-retired)
   Milwaukee, WI

Johnny was a scrappy shortstop who was in more than his share of brawls. He came up with the Boston Braves in '51, and was the team's regular shortstop throughout the decade, including the team's two N.L. pennant-winning seasons in 1957 and '58. "Yachta" was traded from Milwaukee to the Pirates in '61 where he hung up his spikes in 1963. He batted a career high .297 in 1955 when he led the league in doubles with 37. His nickname "Yachta" is Ukrainian for John.

Somewhat of a folk hero in Milwaukee, he was famous for his "Loganisms." After receiving an award, he once said, "I will perish this award forever." Speaking at a dinner for Stan Musial he stated, "One of the all-time greats, the immoral Stan Musial." When ordering dessert, "I'll have pie a la mode with ice cream."   .268

LOHRKE, Jack "Lucky"
   Security officer, Lockheed Corp.
   Sunnyvale, CA

The nickname of this one-time N.L. utility infielder was given to Lohrke while in the military during World War II, after he missed an Army transport plane which crashed. In 1946, while playing at Spokane in the Western International League, a team bus crashed killing nine members of the squad. "Lucky" had gotten off the bus at a previous stop after receiving word that he was called up to the San Diego team in the Pacific Coast League.

He hit for a .242 average, mainly in a utility role for the N.Y. Giants from 1947–51, and for the Phillies 1952–53.

LOLLAR, John "Sherman"
    Died September 24, 1977, at age 53 in Springfield, MO

Lollar was a long time A.L. catcher (1946–63) spending
most of those seasons as the number one receiver for the
Chicago White Sox. He was originally with the Indians in
'46 before becoming a Yankee in 1947. Sherm was the
starting catcher in the first game of the '47 World Series,
and went 3-for-4 in helping the Yanks to a win. He was
with N.Y. again in '48, but since Yogi Berra had taken
over behind the dish, Lollar was dealt to the Browns. He
joined Chicago in 1952 and was a fixture there for another
decade. In 1954 Sherm threw out the last 18 runners who
tried to steal on him, from May until the end of the season.
On April 23, 1955, he picked up two hits in an inning twice
in the same game.
    Lollar coached for the Orioles and White Sox following
his playing days, and later was a manager in the Pacific
Coast League before his death in 1977. Sherm attended
Pittsburgh State Teachers College.   .264

LOMBARDI, Vic
    Golf pro—Palm Lakes Country Club
    Fresno, CA

Vic won 35 games for Brooklyn from 1945–47. The southpaw spent the remainder of a six-year N.L. career with
Pittsburgh from 1948–50.   50-51

LONG, Dale
    Field representative for minor league baseball's Na-
tional Association

Dale was a first baseman who distinguished himself as the
first man since 1906 to ever catch despite throwing left-
handed, when he went behind the dish in 1958 as a member of the Cubs. The experiment lasted for only two games.
The idea first occurred to Branch Rickey when Dale was
with the Pirates earlier in the decade.
    Long was originally with the Pirates and Browns in
1951. Back in Pittsburgh in 1955, he was their regular

first baseman for several seasons, and led the N.L. in triples (with 13) that year. It was in May of 1956 that his name became the biggest in baseball during an eight-game stretch when he established a still-standing record of homering at least once in eight straight games. In 1959 Dale hit two consecutive pinch-hit home runs with the Cubs. He helped the Yankees down the home stretch with some timely pinch-hitting in their A.L. pennants of 1960 and '62.

A career average of .267 and 132 roundtrippers, Dale was the last left-handed throwing catcher before Mike Squires went behind the plate on May 4, 1980, for the White Sox.

LONNETT, Joe
Pittsburgh Pirates coach

Between 1956–59, Joe was a catcher with the Phillies in 143 games. He has remained in the majors as a coach with the White Sox and currently is with the Pirates under Chuck Tanner.   .166

LOPAT, Ed
(born Edmund Lopatynski)
Montreal Expos
Special Assignment scout

"Steady Eddie" was a key member of the Yankees pitching staff along with Raschi, Reynolds, and Ford in the early 1950s. Known as the "Junk Man," he was the premier pitcher in the league among off-speed throwers during this period.

He was just a game over .500 as a member of the White Sox in the mid-forties, going 50-49, but from 1948–54 with the Yankees he was a winner twice as many times as he was a loser, going 109-51. Ed was a 21-game winner in '51, and then beat the Giants twice in the World Series. In '53 he was 16-4 for the highest winning percentage in the A.L. while compiling the best ERA in the league at 2.42.

He has remained in baseball the past 25 years since his pitching days ended as a minor league manager, pitching instructor, and currently a scout. Lopat managed the Kansas City A's under Charlie Finley in 1963 and '64.

If there was ever an Indian killer, it was "Steady Eddie," who holds a 40-12 lifetime mark against the Tribe. By 1951 he had beaten the "Injuns" eleven in a row. In an attempt to hex the scalper, 40,000 fans showed up one night in Cleveland, each carrying a rabbit's foot. Eddie recalled, "While I was warming up before the game, a drunk came on the field and threw a black cat at me, and it clung to my uniform jersey." Apparently the whammy gimmickry proved successful as the Indians defeated the Yankees, 4-3. However, black cats and rabbits' feet couldn't crush Lopat's season as the Yankee junk ball ace went 21-9 that year.

Lopat shows a lifetime log of 166-112. He was 4-1 in World Series play.

LOPATA, Stan "Big Stash"
    Salesman, J.D.M. Materials Company
    Abington, PA

"Big Stash" was a N.L. catcher from 1948–60, all but the final two seasons with the Phillies. He was Andy Seminick's backup in 1950. His finest season was 1956 when he took over full time and established a club record for most home runs in a season by a catcher with 32.

Stan broke Brooklyn pitcher Don Newcombe's streak of consecutive scoreless innings (39⅔) with a long two-run homer for the Phillies on Aug. 11, 1956.

Lopata ended with the Milwaukee Braves in 1959 and '60.   .254

LOPEZ, Hector
    Department of Recreation
    West Hempstead, NY

This Panamanian-born third baseman-outfielder was a valuable player for the Yankees' A.L. pennant winners of the early 1960s. Originally with the Kansas City A's in 1955, he moved to the Bronx during the days of the K.C.-

New York connection. Hector was labeled as a good stick, weak glove type of player.

Lopez hit .333 in the 1961 World Series against the Reds including a three-run homer in the fifth and final game.

Hector owned a cocktail lounge but said, "I gave it up when someone stuck a .38 in my nose."   .269

LOVENGUTH, Lynn
Secretary-treasurer for Ideal Quality Meats
Beaverton, OR

Lynn was a part of the big league baseball life in 1955 (Phillies) and '57 (Cardinals) when he went 0-2 in 16 games.

LOWN, Omar "Turk"
Post office employee
Pueblo, CO

Turk spent almost his entire eleven-year run in Chicago. Beginning with the Cubs as a starter in '51, he never started another game after his first three years. Lown led the N.L. in appearances with 67 for the Cubs in 1957. After a brief period with Cincinnati in 1958, he returned to the Windy City with the White Sox. Turk became an important part of the 1959 pennant race with a 9-2 record and a league-leading 15 saves. The right-hander hurled three scoreless innings of relief against the Dodgers in the World Series. Overall record: 55-61, with an additional 73 saves.

LOWREY, Harry "Peanuts"
Ex-Chicago Cubs coach
Retired in Inglewood, CA

Primarily an outfielder from 1942–55, "Peanuts" also played every infield position. He was with the Cubs throughout most of the 1940s, and was a member of the last Cubs N.L. pennant winner in 1945. He hit .310, going 9-for-29 in the World Series against Detroit. From 1950–55 he was with the Reds, Cardinals, and Phillies. In 1953 with St. Louis, Lowrey led the N.L. in pinch-hits with 22.

As a youngster, Peanuts acted in *Our Gang* comedies. He's played bit parts in numerous movies dealing with sports personalities and even had a speaking role in "The Winning Team" which was the story of one-time great pitcher Grover Cleveland Alexander, portrayed by President Ronald Reagan. Lowrey's line was two words, "Thanks Alex." .273

LUMENTI, Ralph
Bowling lanes employee
Milford, MA

Ralph was 1-3 in parts of three seasons with the Washington Senators from 1957–59. Known as "The Commuter," Ralph was with the team only on weekends in '57 while attending classes during the week at the University of Massachusetts.

LUMPE, Jerry
Banking and insurance business
Springfield, MO

Jerry was an A.L. second baseman from 1956–67 and also played in over 100 games each at shortstop and third base. Originally with the Yankees, he hit .340 in 1957 in 40 games. He played in both the 1957 and '58 World Series for the pinstripers.

In '59 Wilbert Harrison was singing "I'm Going to Kansas City," the same year Jerry went to K.C. He had his best year in '62 when he hit .301. Lumpe walked out with the Tigers. .268

LUNA, Memo
Los Mochis, Sinoloa, Mexico

Memo lost his only game as a big league chucker with the St. Louis Cardinals in 1954.

LUND, Don
>   Associate athletic director
>   University of Michigan

A seven-year outfielder, Don started out with the Dodgers
in the mid-forties, then had a brief stop with the St. Louis
Browns before playing before home town fans in Detroit
from 1952–54.

Lund was a coach for the Tigers in 1957–58, then took
over as the head baseball coach at the University of Michigan. In 1962 he led the Wolverines to the NCAA championship in the College World Series.

As a student at Michigan, Don was a running back and
was drafted by the Chicago Bears of the NFL, but elected
to play baseball.   .240

LUTTRELL, Lyle
>   Chattanooga, TN

Breaking in as a shortstop with the Senators in 1956, Lyle
was all done in '57 after a 57-game career that produced a
.192 average.

LUTZ, Joe
>   Executive director of a Boys Club
>   Sarasota, FL

Joe batted .167 in 14 games as a St. Louis Browns' first
baseman in 1951. He was an Indians' coach in the early
seventies, and also coached in the Japanese Baseball
League in the mid 1970s. Lutz piloted Southern Illinois
University into the College World Series in the late 1960s.

LYNCH, Jerry
>   Operates Champion Lakes 18-hole golf course with
>   former teammate Dick Groat in Ligonier, PA

One of the premier pinch-hitters in baseball history, Jerry
broke in with Pittsburgh in 1954. From 1957, until traded
back to the Pirates in 1963, he was with the Reds. Lynch

GUS BELL was a part of
the homer-happy Reds in the mid-
fifties. *(Baseball Bulletin)*

(center) JOHN BERARDINO is better
known as Dr. Steve Hardy on the
"General Hospital" afternoon soap
opera. *(Baseball Bulletin)*

RAY BOONE hit four grand slam
home runs in 1953. *(Baseball
Bulletin)*

"ROCKY" BRIDGES was a popular utility infielder recognized by his big chaw of tobacco. *(Baseball Bulletin)*

In the '58 World Series, BILL BRUTON led all batters, going 7 for 17 with the Braves. *(Baseball Bulletin)*

"SMOKY" BURGESS had 145 career pinch-hits, a record broken by Manny Mota in 1979. *(Baseball Bulletin)*

ANDY CAREY at Old-timers' Day, Yankee Stadium, 1981. *(Joe Cuda)*

As a White Sox shortstop in 1951, CHICO CARRASQUEL went 53 games without an error. *(Baseball Bulletin)*

DEL CRANDALL, DON McMAHON, ANDY PAFKO, and BOBBY AVILA celebrate after a Braves' victory in 1959. *(Baseball Bulletin)*

The "Little Professor," DOM DiMAGGIO, hit .316 in 1946, helping the Red Sox to the A.L. flag. *(Baseball Bulletin)*

Until Mike Schmidt came along, DEL ENNIS was the Phillies' all-time home run swatter. *(Baseball Bulletin)*

FERRIS FAIN won back-to-back A.L. batting titles in 1951 and 1952. *(Baseball Bulletin)*

MIKE GARCIA, the "Big Bear," was the A.L. ERA leader in 1954 with the pennant-winning Indians. *(Baseball Bulletin)*

SID GORDON walloped 30 homers for the New York Giants in 1948. *(Baseball Bulletin)*

BILLY GOODMAN won the A.L. batting title in 1950, hitting .354. *(Baseball Bulletin)*

SAM JETHROE was the N.L. Rookie-of-the-Year in 1950. *(Baseball Bulletin)*

(below) WILLIE "Puddin' Head" JONES helped lead the 1950 Whiz Kids to the N.L. flag. *(Baseball Bulletin)*

(above) ELLIS KINDER went 23–6 with the Red Sox in 1949. *(Baseball Bulletin)*

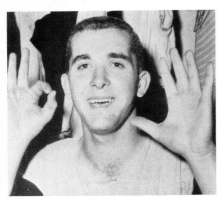

MIKE McCORMICK holds up five fingers to indicate his rain-shortened 5-inning, no-hitter on June 12, 1959. *(Baseball Bulletin)*

WILMER "Vinegar Bend" MIZELL served in the U.S. Congress following his pitching days. *(Baseball Bulletin)*

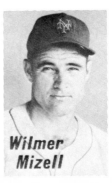

Wilmer Mizell

WALLY MOON'S "Moon Shots" at the Los Angeles Coliseum helped the Dodgers skyrocket to the '59 World Championship. *(Baseball Bulletin)*

DAVE PHILLEY developed into one of the American League's premier pinch-hitters. *(Baseball Bulletin)*

(left to right) DAVE POPE, DAVE PHILLEY, WALLY WEST-LAKE, LARRY DOBY, and AL SMITH. *(Baseball Bulletin)*

WALLY POST was part of the Reds' power machine in the mid-fifties. *(Baseball Bulletin)*

(far left) In 1952, BOBBY SHANTZ was the A.L. MVP, going 24–7 with the Philadelphia Athletics. *(Baseball Bulletin)*

(left) ROY SIEVERS was the A.L. Rookie-of-the-Year in 1949 with the Browns. *(Baseball Bulletin)*

VIC WERTZ recovered from a polio attack to hit 32 homers for the Indians in '56. *(Baseball Bulletin)*

(right) MAURY WILLS led the N.L. in stolen bases for six straight seasons. *(Baseball Bulletin)*

twice hit over .300 but had definite shortcomings as an outfielder.

Jerry led the N.L. in both 1960 and '61 with 19 pinch-hits each year. He completed his thirteen-year career in 1966 with the Pirates and a .277 lifetime average, including 116 pinch-hits, third only to Smokey Burgess and Manny Mota. His 18 pinch-hit home runs are the all-time high.

M

MAAS, Duane "Duke"
    Died December 7, 1976, at age 45 in Mount Clemens, MI

Duke was around for seven seasons starting with the Tigers in 1955. The right-hander was traded to the Kansas City A's after the 1957 season, then moved on to the Yankees midway through '58 and helped them to a pennant with a 7-3 record. Maas enjoyed his best season in 1959 when he went 14-8 for the Yankees.   45-44

MABE, Bob
    Department overseer, Dan River Mills
    Danville, VA

A right-hander with the Cardinals, Reds, and Orioles (1958–60), Bob went 7-11 in 51 games. He lost the sight in his right eye, the result of a childhood accident, but did not allow his handicap to overcome his desire to play in the big leagues.

MACDONALD, Bill
    Walnut Creek, CA

Bill was 8-10, including a pair of shutouts for the Pirates in 1950. In 1953 he lost his only decision in four games with Pittsburgh.   8-11

MACKENZIE, Eric
    Ontario, Canada

In 1955 Eric made a fruitless attempt to make it in the big
time as a one-game catcher for the K.C. A's.   .000

MACKINSON, John
    Location unknown

In 1953 John pitched in one game with the Philadelphia
Athletics. Back for another try in '55, he lost his only decision in 8 games with the Cardinals.

MADDERN, Clarence
    Insurance agent, Farmers Insurance
    Bisbee, AZ

Clarence chased fly balls with the Cubs in the late forties,
and did likewise with the Indians in 11 games in 1951.
Clarence finished with a .248 average.

MADISON, Dave
    New York Mets scout

"The Squeakin' Deacon" appeared in one game for the
Yankees in 1950. He then transferred to the Browns and
Tigers in '52 and '53. After 74 games, he was 8-7.

MAGLIE, Sal "The Barber"
    Retired; worked with Niagara Falls Convention Bu-
    reau
    Grand Island, NY

Sal was already 33 years old when he became one of the
more effective pitchers in 1950 with an outstanding 18-4
season. His biggest year was with the '51 Giants when he
was 23-6. He was 41-10 over that two-year period for a winning percentage of over .800 on his way to a 119-62 life-

time mark, with a winning percentage of over .652 (ninth best of all time). Maglie's late start came after several years in the minors, World War II, and a jump to the "outlaw" Mexican League in 1946.

Oddly enough, Maglie pitched for all three New York teams in the 1950s. While with the Dodgers, he hurled a no-hitter over the Phillies on Sept. 25, 1956. Two weeks later he was the losing pitcher in Don Larsen's 2-0 perfect game in the World Series, although giving up just 5 hits to the Yankees. Late in the '57 season, Maglie was acquired by the Yankees.

"The Barber" was a pitching coach for the Red Sox in the 1960s and for the Seattle Pilots in 1969. Maglie was labeled "The Barber" because of his ability to brush back batters with close-shave pitches, and also because he had the ability of "shaving" the corners of the plate. Sal usually sported a heavy beard on days he would pitch.

The Niagara Falls, NY, City Council voted in 1982 to rename its Hyde Park Stadium in honor of Maglie.

MAGUIRE, Jack
    Gainesville, FL

Jack landed with the N.Y. Giants in 1950. An infielder-outfielder, Maguire was dealt to the Pirates in '51, depriving him of the playoff and pennant-winning excitement. From Pittsburgh he went to the Browns that season where he made his last landing.   .240

MAHONEY, Bob
    District manager for Graves Truck Lines
    Lincoln, NE

Before his 1951 major league debut with the White Sox, Bob compiled a fine 20-7 record for Omaha of the American Association in 1950. The right-hander left the majors in '52 after a short visit with the Browns.   2-5

MAHONEY, Jim
    Former manager of Denver of the American Association

Jim Mahoney came up as a shortstop for the Red Sox in 1959. He also played with the Senators, Indians, and Astros in the early sixties before he was knocked out with a .229 average.

MAIN, Forrest "Woody"
    Liquor store employee
    Fresno, CA

"Woody" was a Pirates' hurler who went 4-13 during his 79-game career that covered the years 1948, '50, '52, and '53.

MAJESKI, Henry "Hank"
    Staten Island, NY

Hank is another in a long list of players who lost what might have been peak years to military duty in World War II. He broke in as a third baseman for the Boston Braves in 1939. His finest seasons were with the Philadelphia Athletics in the late 1940s, including a .310 mark in 1948 when he hit a record six doubles in a doubleheader, the last player to ever do so. After a .310 performance for the White Sox in 1950, Hank became a utility player back with the Athletics and Indians. Majeski closed with the Orioles in 1955.
    Hank has scouted for the Dodgers and Astros, and managed in the minors, most recently in the New York-Penn. League. He set a fielding percentage record for third basemen in 1947 with the A's.   .279

MALKMUS, Bobby
    Cleveland Indians scout

Bobby was a utility infielder with the Braves and Senators in the late 1950s and with the Phillies in the early sixties. He has managed in the minors for several years.   .215

MALLETT, Jerry
Principal, Forest Park High School
Beaumont, TX

Frankie Avalon was singing "Venus" in 1959, and Jerry was in heaven for four games as an outfielder with the Red Sox.   .267

MALLETTE, Mal
American Press Institute
Reston, VA

Mal appeared in two games without a decision for Brooklyn in 1950. A journalism graduate from Syracuse University, he became a sports writer following his pitching days. In 1957 Mal did an article for *The Saturday Evening Post* on Walter Alston, who had been his manager at Montreal (I.L.).

MALMBERG, Harry
Died October 29, 1976, at age 50 in San Francisco, CA

"Swede" vanished after 67 games with the Tigers in 1955. He coached for the Red Sox in 1964.   .216

MALONE, Eddie
Whittier, CA

The extent of Eddie's life as a catcher with the White Sox lasted from 1949–50. He made his exit with a .257 average.

MALZONE, Frank
Super scout—Boston Red Sox

Frank was the Boston Red Sox steady third baseman from the mid-fifties until the mid-sixties when he was traded to the California Angels, where he departed in 1966. He never played another defensive position other than third base in over 1,400 games.

Consistency was a strong point, especially between the '57 and '64 seasons when he played in over 150 games every year but one. Frank was generally good for 15 to 20 homers and 80 to 90 RBIs each year. His career high average was in 1958 when he hit .295, with a league-leading 627 at-bats.

Malzone made a dandy debut with the Red Sox on September 20, 1955, when he racked up six hits in ten at-bats against Baltimore in a twin bill. He led the A.L. third basemen in double plays from 1957–61. The Red Sox pilfered Malzone right from under the Yankees' noses when they signed him out of Samuel Gompers High in the Bronx. Malzone was voted the Red Sox All-Time third baseman in 1969.   .274

MANGAN, Jim
    School teacher
    San Jose, CA

Jim had a see-saw career as a catcher with the Pirates (1952 and '54) and the N.Y. Giants ('56).   .153

MANTILLA, Felix "The Cat"
    Bartender
    Milwaukee, WI

Felix was mainly a utility man from 1956–66. His first six seasons were with the Milwaukee Braves where he replaced Johnny Logan at shortstop. He played the outfield and infield for them, and was a member of both the 1957 and '58 N.L. champions.

In eight seasons in the biggies he hit 35 homers. In '64 and '65 Felix got the chance to play on an everyday basis, and found the short left field wall at Fenway Park to his liking as a member of the Red Sox. He nearly matched his home run total for his previous eight years when he hit 30 in 1964. He added 18 in '65, then made his exit in '66 with the Astros.   .261

MANTLE, Mickey
>   Public relations executive
>   Reserve Life Insurance, Dallas, TX

Mickey is considered by many as the greatest switch-hitter in the history of the game. Against a career total of 536 home runs, Mickey won the triple crown in 1956 (.353; 52; 130).

Mantle, who spent his entire eighteen-year career (1951–68) with the Yankees, switch-hit home runs in the same game ten different times.

Everyone knows about Mantle's 565-foot home run in the Yanks' 7-3 victory over Washington at Griffith Stadium on April 18, 1953. However, in the same game, the sinewy kid from Oklahoma may well have hit the longest bunt in history when his drag bunt landed just in front of second base, and he beat it out for a single.

On April 9, 1965, Mick hit the first home run ever in the Houston Astrodome during an exhibition game against the Astros. The holder of numerous World Series records, including home runs (18) and strikeouts (54), Mantle was named after Philadelphia Athletics' catcher Mickey Cochrane, because his father was a big fan of the famed receiver. Cochrane and his teammates lost the '31 World Series just a week before Mantle's birth in October 1931.

He was plagued by bad legs throughout his 2,401 game career. Mickey was elected to the Hall of Fame in 1974.
>   .298

MANVILLE, Dick
>   Owns Forbes-Manville Furniture Showcase
>   Orlando, FL

Dick failed to gain a decision as a right-handed pitcher in one contest with the Boston Braves (1950) and 11 more games with the Cubs ('52). He is a Yale graduate.

MAPES, Cliff
Retired chemical fertilizer company employee
Pryor, OK

A five-year outfielder (1948–52), Cliff twice had "his" number retired by the Yankees. Mapes was wearing number 3 in the '48 season when that number (previously worn by Babe Ruth) was retired. Cliff was assigned number 7 (which eventually became Mickey Mantle's) which was also retired. Mapes was sent to the St. Louis Browns during the '51 campaign, and concluded in 1952 with Detroit.
.242

MARCHILDON, Phil
Office furniture business
Ontario, Canada

Phil was born in the tongue-twister town of Penetanguishene in Canada. He spent the bulk of the 1940s as a chucker for the Philadelphia A's. His biggest season came in 1947 when he won 19 games.
    Phil's actual playing time in the 1950s consisted of just an inning and a third of pitching for the 1950 Boston Red Sox.
68-75

MARGONERI, Joe
Supervisor, International Paper Co.
Waltz Mill, PA

A southpaw chucker, Joe was 7-7 in 36 games with the New York Giants (1956–57).

MARION, Marty
Manager of Stadium Club Lounge at Busch Stadium, St. Louis

From 1940–50 Marty was "Mr. Shortstop" for the St. Louis Cardinals. A smooth fielder with great range, he helped the Cards to four N.L. pennants and three World Series championships in a six-year period from 1941–46.

In 1951 Marty became the Cardinals manager and led them to a third place finish. He then became a player-coach with Rogers Hornsby and the St. Louis Browns in 1952. Marion was the Browns' last skipper when he replaced Hornsby in that '52 season. In '54 Marty was back to coaching with the White Sox, and then managed them to consecutive third-place finishes in 1955 and '56. His last year as a player came in three games for the Browns in '53 in the role of player-manager.

An older brother, John "Red" Marion, was an outfielder briefly for the Washington Senators in 1935, and again in 1943.   .263

MARIS, Roger
Budweiser beer distributor
Gainesville, FL

Roger broke in with the Indians in 1957. On the third day of the season he hit a grand-slam home run in the eleventh inning against the Tigers. What looked like a bright rookie year was hindered when he fractured two ribs in a base path collision. Midway through the '58 season he was traded to the A's along with pitcher Dick Tomanek for Vic Power and Woody Held.

Playing with the Yankees, Maris hit a four-bagger in his first World Series at-bat in 1960 against the Pirates. In his assault on Ruth's single season home run mark of 60 in 1961, he did not connect for his first home run until the eleventh game of the season. He eventually hit his 61 homers in '61.

As a member of five straight Yankee pennant winners (1960–64), Roger once walked five times in a game on May 22, 1962. He spent his last two years with the Cardinals in 1967 and '68. His final game came in the seventh game of the '68 WS when the Cardinals lost to Mickey Lolich and the Tigers.

Maris, who wore number 9, hit his first N.L. home run on May 9th ('67) in Forbes Field. The spectator who caught the ball was sitting in row 9 seat 9 in right field. Roger also

broke into the majors with a 9-game hitting streak. He hit
.260 lifetime with 275 homers. When asked what aspect of
his career has been overlooked he says, "I feel that I was a
good all-around player. I had good speed, a good arm and
could play the outfield."

MARKELL, Duke
Men's shoe business
Rego Park, NY

Born Harry Duquesne Makowsky in Paris, France, Duke
was 1-1 in five games as a righty with the 1951 St. Louis
Browns. He was a New York City policeman while he was
a professional player.

MARKLAND, Gene
Drapery business
Fort Lauderdale, FL

In 1950 the Athletics said goodnight to Gene after he
played in five games at second base.   .125

MARLOWE, Dick
Died December 10, 1968, at age 41 in Toledo, OH

A career mark of 13-15 (1951–56), Dick spent 97 of his
98 games with the Tigers. He closed with the White Sox.
Marlowe had a perfect game, pitching for Buffalo in the
International League in '52 after he returned to the minors.

MAROLEWSKI, Fred
Insurance salesman
Western and Southern Life
Chicago, IL

Fred was a one-game first baseman with the Cardinals in
1953.   .000

MARQUEZ, Luis
Aguadillo, PR

Luis was a flychaser in 99 big league games with the Braves (1951), Cubs, and Pirates ('54).   .182

MARQUIS, Bob
Traffic manager
Union City Transfer Oil Field Trucking Co.
Beaumont, TX

After 40 games and a .273 average, the Reds had Bob going home in 1953.

MARQUIS, Roger
Marquis Oil Company
Holyoke, MA

In 1955 Roger had a one game shot with the Orioles as an 18-year-old outfielder. "Noonie" was 0-for-1.

MARRERO, Connie
Baseball coach
Havana, Cuba

Connie was 33 years old when he came up in 1950 with the Washington Senators. His best year was 1952 when he had an 11-8 record and 2.88 ERA while completing 16 of his 22 starts. The right-hander closed out at 39-40, including seven shutouts and several gray hairs.

MARSH, Fred
Post office employee
Corry, Pa.

Fred scooped 'em up from 1949–56. In 1951 he was the full-time third baseman for the St. Louis Browns. He was traded to the Senators, then back to the Browns during the '52 season. Marsh played for the White Sox, then the Orioles, before finishing.   .239

MARSHALL, Clarence
    Sima, CA

"Cuddles" was a right-handed hurler for the Yankees in the late 1940s and for the Browns in 1950. He was 7-7 overall, but 3-0 for the Yanks in their '49 championship season.

MARSHALL, Jim
    Manager of Nashville in the Southern League

Jim first arrived in 1958 with the Orioles. He was with the Cubs and Giants before becoming a member of the original Mets in 1962. He finished later that year with the Pirates. Marshall played in Japan for three years, then became a minor league manager in the Cubs' organization. He then coached under Whitey Lockman for the Cubs before managing the team. He later piloted the Oakland A's.

Playing at Memphis in the Southern Association in 1956, Jim hit a 475-foot home run which hit a sign at a laundry outside the stadium. It won him $1,000 as the sign read, "Hit our sign for $1,000." Although the sign had been there since 1942, Marshall was the first to hit it.
.242

MARSHALL, Willard
    Real estate salesman
    Fort Lee, NJ

A long-ball hitting outfielder, Willard's career spanned the 1942–55 seasons, with three years out for military duty during World War II. His biggest year was in 1947 as a member of the N.Y. Giants, which established a then N.L. record of 221 home runs. Marshall contributed 36 on a team on which Johnny Mize hit 51, and Walker Cooper 35, making a great 1-2-3 home-run punch. On July 18th, he hit three consecutive homers in a game. Willard hit .309 in '49 for his career high, but then was traded to the Boston Braves. After three years in Boston, he played two years each for the Reds and White Sox. He owns a lifetime average of .274, with 130 home runs.

MARTIN, Barney
    Retired from Atlanta Seaboard Railroad
    Columbia, SC

Barney was a one-game pitcher for the 1953 Reds. His son
Jerry was a major league outfielder for four teams in the
1970s and early '80s.   0-0

MARTIN, Billy
    (born Alfred Manuel Pesano)
    New York Yankees consultant

Billy was a .257 lifetime hitter, but hit .333 in World
Series play as a member of the Yankees from 1950–57.
When he missed the '54 season due to military duty, the
Yankees also missed the A.L. pennant—the only year dur-
ing his tenure as a Yankee. His debut came at Fenway
Park in Boston when he replaced Jerry Coleman at second
base late on opening day with the Yankees down, 9-0. He
singled and doubled during the seventh inning rally as the
Yankees came back to win, 15-10. Billy returned to the
bench the next day, and to the minors later that season.
    Among the teams that he played for were Kansas City,
Detroit, Cleveland, Cincinnati, the Milwaukee Braves and
Minnesota Twins. He has also managed teams in Minnesota, Detroit, Texas and Oakland, along with the Yankees.
Billy's book described it all in the title, *Damn Yankee*, one
of the three books published on his life.
    Among his many on and off the field brawls, the most
memorable quote probably came after the Cubs' owner
sued him for $1,000,000 following his punch which broke
the jaw of Cubs' pitcher Jim Brewer. "How do they want it,
by cash or check?" laughed Billy.

MARTIN, Boris "Babe"
    (born Boris Martinovich)
    Location unknown

A catcher-infielder-outfielder, "Babe" saw sporadic playing time with the Browns and Red Sox in the late 1940s.
He was quite successful as a pinch-hitter for the Browns

from 1944–46, going 1-for-1 in each of those seasons as a pinch-hitter. He returned to play four games with the Browns in 1953.   .214

MARTIN, Fred
   Died June 11, 1979, at age 64
   Chicago, IL

A right-handed pitcher, Fred compiled a 12-3 record in his limited career as a pitcher for the Cardinals in 1946, '49 and '50. He won all six of his decisions in 1949. Fred was a Cubs' pitching coach in the early '60s. He was a pitching instructor for the Cubs at the time of his death in 1979.

MARTIN, Joseph Clifton "J.C."
   Cleaning business
   Chicago, IL

For 14 years (1959–72), J.C. was mainly a catcher who also played some first base and third base. He spent most of his time in Chicago with the White Sox, although he spent his last three seasons with the Cubs. In 1968 and '69 he was with the New York Mets. As a member of that '69 miracle team, he played in just one World Series game against the Orioles, which led to an explosion.

In the fourth game of the '69 WS, the Mets were batting in the bottom of the tenth with the score tied, 1-1. Jerry Grote was on second, and Al Weis on first, when Martin bunted the ball toward the first base line. Orioles' pitcher Pete Richert fielded the ball and threw to first. The sphere struck Martin on the wrist as he was running the entire distance from home to first base illegally (inside the baseline) according to Baltimore skipper Earl Weaver. The ball bounded into foul territory, and Grote raced across home with the winning run. The umpires did not support Weaver's post-game protest. Earl must have watched it on the clubhouse TV as he was ejected from the game earlier.
                                                              .222

MARTIN, Morrie
    Meat packing business
    Washington, MO

A left-handed pitcher, Morrie spent ten seasons in the big
time beginning with Brooklyn in 1949. His finest campaign came in '51 when he won 11 games for the Philadelphia A's. He was also with the White Sox, Orioles, and
Indians, before closing with the Cardinals and Cubs. At
38-34 lifetime, this meat packer was no "hot dog."

MARTIN, Paul
    Location unknown

Paul lost his only decision in 7 games for the 1955 Pirates.
The 6'6" 240-pound chucker was studying for the ministry
at the time he was signed.

MARTINEZ, Rogelio
    Brooklyn, NY

Nat King Cole was singing "Mona Lisa" in 1950, while
Rogelio Martinez was moaning after pitching only two
games for the 1950 Senators, when he went 0-1 with a
27.00 ERA.

MARTYN, Bob
    Personnel director for Tektronix Inc.
    Beaverton, OR

Between 1957–59 Bob was dancing around the outfield of
the K.C. A's. During that time he hit for a .263 average.

MASI, Phil
    Mount Prospect, IL

"Feller and Boudreau worked the pickoff play very well,
but I'm sure I was safe." In one of the more controversial
plays in World Series history, Phil was a pinch-runner for
the Boston Braves in the 1948 World Series. Boston's

Johnny Sain and Cleveland's Bob Feller were in a scoreless duel. In an attempted pickoff at second, Masi was ruled safe in a very close play. He subsequently scored on a base hit for the game's only run. Feller was never to win a World Series game.

Although he was a pinch-runner in this game, he was a 14-year catcher from 1939–52. The first ten of those seasons were with the Braves. Masi's best year was in 1947 when he hit .304.

Phil was traded to the Pirates during the 1949 season, then spent his final three big league campaigns from 1950–52 with the Chicago White Sox.   .264

MASON, Hank
Marshall, MO

In 1958 Hank arrived as a pitcher with the Phillies. In a four-game career in parts of '58 and '60, Hank failed to gain a decision.

MASSA, Gordon
Employed in sales department
Ashland Chemical Co.
Cincinnati, OH

As a left-handed hitting catcher, Gordon was 7-for-15 in six games for the Cubs in 1957. The following year, NASA (National Aeronautics and Space Administration) appeared and Massa disappeared after pinch-hitting in two games.

Gordon departed with an impressive .412 average. The 6'3" 210-pound bruiser was a star lineman on the Holy Cross University football team.

MASTERSON, Walt
Ex-head baseball coach at George Mason College, VA
Retired in 1981

This right-handed chucker spent fourteen seasons in the biggies beginning in 1939 with Washington. In 1942 he was 5-9 for the Senators, but four of his five victories were shutouts. Walt was with the Red Sox from 1949–52. In 1951 he once struck out Mickey Mantle five straight times which led to Mickey's return to the minors. He was back with Washington in '53. After a two-year absence, he returned for one last stint with Detroit in 1956.   78-100

MATARAZZO, Len
Lynbrook, NY

In 1952 Len hurled one scoreless inning with the Philadelphia Athletics.   0-0

MATHEWS, Eddie
Oakland A's scout

As a rookie for the Boston Braves in 1952, Eddie became the first rookie in N.L. history to have a three-home-run game. The only Brave to play in Boston, Milwaukee, and Atlanta, Mathews hit 47 homers in 1953, then a record for a third baseman. He also holds the N.L. mark of homers hit on the road when he hit 30 in '53. Eddie owns the N.L. record for nine straight seasons with at least 30 round-trippers.

Eddie's last appearance in uniform as a player came in the 1968 "Fall Classic" with the Detroit Tigers.

Elected to the Hall of Fame in 1978, Eddie collected 512 home runs and had a lifetime .271 average.

MAUCH, Gene
California Angels Director of Player Personnel

"My players say I'll never have a heart attack because I have no heart." Mauch is considered to be one of the best managers of the past two decades despite the fact that he holds the major league record for managing the longest without ever winning a pennant. Gene suffered through the longest losing streak of modern times with 23 straight losses as field general of the 1961 Phillies. In 1962 the Phils improved to an 81-80 mark, and despite a seventh-place finish in a ten-team league, he was named "Manager of the Year." Mauch came very close to winning a pennant in '64 as his Phillies led most of the way, only to lose out to the Cardinals in the final week.

Gene was the first manager of the expansion Montreal Expos and later managed the Twins and Angels. He led the Angels to the A.L. West title in 1982, but resigned after his team lost to the Milwaukee Brewers in the A.L. Championship Series.

Mauch played parts of nine seasons, from 1944 to '57. He spent time with the Dodgers, Pirates, Cubs, Braves, and Cardinals, and closed with the Red Sox in 1957. Primarily a second baseman, he also played shortstop and third base.

.239

MAURIELLO, Ralph "Tami"
 Computer design engineer
 Canoga Park, CA

Lots of "ones" for "Tami," who had a three-game pitching career with the '58 L.A. Dodgers. He was 1-1 with 11 strikeouts in a total of 11 innings. During this time, he pursued an electrical engineering degree at USC in the off season.

MAURO, Carmen
 Division chairman—athletic director—baseball coach
 Cuesta College
 San Luis Obispo, CA

An outfielder with the Cubs in the late forties and early fifties, Carmen made stops at Brooklyn, Washington, and Philadelphia (Athletics), where he played his last game in 1953. As a member of the Cubs in '48, his first big league hit was an inside-the-park home run against Murry Dickson and the Cardinals, at Sportsman's Park in St. Louis.

.231

MAXWELL, Charlie "Paw Paw"
Sales manager for die casting company
Paw Paw, MI

An A.L. outfielder (1950–64), Charlie's brighter days came in the late 1950s with Detroit when he became well known for his Sunday home run hitting. On May 3, 1959, he homered in his final time at bat in the first game of a doubleheader against the Yankees, and then in his first three times to the plate in the nightcap. He had career highs of 31 homers and 95 RBIs for the Tigers that season.

Charlie was originally with the Red Sox, where he backed up Ted Williams in the early 1950s. During the '51 season he hit three pinch-hit homers, and all three were hit off future Hall of Famers—"Satchel" Paige, Bob Feller, and Bob Lemon. He also played with the Orioles and White Sox.

Prior to the 1960 season, "Paw Paw" hit 23 of his homers against the Yankees. Maxwell, who attended Western Michigan, banged out 148 homers—40 of which came on Sunday—to go with a .264 average.

MAYE, Arthur "Lee"
Sales representative for a clothing firm
Los Angeles, Calif.

Lee hit an even .300 in his maiden season in 1959 for the Milwaukee Braves. His finest campaign came in 1964 when he led the N.L. in doubles with 44 while hitting .304 for the Braves. He then played for the Astros, Indians, Senators, and White Sox, before wrapping it up in 1971.

Lee was the lead singer of a professional singing group in the mid-fifties called "Arthur Lee Maye and the Crowns." Their recording of "Truly" sold 90,000 copies.   .274

MAYER, Ed
School teacher
Corte Madera, CA

In '57 Ed came up with the Cubs. Gone after the '58 season, Mayer was 2-2 in a 2-year 22-game career.

MAYO, Jackie
    Land developer/real estate broker
    Mayo & Orvets Realtors
    Youngstown, OH

A 1948 graduate of Notre Dame, Jackie spent his entire
six years (1948–53) with the Phillies. He hit a home run in
the September drive for the 1950 pennant, only to have it
washed out by rain.   .213

MAYS, Willie "The Say Hey Kid"
    Hotel public relations
    Atlantic City, NJ

Willie started slowly in his rookie year of 1951, going
hitless in his first 12 big league games. He had been
hitting .477 for Minneapolis of the American Association
when he was called up by the New York Giants. Mays was
the on-deck batter when Bobby Thomson's home run lifted
the Giants into the '51 World Series. In that Series, Willie
hit into a record three double plays against the Yankees.

Among his 660 career homers, a record 22 came in extra
innings. Willie's most dramatic extra-inning blast was in
a 1963 game in the 16th inning, breaking up a scoreless
duel between Warren Spahn and Juan Marichal.

Willie is one of five players in big league history to
gather 20 or more doubles, triples, and homers in the same
season (which he did in 1957).

Inducted to the Hall of Fame in 1979, he won eleven
Gold Gloves for his circus-type catches, and was a two-time
MVP. Mays is the only player in the history of baseball be-
sides Hank Aaron to achieve both 500 or more homers and
collect 3,000 or more hits. Willie was the youngest player
to hit 50 or more home runs in one season when he hit 51
in 1955 at the age of 24. Mays, who wore No. 24, played in
24 All-Star Games. He is also the only player to hit a home
run and steal a base in the same All-Star Game. Considered by many as one of the greatest of all time, he finished
with a .302 lifetime average.

MAZEROSKI, Bill

Owns a 9-hole golf course in Rayland, OH and Bill's Bar in Yorkville, OH; infield instructor in the Montreal Expos organization

Who can forget Bill's dramatic ninth-inning home run off Ralph Terry in game seven of the 1960 World Series which gave the Pirates the championship. He hit well in that Series, going 8-for-25 for a .320 mark. Lifetime, "Maz" collected 2,016 hits and a .260 average.

From the mid-1950s until the early 1970s, "Maz" was considered by many the finest defensive second baseman of his era. The holder of numerous personal records for his defensive play at the keystone sack, he'll always be best remembered for the home run which ended the 1960 Series. Nicknamed "No Hands" because of his lightning quick movements when getting rid of the ball, "Maz" also played with the Pirates in the '71 "Fall Classic."

McANANY, Jim

Insurance agency
Culver City, CA

Jim was a flychaser with the White Sox (1958–60) and Cubs (1961–62). The majority of his playing time came in '59 with the pennant-winning White Sox when he hit .276 in 67 games. Overall he hit .253 in 93 games.

McAVOY, Tom

Retired; former chemical salesman with the North American Co.
Stillwater, NY

In 1959 Tom hurled three scoreless innings as a 22-year-old with the Washington Senators. Twice in Tom's career he broke his arm throwing pitches.   0-0

McBRIDE, Ken
        Operates Norris Bros. Co.
        Cleveland, OH

A right-handed chucker, Ken was around from 1959–65.
He lost his only decision for the pennant-winning White
Sox in '59, but then became a rarity when he compiled a
record of better than .500 as a pitcher for an expansion
team, winning 11, 12, and 13 games for the L.A. Angels in
their first three seasons.   40-50

McCALL, John "Windy"
        Realtor and property manager
        Sierra Vista, AZ

Signed by the Red Sox in 1943, John "Windy" McCall
made his debut with the Sox in 1948. He went to the Pirates in '50, then was not around until '54 when he became
a relief specialist with the N.Y. Giants until '57. He was
given the name "Windy" by Ted Williams because of his
constant questions about the bats used by "The Splendid
Splinter."   11-15

McCARDELL, Roger
        Carpenter
        Rising Sun, MD

Roger drifted away after a four-game career with the San
Francisco Giants in 1959.   .000

McCARVER, Tim
        New York Mets announcer

The youngest of all the players ever to play in the 1950s,
Tim was just 18 when he first appeared in a game for the
Cardinals in 1959. However, his first full season was in
1963. In the 1964 World Series he was 11-for-23 in leading
the Cardinals past the Yankees.
    Following the '69 season, he was traded to the Phillies in
a deal in which Curt Flood was also traded but wouldn't re-

port. McCarver did, but later returned to the Cardinals. He then parted in '79 as Steve Carlton's "personal" catcher, as a member of the Phillies.

The Memphis Chicks team in the Southern League plays its home games at Tim McCarver Field.

Tim was reactivated by the Phillies in September of the 1980 season for the purpose of becoming a four-decade player. In one of the games he was ejected which prompted McCarver to say, "I must be the only player to ever be ejected from a game in four different decades."   .271

McCORMICK, Mike F.
      Brokerage company
      Mountain View, CA

This 1956 N.Y. Giant bonus baby finally reached stardom in 1967 with the S.F. Giants. A 22-game winner, including five shutouts, he was selected as the N.L. Cy Young Award winner.

On June 12, 1959, he hurled a rain-shortened five-inning no-hitter against the Phillies. Mike had 15 wins in 1960 and the best ERA in the N.L. at 2.70. On September 13th, he struck out 13 Phillies for his 13th win of the season. Traded away to the Orioles, he developed a sore arm and eventually spent time in the minors. He returned to the Senators in the mid-sixties with mediocre success. McCormick then went to the Giants' organization where he was the surprise star in '67. Mike fell off after that and was back in the A.L. with the Yankees and Kansas City in the early 1970s.   134-128

McCORMICK, Myron "Mike"
      Died April 14, 1976, at age 58 in Los Angeles, CA

A ten-year outfielder, Mike played on three different World Series teams in his career which spanned the years 1940–51. He is not related to the slugging first baseman, Frank (Buck) McCormick, a teammate on the Cincinnati Reds in the early 1940s.

Mike hit an even .300 for the 1940 N.L. champion Reds, and also hit well in the Series, going 9-for-29. After World

War II, he was traded to the Boston Braves in 1946 and was a member of the 1948 N.L. champions, hitting .303. In 1949 he was with his third pennant winner and was a Series participant with Brooklyn. A .275 lifetime hitter, Mike was with the Senators in 1951.

McCOSKY, William "Barney"
   Automobile salesman
   Dearborn, MI

A solid hitting outfielder whose career spanned from 1939–53, Barney finished with a most respectable .312 lifetime average. His peak year was in 1940 when he hit .340. McCosky lost three years in his mid-twenties during World War II, but continued to hit well over the .300 mark for three consecutive years in the late forties when he returned. He spent the 1949 season out of action with displaced vertebrae. In the early 1950s, Barney was a part-time player with the A's, Indians, and Reds.

McCOVEY, Willie "Stretch"
   Vice president
   Ramallah Linen Company
   San Francisco, CA

On June 30, 1959, Willie arrived with the S.F. Giants with a big 4-for-4 day against future Hall of Famer Robin Roberts. Willie extended his career into a fourth decade, retiring in 1980. He ended with a .354 mark in 1959, but then was back in the minors for a period of time the following season. Willie was back to stay for good in 1961.

A dramatic moment in the 1962 World Series came with two out in the bottom of the ninth inning. The Giants had runners on second and third (the potential tying and winning runs). Willie's line drive went directly into the glove of Yankee second baseman Bobby Richardson. A few inches in either direction would have resulted in a 2-1 Giants' victory and a World Championship for San Francisco.

McCovey, who signed a contract in 1955 for $500 and a

bus ticket, says, "Sandy Koufax was the best pitcher I ever faced."

Willie blasted two four-baggers in the 1969 All-Star Game off "Blue Moon" Odom and Denny McLain. McCovey, they said, "is the kind of hitter who can make a pitcher's arm go sore before he begins warming up." Willie retired with a .270 average and 521 home runs. Eighth on the all-time home run list, his home run total ties him with his idol—Ted Williams.

McCRABB, Les
    Location unknown

"Buster" threw from the port side with the Philadelphia Athletics in parts of only five seasons, but also in parts of three decades. He was with the A's from 1939–42, then again in two more games in 1950.   10-15

McCULLOUGH, Clyde
    Scout for San Diego Padres when he died Sept. 19, 1982, at age 65, in San Francisco, CA

Clyde was a 15-year catcher (1940–56), all with the Cubs, except for a four-year period from 1949–52 which he spent with the Pirates. He missed the 1944 and '45 seasons while in the military. The major league rule at the time was that returning war veterans could be on the roster without being charged to the roster limit. This made Clyde eligible for the '45 World Series although he hadn't played in a regular season game. He made one appearance as a pinchhitter in the Series against Detroit.

Clyde coached for the Twins in 1961 and the Mets in 1963. Ralph Kiner called Clyde "the toughest man I ever knew in baseball."   .252

McDANIEL, Lindy
    Bible book store
    Kansas City, MO

Lindy is one of the all-time premier bullpen aces in a career which began as a starter for the Cardinals in 1955.

"Fireman of the Year" in both 1960 and 1963, Lindy led the league in saves both seasons. However, his career high in saves came later with the Yankees in 1970, when he had 29. In '73 for the Yanks, McDaniel hurled a complete game in a rare start, his first complete game since 1960. At one point in 1968 he retired a record 32 consecutive batters.

Lindy, who was salutatorian of his senior class at Arnett High School in Oklahoma, was named by his father after the famed aviator Charles Lindbergh. Before signing a $50,000 bonus with the Cardinals he had attended the University of Oklahoma, but transferred to Abilene Christian for Bible Study. In 1975 Lindy retired at 141-119 with 172 saves.

McDANIEL, Von
Head of business development for a Houston bank
Pinehurst, TX

Although brother Lindy was the salutatorian of his senior class, Von was one notch better, as he was the valedictorian of his class.

A few weeks after signing a $50,000 bonus contract, Von made a sensational debut for the Cardinals by shutting out the Phillies on one-hit in a four-inning relief stint. Three days later (June 12, 1957), the 18-year-old phenom shut out the Dodgers in his first big league start, hurling a nifty two-hitter. A month later, he blanked the Pirates with one hit.

With a 7-5 mark in '57, fans began to compare the McDaniel brothers to the famed Dean duo. After watching both Von and Lindy pitch during the '57 season, the great Dizzy Dean remarked, "Those fellas are going to go a long way, and one day they'll sure enough win 49 games in a season like me and Paul did in '34, the year the Cards won both the pennant and the World Series." Unfortunately, Dizzy's prophecy never came true. Von, who seemed to be on the verge of greatness, developed tightness in his shoulder that caused a hitch in his delivery. Never effective again as a pitcher, he attempted to return to the majors as an infielder, but never did. He ended his career at 7-5, his record in 1957.

McDERMOTT, Maurice "Mickey"
    Employed with Tino-Barzie, a Las Vegas-based sports agent; Oakland A's scout

This colorful, somewhat eccentric southpaw chucker once sang with Eddie Fisher at Grossinger's in the Catskills in upstate New York. He also did some singing in a Boston nightclub following the 1953 season when he had his one big year of 18-10 for the Red Sox. Mickey was traded with Tom Umphlett to the Senators for Jackie Jensen following the '53 season, and announced to Washington fans, "I'm a triple threat. I pitch, hit and sing." He could hit, having compiled the highest batting average in the A.L. that '53 season of any pitcher at .301. Often used as a pinch-hitter, Mickey played a couple of games at first base for the Kansas City A's later in his career. He once struck out 20 men in a nine-inning game for Louisville in the American Association.

McDermott was a well-traveled player, also wearing the uniforms of the Yankees, Tigers, Kansas City A's, and Cardinals.

Pitching for the Red Sox on July 13, 1951, Mickey pitched 17 innings of a 19-inning contest against the White Sox, but was not involved in the decision. In the 19th inning, the Red Sox scored twice, but Chicago came up with three in the bottom frame to win. The day before, the same two teams played a 17-inning contest, making a total of 36 innings for two games—a major league record.

McDermott's lifetime pitching mark stands at an even .500 (69-69). As a hitter he whacked 9 home runs and had a .252 average. He was last in uniform as a coach for the California Angels in 1968. His father was a pitcher with Hartford in 1924 in the Eastern League, and was a teammate of Lou Gehrig.

McDEVITT, Danny
> Works for U.S. Dept. of Commerce, Economic Develop-
> ment Administration
> Conyers, GA

A lefty chucker, Danny spent six seasons in the big show
from 1957–62. Starting in the Dodgers' organization, he
was 10-8 for the '59 N.L. champions for his finest season.

In the early 1960s he was with the Yankees, Twins, and
K.C. A's. He has an overall big league mark of 21-27, with
just under half of those 21 victories coming in 1959.

On September 24, 1957, in the last game the Brooklyn
Dodgers ever played at Ebbets Field, he shut out the Pirates, 2-0, with a five-hitter. When the final out was recorded, organist Gladys Gooding played "Auld Lang Syne,"
signalling the end of a baseball era.

McDONALD, Jim "Hot Rod"
> Long Beach, CA

A right-handed pitcher, "Hot Rod" spent nine years (all in
the A.L.) from 1950–58. After brief stints with the Red Sox
and Browns, he was with the Yankees for three years. He
was the starter and winner for the Bronx Bombers in game
five of the '53 World Series, an 11-7 slugfest over Brooklyn, highlighted by Mickey Mantle's grand-slam home
run.

Jim also was with the Orioles and White Sox, compiling
an overall record of 24-27, plus that one WS victory.

He was called "Hot Rod" because of his partnership with
one-time Indianapolis 500 winner Johnny Parsons in pro-
moting auto races.

McDOUGALD, Gil
> Owns Yankee Maintenance Co.
> Spring Lake, NJ

Gil was a ten-year infielder (1951–60) all with the Yankees. A highly versatile performer, he played in over 500
games each at second base and third base, and another
200-plus at shortstop. Mr. Versatility led A.L. second base-

men in double plays in 1952, paced third basemen in the same category in 1955, and in '57 was the shortstop leader in DP's.

In 1951 Gil was the A.L. Rookie of the Year with a .306 average. Noted for his unorthodox batting stance, he drove in 6 runs in one inning on May 3rd against the Browns, with a triple and a grand-slam home run. This enabled the Yanks to score 11 runs in the ninth inning, the most runs scored in the final frame of a regulation game. Final score: Yankees 17, Browns 3.

Gil also became the first rookie ever to hit a grand slam in a World Series when he smashed a bell-ringer in the '51 autumnal classic against the Giants. Overall he hit seven home runs in a total of eight World Series. During the decade he was named to All-Star teams for the A.L. at the three infield positions.

In the first All-Star Game played without an extra-base hit, McDougald's pinch-single drove in Frank Malzone with the winning run on July 8, 1958. Gil led the A.L. in triples in '57; the same year the line drive off his bat hit Indians' pitcher Herb Score in the eye.

McDougald, who attended City College of San Francisco, retired at age 32 after the 1960 season to devote time to his family and business. For several years he coached the Fordham University baseball team.   .276

McGHEE, Ed
    Sales representative with Malone and Hyde Ford Service.
    Memphis, TN

Ed roamed the garden with the Athletics and White Sox (1950, 1953–55). After 196 games, he departed at .246.

McGLOTHIN, Pat
    Knoxville, TN

Ezra Mac (Pat) McGlothin, a right-handed pitcher, was 1-1 in 8 games with the Brooklyn Dodgers (1949–50). Pat attended the University of Tennessee.   1-1

McILWAIN, Stover
Died January 15, 1966, at age 26 in Buffalo, NY

In 1957 Stover's dream of reaching the majors was realized as a 17-year-old chucker who hurled one scoreless inning for the White Sox. The following season he started one game for the White Sox and allowed one earned run in four innings, his last big league appearance.   0-0

McLELAND, Wayne
Supervisor, Goodyear Corp.
Houston, TX

Wayne pitched in 10 games for the Tigers in 1951 and '52, losing his only decision.

McLISH, Cal
Milwaukee Brewers pitching coach

Calvin Coolidge Julius Caesar Tuskahoma McLish was born in 1925 when Mr. Coolidge was President. "My parents had six kids before me," Cal said, "and my dad didn't get to name any of them until me. When I came along he tried to catch up. But he called me Buster."

Known as "Buster" to his teammates too, Cal was a right-handed hurler who had several trials with the Dodgers, Pirates, and Cubs in the mid-forties and early fifties. In 1956 he finally returned to stay after several seasons in the Pacific Coast League.

He became a 16-game winner in '58 for the Indians, and had his finest season with 19 victories for the Tribe the following year. It was appropriate that he would find success with the "Injuns" because of his Indian heritage.

Cal also pitched for the White Sox, Reds, and Phils in a career that ended with an even 92-92 mark. He was pitching coach for the Phillies and Expos prior to his current position with the Brewers.

McMAHAN, Jack
    Sales manager, Capital Equipment Co.
    Alexander, AR

In 1956 Jack retired winless, dividing time between the Pirates and the K.C. A's.   0-5

McMAHON, Don
    Cleveland Indians pitching coach

A righty relief specialist, Don had a long run which lasted from 1957–74. He was the bullpen ace for the N.L. champion Milwaukee Braves his first two seasons in 1957 and '58. His 15 saves were the most in the N.L. in 1959.

Don was still effective late in his career as a member of the San Francisco Giants, and at age 43 he had a perfect season with a 4-0 record.

He ranks among the all-time leaders in games pitched and in games saved. He made just two starts in his long trek, both of those in 1963 for the Houston Astros.   90-68

McMILLAN, Roy
    Montreal Expos scout

Roy was the premier fielding shortstop in the N.L. during the 1950s as a member of the Reds. He was with Cincinnati from 1951–60, then with the Milwaukee Braves in the early 1960s, before ending in 1966 with the Mets. He played in a N.L. record 584 consecutive games at shortstop, from Sept. of 1951 to August of 1955.

McMillan signed a professional baseball contract although he had never played any organized baseball. His high school had no baseball team, but he was signed after attending a tryout camp in Texas.

He has managed in the minors, coached in the majors for Milwaukee and the Mets, and also managed the Mets since his playing days ended. Roy, who attended Texas A&M, was sometimes called "The Sponge" because he soaked up so many balls at shortstop.   .243

MEDLINGER, Irv
      Died September 3, 1975, at age 48 in Wheeling, IL

A southpaw flipper, Irv had no decisions in 9 games with
the St. Louis Browns in 1949 and 1951.

MEEKS, Sammy
      Maintenance employee
      Shoney's Restaurant
      Memphis, TN

Sam had a rather meek career as a utility infielder with
the Senators in 1948 and with the Reds from 1949–51.
                                                    .251

MEJIAS, Roman
      Los Angeles, CA

This Cuban-born outfielder spent nine years from 1955 to
'64 with the Pirates, Astros, and Red Sox. He was a part-
time player with Pittsburgh in the late 1950s. He had his
best season in 1962 with the expansion Astros, with a .286
average and 24 homers. He broke away in 1963 and '64 in
the A.L. with Boston. Roman once had a 55-game hitting
streak in Class B in 1954.   .254

MELE, Sabbath Anthony "Sam"
      Boston Red Sox scout

S.A.M. was a ten-year outfielder, 1947–1956. He hit
.302 as a rookie for the Red Sox in 1947. Later traded to
Washington, he led the A.L. in two-base hits in 1951
with 36.
   On June 10, 1952, he had a record 6 RBIs in one inning
as a member of the White Sox. He had a three-run homer
and a bases-loaded triple in the inning. His well-traveled
career also saw him wear the uniforms of the Orioles,
Reds, and Indians.

The Minnesota Twins manager from 1961–67, Sam led them to their only A.L. pennant, in 1965.

Mele was a star basketball player at New York University in the early 1940s before turning to professional baseball. During his playing career he was an off-season sports writer and had a column in the Quincy, Mass. *Ledger* called "The Mele Ticket."   .267

MELTON, Dave
Probation officer for San Francisco adult probation department

A graduate of Stanford University, Dave played in a dozen games in the big time as an outfielder for the K.C. A's in 1956 and '58. He created interest by hitting the first pitch thrown to him as a professional for a home run for the S.F. Seals in 1950.   .111

MERRIMAN, Lloyd
Insurance business
Fresno, Calif.

A World War II and Korean War veteran, Lloyd was an All-American fullback at Stanford in 1946. He was drafted by the Chicago Bears of the NFL, but chose pro baseball instead.

Merriman was an outfielder with the Reds from 1949–51, and again in '54. The following year he completed his playing days with the White Sox and Cubs.

Lloyd, who flew over 80 jet missions in Korea, closed out with a .242 average.

MERRITT, Lloyd
Manager at Gastonia (South Atlantic League) in St. Louis Cardinals organization

In 1957 Lloyd had his fill, going 1-2 for the Cardinals.

MERSON, Jack
      Correction supervisor for the state of Maryland
      House of Correction
      Elk Ridge, MD

An infielder with the Pirates (1951–52) and playing one
game with the Red Sox in '53, Jack experienced a brief
taste of the biggies. In 125 games he batted .257.

METKOVICH, George "Catfish"
      Vice-president of a freight company
      Fountain Valley, CA

This ten-year performer was an outfielder and first baseman from 1943–54. He was a regular in the Red Sox outfield in the mid-1940s, and during the 1944 season had a
28-game hitting streak. He was with the Indians and
White Sox in the late 1940s before going over to the N.L.
where, in 1951, he hit for a career-high .293 for Pittsburgh.
He also played for Milwaukee and the Chicago Cubs.
      Playing first base for the Red Sox in '45, George suffered
through an embarrassing inning, committing three errors.
                                                              .261

MEYER, Jack
      Died March 9, 1967, at age 34 in Philadelphia, PA

Jack spent his entire seven year (1955–61) hitch with the
Phillies. As a rookie in 1955 he went 6-11, but led the N.L.
in saves with 16.
      Pitching in relief for the Phils on Sept. 22, 1958, in a
game against the Pirates, the right-hander fanned the
first six batters he faced, establishing a then-major league
record for relief pitchers.   24-34

MEYER, Russ "Mad Monk"
      Pitching instructor in Yankees organization

Russ spent thirteen seasons between 1946–59 pitching for
the Cubs, Phillies, Dodgers, Reds, Red Sox, and A's with a

lifetime 94-73 record. Originally with the Cubs, he had his
finest years with the Phillies and Dodgers. He returned to
the Cubs in '56 after having beaten them 18 straight times
since leaving them after the '48 campaign. He won a
career-high 17 games for the '49 Phils.

In an amazing pitching staff streak, the Phillies recorded four consecutive shutouts in 1951, with Meyer rack-
ing up the fourth. As a member of the Phils, he once
teamed up with Jim Konstanty to pitch a one-hitter
against the Dodgers. However, the one hit, a two-run triple
in the third inning, was good enough to give the Dodgers a
2-0 victory.

Joining Brooklyn in 1953, he was 15-5. In '55 he was 6-2
for the World Champion Dodgers, and hurled six scoreless
innings in relief in the Series.

Looking back on his career, Russ says, "My biggest
memory was when I pitched a one-hitter against the
Braves. Sibby Sisti got a hit to start the game, then I retired the next 27 batters in a row."

Known for his hot temper, Russ once threw the resin bag
in the air after being removed from a game. To his embarrassment, the bag landed on his head. In reference to his
nickname he stated, "There was a great football player at
Army named Monk Meyer. I was a halfway decent football
player in high school so they called me 'Monk.' It just
stuck with me during baseball."

MICELOTTA, Mickey
   Employed with the Hudson Carpet Co.
   Bronx, NY

In 1954 Mickey began a limited 17-game crusade as a
shortstop with the Phillies (1954–55).   .000

MICHAELS, Cass
   (born Casimir Eugene Kwietniewski)
   Employed by Department of Public Works, Grosse
   Pointe, MI, until his death on Nov. 12, 1982, at age 56

A 12-year infielder, who first appeared at third base for the
White Sox in 1943 at the age of 17, Cass also played short-

stop. By the late 1940s he was a full-time player for the White Sox and had his finest season in 1949 when he hit .308, playing in all 154 games.

In the early 1950s he was with the Senators, St. Louis Browns, and Philadelphia Athletics. He returned to Chicago in '54 where his career came to a premature end as he suffered some loss of vision due to a beaning. In just under 1,300 games by age 28, he hit .262.

MICKELSON, Ed
Counselor and coach at Parkway Central High School, Creve Coeur, MO

A first baseman with the Cardinals in 1950, Ed played with the Browns in '53 and the Cubs in '57. With all that jumping around, he played just 18 games and batted .081.

MICKENS, Glenn
Assistant baseball coach at U.C.L.A.

Glenn lost his only decision in four games with the Brooklyn Dodgers in 1953. Pitching for Fort Worth in a game against Shreveport on April 21, 1954, he was charged with a home run after he left the mound. After throwing two "balls" to Harry Heslet, Carroll Beringer relieved Mickens and promptly served up a home run to Heslet. The scorer charged the four-bagger to Mickens under the old erroneous interpretation of rule 10.14(g), which was clarified a few years ago.   0-1

MIERKOWICZ, Ed
Heavy equipment mechanic
Grosse Ile, MI

Ed was a flychaser with the Tigers in portions of three seasons in the late '40s. He qualifies here as a one game pinch-hitter with the Cardinals in 1950.   .175

MIGGINS, Larry
Chief probation officer, U.S. District Court, Southern
District of Texas
Houston, TX

Larry played in a total of 43 games with the Cardinals in
1948 and '52. Handcuffed with a .227 average, Larry was
gone after '52.

MIKSIS, Eddie
Freight company sales manager
Huntingdon Valley, PA

This fourteen year warrior played every infield position
and the outfield from 1944, when he broke in with Brooklyn at just 17 years of age, until 1958.
Eddie was traded to the Cubs during the 1951 season
and was a full-time player for them the next few years. His
last two seasons (in 1957 and '58) were spent with the Cardinals, Orioles, and Reds.
During his Brooklyn days he was called the "Fixit
Man." Miksis, who attended Kent State University, batted .236.

MILES, Don
Houston, TX

Don played in eight games with the L.A. Dodgers as an
outfielder in 1958.   .182

MILLER, Bill
Meat business
Hatboro, PA

What can you say about a guy who pitches a one-hitter and
loses? Not much when the opposing pitcher hurls a no-
hitter! That was the case in 1952 when Bill allowed the Tigers just one hit while pitching for the Yankees. However,
his mound opponent that day, Virgil Trucks, didn't allow
any.

A southpaw thrower with the Yankees (1952–54) and
Orioles ('55), Bill was 6-9 overall.

*Talk about confusion, bewilderment, or whatever—how
would you like to be a kid growing up in the fifties with
three Bob Millers? (Bob G., Bob J., and Bob L.)*

MILLER, Bob G.
Vice-president, marketing and sales, Barton Brands
Limited
Chicago, IL

The only left-handed pitcher of the three Bob Millers, this
Miller was a $60,000 bonus player for Detroit in 1953
when he broke in with the Tigers as a 17-year-old, making
him the youngest player to appear in the majors that season. He was with the Tigers until 1956, then returned to
the majors a half dozen years later with the N.Y. Mets. For
a short time in '62, both he and Bob L. Miller were members of the pitching staff for the expansion Mets. He was
6-8 overall.

MILLER, Bob J.
Insurance agent; University of Detroit baseball coach

Blessed with a good slider, Bob spent ten years in the
biggies from 1949–58, all with the Phillies. He was 42-42
overall, with his best season coming in his first full year in
1950 when he was 11-6 for the "Whiz Kids."

MILLER, Bob L.
Front office aide, San Francisco Giants

Bob L. had the longest and most successful career of the
three Bob Millers who pitched in the biggies. Bob was
mostly a reliever in a long career which started with the
Cardinals in the late 1950s. He suffered through a 1-12
year in 1962 with the fledgling Mets. Bob L. had his greatest success in the mid-1960s working out of the Dodgers'
bullpen. He was in both the '65 and '66 World Series with

the Dodgers, and the 1971 "Fall Classic" as a member of the Pittsburgh Pirates (just two of the ten teams he played for in his career—equalling the then major league record held by Dick Littlefield). Since that time, Tommy Davis and Ken Brett have equalled the travels of both Miller and Littlefield, playing with ten teams.

When he played for the Mets, Lou Niss, the traveling secretary, assigned Bob L. Miller and Bob G. Miller as roommates on road trips. "That way, if somebody calls for Bob Miller, he's bound to get the right one," said Niss.

69-81

MILLER, Eddie
Lake Worth, FL

A fourteen-year performer (1936–50), Eddie was the regular shortstop for the Reds, Boston Braves, and Phillies during the 1940s. Offensively he had his best year in 1947 with Cincinnati when he led the league in doubles with 38, and hit a career high of 19 homers. The year 1950 brought his last hurrah, playing for the Cardinals. As a batter, he once caught a Rip Sewell "eephus" pitch and fired the ball back to the mound.   .238

MILLER, Rod
Salesman, Shultz Steel Co.
South Gate, CA

"Wagon Train" made its TV debut in '57 when Rod Miller took a train from Brooklyn after striking out as a 17-year-old pinch-hitter for the Dodgers in his only game in the biggies.   .000

MILLER, Stu
Liquor store owner
San Carlos, CA

A right-handed chucker from 1952–68, Stu broke in by pitching a shutout for the Cardinals in his first start in '52.

He later became one of the top relief hurlers in the game as master of the tantalizing off-speed pitch. Miller is best remembered for being blown off the mound by a gust of wind at Candlestick Park in San Francisco in the 1961 All-Star Game (in which he was the winning pitcher). He was the N.L. "Fireman of the Year" that season, an award he would later win in the A.L. for the Baltimore Orioles (the only pitcher to win the trophy in both leagues). His honored season in 1963 was the year he had career highs in both appearances (71) and saves (27).

With an overall record of 105-103 and an excellent 3.24 ERA, he ranks among the all-time leaders with 154 saves.

MILLIKEN, Bob

> St. Louis Cardinals pitching instructor in the minor leagues

Bob broke in with the Dodgers in 1953. A right-handed chucker, Bob spent just two years in the majors, but both were winning ones.   13-6

MILNE, Pete

> Owns the Pete Milne Insurance Agency
> Mobile, AL

Pete made his way into the biggies as an outfielder with the N.Y. Giants in 1948. From 1948–50 Pete played in 47 games with a .233 average.

MINARCIN, Rudy

> Partner in a butcher shop
> North Vandergrift, PA

Between 1955–57 Rudy pitched in 70 games with the Reds and Red Sox. He finished at 6-9.

MINNER, Paul
> Chief of Field Investigation for the Pennsylvania Insurance Dept.
> Harrisburg, PA

Paul spent ten years in the N.L. from 1946–56. He was originally with Brooklyn and was 3-1 for the 1949 N.L. pennant winners, pitching one scoreless inning in relief in the World Series. Traded to the Cubs, he became a regular member of their starting rotation in the early 1950s. Paul won a career-high 14 in 1952.   69-84

MINNICK, Don
> Rocky Mount, VA

In 1955, Don won his first 16 decisions en route to a 20-4 season with Reading (Eastern League). He lost his only decision in two games for the 1957 Washington Senators.

MINOSO, Saturnino Orestes Arrieta Armas "Minnie"
> Chicago White Sox front office

Minnie was already close to 30 years old when he arrived with Cleveland in 1949. Early in his first full season in 1951, Minnie was traded to the White Sox where he had many outstanding years. Selected by the *Sporting News* as "Rookie-of-the-Year" in '51, he hit for a career-high .326 and led the league in both stolen bases and three-base hits. The colorful Cuban outfielder led the A.L. in both categories another two times in his career. Traded back to Cleveland in 1958, Minnie hit over the .300 mark in both 1958 and '59 for the Indians. However, he missed out on being part of the '59 White Sox pennant winners. Traded back to Chicago for the 1960 season, he had a pair of homers and six RBIs in his debut back as a member of the Hose. He was close to 40 years old then, but still hit .311. Minoso was with the Cardinals and Senators, before returning to the White Sox in 1964, his farewell season. He had a lifetime .298 average with 1,963 hits. Hit number 1,963 came as a designated hitter in 1976 when he was activated at the age of 53 for the purpose of becoming a four-decade player. But in 1980 he was reactivated, going 0-for-2 against the Angels, making him a five-decade player. One of the pitchers he faced was Frank Tanana, who, remarkably, pitched against Minnie in 1976 when he joined the four-decade club.

Minnie was known for crowding the plate and getting plunked frequently. He once said in his Latin tongue, "All the times I get hit, those pitchers don't mean it. Is accident every time. Anyway I'd rather die than quit playing."

MIRANDA, Willie

Owns unisex hair styling establishment in Baltimore, MD

This Cuban-born shortstop spent 9 years in the A.L. mainly because of his skillful defensive play. The epitome of the "good field—no hit" player, Willie was especially proficient at making the play deep in the hole and throwing out the runner from the outfield grass.

Miranda wore Number 7, was the 7th of eight children, had a size 7 hat, and a size 7 shoe. He broke into the majors in 7 games with the Senators in '51. The following year he was in 7 games with the Browns and 70 more with the White Sox, for a total of 77 games. What's in a number?

Willie also played with the Yankees and Orioles and had a career average of .221. In 1980 he made a dangerous rescue mission to Cuba to bring several relatives into the U.S.

MITCHELL, Dale

Retired after serving as manager with an Oklahoma oil drilling equipment company

Dale was an 11-year major league outfielder, primarily with the Cleveland Indians from 1946–56. Near the end of the '56 season he was sold to the Brooklyn Dodgers and wound up his career that fall as a pinch-hitter in the World Series. An extremely difficult batter to strike out (just 119 times in over 4,000 plate appearances), Mitchell is, unfortunately, best remembered as the answer to the popular trivia question: "Who was the final out of Don Larsen's perfect game in the 1956 World Series?" He did take the called third strike in that instance, but the southpaw swinger was generally a good contact hitter who hit over .300 six times during his career, including a career-high .336 in 1948 to help the Indians to a pennant. In 1949 Dale led the league with 203 hits, including a league-high of 23 triples—most in that department since 1912 and a figure which hasn't been equalled since. He wound up with a .312 average for 1,127 big league games.

MIZE, Johnny "The Big Cat"
    Retired
    Demorest, GA

"Big Jawn" finally attained entry into the Hall of Fame in 1981, although his statistics were certainly worthy of an earlier enshrinement. He is the holder of numerous records including the all-time homer mark for a left-handed N.L. hitter—he parked 51 in 1947. Mize was a rarity among long ball hitters in that he was very difficult to strike out. He fanned just 42 times in that '47 season. John also holds the record of six times hitting three homers in a game during a career which began with the St. Louis Cardinals in 1936. "The Big Cat" was the N.L. batting champion in 1939 with a .349 average.

His last five seasons were spent as a part-time first baseman and pinch-hitter with the A.L. pennant winning and world champion Yankee teams of 1949 to 1953. Although he played in just 90 games in 1950, he had 25 homers and 72 RBIs on just 76 base hits. During the 1952 World Series, Mize homered in games three, four, and five. In his final season (1953) he was the pinch-hitter deluxe in the A.L., going 19-for-61.

In the early '50s, John was an agent for a clothing manufacturer and was often seen in gaudy Hawaiian shirts at a time when men's fashions might be considered somewhat bland. The first cousin of Mrs. Babe Ruth, John collected 2,011 career hits and 359 home runs to go with his lifetime .312 batting average.

As late as 1961, he was a hitting coach for the K.C. A's.

MIZELL, Wilmer "Vinegar Bend"
   Assistant Secretary of Agriculture for Government
   and Public Affairs

Wilmer was the star player in the annual baseball game
played between the Republican and Democratic congress-
men in Washington, D.C. during the late 1960s after being
elected to Congress from North Carolina. Never quite a
star, Mizell started with the Cardinals before being traded
to Pittsburgh. His 13-5 record helped the Pirates to the
1960 N.L. pennant. He also played briefly with the Mets.
   His nickname comes from his small home town of the
same name in Mississippi.   90-88

MOELLER, Ron
   Sales manager for STP Corp.
   Cincinnati, OH

In 1956 Ron entered at age 17 with the Orioles, who had
signed him out of high school. In the early sixties he was
with the expansion Angels and Senators. Overall he was
6-9 in 52 games, with one of his 6 wins a shutout against
the Orioles, his original team.

MOFORD, Herb
   Farmer
   Dover, KS

Herb entered the big time as a right-handed hurler with
the '55 Cardinals. Before it all ended at 5-13, he made
stops with the Tigers, Red Sox, and Mets in 1962.

MOISAN, Bill
   Nuclear material manager for the Portsmouth Naval
   Shipyard
   Portsmouth, NH

Bill pitched in three games for the Cubs in 1953. He left
the way he came in at 0-0.

MONAHAN, Ed
> Senior vice-president of Equitable Life Insurance
> New York City

"Rinty" Monahan hurled four games for the Philadelphia
Athletics in 1953 with no decisions.

MONBOUQUETTE, Bill
> New York Mets scout

Bill was with us from 1958–68 and was a key member of
the Red Sox pitching staff in the early 1960s. A 14-game
winner in 1960, he was the starter for the A.L. in the first
All-Star Game that summer. In 1961 he won 14, and on
May 12th struck out 17. The 17 Ks was just one short of the
league record at the time. Bill won 15 in '62, including a
no-hitter over the White Sox on August 1st. He was a
20-game winner in 1963, and although he led the league in
losses with a 10-18 log in '65, his ERA was actually lower
than it had been in his 20-win season.
  "Monbo" was with the Tigers, Yankees, and Giants in
his final years, finishing 114-112 lifetime.
  His .984 fielding average ranks among the all-time leaders for pitchers.

MONROE, Zack
> Sales manager for hydraulic manufacturing company
> Bartonville, IL

Zack spent only two seasons (1958–59) in the big arena,
but played an important role in helping the Yankees to the
World Championship in 1958.
  Appearing in 21 games for the Yanks in his rookie season, Zack posted a 4-2 record with a 3.26 ERA, being uti-
lized as a starter and reliever by manager Casey Stengel.
After playing three games for the Yanks in '59 he was sent
back to the minors and never returned.   4-2

MONTEMAYOR, Felipe
Sports reporter
Monterey, Mexico

In 1953 Felipe began a short career with the Pirates. He also played briefly in the outfield with the Bucs in '55, closing out with a .173 average.

MONZANT, Ramon
Edo Zulia, Venezuela

"The Lineup" was aired on TV between 1954–60 when Ramon appeared on big league lineup cards. The Venezuelan right-hander with an excellent curve ball pitched for the N.Y. and S.F. Giants, and finished at 16-21.

For New York Giants' baseball buffs, Ramon appeared on an important lineup card as the starting pitcher in the Giants' Polo Grounds farewell game on September 29, 1957, against the Pirates. Although the starter that sad day, Monzant was not charged with the 9-1 loss.

MOON, Wally
Consultant to the San Antonio team in the Texas League

St. Louis Cardinals' fans were chanting "We want Slaughter" when Wallace Wade Moon came to the plate for the first time in 1954. Popular Enos Slaughter had been sold to the Yankees to make room for Moon, a rookie outfielder, who had been named after football coach Wallace Wade. Wally then homered in his first major league at-bat to silence the crowd. He went on to hit .304, and was named N.L. "Rookie-of-the-Year." Traded to the Dodgers in the late 1950s, he made good use of the short left field fence at the L.A. Coliseum despite being a left-handed hitter. He had 19 homers or "Moon shots" as they were called. Wally also led the league in triples with 11 as L.A. won their first N.L. flag on the west coast. He also homered in the sixth and final game of the World Series win over the White Sox. Triviots will tell you that he became the first Dodger to hit .300 in Los Angeles when he hit .302 in 1959. In 1965 he completed his 12-year voyage with a .289 average.

MOORE, Ray
  Tobacco farmer
  Upper Marlboro, MD

Ray spent twelve seasons under the big top from 1952–63. Originally with Brooklyn for trials in 1952 and '53, the right-hander had his most success with the Orioles from 1955–57 when he averaged 11 wins per season.

In June of 1957, Orioles pitchers Hal Brown, Billy Loes, and Connie Johnson had three consecutive shutouts. Moore then hurled a fourth straight for the Baltimore staff. He was with the A.L. champion White Sox in 1959. In 1960 Ray won a game in relief by throwing just one pitch.   63-59

MORAN, Billy
  General agent
  East Point, GA

A seven-year A.L. second baseman from 1958–65, Billy was with the Indians in 1958–59. Gone from the big time for a couple of years, he joined the expansion Los Angeles Angels in 1961, and in '62 helped them to a surprising first division finish when he hit 17 of his career total 28 homers, and hit for a .282 average, playing in 160 games. He was the first member of the Angels to collect a hit in an All-Star Game when he singled in the first of two All-Star contests played in 1962.   .263

MOREHEAD, Seth
  Vice-president, Commercial National Bank
  Shreveport, LA

Seth launched his career (1957–61) with the Phillies. A 5-19 mark, he also spent time with the Cubs and Milwaukee Braves before his permanent trip into orbit.

MOREJON, Dan
  Labor work
  Miami, FL

An outfielder, Dan hit .192 in a dozen games for the 1958 Cincinnati Reds.

MORENO, Julio
> Employed with the Rejal Wood Co.
> Miami, FL

Julio came to the Washington Senators in 1950. The Cuban right-hander was 18-22 in 73 games from 1950–53.

MORGAN, Bobby
> Manager of Whistler's Restaurant
> Oklahoma City, OK

An eight-year infielder in the N.L., Bobby was a part-time player as a third baseman for Brooklyn in the early fifties. In both 1950 and '52 he played in 67 games, had 45 base hits, and 7 home runs. He appeared in both the 1952 and '53 World Series for the Dodgers. Bobby was a full-time shortstop for the Phillies in '54 when he had a career high 14 homers and a .262 average. He also played for the Cardinals and Cubs.   .233

MORGAN, Joe
> Boston Red Sox special assignment scout

Not to be confused with the Joe Morgan who starred in the 1970s, this Joe Morgan was an infielder from 1959–64 with five different teams in parts of four seasons, compiling a .193 batting average in 88 games. He played with the Braves, A's, Phils, Indians, and Cardinals. An All-American hockey player at Boston College, he turned down offers from NHL teams to play pro baseball.

Joe coached for the Pirates in 1972. In 1981, his Pawtucket team won the longest game in organized baseball history, a 33-inning marathon against Rochester.

MORGAN, Tom "Plowboy"
> Retired as California Angels pitching coach following
> 1983 season

Tom spent thirteen seasons in the A.L. from 1951–63. Originally with the Yankees as a starter, the right-hander became primarily a relief hurler. His most victories were 11 in '54 for the Yanks. That season he had the dubious distinction of hitting three Red Sox batters in one inning. He was also with Kansas City, Detroit, Washington, and the expansion L.A. Angels. "Plowboy" has since been a pitching coach for San Diego and California. He returned to a Yankee uniform in that capacity in 1979.

Tom once lived on Baseball Avenue in El Monte, California. His father owned property and laid out the street where homes were built. There was already a Morgan Street, so he named it Baseball Ave. since his sons, Tom and Dick (who made it to AA) played pro baseball.   67-47

MORGAN, Vern
Died November 8, 1975, at age 47 in Minneapolis, MN

"Davey Crockett," with Fess Parker and Buddy Ebsen, came on TV in 1954 when Vern began his 31-game adventure as a third baseman for the Cubs. He was a coach for the Minnesota Twins from 1969 until his death in 1975.
.225

MORTON, Guy, Jr.
Baptist minister
Wooster, OH

Guy Morton, Sr. pitched for the Indians from 1914–24. His son, Guy Morton, Jr., made a pinch-hitting appearance in his only big league game with the Red Sox in 1954. Morton, who played football and basketball at the University of Alabama, went hitless in his only at-bat.

MORYN, Walt "Moose"
Liquor and bar business
Cicero, IL

Eight years in the N.L. as an outfielder, Walt had his best season as a full-time player with the Cubs in 1957 when he hit .289. The following year he hit 26 homers. He played briefly with Brooklyn prior to joining the Cubs. Moryn fin-

ished with the Cardinals and Pirates in 1961. He walloped
101 home runs.   .266

MOSES, Wally
Philadelphia Phillies hitting instructor

Wally started out in 1935 as a .325 hitter and in '37 collected 208 hits, including 25 homers. After seven consecutive campaigns of hitting over .300, he was traded to the
White Sox in 1942. Moses later played for the 1946 A.L.
pennant-winning Red Sox, and was 5-for-12 in the World
Series. In the late 1940s and early '50s he was back with
the Athletics to wind up his playing days with a .291 career average. He then coached for several teams throughout most of the 1960s.

MOSS, Les
Houston Astros pitching coach

This thirteen-year catcher lasted from 1946–58. He was
originally with the St. Louis Browns until traded to the
Red Sox during the 1951 season. Les was with the Browns
long enough into the '51 campaign to be the catcher for
Bobo Holloman's somewhat legendary no-hitter. He returned to St. Louis in 1952 and stayed with them through
their franchise shift to Baltimore. He then finished with
the White Sox. His shot at managing in the majors was cut
short when he was let go early in the 1979 season by the
Detroit Tigers in favor of Sparky Anderson. Moss had a
winning record at the time he was fired.

A brother, Perry Moss, played for the Green Bay Pack-
ers in the NFL.   .247

MOSSI, Don
Masonite installer
Ukiah, CA

Don began as an outstanding relief pitcher for the 1954 Indians, where he teamed with Ray Narleski to form the best
one-two relief staff in the A.L. He won 6 of 7 decisions in 40

appearances for the A.L. pennant winners while compiling an excellent 1.94 ERA. Mossi held the Giants scoreless in four innings of work as he appeared out of the bullpen in three of the four World Series games. He continued to be a successful bullpen ace for Cleveland until traded to Detroit, where he was placed in the Tigers' starting rotation. He was a 17-game winner in that '59 season. Don wrapped up his 12-year stay in the mid-sixties after pitching for the White Sox and Kansas City. His .990 career fielding average was the best ever in big league history at the time of his retirement.   101-80

MOSSOR, Earl
   Union sheet-metal worker
   Bethel, OH

Earl didn't have a long time in the sun—only three games as a pitcher with the Dodgers in 1951.   0-0

MROZINSKI, Ron
   Phillipsburg, NJ

Ron broke in with the Phils in 1954. His brief trip ended in '55. Overall he was 1-3.

MUELLER, Don
   The Insurance Service Office
   St. Louis, MO

"Mandrake the Magician," as Don was known because of his amazing bat control and timely hits, walloped three homers against Brooklyn on September 1, 1951. The next day he added two more four-baggers off the Dodgers, for 5 in two games. Don had been informed that he had become a father for the first time just prior to hitting No. 5. "The fifth home run was just after we got a call in the dugout that my wife had a baby boy. I hit the next pitch for a home run," recalled Don. He had 16 roundtrippers that year, but just 65 in his 12-year career.

This sudden display of power came during the Giants'

miracle pennant run at the Dodgers. In the ninth-inning rally in the third and final playoff game (culminated by Bobby Thomson's home run), he had singled, but cracked his ankle sliding into third base and was removed from the game on a stretcher. He had to settle for hearing the dramatic blow on the radio in the clubhouse. Don had to sit out the World Series but made the most of his opportunity in the '54 Classic when he set a Series mark of 7 singles in a four-game Series. That season was his finest as he hit .342 but lost out to teammate Willie Mays in a close race for the N.L. batting title.

Mueller closed in 1958 and '59 with the White Sox. One of the most difficult ever to strike out, Don fanned just 146 times in 4,364 at-bats.

His father, Walter, was an outfielder for the Pirates in the mid-1920s. A son, Mark, played in the Cardinals' minor league organization during the 1970s, and his uncle, Clarence "Heinie" Mueller, also played in the N.L. as an outfielder during the 1920s. On July 1, 1954, he hit for the cycle against Pittsburgh, with each of his four hits coming off a different Pirates pitcher.   .296

MUELLER, Joseph G. "Gordy"
    Commercial real estate
    Towson, MD

Gordy pitched in eight games without a decision for the Red Sox in 1950.

MUELLER, Ray
    Philadelphia Phillies scout

A fourteen-year catcher, Ray began as a part-time receiver for the Boston Braves in the mid-thirties. After a brief stint with the Pirates, he was with the Reds in the midforties and was anything but a part-time player during the war years. In 1944 he was tagged the "iron man" as he caught 155 games, one over the then 154-game schedule. Mueller was with the Giants in '49, then worked his way back to his original teams, the Pirates and Boston Braves, in the early 1950s. He was a coach with the Yankees in 1956, and the Cubs in 1957.   .252

MUFFETT, Billy
Detroit Tigers minor league pitching instructor

Billy was around from 1957 to 1962 primarily as a relief pitcher. He was with the Cardinals and Giants in the late 1950s, and from 1960 to '62. He was both a starter and reliever for the Red Sox. He was the Cardinals' pitching coach from 1967–70 and held the same position for the Angels in the mid-seventies.   16-23

MUIR, Joe
Died June 25, 1980, at age 57 in Baltimore, MD

"I Love Lucy" made its debut in 1951 and became one of the all-time TV favorites among viewers. Joe also came along at the same time but wasn't one of the all-time favorites among Pirates' fans as he was out of the majors in 1952. The southpaw was 2-5.

Prior to his death he was a sergeant with the Maryland State Police.

MULLIN, Pat
Montreal Expos minor league batting coach

Pat was a ten-year outfielder (1940–53) all with the Detroit Tigers. Missing four years in World War II military service, Pat had a .345 average in 54 games in 1941, but never approached that figure again after returning from the war. His finest season was in 1948 when he hit .288 with 23 homers.

He was the last Detroit player to wear No. 6 before Al Kaline wore it. A lifetime .271 hitter, Pat was a coach for the Tigers from 1963–67.

MUNCRIEF, Bob
   Automobile salesman
   Dallas, TX

Bob came up in the late 1930s with the St. Louis Browns. From 1941–47 he was a regular in the Browns' rotation. Four of those years he won the same number of games (13), which was his career high.

In the 1948 Series he hurled two scoreless innings in relief for the Indians. He was 5-4 as a spot starter and reliever that year. Bob was with the Cubs and Pirates in 1949, then completed his tour with a couple of appearances with the Yankees in 1951.   80-82

MUNGER, George "Red"
   Inspector for health department
   Houston, TX

"Red" spent most of his ten years with the Cardinals, starting in 1943. In '44 he had an excellent 1.34 ERA. However, he never made it into a World Series game either year. Ironically, in 1946 he was just 2-2 in only 10 games for the Cardinals, but was given the start in the fourth game of the WS, and was a 12-3 complete game winner. That contest saw him supported by the all-time Series record of 20 hits, with Joe Garagiola contributing four. His finest season was in '47 at 16-5 with six shutouts. He remained with St. Louis until traded to Pittsburgh in 1952. Munger was then out of the majors until returning for the 1956 season with the Pirates.   77-56

MURFF, John "Red"
   Montreal Expos scout

This Texas-born chucker didn't begin his professional baseball career until he was 28. A half-dozen years later he was a 34-year-old, 27-game winner in the Texas League. "Red" was purchased by the Milwaukee Braves and was a 35-year-old rookie in 1956. He had no decisions that season. In '57 Murff was 2-2 for the N.L. pennant winners and said "Sayonara" to his short big league career.

MURPHY, Dick
    Cincinnati, OH

Dick signed out of Ohio State University. Playing in six games as a pinch-hitter and pinch-runner for his home town Reds in '54, Murphy finished at .000.

MURRAY, Joe
    Roofer
    San Clemente, CA

Joe went 0-3 in eight games for the Athletics in 1950.

MURRAY, Ray "Deacon"
    County sheriff
    Fort Worth, TX

Ray was a six-year catcher who was already past age 30 when he joined the Indians in 1948. Traded to the Athletics after just one game for Cleveland in '51, he had his best season in '53, hitting .284. Murray made his exit in 1954 with the Orioles. He was a player-manager in the Texas League for the remainder of the decade.   .252

MURTAUGH, Danny
    Died December 2, 1976, at age 59 in Chester, PA

Best remembered as the former manager of the Pittsburgh Pirates from the late 1950s until the early '70s, Danny's playing career was not as successful as his managing career, but he did hit over the .290 mark as the Pirates' second baseman in 1948 and 1950. In 1941 he made his debut with the Phillies when he was recalled from the minors in mid-season. Despite playing just half a year, he still led the N.L. in stolen bases with 18.   .254

MUSIAL, Stan
   Cardinals vice-president; restaurant business
   St. Louis, MO

"The Man"—Hall of Fame—1969.

With 475 career home runs, Stan ranks among the all-time leaders, but oddly enough never led the league in that category during his 22-year career. He came close in 1948 with a career high 39, but Mize and Kiner tied for the lead at 40. Of over 20 great years 1948 was his dream season. Musial led the N.L. with career highs in average (.376), runs scored (135), RBIs (131), base hits (230), slugging percentage (.702), and total bases (429). He still found time to pound out league leading totals in doubles (46) and triples (18).

A minor league pitcher at the start of his professional career, he once pitched in a game for the Cardinals in 1952. "Stash" holds the record for most home runs in All-Star competition with six. One of his All-Star four-baggers was a twelfth-inning shot that ended the 1955 July classic at Milwaukee. All totaled, Stan played in 24 of the mid-summer extravaganzas.

A three time MVP in the N.L. (1943, '46, '48), he won his seventh batting title at the age of 37 in 1957 with a glossy .351 average.

Musial, who departed with a .331 lifetime average, once said, "Hitting is like riding a bicycle. Once you have it, you never forget how to do it, even if you have spells when the hits don't drop safely." Of his 3,630 career base hits, 1,815 came at home, 1,815 on the road.

MYERS, Richie
   Supervisor-city employee
   Sacramento, CA

How do you follow an act like Stan Musial? You don't!

Richie played in four games with the Cubs in '56 as a pinch-hitter and pinch-runner.   .000

N

NAGY, Steve
    Buyer for department store
    Seattle, WA

The namesake of a popular bowler of the same era, this Steve Nagy was a southpaw chucker who tried throwing strikes for the Pirates in 1947 and Senators in '50.   3-8

NARAGON, Hal
    Owns Hal Naragon's Barberton Sporting Goods
    Barberton, OH

A ten-year catcher who was a backup receiver for the 1954 pennant-winning Indians, Hal had his finest season, hitting .323, the following year. Traded to Washington in '59, he went with the franchise to Minnesota and again hit over .300 in 1961. Naragon wore the uniform of two more World Series teams as coach with the Twins ('65) and Tigers (1968).   .266

NARANJO, Cholly
    Havana, Cuba

Cholly went 1-2 for the Pirates' mound corps in 1956.
    As a member of the Senators, he was assigned to sit in the Presidential box to guard President Eisenhower from being hit by a foul ball in the 1954 season opener.   1-2

NARLESKI, Ray
    Truck body mechanic
    Laurel Springs, NJ

A right-handed pitcher, whose career closely paralleled Don Mossi's, Ray teamed with Mossi to give Cleveland strong relief in the Indians' 1954 championship season, when he saved 13 games in his rookie year. However, the following year he was even more effective with league leading totals of 60 appearances and 19 saves, while compiling a 9-1 mark. Like Mossi, he became a starter after beginning his career as a reliever. Ray was an 11- and 13-game winner for the Indians, then was traded along with Mossi to Detroit.

His father, Bill, was an infielder for the Red Sox in 1929 and '30.   43-33

NATON, Pete
    Salesman, Trico Co.
    Buffalo, NY

After six games with the Pirates in 1953, catcher Pete Naton departed with a .167 average.

NEAL, Charlie
    Securities business
    Dallas, TX

An infielder from 1956 to 1963, Charlie originally was groomed to replace the aging Pee Wee Reese at shortstop for Brooklyn. However, he moved over to second base and had one outstanding season in 1959, when the L.A. Dodgers jumped from a seventh place finish in 1958 to the N.L. pennant. He hit .287 with a league-leading 11 triples. Neal also sparkled in the World Series, helping lead the Dodgers past the White Sox in six games. His two homers in game two sparked the win that evened the Series. He finished with a .370 average at 10-for-27. Defensively he set records for double plays and assists.

That was the zenith for Charlie. He was later placed in the expansion draft and played for the New York Mets in 1962 and '63. Neal split his last season between the Mets and Reds.   .259

NECCIAI, Ron
Sporting goods store
Monongahela, PA

Ron never made much noise as a major leaguer, but may have pitched the most earth-shattering of all professional baseball games while at Bristol, Tennessee in the Class D Appalachian League in 1952. He was a 19-year-old Pirates' prospect when he struck out 27 batters in a nine-inning no-hitter. One opposing batter did ground out, but a dropped third strike by catcher Harry Dunlop (later a major league coach), allowed for the extra batter. Ron followed that sensational effort with 24, 20, and 19 strikeout games. He was called all the way up to the struggling Pirates that season, but was just 1 and 6 in 12 games for the extent of his big league stay.

NEEMAN, Cal
Salesman for school supply publisher
Cahokia, IL

A seven-year catcher (1957–63), Cal was the Cubs' regular receiver in his rookie year of 1957. He also played for the Phillies, Pirates, Indians, and Senators.

Neeman attended Illinois Wesleyan University. .224

NEGRAY, Ron
Manufacturer's representative for athletic equipment
Akron, OH

This Kent State graduate was a right-handed chucker with the Brooklyn Dodgers in four games in 1952, and four games with the L.A. Dodgers in '58. In between, he pitched with the Phillies in '55 and '56.

Numerologists would certainly pay attention to Ron's career since he played with the Dodgers 6 years apart, was 6-6 with the Phillies, and pitched in a career total of 66 games, with a final record of 6-6.

NELSON, Bob
>   East Texas Motor Freight
>   Dallas, TX

In 1955 Bob joined the Orioles as an 18-year-old bonus
player. Hailed as "The Babe Ruth of Texas," Bob became
the "Babe Ruse" of the majors, hitting .205 in 79 games
with no home runs.

NELSON, Rocky
>   Painting contractor
>   Portsmouth, OH

A perennial minor league slugging star, Rocky still managed to play in parts of nine seasons as a first baseman. A
three-time MVP in the International League during the
1950s, he never reached star status in the biggies. He was
with the Pirates, Cardinals, Dodgers, Indians, and White
Sox for trials from 1949 until 1959, when he again joined
Pittsburgh. Alternating with Dick Stuart as the Pirates'
first baseman, he hit an even .300 in their 1960 N.L. championship season. He was 3-for-9 in the World Series, and
had a two-run homer in the dramatic seventh game, won
by Pittsburgh, 10-9.
   Once, when he tried to steal home and was thrown out
by a wide margin, he was asked why he had tried, and
responded, "Now you know why they call me Rocky."
.249

NEVEL, Ernie
>   Retired; former instructor at the Sho-Me baseball
>   camp
>   Branson, MO

A right-handed chucker, Ernie lost his only decision in 14
total games split between the Yankees (1950–51) and
Cincinnati ('53).

NEWCOMBE, Don
> L.A. Dodgers' director of community relations; lectures on alcoholism

The only pitcher to ever win Rookie of the Year, Cy Young, and MVP honors in a major league career, Don was a 17-game winner in 1949, his rookie season. He lost the opening contest of the '49 World Series in a great pitching duel, 1-0. That was the start of what would be frustrating attempts in "Fall Classics" for Don. "Newk" also lost another game to the Yankees in that Series. A 19- and 20-game winner in 1950 and '51, Don was kept out of post-season play as Brooklyn lost out in N.L. races to the Phillies and Giants in dramatic fashion. He hit his peak in the mid-fifties when he was 20-5 in '55 for a league-leading .800 winning percentage. Although the Dodgers finally beat the Yankees, he wasn't used again after losing the opening game of the Series.

For Cy Young and MVP honors, 1956 was his season, going 27-7. Yet in October he once again struggled against the Yankees, losing the seventh game. He tailed off after that great season and was eventually dealt to Cincinnati early in the Dodgers' first season in L.A. (in 1958).

Newcombe had a ten-year record of 140-90 for a fine .623 winning percentage, but was 0-4 in World Series action. One of the best-hitting pitchers during his day, Don ended with a .271 lifetime average and 15 home runs. Nearly half of his homers came in 1955 when he hit a N.L. record 7, tied twice by Don Drysdale.

Newcombe was the last pitcher to steal home when he did it on May 26, 1955, against the Pirates (with Elroy Face on the mound).

One of the great hitting pitchers of all time, Don also hit the "ol' demon rum" pretty hard. Quoted from *The Diamond Report,* he says, "I was a wild one in my day. Some people are sophisticated drinkers. Some just sit and soak up the stuff. Others get belligerent. Me? I was just a damn drunkard. It shortened my career. It bankrupted me in business. Worst of all, it almost broke up my home. My marriage at one time hung by a very slender thread. I am lucky my whole life wasn't ruined." The 6'4" 240-pound ex-right-hander persuaded the Dodgers to set up an Alcoholic Rehabilitation program. Commissioner Bowie Kuhn named Newcombe a consultant to work with Leslie C. Gray, a staff member of the National Institute on Alcohol Abuse and Alcoholism in Washington, D.C. Both Gray and Newcombe tour big league training camps as barnstorming evangelists preaching the evils of alcohol.

NEWHOUSER, Hal
Bank vice-president
Bloomfield Hills, MI

Hal was to the 1940s what Sandy Koufax was to the mid-sixties: baseball's premier pitcher. Whereas Koufax was voted into the Hall of Fame immediately, "Prince Hal," as he was known, has never been given strong support for election. Newhouser had the misfortune of having his outstanding years during World War II when many of the game's top players were away in military service. Like Koufax, he started slowly. He began as an 18-year-old in 1939, and for the next several years was well under .500 at 34-52 until 1944 when he had his first of three magnificent seasons. In '44 he was 29-9, leading the league in victories and strikeouts. In '45 he won four fewer at 25-9, but was even more impressive with league leading figures in most pitching departments. He then won 2 of 3 decisions in the World Series, including the seventh and decisive game over the Cubs.

In 1946, with everyone back from the war, Hal still sparkled at 26-9 and had the league's best ERA at 1.94. His 21 wins in 1948 were again the most in the A.L. Sold to Cleveland after the '53 campaign, he had one last fine year as a member of the Indians' great 1954 pitching staff when he was 7-2 to help them to the A.L. flag.

"Prince Hal" is the only pitcher in major league history to win back-to-back MVP awards as he did in 1944 and '45.
207-150

NEWSOM, Louis Norman
Died December 7, 1961, at age 55 in Orlando, FL

"Bobo" was one of the most colorful and eccentric men ever to wear a major league uniform. The legendary stories about him could constitute a book of their own. He once arrived at a spring training camp in a car which had "Bobo" in neon lights on the door with a horn playing "Tiger Rag."

There's nothing boring about his statistics either. "Bobo" spent 20 years in the big time as an exclusive member of a four-decade group of players as he started with Brooklyn in 1929. He is the only player who played during the 1950s, who also pitched in the majors during the 1920s.

In all, he was with nine different teams, including five stints with the Washington Senators. His peak years came from 1938–40 when he won at least 20 all three years. In 1938 Newsom was a 20-game winner despite an inflated ERA of over 5.00—the only time a pitcher has won 20 with that high an ERA. In a 1934 game for the Browns, he hurled nine innings of hitless ball, only to lose in the tenth inning. Three times he was a 20-game loser. It all ended in 1953 with the Philadelphia Athletics when he was 46 years old. His overall mark of 211-222 makes him and Jack Powell (247-253) the only career 200-game winners with more losses than victories.

He won 2 out of 3 decisions for Detroit in the 1940 World Series against Cincinnati. "Bobo" pitched brilliantly with complete-game victories of 7-2 and 8-0. The loss was in the seventh and decisive game by a 2-1 score. He lost a start for the Yankees against the Dodgers in the 1947 Series.

Since he called everyone "Bobo," the moniker was pinned on him.

NIARHOS, "Gus"
    Retired in Harrisonburg, VA

A nine-year catcher, Gus was originally with the Yankees in the late 1940s. He went to the White Sox, Red Sox, and Phillies in a tour that ended with a .252 lifetime average. Gus was a coach for the Kansas City A's from 1962–64. He attended Auburn University before entering pro ball.

NICHOLAS, Don
  Garden Grove, CA

Don had a brief glimpse of the big time in 1952 with the
White Sox. Overall he pinch-hit and ran in ten games for
the Sox in 1952 and '54, but departed hitless.

NICHOLS, Chester Raymond "Chet," Jr.
  Assistant vice-president, Rhode Island Hospital Trust
  National Bank
  Lincoln, RI

This southpaw chucker spent parts of nine years in the
biggies from 1951–64. Chet had his greatest success as a
cool 20-year-old rookie in 1951 for the Boston Braves, as he
was 11-8 with the best ERA in the N.L. at 2.88. He was
with the Braves in Milwaukee in the mid '50s, then after a
three-year absence, returned to Boston with the Red Sox in
1960 for a few more years, before finishing with the Reds
in 1964.
  His father, Chet Sr., was a right-handed pitcher for the
Pirates, Giants, and Phillies in the late 1920s and early
'30s. He also resides in Lincoln, R.I., and is 83 years old.
Chet is a graduate of the Williams College of Banking.
                                                    34-36

NICHOLS, Dolan
  Memphis, TN

The Kingston Trio was singing about a guy named "Tom
Dooley" when a guy named Dolan Nichols went 0-4 for the
Cubs in 1958.

NICHOLSON, Bill "Swish"
  Tobacco farmer
  Chestertown, MD

Although he struck out a league-leading 83 times in 1947,
the real "Swish" Nicholson should have been Dave, who

came along later and K'd a record 175 times in 1963. The two are not related.

Originally with the Philadelphia Athletics, briefly, in 1936, he had his best years from 1939-48 with the Cubs. He was most productive during the 1943-44 talent-depleted war era when he led the N.L. in both home runs and RBIs both years. In '44 his totals were career highs of 33 homers and 122 RBIs. He also had four homers in four straight plate appearances on July 22-23. Bill missed MVP honors by a single vote to Cardinals' shortstop Marty Marion in '44. He tailed off in the Cubs' pennant-winning season in 1945, but still drove home 88 runs and added 8 more in the World Series (although the Cubs lost to Detroit).

"Swish" spent his final five seasons with the Phillies from 1949 to 1953 as a part-time outfielder/pinch-hitter. Bill came down with diabetes on Labor Day in 1950, causing him to miss the remainder of the season. He had 235 career home runs and a .268 lifetime batting average.

NIELSON, Milt
Chevrolet-Oldsmobile dealership
St. Peter, MN

Milt harnessed his saddle with the Indians in 1949. He played again briefly in '51 before he rode out into the sunset with a .067 average.

NIEMAN, Bob
New York Yankees scout

This well-traveled, solid-hitting outfielder, who played from 1951-62, hit home runs in his first two major league at-bats when he was called up to the St. Louis Browns in September 1951. The feat has never been duplicated. He traveled to several A.L. teams, only to return to the Browns (who were now the Orioles) in 1956. Bob hit over the .320 mark twice in the late 1950s for the Orioles before moving over to the Cardinals in 1960.

Nieman's final season in '62 was with the pennant-

winning Giants as he hit an even .300 as a part-time outfielder and pinch-hitter. His final appearance was a
pinch-hitting role in the '62 Series.

Bob later played in Japan, managed in the minors, and
scouted in the Dodgers' and Indians' organizations before
joining the Yankees' scouting staff.   .295

NIXON, Russ
Montreal Expos coach

A twelve-year catcher, Russ began as a member of his
home-town Cleveland Indians in 1957. Nixon hit over .300
in '58 as the team's regular receiver. From 1960 to 1965 he
was with the Red Sox, then after a couple of seasons in
Minnesota, was back in Boston in '68, his final year.

Strange but true, Russ never stole a base in his 906-
game career. More admirable is his record three sacrifice
flies in a game in 1965. Another unusual aspect of his career came on May 4, 1962, when he connected for two hits
and scored two runs in the same inning.

Following his playing career, Nixon was a minor league
manager for six years and a coach with the Cincinnati
Reds for 5½ before being promoted to manager. He was released as Reds' manager following the 1983 season.   .268

NIXON, Willard
Director of transportation
Floyd County public schools
Rome, Ga.

A right-handed hurler whose career lasted from 1950 to
1958 (all with the Boston Red Sox), Willard was in the
limelight in 1955 and '57 when he won a dozen games each
year. In 1954 Willard beat the Yankees four straight
times, allowing just five runs in four games.   69-72

NOBLE, Ray
Brooklyn, NY

Ray came up with the 1951 Giants as the backup catcher
for Wes Westrum. He hit 5 homers, playing in 55 games.

After spending two more years with the Giants, Ray was among the missing. Cuban-born, his name is pronounced "No-blay."   .218

NOREN, Irv
Breeds thoroughbred horses; owns a trophy store
West Covina, CA

This eleven-year outfielder broke in with the Washington Senators in 1950. Irv was traded to the Yankees during the 1952 season, and was a member of both the '52 and '53 Series champions. But like Andy Carey and Bob Grim, he had his most outstanding year in 1954 when the Yankees failed to capture the A.L. pennant, as he hit .319. Irv fell off after that and was traded to Kansas City. Noren then went to the Cardinals, Cubs, and Dodgers where it all ended in 1960. With the Cardinals, he collected 8 hits in his first 16 at-bats.

He was a coach for the World Champion Oakland A's in 1972 and '73, but was ousted in mid-season by manager Alvin Dark in 1974. He then coached for the Cubs in the mid-1970s. Irv had the rather dubious distinction of hitting into five double plays in the '55 WS.   .275

NORTHEY, Ron
Died April 16, 1971, at age 50 in Pittsburgh, Pa.

A stocky left-handed hitting outfielder known as the "Round Man," Ron participated a dozen years, starting with the Phillies in 1942. He had 22 homers and 104 RBIs in '44, his most productive season. Northey, who was with several N.L. teams in the late 1940s and early '50s, gained a reputation as a dangerous pinch-hitter. He established a major league career record with three pinch-hit grand slams (since equalled by Rich Reese and Willie McCovey). In 1956, near the end of his playing days, he had a league-leading 15 pinch-hits for the White Sox.

Ron signed as a free agent with the Phillies on July 10, 1957. To show his appreciation he tied a then big league record that night when he belted his ninth career home run as a pinch-hitter to help the Phils beat the Reds, 8-5.

His son, Scott Northey, was an outfielder for the Kansas City Royals in 1969.

Northey coached for the Pirates from 1961–63.   .276

NUNN, Howie
   Westfield, NC

The Crests had a big hit with "16 Candles" in 1959 when Howie entered with the Cardinals. A right-hander, Nunn was employed with the Reds as a relief pitcher in '61 and '62. When Howie blew out the candles he was 4-3 in 46 games.

NUXHALL, Joe
   Cincinnati Reds announcer and batting practice
   pitcher

Always remembered as the youngest ever to appear in a big league game when he pitched two-thirds of an inning for Cincinnati on June 10, 1944, Joe was just 15 years, 10 months, and 11 days old. It was another eight years before he returned in 1952.

Joe gained respectability at this point, and had his best year in 1955 when he won 17 games, including a league-leading 5 shutouts.

Cast off by the Reds after the 1960 season, and missing out on the team's 1961 N.L. pennant, he looked to be at the end of the line at age 32 after stints with Kansas City and the expansion L.A. Angels. However, after a trip back to the minors, he again returned to the Reds in 1963. This time he was a seasoned veteran—in his mid-thirties—and was a 15-game winner. Joe pitched three more years, finishing up in 1966—22 years after his debut as a teenager—with a lifetime 135-117 mark. An incredible aspect about his career is that, after pitching in the majors at age 15, he was later reinstated to amateur status and played football, basketball, and baseball during his senior year in high school, two years after pitching in the big time. In 1959, Joe had a four-strikeout inning hurling for the Reds.

O

Six sets of twins have dotted our national pastime. The O'Brien twins were well known in the fifties.

O'BRIEN, Eddie
　　Energy consultant for the Alaskan shipping industry
　　Bellevue, WA

O'BRIEN, John
　　Head of security at the Kingdome in Seattle, WA

Although just 5'9", John was an All-American basketball choice in the early 1950s. Ed was also a fine player on the same Seattle University team. Both were signed by the Pirates as bonus players. Both also stepped from the college campus to the majors in the summer of 1953. Both played in 89 games that summer; John as a second baseman, Eddie at shortstop.

They each missed the '54 season because of military service, but returned together in mid-summer in '55, and each had two hits in their first game back. As it became apparent that another former college basketball All-American, Dick Groat, and young Bill Mazeroski were the Pirates' shortstop-second baseman of the future, both O'Briens turned to pitching.

From high school in New Jersey to college in the Pacific Northwest, to the major leagues, the twins' athletic careers had been as teammates until 1958 when Ed's playing days ended with a .236 average, and a 1-0 mark as a pitcher.

John was dealt to St. Louis early in '58, and had his final season in 1959 with the Milwaukee Braves. He closed with a .250 batting average and a 1-3 mark on the mound.

Both played for Seattle in the Pacific Coast League before ending their careers. Eddie coached for the Seattle Pi-

lots in 1969. John was a county councilman in Seattle
before joining another former big leaguer, Ted Bowsfield,
on the management staff of the Kingdome. Ed has been
both baseball coach and athletic director at Seattle University.

O'BRIEN, Tommy
Died Nov. 5, 1978, at age 59 in Anniston, AL

An outfielder with the Pirates (1943–45), Red Sox, and
Senators ('49 and '50), Tommy had a .277 batting average
after 293 contests.

O'CONNELL, Danny
Died October 2, 1969 in an auto accident at age 42 in
Clifton, NJ

A ten-year infielder from 1950–62, Danny hit .292 as a
rookie for Pittsburgh in 1950. After two years of military
service, he swatted a career high .294 in 1953. Danny then
danced over to Milwaukee and the Giants before playing
in the Pacific Coast League. O'Connell returned with
Washington in the early 1960s, finishing with a career
.260 average. He was a coach for the Senators in 1963 and
'64.

O'DELL, Billy "Digger"
Farmer
Newberry, SC

A southpaw flipper, Billy was the Baltimore Orioles' first
bonus player ever, when he was selected in 1954 out of
Clemson University. He never played in the minors and as
a major leaguer was a pitcher for 13 seasons.

He suffered from hay fever early in his career and was
allergic to natural grass. This was before astroturf was in
vogue. O'Dell took injections to counteract the allergy.

Traded to the S.F. Giants after the 1959 season, he had
his finest year as a 19-game winner for the 1962 N.L.
champions. Billy lost the opening game of the Series to the
Yankees, but was credited with a save in game four.

"Digger" became a successful relief pitcher for the Milwaukee Braves in 1965, with 10 wins and 18 saves in 61 appearances out of the bullpen. With a lifetime record of 105-100, he was nicknamed "Digger" after a radio character.

O'DONNELL, George
Employed with the office of the Illinois secretary of state
Winchester, IL

In 1954 George was 3-9 with the Pirates, his only season in the sun.

OERTEL, Chuck
Automobile salesman
Clarkston, MI

Chuck flew around the outfield with the Orioles in 1958. This "Bird" disappeared after 14 games in which he collected two hits (one being a home run).   .167

OKRIE, Len
Fayetteville, NC

Len was a catcher with the Senators in 1948, '50, and '51. The following year he had one game with the Red Sox.
   Okrie was a coach for the Red Sox in the early 1960s and for the Tigers in 1970, exactly 50 years after his father Frank Okrie pitched for them.   .218

OLDHAM, John
Instructor, San Jose City College
San Jose, CA

This left-handed chucker out of San Jose State never pitched in the majors, but was used as a pinch-hitter in his one and only big league game with the Reds in 1956.   .000

OLDIS, Bob
    Montreal Expos scout

Bob was a catcher for parts of seven seasons, beginning
with the Washington Senators in the mid-fifties. He was
with the Pirates and Phillies in the early sixties. From
1964 to 1969 Bob coached for the Phillies, Twins, and
Expos. He has scouted for the Expos for the past decade.
                                                    .237

OLIVER, Gene
    Owns clothing store
    Rock Island, IL

A catcher-first baseman-outfielder for 11 seasons (1959–69),
Gene was with the Cardinals, Braves (in Milwaukee and
Atlanta), Phillies, and late in his career was with the Red
Sox and Cubs. He hit 93 homers, including a big one on the
final day of the 1962 season off Johnny Podres of the Dodgers. The blast gave St. Louis a 1-0 victory, and forced a
playoff between L.A. and the S.F. Giants for the N.L. pennant. During his playing days, Gene had the reputation as
a rather mischievous character. One of his pranks was
"playfully" burning his teammates with cigarettes. A big
man himself, the clothing store he operates is one which
specializes in clothes for big and tall men. Gene played
football at Northwestern.   .246

OLMO, Luis
    Santurce, PR

This Puerto Rican-born outfielder was with the Brooklyn
Dodgers from 1943 to 1945, then again in the pennant-
winning season of 1949. In '45 he hit .313, and led the N.L.
in triples with 13. In the '49 World Series he was 3-for-11,
including a home run off Yankee ace reliever Joe Page. He
ended his travels with the Boston Braves in 1951. In 1958
he operated an off-track betting facility in San Juan,
Puerto Rico.   .281

OLSEN, Karl
    General building contractor in Gardnerville, NV

Karl's career took him to such A.L. cities as Boston, Washington, and Detroit from 1951–57.   .235

ORAVETZ, Ernie
    Postal service employee
    Tampa, FL

The comic strip "Peanuts," by Charles Schulz, first appeared in the early fifties shortly before this 5'4", 140-pound "peanut" made his debut in the outfield with the Senators. Gone after the '56 campaign, he hit for a .263 average in two big league seasons.

ORTIZ, Roberto
    Died September 15, 1971, at age 56 in Miami, FL

Roberto played in the Senators' outfield in the early forties and again in '49. He closed with the Philadelphia Athletics in 1950. Señor Ortiz batted .255. A brother, Oliverio (Baby) Ortiz, pitched briefly for the Senators in 1944.

OSBORNE, Larry "Bobo"
    Southeast Major League Scouting Bureau
    Atlanta, GA

"Bobo" was a first baseman for the Tigers from 1957 to 1962. He was a regular for the Senators in his final campaign in 1963. His father, Ernest "Tiny" Osborne, was a pitcher for the Cubs and Dodgers in the mid-twenties.   .206

OSTEEN, Claude
    Philadelphia Phillies pitching coach and owner of a
    chicken farm near Annville, PA

A southpaw chucker, Claude was one of the premier pitchers for the Dodgers during the 1960s and well into the '70s.

He first appeared as an 18-year-old for the Cincinnati Reds in 1957. A key member of the Dodgers' staff (although not as well publicized as Koufax and Drysdale), he came to L.A. from the Washington Senators in a trade for home-run slugger Frank Howard.

Osteen shut out the Twins in game three of the '65 autumnal classic, and later lost a game in that Series. In '66 he allowed just three hits, but was a 1-0 loser to the Orioles in the WS. He was a 20-game winner in both the 1969 and 1972 seasons.   196-195

OSTER, Bill
     Centerport, NY

Bill pitched in eight games as a 21-year-old member of the 1954 Athletics. A product of New York University, Bill lost his only decision.   0-1

OSTROWSKI, Joe "Professor"
     Retired school teacher
     West Wyoming, PA

A southpaw chucker, Joe was with the St. Louis Browns in 1948 and '49, and then had the good fortune of being dealt to the Yankees midway through the 1950 season. He was aboard ship for three A.L. pennants and World Series championships through 1952.   23-25

OSTROWSKI, John
     Retired
     Chicago, IL

Ostrowski was a third baseman and outfielder, who spent parts of seven seasons with the Cubs from 1943–46 and in the A.L. with the Red Sox, White Sox, and Senators from 1948 till he was nosed out in 1950.   .234

O'ROURKE, Jim
> Investment business
> Walla Walla, WA

Jim twice made pinch-hitting appearances for the 1959 Cardinals, but made outs both times.

O'TOOLE, Jim
> Real estate salesman
> Cincinnati, OH

Jim spent 10 seasons—all with the Reds except his final one with the White Sox in 1967. Never a 20-game winner, the southpaw twice won 17, and once won 16. His best season was in 1961 with the N.L. champion Reds when he was a 19-game winner.

O'Toole, who received a $50,000 bonus from the Reds out of the University of Wisconsin, had his career cut short at age 30 due to a sore arm. His lifetime mark reads: 98-84.

OVERMIRE, Frank "Stubby"
> Died March 3, 1977, at age 57 in Lakeland, FL

"Stubby" was a lefty chucker for 10 years from 1943–1952. From 1943 to '49 he was with Detroit, twice winning a career high of 11 games.

"Stubby" was with the Browns from 1950–52 except for a period down the stretch in 1951 when he was with the Yankees' A.L. pennant winners. He coached for the Tigers from 1963–66.   58-67

OWEN, Arnold Malcolm "Mickey"
> Retired; former Green County sheriff
> Springfield, MO

A 13-year performer, Mickey had a reputation as a fine defensive catcher, especially in 1941 with Brooklyn when he went 100 consecutive games, handling nearly 500 chances without an error (an N.L. record). Unfortunately, he became best known for dropping the third strike and losing the ball in the World Series in game four. The Dodgers were one run up on the Yankees with two out in the ninth inning when Mickey had difficulty handling a Hugh Casey "spitball." Tommy Henrich reached first on the passed ball. DiMaggio, Keller, and Gordon followed with hits. The Yanks won the game, and the next day, the Series.

Owen came up with the Cards in 1937. He left the Dodgers in '46 for the Mexican League. Mickey returned to the Cubs in 1949 and played for them until 1951. In '54 he was with the Red Sox as a backup receiver. He coached for them in 1955 and '56. Owen later scouted for Baltimore, and ran a baseball camp before his election as sheriff in Springfield, Missouri, where he chased criminals instead of passed balls.　　　　　　　　　　　　　　　.255

OWENS, Jim
　　Bartender in Houston, TX

A right-handed pitcher for 13 years (1955–67), Jim had his winningest season in 1959 with the Phillies at 12-12.

Owens was with the Reds in 1963, then departed as a member of the Astros from 1964 to '67. Jim was the Houston pitching coach from 1967–72.

As a member of the '61 Phillies, he saw some action in the outfield. His pitching mark stands at 42-68. His batting mark blushes at .101.

P

PAFKO, Andy
　　Retired
　　Mount Prospect, IL

A 17-year flychaser (1943–59), Andy had the distinction of playing in four World Series with three different teams (Cubs, Dodgers, and Braves). Pafko played in two of the more memorable games of the 1950s. He was in left field and watched Bobby Thomson's dramatic home run sail over his head to give the Giants the pennant in 1951. In 1959 he was in the Braves' lineup the night Harvey Haddix pitched 12 innings of perfect baseball for the Pirates.

Primarily an outfielder, Andy spent the entire 1948 season as the Cubs' third baseman when he hit a career-high .312. His tops in home runs came in 1950 with 36, including three in one game on August 2nd. Traded to Brooklyn during the '51 campaign, he played in his second World Series for his second team the following year. Andy was with the Milwaukee Braves from 1953 until the end of his playing days in 1959 and participated in the 1957 and '58 Series for them.

While a member of the Dodgers, broadcaster Red Barber gave him the name "Handy Andy" because of his fancy sliding catches. Pafko had a career average of .285, with 213 home runs. He coached for the Braves from 1960–62 and later managed in the minors along with scouting for the Montreal Expos.

PAGAN, Jose
  Manager at Ogden in Pacific Coast League

This Puerto Rican-born jack-of-all-trades began with the S.F. Giants in 1959. Mainly a shortstop, he also played the other infield positions, the outfield, and even caught in one game. Jose was a key member of the '62 Giants N.L. pennant winners, leading all N.L. shortstops in fielding. Pagan hit only .259 during the season but was hot in the WS against the Yankees, hitting .368, including a home run.

Traded to the Pirates in 1965, he was a versatile performer for the Bucs through 1972. Usually a sure-handed fielder, Jose tied the major league record with three errors in an inning playing third base in a 1966 game. However, in 1971 he delivered the key blow in the seventh game of the WS, doubling home Willie Stargell with the game and Series winning run in the eighth inning, breaking up a 1-1 tie.   .250

PAGE, Joe "Fireman"
    Died April 21, 1980, at age 63
    Latrobe, PA

Joe was an early day relief pitching ace even before Jim
Konstanty set the pattern for the importance of the job in
1950. As a member of the Yankees in 1947 and '49, he was
outstanding with 14 wins and 17 saves in '47, and 13 wins
and 27 saves in '49.

His work was a key factor in the Yankees' A.L. pennants
and World Series triumphs over the Dodgers. In '47 he relieved in four of the contests. He was charged with the loss
in game six, but in the seventh game he hurled five innings of one-hit relief to gain the win. Page had a win and
a save in the '49 WS as the Yanks won the "Fall Classic"
in five games. His last year with the Yankees was in 1950.
One last comeback attempt was unsuccessful for the Pirates in 1954. He owned and ran a hotel-bar in Ligonier,
Pa., for many years following his baseball retirement.
                                                      57-49

PAGLIARONI, Jim
    Beer distributorship
    Grass Valley, CA

Jim was a catcher who spent most of his career during the
decade of the 1960s with the Red Sox, Pirates, A's, and, in
1969, with the Seattle Pilots. However, in 1955 Pagliaroni
caught in one game for the Red Sox after signing with
them at the age of 17.   .252

PAIGE, Leroy "Satchel"
    Died on June 8, 1982, at age 75 in Kansas City, MO

Sporting News editor Taylor Spink wrote a most critical
editorial on Bill Veeck for signing Paige in 1948, calling it
a travesty since Paige was well past his 40th birthday at
the time, and possibly closer to 50. He had spent the previous quarter of a century as a top pitcher in the Negro
Leagues.

On August 13th of that year, before over 50,000 at

Comiskey Park, he threw a five-hit shutout over the White Sox. A week later, before some 78,000 fans in Cleveland, the 42-year-old rookie shut out the White Sox. He finished up 6-1 for the pennant-winning Indians, and Mr. Spink later wrote another editorial apologizing for his first one.

Satchel's final appearance in the majors was a three-inning scoreless outing for the Kansas City A's in 1965 when he was listed at 59 years of age (and was possibly even older).

In 1966 the Methuselah of baseball appeared in one game for the Peninsula club of the Carolina League at age 60. Paige pitched in the 1953 All-Star Game at age 47, making him the oldest player ever to perform in the July Classic.

His autobiography, *Maybe I'll Pitch Forever*, was made into a TV movie with actor Lou Gossett, Jr., portraying the Hall of Fame pitcher. In 1959 Paige acted in a Western with Robert Mitchum called *The Wonderful Country*.

28-31

PAINE, Phil "Flip"
Died February 19, 1978, at age 47 in Lebanon, PA

A right-handed flipper, "Flip" spent parts of six years in the big time, appearing in 95 total games. In that time he compiled the enviable career record of 10-1. He was 2-0 for the Boston Braves in 1951, 1-0 for the Braves in Milwaukee in '54, and then 2-0 in '55. In 1958 he was with the Cardinals, winning 5 of his 6 decisions. All 95 appearances were as a relief pitcher.

PALICA, Erv
(born Ervin Martin Pavliecivich)
Longshoreman until his death on May 29, 1982, at age 54 in Huntington Beach, CA

Erv spent 9 years in the biggies from 1947 to '51, and again in 1953 and '54 with Brooklyn. He flew out in 1955–56 with the Orioles. The right-hander threw two innings of scoreless relief in the 1949 World Series. His fin-

est year was in 1950 for the Dodgers when he was 13-8.
                                                       41-55

PALYS, Stan
    Purchasing agent for the Northeastern Education In-
    termediate Unit
    Scranton, PA

Born in Moscow—Moscow, Pa., Stan broke in with the
Phillies in 1953. Two years later Palys was traded to the
Reds along with Smoky Burgess and Steve Ridzik for Jim
Greengrass, Glenn Gorbous, and Andy Seminick.
    Overall Stan batted .237 from 1953–56 as an outfielder.

PAPAI, Al
    Postman
    Springfield, IL

Al was with the Cardinals and Browns in the late forties
and with the Red Sox in 1950. The right-hander then
pitched briefly with the White Sox in 1955.   9-14

PAPISH, Frank
    Deputy sheriff of Pueblo, CO, when he died August 30,
    1965, at age 47

A southpaw chucker, Papish was with the White Sox and
Indians in the late 1940s, and closed with the Pirates in
1950. He finished 26-29, with 12 of those wins coming with
the '47 White Sox.

PAPPAS, Milt
    Sales representative
    Wimod Co.
    Northlake, IL

Milt came up with the Baltimore Orioles as a teenager in
1957. He came agonizingly close to two milestones, but
missed in each instance. Only Cy Young, Jim Bunnings,
Ferguson Jenkins, and Gaylord Perry have won over 100

games in each league. Milt won 110 in the A.L., but only 99 in the N.L. His 209 career victories make him one of only two pitchers in big league history to win 200 or more games without achieving a 20-victory season. Jack Quinn won 212 games and never had a 20-win campaign.

Milt's other "just miss" came in September of 1972 when he no-hit the San Diego Padres. He had a perfect game until two were out in the ninth inning when pinch-hitter Larry Stahl worked him for a walk.

Traded by the Orioles to the Reds for Frank Robinson following the 1965 season, Milt won a high of 17 games for the Chicago Cubs in 1971 and '72. The right-hander also won 16 three times and 15 twice. Pappas also pitched for the Braves during his 17-year career. He finished with a record of 209-164 and a 3.40 ERA.

PARNELL, Mel
Operates Parnell and Tullier Pest Control Service
New Orleans, LA

The "Green Monster" has made Fenway Park a difficult place for left-handed pitchers. But Mel Parnell was an exception. In 1949 he was particularly effective, going 25-7 with an ERA of 2.77 in 295 innings, all league-leading figures. In '53 he won 21, including four shutouts over the powerful Yankees. In his tenth and final season (all spent with the Red Sox), he threw a ho-hitter at Fenway over the White Sox on July 14, 1956.

A 123-75 career mark, Parnell managed in the Boston farm system, and was an announcer for Red Sox games following his pitching days.

During the 1955 season Mel once slept through a game. Thinking the Red Sox were playing a night game, Parnell snoozed in his room while his teammates were playing a day contest.

PASCUAL, Camilo
Oakland A's scout

This Cuban-born right-hander was just 28-66 in his first five seasons with the Washington Senators from 1954–58.

He then put it all together in 1959 and ultimately finished above the .500 mark at 174-170. Three times he was the A.L. leader in strikeouts, complete games, and shutouts. He was a 20-game winner in both the 1962 and '63 seasons.

Camilo lost his only decision in the 1965 World Series for the Twins. The late 1960s saw him back in Washington, this time for the expansion Senators. Not afraid to swing the bat, Pascual had two career grand slams.

PASCUAL, Carlos
    Baltimore Orioles scout

The older brother of Camilo, Carlos pitched in two games with the Senators in 1950. His two games were both complete ones, winning one and losing one, with a fine 2.12 ERA.

PATTON, Tom
    Pepperidge Farm Bakery
    Downingtown, PA

Tom caught in one game for the Orioles in 1957.   .000

PAULA, Carlos
    Miami, FL

Noted for his great throwing arm, Carlos was another of the numerous Cuban-born players who spent time with the Washington Senators during the 1950s. He was the first black to play for the Senators. Carlos had his best season in '55 as a regular in the Washington outfield when he hit .299. From 1954–56 he swatted .271 in 157 games.

PAVLETICH, Don
    Loan officer, Universal Mortgage Corp.
    Milwaukee, WI

Don played mostly in the sixties, but played in one game for the Reds in each of the 1957 and '59 seasons. He en-

joyed a 12-year trip as a backup catcher-first baseman with
the Reds (1962–68), White Sox ('69), and Red Sox (1970–71).
In '65 he batted .319 with the Reds, and finished .254 lifetime.

PAWLOSKI, Stan
    Sales engineer with Penn Ventilator Co.
    Philadelphia, PA

The Indians showcased Stan in two games at second base
in 1955.   .125

PEARCE, Jim
    Heat treater at the Westinghouse Meter Plant in
    Raleigh, NC

Jim Pearce played in parts of five seasons (1949–55) with
the Senators and Reds. The right-hander was 3-4 overall.

PEARSON, Albie
    Minister of non-denominational church
    Mammoth Lakes, CA

Albie was originally signed by the Red Sox as a southpaw
chucker in 1952. The diminutive outfielder won Rookie of
the Year honors in the A.L. with the Washington Senators
in 1958.

    A colorful and popular player, he was a roommate of
playboy Bo Belinsky. Pearson, who once cut a record, plays
par golf. He shares a record along with immortals Babe
Ruth and Lou Gehrig for most consecutive extra-base
hits—6. Albie's were 5 doubles and a triple. Pearson became the expansion Angels' first-ever .300 hitter in 1963.
A grandfather when he was just 37, he is the father of five
daughters, all of whose names begin with the letter "K." He
was once quoted as saying, "The K represents a strikeout
in an attempt to produce a son."   .270

PEDEN, Les
> Director of Eagle Mountain Lake of the Fort Worth, TX, Boys Club

Les caught in nine games with the Washington Senators in 1953. In his brief stay he hit .250, and belted one home run. Les remained in baseball as a minor league manager and scout for several years. He is a former basketball and football player at Texas A&M.

PEETE, Charlie
> Died November 27, 1956, at age 25 in Caracas, Venezuela

An outfielder with the Cardinals in 1956, Charlie batted .192 in 23 games. He died at age 25 (a few weeks after the '56 season) in an airplane crash in Caracas, Venezuela while on his way to play winter league baseball. The first big leaguer ever killed in a commercial airline crash, his wife and three children also perished.

PELLAGRINI, Eddie
> Baseball coach at Boston College; realtor

Eddie was around from 1946–54, mostly as a utility infielder with the Red Sox, Browns, Phils, Reds, and Pirates. On April 22, 1946, he hit a home run in his first major league at-bat as a member of the Red Sox in a game against the Senators.

> Eddie, who was born on March 13th, wore No. 13 in his 13th year in pro ball with the '53 Pirates. His career major league totals include 13 triples and 13 stolen bases. He finished with a .226 average.

PENA, Orlando
> Detroit Tigers scout

This Cuban-born right-handed pitcher was in and out of the majors with seven different teams beginning in 1958. In 1963 Pena did not shine too brightly as he was 12-20 for the Kansas City A's, leading the A.L. in losses.　　　56-77

PENDLETON, Jim
    California Tanning Co.
    St. Louis, MO

An eight-year major leaguer, Jim was already close to 30 years old when he hit .299 as a rookie for the Milwaukee Braves in 1953. He was with the Pirates and Reds later in the decade, and in 1962 was with the expansion Astros. Jim played every infield position and also covered the outfield in his journey.   .255

PENSON, Paul
    Kansas City, KS

In 1955 Paul pitched in five games as a 22-year-old with the Phillies. The right-hander ended his brief stint at 1-1.

PEPPER, Laurin
    Teacher and football and golf coach at Ocean Springs
    high school
    Ocean Springs, MS

Hugh McLaurin Pepper III was a Pirates' bonus player in 1954 out of Mississippi Southern where he was also a Saturday afternoon football hero.
    Between 1954–57, Pepper was 2-8 in 44 games with the Pirates.

PEREZ, George
    Leona Valley, CA

George lost one decision in four games with the 1958 Pirates.   0-1

PERKOVICH, John
    Chicago, IL

Pedal pushers and bolero pants were in vogue in 1950 while John wore his White Sox for one game as a right-handed pitcher.   0-0

PERKOWSKI, Harry
    West Virginia Highway Dept.
    (weight enforcement division)
    Beckley, WV

This southpaw hurler was with us from 1947–55. With the exception of his final season (in which he was with the Cubs), Harry spent the bulk of his time with the Reds. He finished 33-40, with his best years coming in 1952 and '53 when he won 12 games each season for Cincinnati.

PERRY, Jim
    Oakland A's minor league pitching instructor

Gaylord's older brother, Jim won 215 games in a long career which began in 1959 with Cleveland. The Perrys are the winningest brother combination in major league history, with Gaylord contributing 314 victories to their total of 529. Jim's best seasons came well into his career in 1969 and '70 as he won 20 and then a league-high 24 games for the Minnesota Twins. In '70 Jim captured the A.L. Cy Young Award. He also led the A.L. in wins (18) in 1960.

215-174

PESKY, John
    (born John Paveskovich)
    Boston Red Sox coach

John had an impressive ten-year career that was interrupted by military service during World War II. He led the league in hits in each of his first three seasons. As a rookie with the Red Sox in 1942, Pesky led the majors with 205 hits. After a hitch in the military, John returned in 1946 to lead the A.L. in hits with 208, and repeated again in '47 with a league-leading 207 safeties.

Pesky is well remembered for hesitating on a relay throw in the '46 World Series while Enos Slaughter of the Cardinals scored the winning run from first base. The story goes that Pesky was at a college football game in his native Oregon that fall. The home receivers were having trouble hanging on to the pigskin when he overheard a fan yell, "Throw it to Pesky, he'll hold it."

In 1946 Pesky once had a streak of 11 consecutive hits. On May 8th that year he scored six runs in a game. He hit over .300 in six of seven years with the Red Sox before being traded to Detroit in 1952. John played second base, shortstop, and third base in a career that ended with the Senators in 1954.

Pesky has remained in baseball since his playing days as a minor league manager, Red Sox skipper (1963–64), Pirates coach, radio and TV announcer for Boston games, and currently as a coach for the Bosox. John closed at .307 lifetime.

PETERS, Gary
    Construction company foreman
    Sarasota, FL

Gary was the "Rookie-of-the-Year" in the A.L. in 1963. He previously had shots with the White Sox, starting in 1959.

In '63 he was 19-8, including 11 consecutive wins at one point. His 2.33 ERA was tops in the A.L. Gary reached the 20-win mark the following year. Those were his finest seasons, but his excellent ERA of 1.98 was tops in the A.L. in 1966. Peters was dealt to the Red Sox after 1969, and was with Boston the final three years of his career.

Originally a first baseman in his first season in pro ball in the mid-1950s, he was a good hitting pitcher, often used as a pinch-hitter. Gary hit 19 homers in the A.L. With four pinch-hit roundtrippers, he has the distinction of hitting more pinch-homers than any other chucker in big league history. One of his pinch-hit wallops came on July 19, 1964, in the 13th inning, to give the White Sox a 3-2 win over K.C.   124-103

PETERSON, Carl "Buddy"
    Central Scouting Bureau
    Sacramento, CA

In '55 "Buddy" broke in as a shortstop with the White Sox. He didn't play in the big show the following year, and made his exit with the Orioles in '57 after playing in seven games. His 13-game career saw him hit .237.

PETERSON, Harding
Pittsburgh Pirates executive vice-president

Harding was a catcher during four seasons with the Pirates in 1955, and from 1957–59. Following his 66 game career, he remained in the Pirates' organization in several capacities.   .273

PETERSON, Kent
Employed in home improvement business
Orem, UT

This lefty hurler spent parts of eight seasons in the N.L. with the Reds and Phillies from 1944–53.   13-38

PETTIT, Paul
High school teacher/coach
Lomita, CA

Paul was the first of the $100,000 bonus players signed by the Pirates in 1950 after a sensational pitching record in high school in California. Labeled a sure bet for stardom, he was under contract to a Hollywood agent for a life story before he had ever thrown a pitch in professional baseball.

An elbow injury cut short his career as a pitcher. Paul pitched in a pale total of 13 games for the Pirates, paying off at $100,000 per win, with a 1-2 lifetime mark in parts of the 1951 and '53 seasons. But to his credit, he didn't just take the money and run. He went to the low minors in an attempt to work his way back up to the big leagues as a first baseman-outfielder. The hard-luck bonus baby struggled his way up to the Triple-A level in the Pacific Coast League before calling it quits in the early 1960s.

He returned to college and earned a master's degree at California (Long Beach) following his playing days.

PHILLEY, Dave
   Red Sox scout and cattle rancher
   Paris, TX

An 18-year outfielder, Dave started in 1941. After military service in World War II, he returned in '46 and extended his career until age 42 in 1962 as he became one of the top pinch-hitters in the game.

Philley was a regular in the White Sox outfield in the late 1940s until he was traded to the Philadelphia Athletics. He was in the Indians' outfield during the 1954 A.L. championship season. Dave made stops in the late 1950s with the Orioles, Tigers, and White Sox again. During his career he also wore the uniforms of the Phillies, Giants, and Red Sox.

His pinch-hitting statistics were unmatched in the late '50s. In 1957 he was 12-for-29 (.413); 1958, 18-for-44 (.409) including 8 straight hits at the end of the season. He then picked up where he left off with a pinch-hit double on opening day of the '59 campaign. This established a record of 9 straight successful pinch-hit appearances. In 1961 as a member of the Orioles, Dave set an A.L. record with 24 pinch-hits. His total record as a pinch-batter is 93-for-311. His overall mark stands at .270 in an even 1,700 games.

PHILLIPS, Howard "Eddie"
   Supervisor, American Cyanamid
   Hannibal, MO

In 1953 Earl Warren was appointed to the Supreme Court. *The Moulin Rouge* was a box office attraction while Eddie Phillips was a baseball attraction in his home town for the last edition of the St. Louis Browns. Used exclusively as a pinch-runner in 9 games, he scored four runs, without an official big league plate appearance.

PHILLIPS, Jack
   Baseball coach at Clarkson College
   Potsdam, NY

A first baseman who spent parts of nine seasons in the big time, beginning in 1947 with the Yankees, Jack also saw

action with the Pirates in the late 1940s and early '50s.
His last stop was Detroit, from 1955–57.   .283

PHILLIPS, John "Bubba"
    Real estate
    Hattiesburg, MS

Bubba was a ten-year A.L. third baseman-outfielder. He
started with the Tigers in 1955. Phillips was with the
White Sox from 1956 through their pennant-winning year
in 1959. He played in 100 games as a White Sox third baseman that season, sharing the position with Billy Goodman
and Sam Esposito. In the World Series against L.A. he hit
an even .300, going 3-for-10.

In the early 1960s he was with Cleveland, then made his
last stop back in Detroit in 1963 and '64. Bubba made
"little" All-American as a football star at Mississippi
Southern.   .255

PHILLIPS, William Taylor
    U.S. post office employee
    Lithia Springs, GA

A southpaw chucker, Taylor was with the Braves, Cubs,
Phillies, and White Sox from 1956–63. After 147 games he
was 16-22. His first shutout in eight years of pro ball came
in May of '58 while pitching for the Cubs in a game against
the Braves, the team he started with.

PICONE, Mario
    Aluminum siding business
    Brooklyn, NY

A Brooklyn native, Mario pitched for the rival New York
Giants in 1947. Picone reappeared with the Giants in '52
and then again in '54 when he split the season between
New York and Cincinnati. He was 0-2 in 13 games.

PIERCE, Billy
>   Director of social services for an envelope company
>   Evergreen Park, IL

Billy broke in as a teenager with Detroit in 1945. He won
all three decisions for the Tigers in 1948, then was sent to
the White Sox for catcher Aaron Robinson in one of the
more one-sided trades in big league history. He started
slowly but in '53 he won 18 and led the league in strikeouts. The polished lefty also had seven shutouts. In 1955
his excellent 1.97 ERA was best in the league. That year
he lost four games by a 1-0 score. He was a 20-game winner
in both 1956 and '57. In 1958 he just missed a perfect game
no-hitter when he retired the first 26 Senators to face him.
Pinch-hitter Ed Fitzgerald then doubled to ruin both the
no-hitter and perfect game.

The classy southpaw remained in Chicago for two more
years before being traded to the S.F. Giants after the '61
season. In '62 he was undefeated at Candlestick Park in
compiling a 16-6 mark for the N.L. champs. He then
hurled a three-hit shutout over the Dodgers in the first of a
2-out-of-3 playoff to break the tie for the N.L. pennant.
Billy also pitched well in the Series against the Yankees,
winning one and losing one.

Even in his final year ('64) he was still effective at 3-0
with a 2.20 ERA.   211-169

PIERETTI, Marino
>   Died January 30, 1981, at age 60
>   San Francisco, CA

Born in Lucca, Italy, "Chick" Pieretti was a boyhood
friend of Billy Martin in the San Francisco Bay area. A
long-time pitcher in the PCL, "Chick" spent six seasons in
the late '40s with the Senators and White Sox, having his
best year in '45 with Washington (when he won 14). His
last season in the big top was in 1950 with Cleveland.
                                                          30-38

PIERRO, Billy
    Auto mechanic
    Brooklyn, NY

Bill came on the scene as a right-handed pitcher, losing his only two decisions in 12 games with the Pirates in 1950. A great prospect in the Pirates' chain, he once had 300 strikeouts in a season while in the minors, including a 21-strikeout game. However, he was plagued by encephalitis, which ended his career.

PIERSALL, Jimmy "The Waterbury Wizard"
    Hosted pre- and post-game pay TV shows for Chicago White Sox in 1983—since been released from his position

A colorful and sometimes eccentric outfielder, Jimmy first came up to the Red Sox in 1950. He suffered a mental breakdown shortly after. The story of his life, *Fear Strikes Out,* was made into a motion picture, with actor Tony Perkins playing Piersall. Another version was made for TV on "Climax," with Tab Hunter portraying the volatile Piersall in the 60-minute series.

Jimmy returned in '52 and played 30 games at shortstop before moving to center field where he became one of the top notch defensive players. He remained with Boston throughout most of the 1950s in an outfield flanked by Ted Williams in left and Jackie Jensen in right. His 40 doubles led the A.L. in 1956. On June 10, 1953, he had five singles and a double, going 6-for-6 for the Bosox (making him the only player in Red Sox history to collect six hits in a nine-inning game). He was with Cleveland and Washington in the late fifties and early sixties. As a member of the Mets in 1963, Piersall hit his 100th career home run and ran backwards around the bases to mark the occasion. He was released by the Mets and his career appeared to be at an end. But he signed with the Angels, where he made a strong comeback in 1964, hitting .314. He played several more seasons there, finishing his career with a .272 average.

PIGNATANO, Joe
    Atlanta Braves coach

A six-year catcher starting with Brooklyn in 1957, Joe remained with the Dodgers as backup to John Roseboro from 1958–60. After being with Kansas City and the S.F. Giants, he finished with the Mets in 1962. His final plate appearance came at Wrigley Field in Chicago against the Cubs when he hit into a triple play.

Joe coached for the Senators in the mid-1960s, then moved to the Mets and on to the Braves in the same capacity. "Piggy" is the cousin of Braves' pitcher Pete Falcone.

.234

PIKTUZIS, George
    Downey, CA

George was floored after pitching in only two games with the Cubs in 1956.
        0-0

PILARCIK, Al
    School teacher/coach
    St. John, IN

A six-year outfielder from 1956–61, Al was originally with K.C. in 1956. He was traded to Baltimore where he was the club's regular right fielder for three seasons. The studious flychaser was sent back to the A's in '61. He split his last season ('61) between K.C. and the White Sox.

Al ended with a .256 career average with his best season coming in 1959 with the Orioles, when he hit .282.

PILLETTE, Duane Xavier "Dee"
    Owner and manager of a mobile home dealership
    (Sundance Homes)
    San Jose, CA

A right-handed pitcher in the biggies from the late

1940s through the mid-1950s, "Big D" was the son of another former big league pitcher, Herman Polycarp (Old Folks) Pillette, who was with Detroit in the 1920s. Dee was with the Yankees in 1949 before being traded to the Browns the following year. He remained with them through the franchise shift to Baltimore in 1954. Duane had an overall record of 38-66, but his 3-2 complete game victory over the Tigers was the first-ever win in Orioles' history in 1954.

PINSON, Vada
Seattle Mariners minor league hitting instructor

Vada first came up to the Reds in 1958 as a 19-year-old. His first major league home run in his second big league game was a grand slam which gave the Reds a 4-1 win over Pittsburgh. He returned to the minors for the balance of that season, but came back to stay the following year, rejoining former high school teammate Frank Robinson in the Cincinnati outfield. Vada was outstanding as a rookie with a healthy .316 average, and league-leading totals in runs scored and doubles. He also had his first of four 200-plus hit seasons.

His career high average came in the 1961 pennant-winning year, with a .343 mark. In the late 1960s and early 1970s he played with the Cards, Indians, and Angels. Vada closed out with a .286 average and 2,757 hits, including 256 home runs. Both base hit number 1,000 and 2,000 of his career were home runs. Odds, anyone?

PISONI, Jim
St. Louis, MO

In 1953 Jim made his climb to the top. He hung on for parts of five seasons with the Cardinals, K.C. Athletics, Milwaukee Braves, and Yankees between 1953-60. He played in 103 games and batted .212.

PITULA, Stan
> Died August 15, 1965, at age 34
> Hackensack, NJ

The Diamonds had a big hit with "Little Darlin' " in 1957. That same year, this young jewel pitched in 23 games with the Indians. Overall the right-hander was 2-2.

PIZARRO, Juan
> Director of youth baseball program
> San Juan, PR

This Puerto Rican-born lefty began as a 19-year-old with the N.L. champion Milwaukee Braves in 1957. He had his finest years in the 1960s with the Chicago White Sox. Juan went 19-9 in 1964. After a time in the minors in the early 1970s, he returned to the biggies with the Cubs and outdueled Met ace Tom Seaver, 1-0, in a game in which he homered for the game's only run.

A 131-105 career record-holder, he was still pitching in the Mexican League in the late 1970s.

PLARSKI, Don
> Former sports editor of the *Alton* (IL) *Telegraph*; died December 29, 1981, at age 52 in St. Henry, OH

The K.C. A's decided to scratch Don after eight games in 1955. The outfielder had a .091 average.

PLESS, Rance
> Security chief for Magnavox Corp.
> Greenville, TN

A flash in the minors, Rance was never able to crack the Giants' infield of the 1950s which included Davey Williams, Hank Thompson, and Al Dark. In 1955 he won the American Association's MVP award. However, his big league taste consisted of only 48 games with the '56 K.C. A's when he hit .271.

PLEWS, Herb
> Laboratory employee of Martin Marietta Cement Co.
> Longmont, CA

A graduate of the University of Illinois, Herb is one of the few Montana-born major leaguers. He was an infielder with the Washington Senators from 1956 until traded to the Red Sox in 1959. He batted .262 in his four big league campaigns. Herb was the third captain of the University of Illinois baseball team to reach the biggies, preceded by Lou Boudreau and "Hoot" Evers.

PODBIELAN, Bud
> Construction worker until his death on October 27, 1982, at age 58, in Syracuse, NY

Clarence "Bud" Podbielan pitched with the Brooklyn Dodgers, Cincinnati Reds, and Cleveland Indians in a eleven-year period spanning the 1949–59 seasons. Overall, the right-hander was 25-42.

PODRES, Johnny
> Minnesota Twins pitching coach

A southpaw chucker with a great changeup, John first arrived with Brooklyn in 1953. He was just 9-10 during the 1955 season, but on September 30th, on his 23rd birthday, he started and defeated the Yankees, 8-3, in game three of the World Series after the Yanks won the first two games. A few days later, with the aid of Sandy Amoros' great game-saving catch in left field, Podres shut out the Bronx Bombers, 2-0, as the Dodgers finally won their first Series. Riding to the game on the bus to Yankee Stadium he told his teammates, "Just get me one run." He was right!

That winter he was in great demand for appearances—including one in front of the draft board. Previously classified 4-F, he was suddenly 1-A. Returning from military duty in '57, he had the best ERA in the N.L. at 2.66, and a league leading six shutouts. His 18-5 mark in 1961 was the best winning percentage in the N.L. at .783. On July 2, 1962, he struck out eight Phillies in succession.

Along with his 1955 WS heroics, he also helped the Dodgers to Series wins in 1959 and 1963, with victories over the White Sox and Yankees. Podres was with the Tigers and the expansion San Diego Padres in the late 1960s. Johnny previously was a pitching coach for San Diego and Boston.   148-116

POHOLSKY, Tom
> Manufacturer's representative
> St. Louis, MO

A graduate of Washington University in St. Louis with a degree in civil engineering, Tom appeared in 159 games and engineered a 31-52 mark. The right-hander was with the Cardinals in 1950–51 and 1954–56. His final season was spent with the Cubs in '57. In 1950, Tom was International League MVP. That year he pitched all 22 innings in a 2-1 victory.

POLLET, Howie
> Died August 8, 1974, at age 53 in Houston, TX

Howie was born and raised in the same neighborhood as Mel Parnell. He spent 14 years in the bigs, starting in 1941 with the Cardinals. In 1943 he was 8-4, and had a string of 28 consecutive scoreless innings when he was called to military duty. His 1.75 ERA was the best in the N.L. that year.

Howie returned in 1946 to win 21 games, and again posted the best ERA in the league at 2.10 as the Cardinals won the pennant. In the opening game of the Series, he lost a 10-inning game, 3-2. He had one last outstanding year in 1949 when he won 20, including a league-leading five shutouts.

In the early 1950s he was with the Pirates, Cubs, White Sox, and Pittsburgh again before culminating his career in 1956 with a mark of 131-116. He was also a pitching coach for the Cardinals and Astros.

POPE, Dave
    Department of Recreation
    Cleveland, OH

Dave arrived with Cleveland in '52. His career (1952–56) was spent with the Indians and Orioles. He was the starting right fielder for the Indians in the opening game of the 1954 World Series. Dave hit for a career average of .265, including a .294 mark in 60 games for the 1954 A.L. champion Indians.

PORTER, Dan
    Postal employee
    San Diego, CA

The Korean War talks started in 1951, but not soon enough as far as Dan was concerned. Breaking in at age 19, he played the outfield for 13 games with the '51 Senators, hitting .211. After two years in the military, he never returned to the majors.

PORTER, J. W.
    Appliance business
    West Palm Beach Gardens, FL

"Jay" signed for a large bonus in 1951 and made his debut at 19 in 1952 with the St. Louis Browns. After two years of military service, he was with the Tigers (1955–57), then the Indians, Senators, and Cardinals before hanging it up in 1959. He had a .228 average in 229 games as a catcher, outfielder, first baseman, and third baseman.

PORTERFIELD, Bob
    Died April 28, 1980, at age 56, in Charlotte, NC

Bob was around from 1948–59. He was a product of the Yankees' farm system before being traded to Washington in 1951. As a member of the Yankees' International League team in 1948 in Newark, he once threw four straight shutouts. But it was in the '53 season, at age 30, that he peaked in that department with a league-leading nine whitewashings for the Senators. He was 22-10 and was named by the *Sporting News* as the outstanding pitcher in the A.L.

Bob fell off to a few losing seasons after that, and finished with the Pirates and Cubs in 1959.

Despite a mediocre overall record of 87-97, he was anything but mediocre in '53 when he also led the A.L. with 24 complete games. Prior to his death, Bob was employed by Westinghouse Electric. He was a paratrooper during World War II.

PORTOCARRERO, Arnold
Manufacturer's representative
Shawnee Mission, KS

Arnold spent seven seasons (1954–60) in the A.L. An 18-game loser as a rookie for the Philadelphia Athletics, he went to Kansas City with the franchise, then was traded to Baltimore where he had his finest campaign in the biggies when he went 15-11 for the '58 Orioles.

On September 24, 1954, he struck out three consecutive Yankee pinch-hitters—Lou Berberet, Gus Triandos, and Frank Leja. The native New Yorker was the last pitcher to strike out 100 batters in a year wearing an A's uniform in Philadelphia.   38-57

POSSEHL, Lou
Palatine, IL

Lou was 2-5 in 15 games, pitching in parts of five seasons with the Phillies from 1946–52.

POST, Wally
Sales manager for the Minster Canning Co. in Minster, OH, until he died January 6, 1982, at age 52 in St. Henry, OH

A long ball hitting outfielder from 1949–64, Wally was originally a pitcher. He once won 17 games in the minors

before switching to the outfield. Wally became a full-time
player for Cincinnati in 1954, and became part of the Reds'
power hitting teams of the era. He smashed 40 homers in
1955, followed up by 36 in '56 when the slugging Reds
(who featured Ted Kluszewski, rookie Frank Robinson,
and Gus Bell) combined to tie the '47 Giants with 221
home runs.

Post was traded to the Phillies after the '57 season, but
returned to the Reds after two years. In 1961, his 20
homers and .294 average helped the team to the N.L. pennant. Although they lost the World Series to the Yankees
in five games, he hit .333, going 6-for-18, including a home
run.

He played briefly in the A.L. with the Indians and Twins
before finishing in 1964. Wally posted a .266 average with
210 home runs.

POWELL, Bob
    Engineer at Nevada nuclear test site

In 1955 and again in '57 this Las Vegas resident rolled
snake eyes, appearing in one game with the White Sox
both years. He had no official plate appearances, but did
score a run. Bob received his degree in engineering from
Michigan State.

POWER, Vic
    Runs baseball clinics; California Angels scout
    San Juan, PR

This Puerto Rican-born player was originally in the Yankees' organization. After some strong hitting at Kansas
City in the American Association in the early 1950s, it appeared that Vic would be the first black to ever wear a
Yankee uniform. However, he was traded to the Philadelphia Athletics and made his debut in 1954. Back in
Kansas City in '55 (but this time with the transplanted
A's), he was over the .300 mark in both '55 and '56. A
flashy fielder, he led all A.L. first baseman in fielding
three years. He was a Gold Glove Award winner from
1958–64.

Vic was traded to Cleveland in 1958. On August 14th he became the first player since Walter Gautreau (1927 Braves) to steal home twice in the same game. The feat hasn't been matched since. Ironically, the two stolen bases were his first two of the season in mid-August. He wound up with 3 thefts for the year. Power ended his career with a .284 average. As for "power," he hit 126 home runs. Along with over 1,300 games as a first baseman, he also played in the outfield, second base, third base, and shortstop. Somewhat of a "hot dog" with his fancy fielding exploits, he retired with the best career fielding mark for first basemen, with a lifetime fielding average of .9941. Vic was noted for his one-handed stabbing catches.

POWERS, Johnny
    Shipping department
    Butler Manufacturing Co.
    Birmingham, AL

Johnny has the distinction of hitting the last home run against the Giants at the Polo Grounds on Sept. 29, 1957, as a member of the Pirates, in the team's 9-1 victory over New York. An outfielder, Johnny spent parts of six seasons playing in the big time with the Pirates, Reds, Orioles, and Indians from 1955–60. He departed with a .195 average in 151 games.

POWIS, Carl
    Baytown, TX

Carl appeared in 15 games as an outfielder with the Orioles, hitting .195 in 1957.

PRAMESA, John
    Sales representative, Helms Express
    Cincinnati, OH

John came up with the Reds in 1949 where he stayed until the end of the '51 season. In his last year (1952) he wore a Cubs' uniform. John hit .307 with the Reds in 1950 when he shared the catching duties with Dixie Howell.   .268

PRESKO, Joe
    Guard with Brinks Armored Car Co.
    Kansas City, MO

Joe pitched with the Cardinals (1951–54) and Tigers
(1957–58). After 128 games the right-hander was 25-37.
Presko led the Texas League in strikeouts with 165 in
1950 while playing for Houston.

PRIDDY, Jerry
    Died March 3, 1980, at age 60
    Long Beach, CA

An A.L. infielder from 1941–53, Jerry came up with the
Yankees. He hit .280 in '42 for the A.L. champions. Traded
to Washington, he played three seasons in the nation's
capital, with time out for military duty. In the late forties
he enjoyed his two finest seasons with the St. Louis
Browns, hitting over .290 each year. Jerry was traded to
the Tigers where he participated in a then-major league
record of 150 double plays at second base in 1950.

A very durable and injury-free career was all but ended
at age 32 in 1952 when he suffered a broken leg. He finished with a career .265 average. Following his baseball
days, he played briefly on the PGA tour.

In later years he was accused of trying to extort
$250,000 from a steamship company by threatening to put
a bomb aboard one of its vessels. He was convicted and sen-
tenced to nine months in prison, and was released after he
had served half of his term.

PRITCHARD, Harold "Buddy"
    Central Scouting Bureau; high school teacher
    Fullerton, CA

In 1957 Buddy received his walking papers after struggling to make it with the Pirates as a shortstop-outfielder.
In his 23-game jaunt, Buddy batted .091.

PROCTOR, Jim
    Naperville, IL

Exodus, by Leon Uris, was a best seller in 1959, the year Jim made his exodus out of the big leagues after pitching two games for the Tigers. The right-hander closed at 0-1.

PURKEY, Bob
    Insurance business
    Bethel Park, PA

Bob did his pitching from 1954–66. He started in the Pirates' organization, and had a record 6 putouts in a '54 game. Following an 11-14 season in '57, he was traded to the Reds where he became a 17-game winner twice, and won 16 on the '61 pennant winners. The Reds failed to repeat in 1962, but Purkey had his best season at 23-5. Traded to the Cardinals after a few mediocre years, he parted where it all started, in his home town of Pittsburgh.
                                                  120-115

PYBURN, Jim
    Former University of Georgia assistant football coach

An outstanding college football star at Auburn University in the mid-fifties, Jim signed to play pro baseball with the Orioles. He was an infielder-outfielder and hit just .190 in 158 big league games.

His son Jeff was a quarterback at the University of Georgia, and was a first-round selection of the San Diego Padres in the 1980 baseball free-agent draft.

PYECHA, John
    Director at the Center for Educational Research and
    Evaluation-Research
    Triangle Institute
    Chapel Hill, NC

John's smoke was put out quickly when he lost the only big league game he ever pitched in, for the Cubs.

In 1968 John received a Ph.D. degree in educational research from the University of North Carolina.

Q

QUALTERS, Tom
Pennsylvania fishing commission
Somerset, PA

The only player in Phillies' history whose last name began with the letter Q, Tom was a bonus baby who had an ERA of 162.00 after a third of an inning of work as an 18-year-old in 1953. Eventually it was lowered to 5.71 but in 34 career games he failed to gain a decision. He made his exit with the White Sox in 1958.

QUEEN, Bill
Owns a local store in Gastonia, NC

This Queen lasted a little more than a day. An outfielder for three games with the '54 Milwaukee Braves, Bill stepped down with a .000 average.

QUEEN, Mel
Died April 4, 1982, at age 64, in Fort Smith, AR

Mel was with us between 1942–52. The right-hander was originally with the Yankees, and later the Pirates from 1948–52, compiling a lifetime mark of 27-40. Could there be a more royal pitching matchup than Mel Queen opposing Clyde King?

His son Mel was originally an outfielder in the Reds' organization in the mid-1960s. He then switched to pitching and won 14 games for the Reds in 1967. He remained in the majors through 1972 with the California Angels.

QUINN, Frank
> Clubhouse director—Century Village Community Center
> West Palm Beach, FL

Frank signed a large bonus out of Yale where he was a teammate of Vice-President George Bush. The right-hander pitched creditably with the Red Sox in eight games in 1949, with an ERA under 3.00, but without a decision. He hurled one more game for the Red Sox in 1950—the extent of his big league story.   0-0

R

RABE, Charlie
> Darien, IL

Charlie came up with the Reds in 1957. Cincinnati didn't get very good mileage from the southpaw chucker as he went 0-4 in 11 games in 1957 and 1958.

RACKLEY, Marv
> Salesman, Mitchell Motors
> Atlanta, GA

After four long years in the N.L. (1947–50), Marv compiled a .317 average. He appeared briefly in '47 with Brooklyn, then in 1948 hit .327 in 88 games. Rackley started the '49 season with the Dodgers, and after a brief time with the Pirates, he returned to Brooklyn for the remainder of the year where he hit .303. In 1950 he finished with the Reds.

RAETHER, Hal
> Lake Mills, WI

Signed by the A's in 1954 out of the University of Wisconsin, this right-hander has the distinction of pitching in one game each for the 1954 Philadelphia Athletics and '57 K.C. A's in his two major league appearances.   0-0

RAFFENSBERGER, Ken
York Capital Distributors
York, PA

Originally with the Cardinals in 1939, he was traded away to the Cubs, for whom he pitched in 1940 and '41. He was with the Phillies starting in 1943, and in '44 his 20 losses were the most in the N.L. However, his ERA was a respectable 3.06. Ken was the winning pitcher in the All-Star Game that summer.

In 1949 with Cincinnati, he went 18-17 with a league-leading five shutouts. In '51 he again led the senior circuit in losses with 17. Then in 1952 he won 17, and again had the most shutouts in the N.L. (with 6).   119-154

RAINES, Larry
Lansing, MI

Larry got his feet wet playing in Japan and the Negro Leagues before a brief stint in the minors.

As a Cleveland rookie in 1957, he was shuttled between various positions in the infield and saw occasional duty in the outfield. All of this shuffling might have dampened his career. Following the '58 season he was gone after batting a soggy .253 overall.

RAMAZZOTTI, Bob
SFK Bearing Company
Altoona, PA

Bob was a utility infielder with the Dodgers and Cubs from 1946-53. He made his exit with a lifetime .230 average.

RAMOS, Pedro "Pete"
> Owned a cigar manufacturing company in Cuba before serving jail sentence for drug possession

For four straight years (1958–61) this Cuban-born right-hander led the A.L. in losses as a member of the Senators with 18, 19, 18, and 20. He then went with the team to Minnesota in '61. Ramos saw action with Cleveland for a few years before joining the Yankees down the stretch in 1964, where his outstanding work out of the bullpen helped the Yanks win the A.L. pennant. In the late 1960s he was in the N.L. with the Phils, Pirates, and Reds. He last appeared back in Washington.

In 1957 he gave up a record 43 roundtrippers. He also could hit the long ball, hitting 15 career home runs. Twice he hit two four-baggers in a game.

An extremely fast runner, Pedro was often challenging and beating some of the games' speedsters in foot races. But the man he wanted to race the most, Mickey Mantle, would never accept the challenge.

Ramos was arrested in 1979 for possession of cocaine in an alleged $2 million drug bust. He received a three-year prison sentence at the Hendry Correctional Institute in Florida.   117-160

RAMSDELL, Willard
> Died October 8, 1969, at age 41
> Wichita, KS

This knuckleball chucker was with the Dodgers in the late forties, and with the Reds and Cubs in the early fifties. Willard was 24-39 in 111 games.

RAND, Dick
> Long Beach, CA

Dick caught with the Cards in 1953 and '55, then with the Pirates in '57.   .240

RANEY, Frank
  (born Frank Raniszewski)
  Warren, MI

Tall and thin (6'4", 190 lbs), Frank was called "Ribs." The right-hander pitched in four games with the St. Louis Browns in 1949 and 1950, and was involved in the decisions in all four, going 1-3.

RAPP, Earl
  Montreal Expos scout

Earl was around from 1949–52 and did his share of traveling, spending time with the Tigers, White Sox, Giants, Browns, and Senators. In '52 he was 10-for-54 as a pinch-hitter—both figures the most in the A.L. that year.   .262

RASCHI, Vic
  Liquor store owner
  Conesus, NY

"The Springfield Rifle," as he was known (having been born in Springfield, Mass.), came up to the Yankees in 1946, and was one of the aces of the championship Yankee teams from 1949–53. The winning pitcher in the 1948 All-Star Game, he also drove in the winning run. In 1953 he had a record-seven RBIs in a contest, most ever in a game by an A.L. pitcher. In that debacle the Yanks beat the Tigers, 15-0. But it was his pitching in the early 1950s for which he deserves to be remembered, not his hitting feats, or for being the answer to the trivia question, "Who served up Hank Aaron's first major league home run?" Raschi threw that pitch as a member of the Cardinals in '54, near the end of his career.

He was a 21-game winner three straight seasons, from 1949–51. His .724 winning percentage in 1950 was the best in the A.L. In '51 he led the junior circuit in strikeouts.

His overall mark of 132-66 puts him in select company

with the likes of Christy Mathewson, Lefty Grove, and Whitey Ford—pitchers who have won at least 100 games, and won twice as many games as they lost.

Vic was extremely tough at World Series time. In 1949 he was a 1-0 loser, but then won the fifth and final game over the Dodgers. He had a 2-hit shutout in the opener of the 1950 Series over the Phillies. Raschi won the sixth and final game in '51 over the N.Y. Giants. In '52 he beat Brooklyn twice, 7-1 and 3-2.

On May 3, 1950, Vic committed four balks in posting a 4-3 victory against the White Sox.

RAYDON, Curt
    Policeman
    Bloomington, IL

In 1958 Curt went 8-4 in 31 games with the Pirates. Following the '58 season he left the big leagues.

RAYMOND, Claude
    Montreal Expos announcer

French speaking "Cloh Ra-Mohn" first arrived in 1959, appearing in three games for the White Sox. During the 1960s he was a relief pitcher with the Milwaukee Braves, Houston Astros, and once again with the Braves (in Atlanta). He finished in the early 1970s with the Expos.

REED, Bill
    Customer services manager, American Can Co.
    Houston, TX

In 1952 Bill had his introduction as a second baseman. His days were numbered, as he appeared in only 15 games for the Boston Braves, hitting .250.

REED, Howie
    Operates a farm with his father-in-law
    Mathis, TX

An All-American chucker at the University of Texas, Howie was 26-29 in 229 games, pitching for the K.C. A's, L.A. Dodgers, California Angels, Houston Astros, and Montreal Expos from 1958–71.

REESE, Harold "Pee Wee"
    Representative of Hillerich & Bradsby, bat makers
    Louisville, KY

Although not big, the nickname came from his prowess as a marble champion at the age of 12. His entire career (1940–58) was spent as the Dodgers' shortstop.

In 1949 he led the N.L. in runs scored with 132, and in 1952 was the league leader in stolen bases with 30. His .309 average in 1954 was his career high. In seven World Series he hit for a .272 average in 44 games.

Reese's swan song was in 1958 (the Dodgers' first year in L.A.). He was a coach for the team in the 1959 championship season. "Pee Wee" later worked several years as Dizzy Dean's partner on the TV "Baseball Game of the Week."

"Pee Wee" is the only man to play in all 44 World Series games—covering seven Series—between the Brooklyn Dodgers and New York Yankees from 1941–56.

When Duke Snider was elected to the Hall of Fame in 1980, he said, "If I'm here, and Jackie and Campy are here, then Pee Wee should be here too. He was the essence of those Dodger teams."   .269

REGALADO, Rudy
    Assistant sales manager
    Bay City Television
    San Diego, CA

Rudolph Valentino Regalado was a third baseman out of USC who played in 91 games with the Cleveland Indians (1954–56), hitting .249. He was 1-for-3 in the '54 World

Series against the New York Giants. Not the most romantic career, but generally interesting.

REISER, Harold Patrick "Pete"
Died October 25, 1981, at age 62 in Thousand Palms, CA

By the early 1950s Pete was somewhat of a legend for his outstanding 1941 season when he had led the N.L. in hitting at .343, while leading the Dodgers to the N.L. flag. He also led the league in doubles, triples, and runs scored.

Reiser led the senior circuit in stolen bases in both 1942 and '46. In '47 he established a record (since tied by Rod Carew) of stealing home seven times.

However, by this time the serious injuries were mounting—most of them the result of crashing into outfield fences chasing fly balls. In 1949–50 he was a member of the Boston Braves; he spent '51 with the Pirates, and in '52 he departed with the Indians.

Pete remained for several years into the 1970s as a coach with the Dodgers, Cubs, and Angels.   .295

RENFROE, Marshall
Died December 10, 1970, at age 34 in Pensacola, FL

Marshall pitched in one game for the S.F. Giants in 1958, and left the way he arrived at 0-0.

RENNA, Bill
Vice-president of a concrete manufacturing company
San Jose, CA

Bill hit .314 in 61 games for the Yankees in 1953. He then played for the Athletics in both Philadelphia and Kansas City. In the late fifties he was with the Red Sox.

Before signing to play professional baseball Bill played on Santa Clara U.'s 1950 Orange Bowl winner. A standout performer on the gridiron, Bill played in the East-West Shrine Game, and turned down an offer to play with the Los Angeles Rams.   .239

REPULSKI, Eldon "Rip"
>Works part-time for Burlington Northern Railroad
St. Cloud, MN

"Rip" was a college football running back at St. Cloud College in Minn. before his pro baseball days. Repulski was a regular in the Cardinals' outfield as a rookie in 1953, hitting .275. He then hit for a career high .283 in 1954. After several years with the Phillies, he spent the 1959 season as a backup outfielder and pinch-hitter for the Dodgers.

He closed with the Red Sox in 1961.   .269

RESTELLI, Dino
>Chairman of parks and recreation commission
San Carlos, CA

An outfielder for the Pirates in 1949 and '51, he went on a home-run tear, with 8 in his first 10 games in 1949. That was the extent of his success however, as he ended up with 12 homers in 72 games, and a .250 average. Dino was back in the minors in 1950. Restelli returned in '51 for 21 games and hit .184 with one homer—the extent of his big league life.

In the late fifties, Dino was a San Francisco policeman.
.241

REYES, Nap
>Manager in Mexican League

Nap was with the New York Giants during the war years (1943–45). The Cuban-born first baseman-third baseman hit for .289 and .288 averages, playing in over 100 games in both '44 and '45. Five years later he became a fifties player when he appeared in one game at first base for the Giants.   .284

REYNOLDS, Allie
    Chairman of the board
    New Park Mid-Continent Drilling Co.
    Oklahoma City, OK

The "Chief," as he was known, was part Indian, but in the late 1940s and early '50s he was all "Yankee."

Allie was a college football star at Oklahoma A&M (now Oklahoma State) in the mid-1930s before signing to play baseball. The hard-throwing right-hander was a .500 pitcher in the mid-40s with Cleveland. From 1947–54 he won twice as many as he lost, going 131-60 for the Yankees. In '47 he went 19-8 for the best winning percentage in the A.L. at .704. He lost more than 8 games just once in his eight seasons with New York. In '51 his 7 shutouts led the A.L., and two of those were no-hitters. One was against his former Cleveland team, 1-0. The second one, which came on September 28th, clinched the pennant. The game was dramatic despite the 8-0 score, as Ted Williams was given a second chance when Yogi Berra dropped his pop foul with two out in the ninth. Williams again popped to Berra, who hung onto the ball the second time. With two days left in the '51 campaign, manager Casey Stengel told Reynolds to take the rest of the season off.

The year 1952 was probably his finest, at 20-8 with a 2.06 ERA (best in the A.L.). He also led the league in strikeouts, and again in shutouts. The "Chief" had 13 wins in '53, and an additional 13 saves working out of the bullpen.

Allie was extremely effective in October, going 7-2 in WS competition.   182-107

RHODES, James "Dusty"
    Oil barge transportation worker
    New York, NY

"Dusty" had a .253 lifetime average in eight seasons with the Giants from 1952–59, but the 1954 season and World Series made him a legendary folk hero as he hit .341, including a 15-for-45, .333 clip as a pinch-hitter (with several of his hits helping the Giants win games in their drive for the N.L. pennant). In the Series sweep over favored Cleveland, his pinch-homer won the opener. He had a pinch-single in game two, stayed in the game, and homered again. Then in game three, the pinch-hitter deluxe had a bases-loaded pinch-hit single. He rested the fourth and final game.

Ironically, baseball literature has been filled with details of Willie Mays' dramatic catch of Vic Wertz' 450-foot drive in the opening game of the '54 "Fall Classic." However, the game was won by "Dusty" with a 270-foot homer which landed in fair territory by only five feet.

Following his monumental performance in the '54 WS, he was sometimes referred to as "The Colossus of Rhodes."

"Dusty" also has the distinction of making the last out in the Giants' final game at the Polo Grounds in 1957, while handkerchiefs waved a last farewell from the bleachers.

RICE, Del
San Francisco Giants scout when he died January 26, 1983, at age 60, in Buena Park, CA

A 17-year catcher in over 1,300 games, Del never played another defensive position. Most of his days were spent with the Cardinals. He hit .500 (3-for-6) in the '46 World Series. Rice, who was Del Crandall's backup on the 1957–58 N.L. champion Braves' teams, was often seen behind the dish when Bob Buhl was on the mound.

Del was a coach for both Cleveland and the Angels in the 1960s, and in 1972 he managed the Angels. He played with the Rochester Royals in the A.B.L. from 1943–46.

.237

RICE, Hal
Retired
Muncie, IN

Hal roamed the outfield with the Cardinals, Pirates, and Cubs from 1948–54. He has been left partially disabled from serious injuries he received in an auto accident. .260

RICHARDS, Fred
Assistant chief for the Warren, OH, Fire Department

"Strike it Rich," with Warren Hull, appeared on TV in 1951 when Fred played in just 10 games as a first baseman with the White Sox. Although he hit a respectable .296 (8-27), he failed to strike it rich, as he never played in the big arena after that season.

RICHARDSON, Bobby
President, Baseball Chapel, Inc.
Asheville, NC

Bobby carried a .266 lifetime average as the second baseman for the Yankees from 1955–66. But come World Series time (he participated in seven), he picked up where Billy Martin left off as a clutch performer. He hit for a .305 average in 36 Series contests, including a 6 RBI game against the Pirates in 1960 in game three of the 10-0 Yankee victory. Overall he had 12 RBIs in the Series, after accumulating 26 on the season.

His finest year was 1962, with a league-leading 209 hits and .302 average. He contributed little offensively in the WS against the Giants, hitting just .148 (4-for-27), but is remembered for catching the Series-saving line drive off Willie McCovey's bat with two out in the bottom of the ninth in game seven.

In 1964 he had 13 hits in the seven-game battle against the Cardinals. He has coached the baseball team at the University of South Carolina, and has been involved with the fellowship of Christian Athletes since his playing days ended.

RICHMOND, Don
Distributor for Genesee Beer when he died May 24, 1981, at age 61, in Elmira, NY

A third baseman with the Phillies in '41 and again in 1946–47, Don returned to play a dozen games with the Cards four years later.   .211

RICHTER, Al
    Salesman for Goldberger Foods in Minneapolis, MN.
    He resides in Norfolk, VA

Al played a total of six games at shortstop with the Red
Sox in 1951 and 1953 before leaving with an .091 average.

RICKERT, Marv
    Died June 3, 1978, at age 57
    Oakville, WA

An outfielder with the Cubs in 1942 and again in '46 and
'47, Marv traveled to the Reds and Boston Braves in the
late 1940s, hitting .292 in '49 (his best season). His career
culminated in 1950, split between the Pirates and White
Sox (his original team).   .247

RICKETTS, Dick
    Manager, business placement for Eastman Kodak Co.
    Rochester, NY

Dick was a first-team basketball All-American in 1955,
when he led Duquesne University to the NIT title. He
played three years in the NBA with the St. Louis Hawks,
Rochester Royals, and Cincinnati Royals. In 1959 the 6'7"
right-hander was 1-6 in 12 games with the St. Louis Cardinals in his only big league fling. His ERA for those 12
games was close to his NBA scoring average.
    Dick's brother Dave, who was also a starter on the same
NIT championship team, caught six seasons (1963–70)
with the Cardinals and Pirates.

RIDZIK, Steve
    Military base supply salesman
    Annandale, VA

This well-traveled sinkerball right-hander first came up as
a part-time starter and reliever with the Phillies in the
early 1950s. He later was with the Reds, Giants, and Indians during the decade, before leaving in 1958. His major

league days seemed to be at an end when he returned five
seasons later with the expansion Senators for whom he did
some fairly effective relief work in the mid-1960s. He
ended in 1966 with the Phillies.   39-38

RIGNEY, Bill
Assistant to the president, Oakland A's; also their TV
announcer

Known as "Cricket" during his playing days, he spent his
entire run with the N.Y. Giants from 1946-53. He was
pretty much a full-time player the first four years, then
was used in a utility role from 1950-53.

Following his playing days, Bill managed in the minors,
then became manager of the Giants in 1956 and went to
San Francisco in the same capacity. "Rig" piloted the Angels and Twins during the 1960s and the early '70s.

His son, Bill, Jr., was the 1979 Executive of the Year as
the General Manager of the Midland team in the Texas
League.   .259

RINKER, Bob
Machinist for Beltrami Enterprises in Eckley, PA

Bob had a three-game snack catching for the 1950 Philadelphia A's, going 1-for-3.

RIVERA, Manuel Joseph "Jim," "Jungle Jim"
Owns Captain's Cabin, a restaurant in Angola, IN

A ten-year A.L. outfielder, Jim first arrived as a 30-year-
old rookie with the St. Louis Browns in 1952. He was
traded to the White Sox that season and spent the rest of
the decade as one of the main cogs of the high octane
"Go-Go" White Sox. His 16 triples in 1953 and 25 stolen
bases in '55 both led the A.L.

Jim was a part-time player in '59 for the A.L. champions. In the World Series he was hitless in 11 at-bats, but is
remembered for his sensational game-saving catch in
game five against the Dodgers.

Rivera's career parallels that of outfielder Ron LeFlore

a generation later, in that he never played pro ball until
his late twenties, and had served some prison time. His
Tarzan-like aggressive play resulted in his nickname of
"Jungle Jim."   .256

RIZZUTO, Phil "Scooter"
New York Yankees announcer

Unable to gain Hall of Fame attention despite being a first-
rate performer, Phil supplanted Frank Crosetti in 1941
and spent 13 seasons as the Yanks' shortstop (with three
years out in the mid-1940s for military duty in World War
II). He had a lifetime batting average of .273, including a
.307 mark as a rookie in 1941. His finest season was in
1950 when he hit .324 and was named the A.L. MVP.

Phil hit for a .246 average in nine World Series, totaling
52 games, the most of any shortstop in big league history.

Rizzuto was considered the finest bunter of his day and
one of the best of all time. The popular Yankee announcer
was called "Scooter" because of the way he scooted after
ground balls. "Holy Cow."

ROACH, Mel
Bank vice-president
Richmond, VA

A former quarterback at the University of Virginia, Mel
was an infielder-outfielder who spent parts of eight seasons in the N.L., and never compiled a batting average in
the .200s in all those years. He was hitless for a .000 mark in
limited plate appearances for the Braves in 1953 and '54.
In 1957 Mel came back with a .167 average, going 1-for-6,
then jumped all the way to .309 as a member of the 1958
N.L. champions. In '59 it was back to .097, but then returned to the .300 class in 1960. He was under .200 with
both the Cubs and Phillies in 1961-62. It all balanced out
to a .238 lifetime average.

ROBERTS, Curt
>   He was killed while fixing a flat tire on a freeway in
>   Oakland, CA, on November 14, 1969, at age 40

The first black ever to wear a Pirates' uniform, Curt was
the team's regular second baseman as a rookie in 1954. He
also played with them in parts of the '55 and '56 seasons.
Lifetime he hit .223.

ROBERTS, Robin
>   Baseball coach at the University of South Florida
>   Tampa, FL

Elected to the Hall of Fame in 1976, Robin made headlines
in the early 1950s by never winning under 20 from 1950–55,
including a 28-7 season in 1952.

When he fell off to a 1-10 mark in 1961, he seemed to be
at the end, but returned to win 10 games in 1962 for the
Orioles, posting the second best ERA in the A.L. The development of a change-up pitch was a big factor in prolonging
his career.

His lifetime mark of 286-245 fell just 14 short of the coveted 300 wins, but he did win 14 in the minors for an even
300 victories in his professional career.

He gave up record totals of 46 homers in 1956, and 502
during his career. From August 28, 1952, to July 9, 1953,
Robin had an amazing streak of 28 complete games. Roberts pitched the distance in the Phillies' dramatic 4-1 victory over the Dodgers on the last day of the 1950 season to
clinch the pennant. He became the Phillies' first 20-game
winner since 1917.

In reference to the storylike 1950 "Whiz Kids," Roberts
responded, "We were trained for the World Series. Winning the pennant was the big thing for us. My biggest dis-
appointment is that I thought we would be in the Series
many years with that ball club in Philadelphia, but the
only time we made it was in 1950."

Robin started 13 season openers in the N.L., twelve of
them with the Phillies, the other with the Astros in 1966.

ROBERTSON, Don
    Glendale, AZ

Don appeared in 14 games with the Cubs in the outfield in 1954.   .000

ROBERTSON, Jim
    Real estate and mobile home park owner
    Peoria, IL

A former football and basketball player at Bradley University, Alfred Jim Robertson caught in 69 games with the 1954–55 Athletics in Philadelphia and Kansas City. For three decades his father was the football, basketball, and baseball coach at Bradley University in Peoria. The field-house at the university is named Robertson Fieldhouse in honor of his father.   .187

ROBERTSON, Sherry
    Died October 23, 1970, at age 51 in Houghton, SD

Sherry was a ten-year infielder-outfielder between the years 1940 and 1952 (most of which was spent with the Washington Senators—the team that happened to be owned by his uncle, Clark Griffith). He was often the victim of the fans' frustrations because of his inept hitting. His only year with another team was in 1952 when he played for the Philadelphia Athletics.

He was coach, farm director, and vice-president for the Twins following his playing days, until his death in an automobile accident in 1970.   .230

ROBINSON, Aaron
    Died March 9, 1966, at age 50
    Lancaster, OH

An nine-year A.L. catcher with four teams from 1943–51, Aaron was originally with the Yankees. He had his finest campaign in 1946, with 16 homers and a .297 average. The following year he shared the catching duties with Yogi

Berra. He was then traded to the White Sox for Eddie Lopat. After one season in Chicago, he was traded to Detroit for Billy Pierce. He finished with a .260 lifetime average after playing for the Red Sox in 1951.

ROBINSON, Brooks "The Vacuum Cleaner"
>   Management position with Crown Petroleum; partner in Personal Management Associates; Baltimore Orioles TV announcer

Up and down between the Orioles and minors in the late fifties, Brooks arrived to stay in 1959. Following his recall after the All-Star break, he was at third base in virtually all of the Orioles' games in the next fourteen and a half seasons until 1973, playing in 2,275 of a possible 2,323.

The holder of virtually every A.L. and major league record for fielding at third base, he also holds the mark for committing three errors in an inning on July 18, 1971, when the "vacuum cleaner" temporarily broke down.

Third base is the position most ignored by the Hall of Fame, but in 1983 Brooks and fellow inductee George Kell (both from Arkansas) joined Pie Traynor, Frank Baker, Jimmy Collins, Fred Lindstrom, Joe Sewell, and Eddie Mathews as Hall of Famers playing exclusively at the "hot corner."

Brooks hit into four triple plays during his career, making him the all-time leader for hitting into triple killings. He had 24 hits in championship playoff competition. Robinson, who attended Little Rock Junior College, played 22 years with the Orioles.

The clever fielding third baseman made only 263 errors in 9,165 chances for a lifetime .971 fielding percentage.

When Graig Nettles broke the A.L. career home-run mark for third baseman in 1980, Brooks remarked, "I wouldn't mind seeing someone erase my record of hitting into four triple plays."   .267

ROBINSON, Earl
> Professor at Laney College
> Berkeley, CA

A college basketball standout in the mid-1950s, Earl was signed by the Dodgers off the University of California campus. He arrived on the Los Angeles scene as a third baseman in '58.

Robinson spent three seasons in the early 1960s as an outfielder for the Orioles, and closed with a .268 average after 170 games.

ROBINSON, Eddie
> Front office aide (special assignments) for the New
> York Yankees

Eddie was a 13-year first baseman (1942–57) with three years out in the mid-forties for military service during the war. Robinson appeared in virtually every uniform in the A.L. during his playing days. He never played for the Red Sox or Browns, but did complete his career with the Orioles in 1957 after the team transferred from St. Louis.

His finest years were with the White Sox in the early fifties, especially in 1951 when he hit 29 homers and collected 117 RBIs. Despite just two and a half seasons in Chicago, he was voted the White Sox all-time first baseman in 1969.

As a member of the Yankees in '54, he was the A.L.'s top pinch-hitter at 15-for-49. His career totals include a .268 average and 172 home runs.

Since his playing career ended, he served the Astros, Braves, and Texas Rangers in an executive capacity before assuming his present position.

ROBINSON, Frank
> San Francisco Giants manager

Frank has numerous distinctions including his rookie record 38 homers for the Reds in 1956. He won MVP honors in both leagues when he led Cincinnati to the pennant in

1961, and the Orioles to the World Championship in '66—a
year he also won the triple crown.

A fierce competitor, Frank is also the only player to hit a
home run for both leagues in All-Star Game competition.
In 1970, he hit two grand-slam homers in the same game,
the last player to do so.

While a member of the Orioles, he used to preside over a
playful "Kangaroo Court" in the locker room after Baltimore victories. Because of his role playing, he was nicknamed "The Judge."

Major league baseball's first black manager, he was
also the first black manager to be fired. He was elected to
the Hall of Fame in 1982. Frank finished with 586 homers
and a .294 lifetime average.

ROBINSON, Humberto
    Panama

The first Panamanian to ever appear in the biggies,
Humberto pitched with the Milwaukee Braves, Indians,
and Phillies between 1955–60. The right-hander was 8-13
in 102 games.

ROBINSON, Jackie
    Died October 24, 1972, at age 53
    Stamford, CT

A star running back at UCLA, Jackie became the major
league's first modern-day black player in 1947. Breaking
this barrier was enough for immortality, but his career on
the field was also noteworthy. A first baseman with the
Dodgers in his first big league season, he won N.L.
"Rookie-of-the-Year" honors. In 1949 his .342 average and
37 stolen bases led the league. The daring base runner pilfered home 19 times in his career. He also stole home in
the 1955 World Series at age 36 against Whitey Ford and
the Yankees.

A man of "firsts," Jackie was the first player ever to hit
into a triple play on national television on the "Game of
the Week" in 1955.   .311

RODGERS, Andre
Nassau, Bahamas

An 11-year shortstop (1957–67), Andre was with the Giants in New York and San Francisco when he first came up in the late 1950s. Sent to the Cubs, he replaced "Mr. Cub" Ernie Banks at shortstop when Ernie switched to first base in the early 1960s. A good lowball hitter, he finished with the Pirates. Andre was an outstanding cricket player in his native Bahamas before turning to baseball.
.249

RODIN, Eric
Location unknown

A quarterback on the 1949 University of Pennsylvania freshman football team, Eric soon signed with the New York Giants. An outfielder, Rodin played in five games with the '54 Giants. .000

RODRIGUEZ, Fernando
Havana, Cuba

Fernando pitched in seven games with the Cubs in 1958. He appeared in one more game the following year with the Phillies. The right-hander had no decisions in his brief trip to the majors.

RODRIGUEZ, Hector
Havana, Cuba

In 1952, familiar names like Eddie Robinson (first base), Nellie Fox (second base), and Chico Carrasquel (shortstop) were regulars in the Chicago White Sox infield. Hector is the answer to the trivia question: "Who played third base for the White Sox in 1952?" He hit .265 in 124 games in his only season.

ROE, Elwin "Preacher"
Grocery store owner
West Plains, MO

Preacher had a losing record in four seasons with the Pirates in the mid-1940s, but he completely turned it around as a member of the Dodgers for seven campaigns from 1948–54. The left-hander was especially effective in '51 at 22-3, the lowest number of losses by a 20-game winner in modern times. He followed that up with 11-2 and 11-3 seasons for a three-year mark of 44-8. Following his playing days, he admitted to throwing a spitball.   127-84

ROEBUCK, Ed
Cincinnati Reds scout

Ed pitched 11 years in the big time. Plagued with a shoulder injury, he appeared washed up in 1958 after three effective seasons of relief work for the Brooklyn Dodgers. Roebuck returned in 1960 and was 20-5 over the next three years in L.A. Ed also pitched for the Senators and Phillies in the mid-sixties. His overall mark stands at 52-31 in 460 games—all but one of them in relief. Not an especially good hitting pitcher (with a lifetime .204 average), Ed was an expert with the fungo bat, and the only man to ever hit the roof of the Houston Astrodome.

ROGOVIN, Saul
English teacher at Eastern District high school
Brooklyn, NY

A right-handed pitcher, Saul spent nine seasons in the big top between 1949–57. Originally with the Tigers, he had his most success with the White Sox in 1951 and '52. His 2.78 ERA was best in the A.L. in '51, and he won a career high 14 games in 1952.   48-48

ROIG, Tony
    Philadelphia Phillies' scout for the state of Washington

Anton Ambrose "Tony" Roig was a utility infielder with the Washington Senators in 1953, and 1955–56. He hit .212 in 76 games.

ROJEK, Stan
    Dairy owner
    North Tonawanda, NY

A shortstop, Stan came up with Brooklyn in 1942 for one game, then was back with the Dodgers in 1946–47 after military service. Since Pee Wee Reese had the Dodgers' shortstop position filled, Stan went to Pittsburgh, where he had his finest season. In 1948 he led the league in at-bats (641) and hit .290. He also played for the Cards and Browns in the early fifties.   .266

ROMANO, Jim
    Retired New York City policeman; employed in payroll accounting for a company in New York, NY

Jim pitched in three games for his home town Brooklyn Dodgers in 1950. The right-hander failed to get a decision in his short stay.

ROMANO, John
    Automobile salesman
    Upper Saddle River, NJ

Originally with the White Sox in the late 1950s, he was a backup to Sherm Lollar on the 1959 A.L. champions. Romano was the Indians' number one catcher in the early 1960s before returning to the White Sox in the mid-1960s. He departed in 1967 with the Cardinals.   .255

ROMBERGER, Allen "Dutch"
    Owned a bar until he died on his 56th birthday, May
    16, 1983, in Weikert, PA

"Dutch" was 1-1 in 10 games for the '54 Philadelphia Athletics.

ROMONOSKY, John
    Sheriff's department
    Columbus, OH

John came up with the Browns in '53. The right-hander
also pitched with the Senators in 1958–59.   3-4

ROSAR, Warren "Buddy"
    Buffalo, NY

A 13-year catcher (1939–51), Buddy was Bill Dickey's
backup during his first four seasons in the majors with the
Yankees. Rosar then played for the Indians several years
before spending five campaigns as Connie Mack's catcher
for the Philadelphia Athletics. An outstanding defensive
backstop, he set the never-to-be-broken record of a 1.000
fielding average in over 100 games in 1946. He made his
exit in 1950 and '51 with the Red Sox.   .261

ROSEBORO, John
    All Sports Management
    Carson, CA

The successor to Roy Campanella as the Dodgers' catcher
in the late 1950s, John is best remembered for the incident
in which Juan Marichal swung his bat at him in Candlestick Park in August of 1965. He was on four Dodgers'
World Series teams, and in game one of the 1963 Series,
John hit a big three-run homer to lead L.A. to a 5-2 win in
the first of a four-game sweep over the Yankees.
    He was a coach for the Senators and Angels in the early
1970s. His autobiography, *Glory Days with the Dodgers,*
was published in 1978.   .249

ROSELLI, Bob
> Baltimore Orioles scout; liquor salesman for Regal
> Beverage Inc.
> Redwood City, CA

"The Lawrence Welk Show" entertained the nation with
its "bubbly" music in 1955 when this bubbly backstop arrived with the Milwaukee Braves. Bob also played sparingly with the Braves in '56 and '58. His 68-game cruise
fizzled with the White Sox in 1961–62.   .219

ROSEN, Al "Flip"
> Houston Astros general manager

A leap year baby, born February 29, 1924, Al was a
26-year-old rookie in 1950 when he led the A.L. in homers
with 37. Cleveland's regular third baseman until retiring
in 1956, Al compiled some awesome statistics, especially
in 1953 when he was named the A.L. MVP and narrowly
missed the triple crown. He was the league-leader in
homers (43) and RBIs (145), but missed the batting title by
just one point, .337 to .336, to Mickey Vernon. His 43
homers is still an A.L. record for most four-baggers in a
season by a third baseman.

He had a pair of homers and 5 RBIs in leading the A.L.
to an 11-9 win in the 1954 All-Star Game, played before
68,751 fans at Cleveland. "Flip" was the first third baseman—since Frank (Home Run) Baker in 1913—to win
homer and RBI titles.

Before making it with the Indians as a regular in 1950,
Al once hit home runs in five consecutive at-bats in a two-
day period on July 26–27, at Kansas City in the American
Association.

After several years with a brokerage firm in Cleveland,
he was back in baseball in a Yankee executive position,
and was often involved in the middle of the Billy Martin-
George Steinbrenner soap opera in the late 1970s. Rosen
was called "Flip" because of his junior high school days
when he was a touted softball pitcher, or "flipper." He was
sometimes labeled "The Hebrew Hammer."   .285

ROSS, Cliff
      Cliff Ross Aluminum Products
      Roslyn, PA

Cliff pitched in four games without a decision for the '54
Reds. He hurled three innings of hitless-scoreless relief in
those four games, and had a spotless 0.00 ERA, but never
again appeared in the biggies.

ROSS, Floyd R. "Bob"
      Assistant superintendent of schools in the Anaheim,
      CA, school district

Bob broke in with the Senators in 1950. The following year
he pitched briefly with Washington and also saw spotty action with the Phillies in '56. He lost two decisions in 20
games. Bob is a graduate of Long Beach State in California.

ROSSI, Joe
      Albany, CA

The famed Rogers Hornsby managed at Seattle in the PCL
in '51 when Joe was a catcher on the Portland team.
Hornsby commented that Rossi would never be a major
league catcher.
      In '52 Joe was brought up by the Reds. Hornsby, fired as
manager of the Browns early in '52, arrived at Crosley
Field in Cincinnati for a special Hall of Fame celebrities
night. Rossi spotted Hornsby and got sweet revenge,
jeering at Hornsby, "I'm in the major leagues, and you're
not." A few weeks later, Rogers replaced the fired Luke
Sewell as manager of the Reds. And you guessed it—Rossi
became an ex-big leaguer. Joe hit .221 in 55 games.

ROTBLATT, Marv
      Insurance salesman
      Chicago, IL

Marv fought his way up in the biggies with his home
town Chicago White Sox in 1948. He also saw action

with the "Hose" in 1950–51. Overall the southpaw went 4-3.

ROY, Norm
Bedford, MA

Do you remember Snooky Lanson and Dorothy Collins as they helped to make "Your Hit Parade" a Saturday night feature beginning in 1950? How about Norm Roy, who was never much of a hit, but did go 4-3 in 19 games with the Boston Braves?

ROZEK, Dick
Manufacturer's representative
Also has own company—Centric Inc.
Cedar Rapids, IA

A southpaw chucker, Dick spent parts of five seasons with Cleveland and the Philadelphia A's from 1950–54, but was involved in just one decision—a win—in 33 career contests.

RUDOLPH, Don
Died in an auto accident, September 12, 1968, at age 37 in Encino, CA

Don was with the White Sox and Reds in the late 1950s. Before becoming a regular in the starting rotation for the expansion Senators, he pitched in one game for the Indians. In 1962 and '63 he compiled marks of 8-10 and 7-19. Noted for being an especially quick worker, this swift lefty was often involved in games lasting less than two hours. He was possibly in a hurry to get home to his wife, who was a striptease dancer known as "Patti Waggin."   18-32

RUFER, Rudy
L.A. Dodgers special assignment scout

A shortstop for the N.Y. Giants in 1949–50, Rudy was with us for two years. In 22 games he had 2 hits, scored 2 runs, collected 2 RBIs, and walked 2 times. He broke in at age 22.   .077

RUNNELS, Pete
Sporting goods store
Pasadena, TX

A 14-year performer, James E. "Pete" Runnels played in over 600 games at both first base and second base and another 400-plus at shortstop. He also played some third base and one game in the outfield. A left-handed line-drive hitter, Runnels was with Washington from 1951 to 1957. From 1958 to 1962 he had five straight .300-plus seasons for the Red Sox. Twice he won the A.L. batting title—in 1960 (.320) and '62 (.326). On August 30, 1960, he tied a major league record with 9 hits in a doubleheader. He finished in 1964 with the expansion Astros. Runnels was the first player in All-Star Game history to execute an unassisted double play (in the second game) in 1959. In 1972, Astros' first baseman Lee May duplicated the feat.   .291

RUSH, Bob
Sales coordinator for Motorola Corp.
Mesa, AZ

A big right-handed chucker, who was generally the ace of the Cubs pitching staff during most of the 1950s, Bob suffered through many losing seasons on losing teams—most notably in 1950 when his 20 losses led the N.L.

His finest campaign was in 1952 when he was 17-13, and was the winning pitcher in the All-Star Game. In 1958 he was 10-6 for the N.L. pennant-winning Milwaukee Braves. He started and lost the third game of the World Series, 4-0, to the Yankees. Bob had an overall mark of 127-152, despite a respectable 3.65 ERA.

RUSSELL, Jim
Sales manager for SCM Typewriters
Belle Vernon, PA

A 10-year N.L. outfielder (1942–51), Jim was a regular in the Pirates' outfield in the mid-1940s, and had his finest season in 1944 when he hit .312. He was with the N.L.

champion Boston Braves in 1948, and ended in 1950 and '51 with the Dodgers.

Playing with the Pirates on opening day in 1945, Jim was deprived of a home run because a base runner had called "Time" to tie his shoe. The opposing pitcher didn't hear "Time" called, and delivered the pitch.   .267

RUTHERFORD, Johnny
Doctor at the River Rouge Clinic
Dearborn, MI

Okay numerologists, check this one out! Not to be confused with the Indianapolis driver, Johnny pitched just one year in the big leagues (1952) with the N.L. pennant-winning Dodgers. He was 7-7 in 22 games. Rutherford was 2-2 in relief, and 5-5 as a starter. He gave up 97 hits in 97 innings pitched. Johnny walked 29 batters and fanned 29. In the '52 World Series he pitched 1 game and in 1 inning gave up 1 hit, 1 walk, and collected 1 strikeout. His birthday comes up on May 5th, that's 5/5. No kidding!

RYAN, Connie
Texas Rangers special assignment scout

A 12-year infielder, Connie was used mostly at second base, although he also played all other infield positions. Originally with the Giants in 1942, he spent the remainder of the '40s as the Boston Braves' second baseman. In the early 1950s he was with the Reds and Phillies, and briefly in the A.L. with the White Sox.

On April 16, 1953, he connected for six hits in six at-bats as a member of the Phils. Unfortunately his efforts were futile as the Phillies lost to the Pirates, 14-12. In the fifth inning of that game, the Phils scored 9 runs and the Pirates 6 to tie a modern N.L. record.

Only he and Warren Spahn were in uniform for both Braves' appearances in the World Series in 1948 and 1957. Ryan was a Braves' coach in '57, and then again wore a Braves' uniform when the team was in Atlanta, when he was on the coaching staff in the early 1970s. Connie was also a coach with the Texas Rangers.   .248

S

SACKA, Frank
Supervisor
Palmer-Smith construction company
Wyandotte, MI

Frank came up as a catcher with the Senators in 1951. He saw brief action again in '53, and finished his 14-game career with a .265 average.

SAFFELL, Tom
Painting contractor
Sarasota, FL

Tom arrived with the Pirates in 1949 where he played until 1951. After an absence of three years, he returned in '55 with the Pirates, and also spent time with the K.C. A's. The outfielder swung for a .238 average.

SAIN, Johnny
Pitching coach for the Richmond Braves of the International League

Of "Spahn and Sain and Pray for Rain" fame, John was a 24-game winner for the 1948 NL champion Braves. He also won over 20 games three other years. Traded to the Yankees in '51, he was an 11- and 14-game winner the next two seasons for the A.L. and World Series champions. He was the winning pitcher in relief in game one of the '53 World Series. Sain was used exclusively in relief in '54 when he led the A.L. in saves with 22. Overall he was 139-116.

John was the starting pitcher for the Boston Braves on

April 15, 1947, vs. Brooklyn, when Jackie Robinson de-
buted for the Dodgers. He also threw the last pitch ever to
Babe Ruth during a war-time fund-raising game at Yankee Stadium.

An outstanding hitting pitcher, among his accomplish-
ments with the bat are a .346 average in 1947 (including a
14-game hitting streak). He was the only pitcher to ever
lead the league in sacrifice hits (with 16 in 1948).

ST. CLAIRE, Ebba
Produced Ebba's Batting Aids; was in the insurance
business when he died on August 22, 1982, at age 61,
in Whitehall, NY

Edward (Ebba) St. Claire caught for the Boston and
Milwaukee Braves from 1951–53. His next stop was the
Polo Grounds, where he played for the champion New
York Giants in 1954.

Catching for the Braves in '51, he once took part in three
double plays in one game. His 164 big league games saw
him bat .249. Of course, that was before Ebba's Batting
Aids were marketed.

SALKELD, Bill
Died April 22, 1967, at age 50
Los Angeles, CA

A catcher with the Pirates and Boston Braves in the late
1940s, he played in one game with the White Sox in 1950.
Several years before he reached the majors, he was a
player-manager at the age of 22 in the Arizona-Texas
League.

His finest season in the big time came as a 28-year-old
rookie with the Pirates in '45, with a .311 average and 15
homers. He shared the catching duties with Phil Masi on
the '48 N.L. champion Boston Braves. In the World Series,
one of his two hits was a home run.　　　　　　　.273

SAMCOFF, Ed
Englewood, CO

In 1951 the Philadelphia A's turned off Ed after 4 games at second base. .000

SAMFORD, Ron
Texas Auto Transmission
Dallas, TX

Ron played in 158 games, enjoying his best season in 1959 with the Senators, filling in at second base and shortstop. Samford broke in with the Giants in 1954. The infielder then wore a Tiger uniform in one game in '55, and 54 contests the following year. .219

SANCHEZ, Raul
Construction worker
Carol City, FL

Raul arrived in '52. During his rookie year, Sanchez hurled a shutout in one of his two starts. He also worked out of the Cincinnati Reds' bullpen in 1957 and 1960. Pitching for the Reds on May 15, 1960, Raul plunked three Phillies' batters in the same inning (the last being pitcher Gene Conley). The beaning spree triggered a wild brawl between the teams. In 49 big league games, Raul was 5-3.

SANDLOCK, Mike
Building contractor
Old Greenwich, CT

Mike started out as an infielder with the Boston Braves and Brooklyn Dodgers in the early 1940s before switching to catching. He returned after several years' absence in 1953 with the Pirates, exclusively to handle the knuckleballs of Johnny Lindell, a former Yankee outfielder who had switched to the mound. The pair had been batterymates at PCL champion Hollywood in 1952. .240

SANFORD, Fred
> Water Department
> Salt Lake City, UT

A right-handed chucker with the Browns in the late forties, Fred was the A.L. leader in losses (with 21) in 1948, then got a reprieve and spent the 1949 and 1950 seasons with the World Champion Yankee teams, winning a dozen games as a spot starter and reliever. In his final campaign in 1951, he went from the Yankees to the Senators, and back to the St. Louis Browns.

Sanford closed out at 37-55, including a pair of shutouts in his first two big league victories in 1946.

SANFORD, Jack
> Baltimore Orioles scout and golf pro
> West Palm Beach, FL

Jack was a 19-game winner as a 28-year-old rookie with the Phillies in 1957, and was named the N.L. "Rookie of the Year." Traded to the S.F. Giants in 1959, his six shutouts led the league in 1960, but his big season came in 1962 when he was 24-7, including 16 wins in a row at one point as the Giants won the N.L. pennant. He later pitched with the California Angels and Kansas City A's. At 137-101 overall, he tied a then-Phillies' record by fanning 13 Cubs in a 1-0 victory on June 7, 1957.

SANICKI, Ed
> Special Education teacher
> Clifton, NJ

As an outfielder in 7 games with the Phillies in 1949, Ed was 3-for-13 at the plate, with all three hits being home runs, including one in his first major league at-bat. He was in 10 more games with the Phils in '51, and went 2-for-4 to finish 5-for-17 for a .294 mark, counting a double and three homers among his five major league hits.

SANTIAGO, Jose
Rio Piedras, PR

Jose Santiago was 3-2 in 27 games for the Indians and
Kansas City A's between 1954–56.

SARNI, Bill
Stock broker
Kirkwood, MO

A catcher, Bill was 23 years old when he arrived with the
Cardinals in 1951. Unknown to many, he played one level
below the majors with Los Angeles (PCL) back in 1943, at
just 15 years of age.

As the regular catcher for the Cardinals, he led N.L.
backstops in fielding percentage, and hit an even .300 in
123 games. Traded to the N.Y. Giants in 1956, his career
was cut short by a heart attack during spring training of
1958.   .263

SAUCIER, Frank
President of Chemical Industries; vice-president and
director for First Savings and Loan Association
Borger, TX

Frank is the only man in big league history who could say
he was pinch-hit for by a midget—Eddie Gaedel went to bat
for him in 1951 for the Browns. The 1950 Southern Association batting champion, Frank was 1-for-14 in his brief
stay.   .071

SAUER, Hank
S.F. Giants scout and hitting instructor

A long-ball-hitting outfielder, Hank was originally with
the Reds in the early 1940s. He returned to stay in 1948
following a 50-home-run season in the International
League in 1947. From 1948–52 he was never under 30
homers per season, and in '52 his 37 tied Ralph Kiner for

the league lead, and his 121 RBIs led the league as he was named the N.L. MVP despite the Cubs' fifth-place finish.

He hit a career high 41 homers in 1954, including a N.L. record 13 against the Pirates (later tied by Joe Adcock in '56). On June 11, 1954, Sauer hit three solo round-trippers off Curt Simmons of the Phils, to beat them, 3-2, at Chicago.

Before calling it quits, Hank played with the Cardinals and Giants. His brother, Ed, was also an outfielder in the forties (with the Cubs, Cardinals, and Boston Braves). Hank's totals read: 288 homers and a .266 average.

SAVERINE, Bob
    Account executive for Merrill Lynch Brokerage
    Stamford, CT

Next to Tim McCarver, Bob is the youngest of the former players of the fifties decade. He was just 18 when he appeared in one game in 1959. Bob later returned to the Orioles, and also played as an infield-outfielder with the Senators in the mid-1960s.   .239

SAVRANSKY, Morris "Moe"
    Steel Distributor
    Chicago, IL

Moe lost his only two decisions in 16 games with the Reds in '54.

SAWATSKI, Carl
    President of the Class AA Texas League

The first Shickshinny, Pa., native to ever reach the big show, Carl spent 11 years in the biggies, generally as a backup receiver with the Cubs, White Sox, Braves, Phillies, and Cardinals. "Swat" was named the top minor league executive at the AA level in 1970 as General Manager of the Arkansas team in the Texas League.   .242

SCALA, Jerry
    Location unknown

Jerry broke in with the White Sox in 1948. He batted .223 in 80 games for the "Hose" from 1948–50.

SCANTLEBURY, Pat
    Truck driver for Hodges-Rental catering company
    Montclair, NJ

The last black player to ever go directly from the Negro Leagues to the majors, this Panamanian southpaw lost his lone decision in six games, pitching for the Reds in 1956. At this writing Pat still remains in the game as a pitching coach for a Clifton, N.J., semi-pro team, and he plays third base.

SCARBOROUGH, Ray
    Special assignment scout for the Milwaukee Brewers
    at the time of his death, July 1, 1983, at age 64, in Mt.
    Olive, NC

A Wake Forest graduate, Ray was with the Senators in the early forties, then again from 1946 until he was dealt to the White Sox in 1950. The right-hander enjoyed his finest year in '48 when he logged a 15-8 mark. He was with the Red Sox, Yankees, and Tigers in the early fifties. After joining the Yankees in '52, he helped them win the pennant by going 5-1 down the stretch as the Yanks nosed out the Indians. Ray finished 80-85.

SCHACHT, Sid
    Retired
    Delray Beach, FL

Sid was listed on the Browns roster in 1950. In his 19-game career, the right-hander pitched briefly with the Boston Braves as well. Sid threw his last big league pitch in 1951 and closed out at 0-2.

SCHAEFFER, Harry
Athletic Director at Cocalico High School
Denver, PA

Harry went 0-1 in five games with the Yanks in '52.

SCHAFFERNOTH, Joe
Production manager, T.R.W. Palnut
Mountainside, NJ

The right-hander was 3-8 in 74 games with the Cubs and
Indians from 1959–61.

SCHAIVE, Johnny
Insurance salesman
Springfield, IL

In 1958 Bobby Freeman was singing "Do You Want To
Dance"; the Elegants had a big hit with "Little Star"; and
Johnny twinkled briefly with the Senators as a utility infielder where he spent parts of five seasons (1958–60,
1962–63). His most sparkling effort came in '62 when he
batted .253.   .232

SCHALLOCK, Art
California Land Title Co.
Novato, CA

This southpaw flipper pitched in part of five seasons with
the Yankees, from 1951–55. He spent most of the 1955
campaign with the Orioles, his last in the biggies.   6-7

SCHANZ, Charley
Petroleum company plant manager
Sacramento, CA

A right-handed chucker, Charley was with the A's (1944–47),
then with the Red Sox in 1950. After 155 games he was
28-43.

SCHEFFING, Bob
  N.Y. Mets special consultant
  Scottsdale, AZ

A manager in the low minors in the late 1930s while just in his twenties, he came up to the Chicago Cubs in 1941 as a catcher. After World War II he was with them from 1946–50, and spent his final year as a player in the N.L. with the Reds and Cardinals. Following his playing days, Bob was a coach for the St. Louis Browns and Cubs, before becoming their manager in the late 1950s. He was at the helm of the Tigers in 1961, leading them to a second-place finish behind the powerful Yankees. He later became general manager and vice-president of the Mets.   .263

SCHEIB, Carl
  Sales representative
  San Antonio, TX

Carl was the youngest player ever to play in the American League. He was a 16-year-old chucker with the Philadelphia A's in 1943. A right-hander, he had his finest season in 1948, going 14-8. A solid-hitting pitcher, who was often used as a pinch-hitter, he played several games in the outfield and hit for a .396 average in 1951 (a year he struggled through a 1-12 mark on the mound).

  Overall he was 45-65 in an 11-year stint which came to an end with the Cardinals in 1954, when he was only 27.

SCHELL, Danny
  Died May 11, 1972, at age 44 in Mayville, MI

Clyde (Danny) Schell came up to the Phillies as an outfielder after winning the Eastern League batting title in 1953. He hit .283 in 92 games for the Phillies in '54, then never reappeared in the big leagues after just two games in '55.   .281

SCHENZ, Hank
  General contractor
  Tillar Brothers, Inc.
  Cincinnati, OH

Hank broke in with the Cubs in 1946. An infielder in parts of six N.L. seasons with the Cubs, Pirates, and Giants, Hank batted .247 during his 207-game journey.

SCHERBARTH, Bob
  Process artist lithographer for Graphics Unlimited
  Milwaukee, WI

The Red Sox used four catchers in 1950—Birdie Tebbetts, Matt Batts, Buddy Rosar, and Bob Scherbarth. Bob caught in one big league game, his only shot in the majors.   .000

SCHMEES, George
  Bernard Food Industries
  San Jose, CA

Invisible Man by Ralph Ellison was a best seller in 1952. George became invisible after the '52 season—his only one in the big time. Schmees was an outfielder with the Browns and Red Sox. He also pitched in a couple of games, including one start for the Bosox. He had no decisions and allowed just two runs in six innings. His .168 batting average might have precipitated his move to the mound.

SCHMIDT, Bob
  Foreman, C. Sansone Co.
  St. Louis, MO

1958 was the beginning of Bob's big league trip as a rookie catcher for the Giants. He also played for the Reds, Senators, and Yankees in the early sixties.   .243

SCHMIDT, Willard
General manager for a Subaru dealership
Norman, OK

Willard spent eight seasons (1952–1959) with the Cardinals and Reds. His finest year was in '57 with a 10-3 mark for St. Louis. On April 26, 1959, Willard became the first player in big league history to get hit by a pitch twice in the same inning. The following frame he was hit on the pitching hand by a line drive while on the mound, and had to leave the game.   31-29

SCHMITZ, Johnny
Golf course greenskeeper
Wausau, WI

"Bear Tracks" was a southpaw starter for the Cubs during the forties, missing three years in the military during World War II. His relatively low figure of 135 strikeouts was the most in the N.L. in 1946. Johnny's 18 losses in '47 also topped the league, but he came back to have his best year in 1948 with 18 wins. From 1951–56 he was with several teams in both leagues, including the Yankees and Dodgers. Because of his strange way of walking, players called him "Bear Tracks."   93-114

SCHOENDIENST, Albert "Red"
St. Louis Cardinals coach

An outfielder in his maiden season in 1945, he led the N.L. in stolen bases with 26 as a Cardinal rookie. He moved to second base on a regular basis the following year for the N.L. pennant winners, and remained a fixture there for the next decade until he was traded to the New York Giants in 1956. The switch-hitting infielder set a record for most two-base hits in three consecutive games when he hit 8 in 1948. In 1950 his 43 doubles led the N.L. Red hit just 7 homers, but his 14th-inning blast gave the N.L. a victory in the All-Star Game that summer.

Traded to Milwaukee during the '57 season, he became a key factor in the Braves' drive to two consecutive N.L.

flags. Stricken with tuberculosis after the '58 campaign, he returned to the Braves late in 1960, then completed his 19-year career with a pair of .300-plus seasons with his old team, the Cardinals.

Red later coached and managed St. Louis, taking over in a tough situation in 1965 when the World Championship team lost their manager, Johnny Keane, to the Yankees. In '67 and '68 Red piloted the Cards to the N.L. flag, winning the World Series in '67.

His 2,449 base hits rank him in the top 60 of all time, but in 1969, when fans across the country voted for their all-time teams in conjunction with baseball's 100th anniversary, Rogers Hornsby was named as the Cardinals' all-time second baseman. Interestingly enough, Red was named as the Braves' all-time second baseman, a team with which he played for only three seasons.   .289

SCHOFIELD, Dick
Member of Illinois Youth Commission
Springfield, IL

"Ducky" Schofield joined the Cardinals in 1953 at age 17, and was tossed out of a big league game before ever appearing in one when umpire Augie Donatelli accused him of being the player who tossed a towel out of the dugout while manager Eddie Stanky was arguing a call with him. Dick did get into over 1,300 games over the next two decades. It is doubtful if any other player of the era played with more distinguished teammates. At one time or another he played with Stan Musial, Roberto Clemente, Willie Mays, Mickey Mantle, Whitey Ford, Sandy Koufax, Bob Gibson, and Carl Yastrzemski.

Primarily a shortstop, he spent most of his career in a utility role. In 1960 he hit .333 and filled in admirably for the injured Dick Groat down the stretch as the Pirates won the N.L. pennant. "Ducky" did likewise with the Dodgers in 1966, and then back with his original team (St. Louis) in 1968. A .227 lifetime average, the $40,000 bonus baby also attended Springfield Junior College.

Dick's son arrived in the majors in 1983 with the California Angels.

SCHOONMAKER, Jerry
    Lebanon, MO

An outfielder with the Senators, Jerry played in 50 games in 1955 and '57 with an anemic .130 batting average. He attended the University of Missouri, where he was a key member of the 1954 NCAA baseball championship team, as well as captain of the football team.

SCHRAMKA, Paul
    Mortician
    Milwaukee, WI

Paul was an outfielder in two games with the Cubs in 1953, which is two more games than most of us ever played in the majors. The former University of San Francisco athlete went hitless.

SCHROLL, Al
    Sears department store employee
    Alexandria, VA

Al made his debut with the Red Sox in 1958. The right-hander was also on the mound staff of the Phillies, Cubs, and Twins during his four-year flight which lasted from 1958–61.   6-9

SCHULT, Art
    District manager—LeaseTex Systems Inc.
    Mount Vernon, N.Y.

"Dutch" was originally Yankee property. In 1953 he appeared in seven games with the pinstripers, all of them as a pinch-runner. Although he never batted or played the field, he did score three runs.
    Art returned in '56 with the Reds, and also played with the Senators and Cubs until 1960. After 164 games, he had a .264 lifetime average. "Dutch" attended Georgetown University.

SCHULTZ, Barney
      Pitching coach for the Nankai Hawks
      Japan

George "Barney" Schultz first appeared on the mound for
the Cardinals in 1955. He returned to the majors a few
years later, and in 1962 tied a then-big league record by
appearing in nine straight games out of the Cubs' bullpen.
But it was late in the '64 season that he had his most success. Recalled from the minors, he was credited with 14
saves down the stretch for the Cardinals as they overtook
the Phillies for the N.L. pennant. Barney was credited
with a save in the opening game of the World Series. In the
third game he was the losing pitcher despite throwing just
one pitch—a home run ball to Mickey Mantle as the first
batter in the bottom of the ninth—which gave the Yankees a 2-1 victory.   20-20

SCHULTZ, Bob
      Died March 31, 1979, at age 53 in Nashville, TN

In 1951 Bob came up with the Cubs to begin a five-year career (1951–55). The right-hander was 9-13 overall, pitching with the Cubs, Pirates, and Tigers.

SCHYPINSKI, Jerry
      Electrician
      Detroit, MI

Bill Haley and the Comets' "Rock Around the Clock," one
of the biggest-selling singles in rock history, appeared on
the charts in 1955. The sound was wild and infectious.
Jerry was rather calm and immune to the whole thing at
shortstop in 22 games for the K.C. A's, in his only season
in the biggies.   .217

SCORE, Herb
      Cleveland Indians announcer

Billed as the left-handed Bob Feller, Herb might have been
one of the greatest pitchers in big league history had his

career not been ruined when he was struck in the eye by a line drive off the bat of the Yankees' Gil McDougald on May 7, 1957.

The Cleveland phenom averaged over a strikeout per inning in leading the A.L. in strikeouts his first two seasons. As a rookie, the brilliant southpaw recorded 245 K's—the most strikeouts ever by a rookie. On March 19, 1957, the Red Sox offered the Indians one million dollars for Score's services.

Following a 16-win season his first year, he was a 20-game winner for the '56 Indians, pitching alongside a famed mound staff of Bob Lemon, Early Wynn and Mike Garcia.

After his accident he struggled to regain his form from 1958-62. Although he did fan 13 White Sox and shut them out early in '58, he never was the same. The White Sox picked him up in 1960, where he called it quits two years later—a dark ending to a bright prospect.   55-46

SEGRIST, Kal
Baseball coach at Texas Tech

Kal came up with the Yankees as an infielder in 1952. He appeared again briefly in 1955 with the Orioles. His 20-game jaunt shows a .125 average.

SEMINICK, Andy
Phillies scout
Melbourne, FL

A long-time catcher, Andy first showed up with the Phillies in 1943. He was a 30-year-old veteran in his eighth big league season as the regular backstop for the 1950 Phillies when he had his finest year, hitting .288 with 24 homers. He was with Cincinnati (1952–1954) before returning to the Phillies where it all ended in 1957.

Andy had a lifetime .243 average in over 1,300 games with 164 home runs, including two in one inning and three in one game on June 2, 1949. Andy was voted as the Phillies' All-Time Catcher in 1969, and has remained in

the organization as a coach, minor league manager, instructor, and scout since his playing days ended.

SEMPROCH, Ray
　　Owns Broglio's Restaurant in Bethel, OH

Roman "Ray" Semproch was 13-11 as a rookie with the
Phillies in 1958. Ray fell off to 3-10 his second year, then
was with the Tigers and Angels in 1960–61.　　　　19-21

SENERCHIA, Sonny
　　School teacher
　　Ocean, NJ

In 1952 Emanuel "Sonny" Senerchia appeared in 29
games as a third baseman with the Pirates. Following his
brief act, "Sonny" became a concert violinist. With a .220
average, "Sonny's" music was not too sweet in the ears of
the Pirates' brass.

SERENA, Bill
　　Central Scouting Bureau

Bill was a Chicago Cubs' second baseman and third baseman (1949–1954) in his six-year stay. He had a .251 average in over 400 games, including 48 homers. Before
arriving in the majors, he was at Lubbock, Texas, in the
West Texas-New Mexico League, where he hit 57 homers,
plus another 13 in 7 post-season playing games for 70
home runs in 1948.

SHANNON, Wally
　　Manufacturer's agent for Industrial Packing
　　Creve Coeur, MO

No relation to former Cards' third baseman Mike Shannon, Wally was a second baseman-shortstop in 65 games
(1959–60) with the St. Louis Cardinals. During this time
his father, Walter Shannon, was the Cardinals' director of
player personnel.　　　　　　　　　　　　　　.263

SHANTZ, Bobby
        Dairy bar manager
        Chalfont, PA

Bobby threw nine innings of hitless relief ball in his second major league game with the Philadelphia A's in 1949. He finished just 6-8 that season, but in 1952, the 5'6" 140-pounder was the big name in baseball as he went 24-7 for a .774 winning percentage—both tops in the league— and was named MVP in the A.L. He suffered a fractured wrist when hit by a pitch late in '52, and the next four years he struggled with a sore arm, winning just 13 games in four seasons. He joined the Yankees in '57 and had a 2.45 ERA (best in the A.L.) to go with his 11-5 record.

The little southpaw was the first player selected in the expansion draft in the early 1960s by the Senators. But he was traded to the Pirates before he ever got a chance to pitch for Washington.

Bobby was 119-99 overall and the winner of eight Gold Gloves for his fielding prowess on the mound.

SHANTZ, Wilmer
        Sporting goods business
        Fort Lauderdale, FL

"Billy" Shantz was Bobby's batterymate in Philadelphia and Kansas City in 1954-55. He also caught in a game for the Yankees in 1960 at the time Bobby was with New York. Bobby's younger but somewhat bigger brother hit for a .257 average in 131 career games.

SHAW, Bob
        New York Yankees scout

Bob had a brief trial with the Tigers in 1957 and '58 before finding success with the White Sox in '59, going 18-6 as a member of the 1959 A.L. champions. Shaw was also with Kansas City and several N.L. teams in a career which culminated in 1967 at 108-98.

When balk rules were being enforced more strictly in 1963, he set dubious records of most-balks in a season (with 8), and in a game (with 5). He also had 3 in one inning. Bob was later a Dodgers pitching instructor, and pitching coach with the Milwaukee Brewers.

SHEA, Frank "Spec," "The Naugatuck Nugget"
　　Recreation director and Superintendent of Parks
　　Naugatuck, CT

"Spec" won't forget his rookie season in 1947 when he won two World Series games pitching for the Yanks. He was part of an all-rookie battery that season when he teamed with Yogi Berra. He went 14-5 his rookie year, and was the winning pitcher in the All-Star Game.

Frank became one of just three rookies to ever start and win a World Series opener, beating Brooklyn 5-3 with relief help from Joe Page.

Traded to the Senators in 1952, he finished in Washington in 1955. The right-hander was called "Spec" because of his freckles as a young boy.　　　　　　　　　56-46

SHEARER, Ray
　　Employed with Preston Trucking Co. when he died on
　　February 22, 1982, at age 52, in Manchester, PA

Ray played in two games for the 1957 Braves. The outfielder collected one hit in two tries for a .500 average.

SHEELY, Bud
　　Restaurant owner
　　Sacramento, CA

Hollis "Bud" Sheely was a catcher in 101 games for the Chicago White Sox from 1951–53. His father, Earl, was the White Sox first baseman throughout most of the 1920s.
　　　　　　　　　　　　　　　　　　　　.210

SHEPARD, Jack
> Executive vice-president and director of finance and
> administration
> TAB Products
> Atherton, CA

A college All-American out of Stanford in 1953, Jack hit
.304 as a rookie catcher in 82 games for the 1954 Pirates.
Slowed by an ankle injury, he remained through 1956 with
a .260 lifetime average.

The Stanford graduate picked up a master's degree in
education and business administration in the off season
during his playing days.

SHERRY, Larry
> L.A. Dodgers minor league pitching coach

Although Lew Burdette had personally won three games
in the 1957 World Series for the Milwaukee Braves, Larry
Sherry had a hand in all four Dodger wins in the '59 Series
against the White Sox, as he came out of the bullpen to
save games two and three for Johnny Podres and Don
Drysdale, and was the winning pitcher in game four, and
in the clinching game six. He had been recalled late in the
year by L.A., and compiled a 7-2 mark down the stretch.
The right-hander continued to work effectively in relief for
the Dodgers and Tigers before ending with the Angels and
Astros. Four hundred of his 416 appearances were in relief.   53-44

SHERRY, Norm
> San Diego Padres pitching coach

The catching end of the last brother battery, Norm was a
Dodger backup receiver (1959–62), and was with the Mets
in '63. He had a .215 average in 194 games.

Norm was later a California Angels coach and manager.
                                                      .215

SHETRONE, Barry
Insurance company employee
Baltimore, MD

A graduate of the same Baltimore high school which produced Hall of Famer Al Kaline, Barry was the first home town product to ever wear an Orioles uniform in 1959. Overall he appeared in 60 games with the Orioles and Senators from 1959–63, hitting .205 as an outfielder.

SHIFFLETT, Garland
Warehouseman for Coors Brewery
Lakewood, CO

A right-handed hurler, Garland had no decisions in six games for the Senators in 1957. His next big league try came with the Twins in 1964 when he went 0-2.

SHIPLEY, Joe
General Motors employee
St. Louis, MO

Joe spent parts of the 1958, '59, and '60 seasons with the S.F. Giants, failing to gain a decision. He finished with the White Sox in 1963 at 0-1 lifetime.

SHOOP, Ron
Rural Valley, PA

Soviet Premier Nikita Khrushchev visited the United States in 1959, but was denied entrance to Disneyland. Ron Shoop was allowed entrance to the big leagues that year for three games, but probably wished he had gone to Disneyland. As a catcher with the Detroit Tigers, Ron was 1-for-7 at the plate.   .143

SHORT, Chris
  Insurance agent
  Wilmington, DE

Chris made his debut with the Phillies in 1959. A stamp collector, the "Philatelist" Phillie was a top-flight chucker in the sixties, combining with Jim Bunning to give the team a formidable front line starting staff. On September 13, 1963, he set a Phillies' club record for a left-handed pitcher by striking out fourteen in a 3-2 victory over the Dodgers.

Short was the winning pitcher in the final game ever played at the Polo Grounds on Sept. 18, 1963, when the Phillies beat the Mets, 5-1. In 1966 he became the Phillies' first southpaw hurler to win 20 games since Eppa Rixey in 1916.

Chris finished in 1973 with the Milwaukee Brewers. Overall 135-132, writers must have had a field day when Short pitched against Long.

SHUBA, George
  Postal employee
  Youngstown, OH

"Shotgun" Shuba is not as readily recalled as some of the other names from those glory days in Flatbush, but in 1952 George hit .305 in 94 games, and was an even .300 in the World Series. He hit a two-run, pinch-hit home run in his only plate appearance in the '53 Series. George spent his entire seven-year run with Brooklyn, closing in 1955, the year the Dodgers finally won a World Series.

A .259 average in 355 games overall, he was known as "Shotgun" because line drive hits jumped from his bat like bullets.

SIEBERN, Norm
  Insurance business; scouts for Kansas City Royals
  Naples, FL

Originally with the Yankees as an outfielder in 1956, he hit an even .300 in his first full season in '58. Despite being

remembered for losing two fly balls in the sun in left field
at Yankee Stadium in game four of the World Series
(which accounted for all the Braves' runs in a 3-0 win),
Norm was the Gold Glove winner for fielding in '58. Following the '59 campaign he was traded to Kansas City in
the deal which saw Roger Maris come to the Yankees.

Siebern became a first baseman for the A's, and had his
finest year in '62 with career highs in homers—25, RBIs—
117, and batting average—.308.

Norm also played for the Orioles, Angels, and Giants before completing his travels with the Red Sox—joining
former teammate Elston Howard down the stretch in the
Red Sox A.L. pennant-winning season of 1967.   .272

SIEVERS, Roy
Truck company supervisor
St. Louis, MO

Several distinctions mark the career of this first baseman-outfielder, who was around from 1949–65. The A.L.
"Rookie-of-the-Year" with the Browns in '49 when he hit a
career high .306, Roy was slowed by a shoulder separation
the next few years before being traded to the Senators after the Browns' final year in St. Louis in 1953. He went on
to have his finest seasons in Washington, and was the "favorite" player of the then-Vice-President Nixon. In '54,
Roy's average of .232 was the lowest ever for a player with
a 100 RBI season. His big year came in '57 for the last-
place Senators with league-leading figures in homers (42)
and RBIs (114). The triple crown eluded him as his .301 average trailed league-leader Ted Williams' .388 by 87
points.

Sievers became the first Senators RBI champion since
Goose Goslin in 1924. That same year, Roy tied a record
set by Ken Williams of the Browns in 1922, when he belted
home runs in six straight contests.

Playing for the White Sox and Phillies in the early
1960s, he became the second player along with Jimmie
Foxx to ever hit a pinch-hit grand-slam home run in both
leagues.

Sievers was called "Squirrel" from his high school basketball playing days, because he was, supposedly, always "hanging around the cage like a squirrel." Roy later managed in the minors, and coached with the Reds for one season. For many years baseball fans in the nation's capital chanted, "Washington first in war, first in peace, and last in the American League." But that was no fault of Roy Sievers: .267 average; 318 home runs.

SILVERA, Al
Beverly Hills, CA

An outfielder, Al joined the Reds in 1955 to begin his 14-game career. Silvera played in 13 games that year and one more the following year. He attended USC where he hit .405.   .143

SILVERA, Charlie
Special assignment major league scout for the Oakland A's

A ten-year catcher from 1948–57, he spent all but the final season with the Yankees, backing up Yogi Berra. Charlie compiled a career average of .282, and from 1949–53 collected five straight winners' shares of the World Series pool, despite appearing in just one World Series game. In '49 he saw his most playing time, hitting .315 in 58 games.

His final year was with the Cubs in '57. After his playing days he managed in the minors and then coached for the Senators, Twins, Tigers, and Texas Rangers.

SILVESTRI, Ken
Pitching coach at Edmonton, Pacific Coast League

Ken was a catcher in parts of eight seasons, his first with the White Sox in 1939. He was then with the Yankees in 1941, and also after World War II in '46 and '47. With the Phillies from 1949–51, he appeared in the 1950 World Series against his former team. He later coached for the Phillies before a long stay as a coach for the Braves in both Milwaukee and Atlanta.   .217

SIMA, Al
>   Pari-mutuel clerk at Sanford-Orlando dog track
>   Brandon, FL

This left-hander had an exact total of 77 innings pitched,
and a 4.79 ERA in both the 1950 and 1951 seasons with the
Senators. He also pitched for the White Sox and the Philadelphia A's in 1954.   11-21

SIMMONS, Curt
>   Manager of Limekiln golf course
>   Meadowbrook, PA

Curt broke in with a complete game victory for the Phillies
in 1947 after signing a $65,000 bonus. After losing sea-
sons, he came into his own in 1950, and was 17-8 as a key
member of the "Whiz Kids." But he was called into military service late in the season, causing him to miss the
World Series. He returned to win 14 games in '52, including a league-leading six shutouts, and hit the only home
run in his 20-year career. A 16-victory season in '53 included a game in which he retired 27 straight Braves after
giving up a leadoff single to Billy Bruton.

Released by the Phillies after 115 victories early in
1960, he began a "second" career with St. Louis where he
won an additional 78 games, including a 18-9 mark in '64,
a key factor in helping the Cards overtake his old team for
the N.L. pennant. The talented southpaw defeated the
Phils four straight times without a defeat that year.
Simmons was also with the Cubs and Angels at the end of
his pitching days.   193-183

SIMPSON, Harry
>   Died April 3, 1979, at age 53 in Akron, OH

"Suitcase" came up with the Indians in 1951 and had
his best campaign with the Kansas City A's (1955–56),
hitting an even .300 in '55. He then packed his bags for
New York (Yankees), back again to K.C. (A's), then to

Chicago (White Sox), and then to Pittsburgh (Pirates) for his final season. His nickname "Suitcase" came about because he was traded five times during his eight-year career.   .266

SIMPSON, Tom "Duke"
    Beer distributorship
    Woodland Hills, CA

Duke was 1-2 in 30 games with the 1953 Cubs.

SINGLETON, Elmer
    Rockery construction business
    Bellevue, WA

Bert Elmer Singleton was in the biggies for parts of eight seasons beginning in the late forties with the Boston Braves, Pirates, and Senators. After several standout years in the PCL, he joined the Cubs in 1957 at 39 years of age. While pitching with the Cubs on May 10, 1959, Elmer was credited with a Cubs' win in the first game of a doubleheader, defeating Lindy McDaniel and the Cardinals. In the nightcap the situation reversed itself with McDaniel gaining the victory, and Singleton the defeat.
                                                    11-17

SISLER, Dave
    Senior Vice President
    A. G. Edwards and Sons brokerage firm
    St. Louis, MO

A Princeton graduate (he also played basketball), Dave is the youngest son of Hall of Famer George Sisler. The right-hander was with the Red Sox and Tigers in the late fifties, and finished with the Senators and Reds in the early sixties. During his career he studied for a master's degree in engineering.   38-44

SISLER, Dick
Resigned as Mets' hitting instructor in 1980 and now retired
Nashville, TN

Dick was born in 1920 in St. Louis, the year his father hit .407 with the Browns. As a rookie with the Cardinals in '46, he hit .260 as a part-time player and appeared in the World Series. His big moment came on October 1, 1950, when his tenth-inning home run on the final day of the season provided the Phillies with the N.L. pennant over the Dodgers. He also played with the Reds, and then, back with his original team (the Cardinals), playing until 1953. A first baseman-outfielder, he later coached for the Reds in the early sixties and then replaced Fred Hutchinson as manager. He then coached for the Cardinals in 1967–68.
.276

SISTI, Sibby
Instructor in Milwaukee Brewers organization (retired)
East Amherst, NY

Yes, there really was and still is a Sibby Sisti (real name: Sebastian Daniel Sisti). He was the ultimate utility infielder in a long run spent entirely with the Braves in Boston and Milwaukee (1939–54), with time away for military duty in World War II. On the '48 N.L. pennant winners, he filled in for Eddie Stanky and Alvin Dark.
.244

SKAUGSTAD, Dave
Detective for the Buena Park, CA, police department

Dave joins Tim McCarver, Rod Miller, and Bobby Saverine as fifties players born in the forties. The southpaw was just 17 when he appeared in two games with the Reds in 1957.
0-0

SKINNER, Bob
　　Pittsburgh Pirates hitting instructor

Bob first came up with the Pirates in 1954 and became a
regular in the outfield in the late fifties and early sixties,
hitting over the .300 mark three times, including a career
high of .321 in 1958. Traded to the Reds in '63, he joined
the Cardinals down the stretch in '64, and helped them
overhaul the Phillies for the N.L. pennant. He was 2-for-3
as a pinch-hitter as the Cardinals beat the Yankees in
seven games. In 1965 Bob's 15 pinch-hits led the N.L.
Skinner's playing days ended in 1966. He then managed in
the minors before becoming the Phillies' skipper in the
late 1960s. He later was a coach and manager for the San
Diego Padres.   .277

SKIZAS, Lou
　　Health teacher at Centennial High School in Cham-
　　paign, IL

Mr. Skizas broke in with the Yankees in 1956. The third
baseman-outfielder was around from 1956–59. Traded
from the Yanks to the K.C. A's in '56, he hit .314 in 89
games. Lou also played with the Tigers and White Sox.
　　Skizas could be called a "Tiger Killer" when he played
for the K.C. A's. Early in the '57 season, Skizas whacked a
ninth-inning home run to beat the Tigers. One month later
he did the same thing to the Bengals in an earlier inning to
win the game. Evidently Detroit saw enough as they
picked him up during the winter prior to the '58 campaign.
                                                        .270

SKOWRON, Bill
　　Sales representative
　　Interchecking Co.
　　New York, NY

That was not "BOO," but cries of "MOOSE" coming from
the stands of Yankee Stadium as the first baseman had
been called Mussolini by his grandfather when Bill was a
toddler. The tag was eventually shortened to "Moose."

He was the punter and extra-point man for the Purdue University football team before turning to professional baseball. In his college days, he played shortstop for the Boilermakers. Although he suffered from back problems throughout most of his career and was overshadowed by Mantle, Berra, Maris, and others, he was a .300-plus hitter during five seasons.

Following the '62 campaign, he was traded to the Dodgers and proceeded to have his worst season, hitting just .203 for L.A., and sharing the first base job with Ron Fairly. But come World Series time he was 5-for-13, including a home run, as the Dodgers swept his former team in four straight. He also played with the Senators, White Sox, and Angels before hanging it up.

On April 22, 1959, Skowron hit a home run in the 14th inning against the Senators to give the Yankees a 1-0 victory. This established a record for the longest A.L. game to end 1-0 on a home run. Whitey Ford struck out 15 Senators to get the victory.   .282

SLAUGHTER, Enos "Country"
    Farmer
    Roxboro, NC

Enos has been frustrated at Hall of Fame election time despite impressive credentials. An outfielder who lasted from 1938 to 1959, he hit over .300 eight times, and finished with an even .300 average.

He is best remembered for his memorable sprint from first to score the winning run in the 1946 World Series. With the Cardinals (1938–53) he led the league in doubles in '39 (52), in base hits in 1942 (188), and also in triples (17) that same year. In 1946 he was the league leader in RBIs with 130. Enos scored an even 100 runs in 1942 and again in 1946–47 after missing three seasons in the military. From 1954–59 he divided time with the Yankees and Kansas City A's. His 16 pinch-hits in '55 were the most in the A.L.

Overall, in five World Series he hit .291 in 27 games. In 1958 he became the oldest non-pitcher to be in a WS game, at age 42. His final stop was back in the N.L. with the

Milwaukee Braves in 1959 at age 43. He was a coach at Duke University in the mid-1970s.

Slaughter made hitting a science. Pitchers didn't like to pitch batting practice to Enos because his philosophy was to hit pitches up the middle. He felt this was good for his timing.

SLEATER, Lou
   Steel company sales representative
   Townsend, MD

Born in St. Louis, but raised in Baltimore, Lou was with both the Browns and Orioles from 1950–58.

The southpaw also pitched for the Senators, A's, Tigers, and Milwaukee Braves. Pitching for Washington in '52 he got Walt Dropo to pop up, ending his record 12 straight hits.   12-18

SMALL, Jim
   Sales manager
   Canadian Lakes Development Co.
   Mecosta, MI

Jim arrived with the Tigers as a youthful bonus baby outfielder in 1955. He hit .319 in 58 games with Detroit in 1956. However, after playing in two games with the K.C. A's in 1958, Jim was among the missing.   .270

SMALLEY, Roy
   Owns Major League Maintenance Co.
   Inglewood, CA

The brother-in-law of Gene Mauch, Roy Smalley is the father of Yankee infielder Roy Smalley III. A shortstop with the Cubs (1948–53), Milwaukee Braves ('54) and Phillies (1955–58), Roy hit for a .227 average in 872 games. He attended Pepperdine College.

SMITH, Al
>   District supervisor of parks
>   Chicago, IL

A great all-around scholastic athlete in St. Louis, Al once
scored ten touchdowns in a high school football game, and
also was a Golden Gloves boxing champion before turning
to professional baseball. A third baseman-outfielder, he
had a .272 lifetime average in his twelve-year stint. He
joins Manager Al Lopez and Hall of Famer Early Wynn as
the only members of both the '54 Indians and '59 White
Sox teams which temporarily stalled the Yankee dynasty
during the decade.

In the '54 World Series he hit the first pitch of game two
for a home run, the only Indian run in a 3-1 loss to the
Giants. He hit .306 in '55, and led the A.L. in runs scored.

He went to the White Sox in '58, and in the '59 WS
starred in a memorable photo in which a cup of beer was
poured on his head as he backed up to the fence for a home
run off the bat of the Dodgers' Charlie Neal. Al hit a career
high of .315 in 1960, finishing second to Pete Runnels' .320
in the A.L. batting race. Smith finished in '64 after spending time with the Orioles, Indians, and Red Sox.

SMITH, Bill
>   Jamestown, NC

When Bill Smith appeared in two games with the Cardinals in 1958, he became the fourth Bill Smith to appear in
the majors, but the first since 1886. The lefty was also with
the Cards in 1959 and Phillies in '62.   1-6

SMITH, Bobby Gene
>   Hood River, OR

An outfielder with the Cardinals in the late 1950s, Bobby
Gene also spent time with the Phillies, Mets, Cubs, and
Cards again in the early 1960s, before appearing last with
the Angels in 1965.   .243

SMITH, Bob G.
Purchasing manager
Boise-Cascade Co.
Vancouver, WA

This Bob Smith came up with the Red Sox in 1955, then later in the decade was with the Cardinals, Pirates, and Tigers—making him a member of the Cardinals team at the same time Bobby Gene Smith was on the roster which must have been very interesting at mail call. The chucker was 4-9.

SMITH, Bob W. "Riverboat"
Constantia, NY

No confusion here with the other left-handed pitcher named Bob Smith. This southpaw was known as "Riverboat," and was with the Red Sox in '58, at which time Bob G. Smith had moved from Fenway to the N.L. But then "Riverboat" sailed over to the N.L. with the Cubs, before voyaging back to the A.L. with Cleveland. Like Bob G., he was also a four-time winner.   4-4

SMITH, Dick
Assistant professor in phys. ed. dept. and assistant
baseball coach at Penn State University

An infielder with the Pirates in parts of five seasons (1951–55), Dick hit for a .134 average in 70 games overall, including a career-high .174 in 1951.

SMITH, Earl
Almond farmer; grocery business
Fresno, CA

Earl had a dream year in the minors, collecting 195 RBIs in 1954. But he had 195 less the following season with the Pirates. A five-game employee of the '55 Pirates, Earl batted .063.

SMITH, Frank
       St. Petersburg, FL

A right-handed relief specialist with Cincinnati in the
early 1950s, Frank was 12-11 in '52, 8-1 in '53, and was
credited with 20 saves in '54. He was dealt to the Cardinals the following year, and then closed shop back with the
Reds in 1956.   35-33

SMITH, Hal R.
       St. Louis Cardinals scout

In a 570-game career, Hal R. spent just about all of his
time in the biggies as a member of the Cardinals, with the
exception of four games with the '65 Pirates. He arrived in
1956. Hal later coached for the Pirates, Reds, and Brewers.
                                                           .258

SMITH, Hal W.
       Steel company sales manager
       Houston, TX

Originally in the Yankees' organization, he's the Hal
Smith who came back to haunt the Yankees in the 1960
World Series with a big three-run, pinch-hit homer in the
seventh game. He had previously played with Yankee
"farm" teams (Oriôles and A's) in the late 1950s, before
finishing in a Pirates uniform. He hit .295 in 1960 as a
backup to "Smoky" Burgess. Hal was with the Astros, and
then the Reds before leaving in 1964.   .267

SMITH, Milt
       Columbus, GA

"Gunsmoke" was big in 1955, the year this third baseman
went up in smoke after hitting only .196 in 36 games with
the Reds.

SMITH, Paul
   Employed with 3M Company
   Conroe, TX

Paul arrived in 1953 with the Pirates, batting .283. A first
baseman-outfielder, Paul was also with the Bucs in 1957,
then split the '58 season between the Pirates and Cubs. He
was MVP in the Southern Association in 1952.   .270

SNIDER, Duke
   Montreal Expos announcer and hitting instructor

The all-time great Dodger center fielder, Duke finally
made it to his den at Cooperstown in 1980. Edwin (Duke)
Snider, called "The Silver Fox" because of his premature
gray hair, piled up some royal totals with his bat in a career which began in '47. Most notably, he had five straight
40-plus home-run seasons (1953–57), 407 lifetime home
runs, and a .295 average.
   Originally a native of Southern California, he returned
home with the Dodgers in '58, and remained with them until playing for the Mets in New York in '63, and then for (of
all teams) the Giants in '64.
   Duke later scouted and managed in the minors for the
Dodgers, and was an announcer and hitting instructor for
the San Diego Padres, before joining the Expos as both a
hitting coach and announcer in '73. "The Dook of Flatbush" hit four homers in a World Series twice. In 36 WS
games, Snider rapped 11 roundtrippers and drove in 26
runs.
   Snider requested uniform number four because his idol,
Lou Gehrig, wore that number. Snider had his first big
league home run nullified in 1948 when he was called out
for stepping on the plate when he made contact with the
ball. Reflecting upon his days in Brooklyn he said, "The
camaraderie we had on our team in Brooklyn is something
you don't see today."
   In his first major league at-bat ever, he collected a pinch-
hit single for Dixie Walker. Duke had a damaged knee operated on during the winter of 1957, but reinjured it in the
spring in an auto accident. Dodger skipper Walt Alston re-

marked at the time, "He'll play somewhere, in left field if not center, and he won't have far to run in the Coliseum in Los Angeles." Between 1950–59, Snider hit 326 home runs, more than any player during the decade.

SNYDER, Gene
    Sales (steel service center)
    Edgcomb Metals
    York, PA

Gene was 1-1 in 11 games with the Los Angeles Dodgers in 1959 before he put his wing to rest.

SNYDER, Jerry
    Texas Plumbing Supply Co.
    Houston, TX

Jerry was a seven-year (1952–58) utility infielder, all with the Washington Senators. He was groomed in the Yankee farm system but was acquired by the Senators in '52.
    Snyder, who attended Oklahoma University, hit .230 in 266 games.

SNYDER, Russ
    Field worker for the government soil conservation office in Nelson, NE

Russ was an A.L. outfielder with five different teams (1959–70). One A.L. team he never played for was the Yankees—the organization he originally signed with. In his first season in pro ball ('53) he hit .432 in the low minors, the highest in all of professional baseball that season. He never approached that figure in the biggies, but three times he did hit over .300 (including his rookie season with K.C. in '59). Russ also hit over .300 with the Orioles in 1962 and 1966. In '62 he once hit safely twice as a pinch-hitter in one inning. Another distinction was scoring from second base on a sacrifice fly off the bat of Brooks Robinson.   .271

SOLIS, Marcelino
   Monterey, Mexico

Marcelino had a cup of Mexican coffee with the Cubs. The southpaw was 3-3 in 15 games.

SOMMERS, Bill
   President of Consolidated Color Press
   New York City

After 65 games as an infielder with the St. Louis Browns in 1950, Bill became an ex-big leaguer.   .255

SOUCHOCK, Steve
   Central Scouting Bureau
   Florida

An infielder-outfielder, Steve hit .302 in 1946 with the Yankees, but then, after having those numbers reversed to .203 in '48, he was dealt to the White Sox. From 1951–55 he was with the Tigers and had another .302 season in '53. In '55 Steve played in one game (his final appearance), and bowed out with a pinch-hit single.   .255

SPAHN, Warren
   Cattle rancher
   Hartshorne, OK

Born in '21, the all-time winningest left-hander was often stuck on that number as he won 21 games in eight different seasons. He also managed to win "just" 20 once, and also added several 22- and 23-game winning seasons during a career which totaled 63 shutouts among his 363 victories. The number of base hits he collected during his lengthy stay is also 363.

About the only distinction which eluded him as his long career was about to end was the failure to hurl a no-hitter. However, in September of 1960, his 20th win of the season was a no-hitter over the Phillies with a 15-strikeout effort at the age of 39. The following April his second win was his second no-hitter, over the S.F. Giants. Although 40 at the time, he was still not the oldest pitcher to throw a no-hitter (Cy Young accomplished the feat at age 41).

Warren broke in with the Boston Braves in 1942. Over two decades later he was with the N.Y. Mets, both times pitching under manager Casey Stengel. Spahn was quoted as saying, "I'm the only guy to play for Stengel both before and after he was a genius." Warren finished with the S.F. Giants in 1965. Among the players he was sometimes called "Hooks," because of a broken nose he acquired in a 1941 exhibition game in Texas.   363-245

SPANGLER, Al
    Divisional manager for Investment Co.
    Houston, TX

This Duke University All-American first arrived with the Milwaukee Braves in 1959 and went 5-for-12. A dozen years later he bowed out with the Cubs in 1971. He was most productive in the early 1960s as a regular with the expansion Astros as an outfielder, hitting over the .280 mark several years. Al also played for the Angels in the mid-1960s.   .262

SPEAKE, Bob
    Executive vice president, American Investors Life
    Topeka, KS

This first baseman-outfielder broke in with the Cubs in 1955. He was also with the Cubbies in '57, and with the S.F. Giants the next two years. After 305 games, he departed with a .223 average.

SPENCER, Daryl
    Semiretired—public relations work for the Wichita
    team in the American Association

Daryl can boast that he hit the first west coast major league home run in the Giants-Dodgers 1958 opener.

Spencer was the Giants' regular shortstop both in the

'57 and '58 seasons (their first on the west coast). He also
played for the Cardinals, Dodgers, and Reds in the early
sixties. Considered a pretty good card player off the field,
Daryl batted .244 in 1,098 games.

SPENCER, George
    Works for a plumbing company
    Columbus, OH

This one-time Ohio State Buckeye quarterback was a right-
handed pitcher with the New York Giants in the early fifties. He was a key man out of the bullpen for the '51 Giants
as he was 10-4 in 57 games. George later pitched for the Tigers in 1958 and 1960.   16-10

SPICER, Bob
    Manager of Divines Sporting Goods store
    Fayetteville, NC

Rebel Without a Cause, starring James Dean and Natalie
Wood, was a giant flick in '55 when this Virginia-born
rebel with a cause appeared in two games with the K.C.
A's. He did likewise in '56 and ended his brief run at 0-0.

SPOONER, Karl
    Citrus packing house manager
    Vero Beach, FL

Karl came in like a roaring lion. On September 22, 1954,
in his first big league start he shut out the Giants on a
three-hitter with 15 strikeouts. Four days later he whiffed
a dozen more in blanking the Pirates on four hits. The
Dodgers won the '55 pennant, but Spooner was just 8-6, although he did throw one shutout. Unfortunately, 1955
turned out to be his only complete season as he developed a
sore arm. His final appearance came in the '55 WS in game
six when he was knocked out in the first inning by the
Yankees. The following day Johnny Podres led the Dodgers to their first World Series championship.
    Referring to his debut, Karl said, "I was on cloud nine.

. . . I hadn't ever seen a major league game before, until the day I pitched" (in reference to his two opening shutout victories).

SPRING, Jack
Athletic director, coach and teacher at West Valley High School
Spokane, WA

A southpaw chucker, Jack was with the Phillies, Red Sox, and Senators, all for brief periods in the late 1950s. From 1961–63 he did some effective relief hurling for the Angels, winning 10 of 12 decisions. He then pitched for the Cubs, Cardinals, and Indians before finishing in 1965, having pitched for seven different teams in eight seasons.

12-5

STALEY, Gerry
Superintendent of parks and recreation
Vancouver, WA

Gerry was around for 15 years (1947–61) and was a 19-, 17-, and 18-game winner with the Cardinals in the early fifties. Later in the decade he became a relief ace with the White Sox after pitching with both the Reds and Yankees in the mid-fifties. The right-hander was 8-5 plus 14 saves in a league-leading 67 appearances for the A.L. pennant winners in '59. He had four appearances in six games against the Dodgers in the World Series, with one save and one loss. He followed with a 13-8 mark in '60 coming out of the bullpen in 64 games. Gerry departed after pitching for the A's and Tigers in '61.

134-111

STALLCUP, Virgil
Chemical company supervisor
Greenville, SC

Virgil broke in with the Reds in 1947 and was the regular shortstop from 1948–51, preceding Roy McMillan. Virgil also played for the Cardinals in 1952–53.

.241

STANKA, Joe
Storm window business
"Energy Specialties"
Houston, TX

Joe won his only decision in two games with the White Sox
in 1959. Later he became a star in Japan, helping his team
to a pennant. When he arrived there, fans would say
"Okii." The 6'6" native of Oklahoma was surprised that
they were aware that he was a native of Oklahoma, not
realizing the term referred to "Big" in Japanese.

STANKY, Eddie "The Brat"
Retired as baseball coach at the University of South
Alabama in 1982

"He can't hit, he can't run . . . all he can do is beat you!"
And in his 11-year career with five teams, he did play on
three different World Series teams. Unfortunately, all
three came up short. He was first with the Cubs in '43 before going to the Dodgers from 1944–47. In '45 he set the
N.L. record for walks (148) in a season, since tied by Jim
Wynn. Eddie was then with the Boston Braves' '48 champions before going to the New York Giants where he was a
member of the '51 team which won the N.L. pennant in
such dramatic fashion.

Three times he was the league leader in bases-on-balls,
and in '45 led the N.L. in runs scored. He hit .320 in '48,
playing in just 67 games, but he also hit an even .300
playing full-time for the Giants in 1950.

He was a player-manager with the Cardinals (1952–53)
and managed the Birds into the '55 season. A decade later
he returned as skipper of the White Sox (1966–68). Another decade later in 1977 he returned to manage the
Texas Rangers. However, he changed his mind after just
one game and returned to college coaching.

His father-in-law, Milt Stock, was a third baseman in
the majors from 1913–26, and later coached for the Cubs,
Dodgers, and Pirates from 1944–52.

Stanky was involved in a famous incident with Phil
Rizzuto of the Yankees in the '51 Series when he kicked
the ball out of Rizzuto's glove in the fifth inning of game

three. The maneuver ignited a 5-run Giant rally. Eddie hit
.268 in 1,259 games.

STARR, Dick
Production control dept. with Allegheny Ludlum
Kittaning, PA

Not a star, but always a STARR, this right-hander was
12-24 in 93 contests with the Yankees (1947–48), St. Louis
Browns (1949–51), and Senators ('51).

STEPHENS, Gene
District manager for the Kerr McGee Refining Corp.
Oklahoma City, OK

A 13-year outfielder (1952–64), Gene was often used as a
late-inning replacement for Ted Williams while with the
Red Sox throughout most of the 1950s. In 1953 he only hit
.204, but on June 18th, when Boston had their record-
breaking 17-run inning, his three hits in the frame set a
standard never equalled.

In a 1959 game against the Yankees, Gene pinch-ran for
Ted Williams. Later in the same inning he hit a grand-slam
home run. Gene then played with the Orioles, A's, and White
Sox, finishing with a .240 average in 964 games.

STEPHENS, Vern "Junior"
Died November 3, 1968, at age 48
Long Beach, CA

A power-hitting shortstop, "Junior" compiled some statistics usually not associated with players at that position.
His 109 RBIs led the A.L. in 1944 as he helped the St.
Louis Browns to their only A.L. pennant. His 24 homers
led the league the following season.

But it was the 1948, '49, and '50 campaign as a Red Sox
player that he took aim at the "Green Monster" in Fenway
to the tune of a career high 39 homers in '49, and RBI figures of 137, 159 and 144 respectively, tying for the league
lead in RBI's in both '49 and '50 with teammates Ted
Williams and Walt Dropo.

His overall totals include a .286 average and 247
homers, closing out in 1955 after playing with the White
Sox, Browns again, and Orioles.

STEPHENSON, Bob
Geologist and co-owner of Potts-Stephenson Explor-
ation Oil and Gas Co.
Oklahoma City, OK

Bob played in 67 games with the Cardinals in '55. A graduate of the University of Oklahoma, Stephenson hit .243 in
his only season.

STEVENS, Ed
San Diego Padres scout

A first baseman with the Dodgers (1945–47) and Pirates
(1948–50), Ed hit .252, appearing in 375 games.

STEVENS, R.C.
Davenport, IA

Called "Cola" by some for obvious reasons, R.C. played
first base with the Pirates (1958–60), and Senators ('61).
He hit .210 in 104 games.

STEWART, Bill
Sylvan Lake, MI

This 5'11" outfielder was born on April 11th. He hit .111
for the 1955 Cubs. How many games do you think Bill appeared in? That's right—11! He is not related to another
Bill Stewart who pitched with the Cubs—would you
believe—11 years earlier! To add some frosting on the
cake, the name Bill Stewart has 11 letters.

STEWART, Ed "Bud"
City of Hawthorne parks recreation director
Inglewood, CA

An outfielder with Pittsburgh in the early 1940s, his 10

pinch-hits were the most in the N.L. in 1941. He returned after World War II to play briefly for the Yankees before joining the Senators and White Sox in the early 1950s. His nine pinch-hits with the White Sox in '51 led the junior circuit.   .268

STEWART, "Bunky"
Real estate salesman
New Bern, NC

Veston Goff Stewart, better known as "Bunky," broke in with Washington in 1952. The southpaw chucker was 5-11 in 72 games in parts of five seasons with the Senators (1952–56).

STIRNWEISS, George "Snuffy"
Died September 15, 1958, at age 39 in Newark, NJ in a train accident

The Yankees have had five different players win batting titles in their illustrious history. Ruth, Gehrig, DiMaggio, and Mantle are four of the most significant names in baseball history. "Snuffy" Stirnweiss was the Yankee second baseman in 1945, and his .309 average was good enough to cop the A.L. batting crown (the lowest average to win a title since Elmer Flick won it with a .306 average in 1905). Stirnweiss entered the last day of the season tied with Tony Cuccinello for the league lead. Cuccinello and the White Sox were rained out the final day, and "Snuffy" picked up three hits to capture the title.

He joined the Yankees in 1943 and hit just .219, but the following year raised his average an even 100 points to .319. Although he didn't win the title in '44, he led the A.L. in four other departments: base hits (205), runs (125), triples (16), and stolen bases (55). He also led the A.L. in all those departments in 1945. Stirnweiss remained with the team through the rest of the decade, but never approached the success of his '44 and '45 seasons. He retired in 1952 after playing for the Browns and Indians, with a .268 lifetime average in 1,028 games.

"Snuffy" was a running back at the University of North Carolina in the late 1930s.

STOBBS, Chuck
   Pitching instructor for Cleveland Indians, minor
   leagues

Chuck's 15-year stay spanned 1947–61. He had three
straight winning seasons with the Red Sox. After a year
with the White Sox, he spent most of his time losing games
with the second-division Senators. His 20 losses in '57
were the most in the A.L. He was the first Senators'
pitcher to lose that many games since Harry Harper lost
21 in 1919. During that '57 campaign, he had lost 18
straight decisions (going back to the '56 season). Stobbs
then switched to uniform number 13 and snapped the losing streak. He is probably best remembered for having
thrown the pitch which Mickey Mantle hit for a colossal,
tape-measure job, some 565 feet at Griffith Stadium in
Washington in 1953.
   Stobbs might have released the wildest pitch in history
on May 20, 1956, while pitching for the Senators against
the Tigers. The southpaw was pitching to Bob Kennedy
with the bases loaded when he threw the ball into the sev-
enteenth row along the first base stands at Briggs Stadium
in Detroit.   107-130

STOCK, Wes
   Oakland A's minor league pitching coach

A right-handed relief pitcher (1959–1967), Wes once went
over two years between defeats. He was 12-0 over a
100-game stretch between July 1962 and July 1964. This
established a big league record, breaking the mark of
Elroy Face, who had gone 98 straight games without a loss
from May 1958 to September '59.
   Stock began with the Orioles before he was traded to
Kansas City for the current prominent hitting coach,
Charlie Lau.
   He had an overall record of 27-13 in 321 games, all but
three from out of the bullpen. Following his pitching days
he became a pitching instructor for the Brewers in 1970
before joining the A's in the same capacity. The past few
seasons he has held that position with the Mariners. Wes

has a son named Jeff who used to work out of the Kingdome as a member of the Seattle Sounders soccer team of
the North American Soccer League.

STONE, Dean
   Landscaping business
   Silvis, IL

Dean was with the Senators, Red Sox, Cardinals, Astros,
White Sox, and Orioles in an eight-year safari from
1953–59, and again in 1962 and '63.

   His best year was in his first full season with Washington in 1954 when he was 12-10. Selected to the A.L. All-
Star team, he entered the game with his team down 9-8,
with the N.L. threatening to add more with runners on
first and third and two away. The runner on third, Red
Schoendienst, attempted to steal home, but was tagged
out. To no avail, the N.L. claimed Stone had balked. The
A.L. then rallied for two runs in the top of the ninth to win,
10-9. In the bottom of the ninth, Virgil Trucks kept the
N.L. from scoring. Stone, who had thrown just a single
pitch and had not officially retired any hitters, was the
winning pitcher.   29-39

STRAHS, Dick
   Banker
   Chicago, IL

Dick was scratched from the big time after appearing in
nine games with the White Sox in 1954.   0-0

STREULI, Walt
   Streuli's Sales Inc., a manufacturer's agent's business
   Greensboro, NC

A catcher with Detroit, Walt played in one game with the
Tigers in '54, two more in '55, and then three more in '56.
That was it, 1-2-3! He wound up 3-for-12, including a pair
of doubles in his brief but interesting career.   .250

STRICKLAND, George
> Mutuel manager at Fairgrounds Race Track and the
> Jefferson Race Track in Jefferson, LA
> New Orleans, LA

Primarily a shortstop (1950–60), George started with the
Pirates in the early 1950s before spending the remainder
of his time from 1953 on with Cleveland. He had a .284 av-
erage in that '53 season, his best ever.
    From 1962–72 he was a coach with the Twins, A's, and
Indians. He managed the Indians following the firing of
Birdie Tebbetts during the 1966 season.   .224

STRIKER, Wilbur "Jake"
> High school baseball coach
> Bucyrus, OH

With his name, he had to be a pitcher. He was in one game
with Cleveland in 1959. Jake started and went seven innings, winning in his only appearance. He had no decisions in two more games with the White Sox the following
year. Six times in his three appearances opposing hitters
went down on strikes. He lived up to his name in the minors when he once struck out 17 in a game.   1-0

STRINGER, Lou
> Retired; former automobile salesman
> San Clemente, CA

A "first stringer" as the Cubs second baseman in his first
two years (1941–42), Lou returned to the Cubs following
World War II in 1946, and then was with the Red Sox
(1948–50) as a utility or "second stringer." Following his
baseball days, he acted as an "extra" in movies and offici-
ated college basketball games.

STUART, Dick
> Securities analyst in New York City

Dick led all first-sackers in putouts and assists in 1963.
However, it was his bat for which he is best remembered.

Back in 1956 he hit 66 homers in the lower minors and, remaining humble, he began signing his autograph "Dick Stuart—66." Arriving in the majors in '58 with the Pirates, his first hit in the big arena was a home run; his second, a grand-slam homer. Dick's best season in Pittsburgh was in '61 when he hit 35 homers and 117 RBIs while batting over .300 for the only time in his career. Joining the Red Sox in '63, he had career highs with 42 homers and 118 RBIs (leading the A.L. in RBIs). He was also the first player to ever hit over 30 home runs and collect over 100 RBIs in both leagues.

On June 28, 1963, playing for the Bosox, Dick established a big league record at first base when he assisted in all three of the first-inning outs. Known as "Dr. Strangeglove," Stuart led or tied the league in errors at first base for seven years. Dick also spent time with the Phils, Mets, and Dodgers before playing in Japan. He returned with the Angels in '69, proclaiming that "nothing bothers me anymore after being the only American player on a team in Hiroshima."

Overall, "Dr. Strangeglove" batted .264 with 228 homers.

STUART, Marlin
    Farmer
    Paragould, AR

From 1949–54, Marlin pitched with the Tigers, Browns, Orioles, and Yankees. He had a perfect game while pitching at Indianapolis in the American Association in 1950. Overall he was 23-17 in 196 games, including an 8-2 mark for the lowly Browns in 1953. He won all three decisions with the Yankees in 1954, his last campaign. In a 1954 poll conducted by the *Sporting News,* no less a hitter than Ted Williams stated that Marlin Stuart was the pitcher who gave him the most trouble.

STUFFEL, Paul
    Operates a Nationwide insurance agency
    Alliance, OH

Paul won his only decision in seven games while pitching for the Phillies in 1950, '52, and '53.

STUMP, Jim
>   Quality control, Oldsmobile Division, General Motors
>   in Lansing, MI

A member of the Tigers in 1957 and '59, Jim won his only
decision, compiling a fine 2.19 ERA in 11 games. As a hitter he went 2-for-3.

STURDIVANT, Tom "Snake"
>   Executive with Rollins Trucking Co.
>   Oklahoma City, OK

A right-handed chucker with the Yankees in the mid-
fifties, Tom started out as a third baseman. In 1956 and '57
he was a 16-game winner for the A.L. champions. His 16-6
mark in '57 was good for a .727 winning percentage (best
in the A.L.).

   In the 1956 World Series, Tom won a 6-2 complete game
over the Dodgers in game four. He later developed a sore
arm, and could have been referred to as "Suitcase Sturdivant" as he was with the A's, Red Sox, Senators, Pirates,
Tigers, and A's again. His last stop reunited him with
Casey Stengel when he joined the Mets.   59-51

SUCHECKI, Jim
>   Location unknown

Jim came up with the Red Sox in 1950. The following year
he did his hurling for the Browns. The right-hander departed after pitching with the Pirates in '52. Overall he
was 0-6 in 38 games.

SUDER, Pete
>   Former jail warden
>   Aliquippa, PA

Pete was an infielder who spent his days with the Philadelphia Athletics (1941–54) with a couple of years out for mili-

tary service during World War II. His last year was with the A's in Kansas City in 1955. After 1,421 games he departed with a .249 average.

SULLIVAN, Frank
    Golf pro
    Kauai, HI

Frank had five straight winning seasons for the Boston Red Sox (1954–58), going 79-52. His best year was in '55 when he led the A.L. in wins with 18. He was the loser in the All-Star Game that summer when he gave up a 12th-inning home run to Stan Musial. The winning pitcher in the July Classic that year was the only chucker in the majors taller than Sullivan—Gene Conley. In the early 1960s Frank was with the Phillies and the Twins, and wound up 97-100 in 351 games.

His batterymate and roommate in Boston was Sammy White. Both are now golf pros in Hawaii. Sullivan, a Korean War veteran, made his debut in '53 after being recalled from the Eastern League. He entered the game in relief against the Tigers with the bases loaded and nobody out. Frank proceeded to retire the side with no runs crossing the plate.

SULLIVAN, Haywood
    Executive vice president and general manager of the Boston Red Sox

An All-Conference football star at the University of Florida, Haywood turned to professional baseball as a catcher and hit for a .226 average in 312 games with the Red Sox in 1955 and from 1957–60. He was with the Kansas City A's in 1961–63. Sullivan managed the A's to a tenth-place finish in 1965.

He stood 6'4". When he teamed up with pitcher Frank Sullivan, who measured 6'7", it was one of baseball's biggest batteries ever.

SULLIVAN. Russ
 Builder-developer
 Fredericksburg, VA

Russ arrived with the Tigers in 1951. The outfielder
played in a total of 45 games in parts of 1951, '52, and '53,
and finished a not too controversial career with a .267 average.

SUNDIN, Gordon
 Sales representative for Viking Materials Co.
 Minnetonka, MN

Gordon pitched to two men and walked them both in his
only big league action, for the Orioles in 1956.

SURKONT, Max
 Tavern owner
 Pawtucket, RI

Max first pitched with the White Sox in 1949. He had his
best years with the Braves in the early 1950s before pitching for the Cardinals, Pirates, and N.Y. Giants. In 1953 he
was 11-5 for the Braves, striking out a total of 83 hitters in
170 innings, an unspectacular total. But on May 25th, he
had his strikeout pitch working when he had a record
(since surpassed by Tom Seaver) eight consecutive strikeouts against the Cincinnati Reds.   61-76

SUSCE, George
 Owner, rental construction equipment firm and oper-
 ates a cemetery
 Needham, MA

George was 9-7 as a Red Sox rookie in 1955. On July 20th
he one-hit the K.C. A's. His father, a former major league
catcher, was on the Athletic coaching staff, and must have
had mixed emotions that day.
 After pitching with Boston, George finished the '58 sea-

son in Detroit, and closed out his career in the Motor City
the following year with a 22-17 record.

SWANSON, Art
Oil lease business in Columbus, MS

A bonus player out of high school, Art was 3-3 in 42 games
with the Pirates from 1955–57. In June of '57 after approx-
imately two years of inactivity in the Pirates' bullpen, he
was given his first start in the big show and beat the
Cards, 8-1. This was shortly after Herb Score was hit in the
eye by Gil McDougald's line drive. Apparently affected by
Score's tragic experience, Swanson went to the mound
looking like something from *Star Wars* as he wore a specif-
ically designed rubber and wire eye protector. At the time,
his father was an assistant football coach and head baseball coach at LSU.

SWIFT, Bob
Died October 17, 1966, at age 51
Detroit, MI

An A.L. backstop for 14 seasons (1940–53), Bob is the
catcher kneeling behind Eddie Gaedel in the famous photo
of Bill Veeck's midget at bat in 1951. Swift hit .231 in
1,001 contests.

He coached for the Tigers, Senators, and Tigers again
following his playing career. He took over as manager of
Detroit for the ailing Charlie Dressen during the 1966 season. Dressen died in August that year and shortly after the
season ended, Swift passed away.

SZEKELY, Joe
Industrial chemical salesman
Paris, TX

Joe appeared in five games with the Reds and carried a
.077 average in 1953.

T

TALBOT, Bob
Personnel director
Early California Foods Inc. in Visalia, CA

Bob sprinted into the biggies in 1953 with the Cubbies, but was gone after '54. The outfielder took home a .247 average.

TANNER, Chuck
Pittsburgh Pirates manager

This Fourth of July baby burst on the scene by hitting a pinch-hit home run on the first pitch he ever saw in the big show in April of 1955 with the Milwaukee Braves. He would hit just 20 more homers. Chuck also played for the Cubs, Indians, and Angels through the 1962 season. Overall he batted .261 in 396 games. He became a manager in the minors, and later with the White Sox and A's before taking over in Pittsburgh.

TAPPE, Elvin
Sporting goods business
Quincy, IL

Elvin was a catcher with the Cubs for parts of six seasons from 1954–56, then in '58, '60, and '62.

As part of the Cubs' coaching staff (which took part in the unique experiment of sharing the Cubs' managing position in 1961–62), he was in charge for the largest amount of games in '61 with 95. In '62 he was the manager at the start of the season, but gave way to Lou Klein when the Cubs went off to a sputtering 4 and 16 start.

Elvin had a twin brother named Melvin who never reached the majors. Writers would have had a picnic with Elvin and Melvin Tappe.   .207

TAPPE, Ted
    Location unknown

Unrelated to either Melvin or Elvin, Ted Tappe was a teammate of Elvin's on the '55 Cubs as an outfielder. But Achilles' heel problems shortened his playing time. Ted broke in with the Reds in 1950 at age 19 and was also with them the following year. Theodore Nash Tappe (TNT) exploded on the scene with a home run in his first major league plate appearance late in the '50 season. A 34-game career man, Ted batted .259, with a third of his 15 base hits being home runs.

TASBY, Willie
    Employed with the American Can Co.
    Oakland, CA

Baltimore fans won't forget that stormy day when Willie played the outfield in his bare feet so that lightning wouldn't strike his spiked baseball cleats. An outfielder with four A.L. teams (Orioles, Red Sox, Senators, and Indians), Tasby was around from 1958–63, hitting .250 in 583 games.

Willie is another in a long list of athletes out of McClymonds H.S. in Oakland. After his playing career he was employed with Trans-Pacific Ocean Aircraft Company in Oakland.

TATE, Lee
    AAA Motor Club
    Omaha, NE

Lee broke in as a Cardinal shortstop in 1958. Also with the Cards in '59, Lee shuffled out with a .165 average.

TAUSSIG, Dan
Long Island, NY

Dan arrived in 1958 with the S.F. Giants. He had his best season in '61, hitting .287 for the Cardinals. Dan flew out with the Astros in '62, with a .262 lifetime average.

TAYLOR, Ben
Production department
Anheuser Busch Co.
Houston, TX

Born in Metropolis, Illinois, this first baseman was certainly no Superman, although he did do his share of flying around. He was with the Browns (1951), Tigers ('52), and Milwaukee Braves ('55). Ben finished with a .231 average.

TAYLOR, Bill
Real estate business
Acton, CA

An outfielder with the N.Y. Giants, Bill was the team's other pinch-hitter during the years Dusty Rhodes was stealing the show. But Bill's 15 pinch-hits topped the N.L. in 1955. He was also with the Tigers in 1957–58. Bill had an overall .237 average in 149 games, playing defensively in the outfield in just 18 of those contests.

TAYLOR, Bob "Hawk"
Equity qualified agent
Equitable Life Insurance Co.
Paducah, KY

The nephew of Ben Taylor, Bob "Hawk" Taylor was also born in Metropolis. "Hawk" had an 11-year flight as a catcher-first baseman-outfielder, in which he hit a mild-mannered, Clark Kent-type .218. Originally a bonus baby with the N.L. champion Milwaukee Braves in 1957–58, he also played for the Mets, Angels, and A's in a career which terminated in 1970. "Hawk" was the first Mets player ever to pinch-hit a grand-slam homer.

TAYLOR, Fred
    Golf course manager in New Albany, OH; runs bas-
    ketball camp at Valley Vista sports camp in OH

Fred was a first baseman who hit .191 in 22 games with
the Senators from 1951–53. He turned to coaching basketball, and had better success as the head coach of his
alma mater—Ohio State. His Jerry Lucas-John Havlicek-
led Buckeyes won the NCAA championship under him.
During his tenure at Ohio State, his teams won seven Big
Ten championships. He retired as the cage mentor in 1979.

TAYLOR, Harry
    West Terre Haute, IN

James "Harry" Taylor was a right-handed pitcher with
the Brooklyn Dodgers (1946–48) and Boston Red Sox
(1950–52). He went 19-21 in 90 games. Harry had his best
season in '47 when his 10-5 mark helped the Dodgers to
the N.L. pennant. Today he is the answer to the trivia
question: "Who started for the Dodgers in the '47 World
Series the day Bill Bevens had his near no-hitter for the
Yankees?"

TAYLOR, Harry E.
    Fort Worth, TX

Not to be confused with James "Harry" Taylor, Harry E.
was a right-hander who pitched in a couple of games for
the K.C. A's as a 21-year-old, and pitched respectably
enough, giving up just 3 runs in 9 innings.
    Taylor attended pre-dental school at the University of
Texas during his playing days.   0-0

TAYLOR, Joe
    Hospital employee
    Pittsburgh, PA

Joe had a reputation as a long-ball-hitting outfielder during much of the decade in the Pacific Coast League. He

also saw playing time with the A's, Reds, Cardinals, and Orioles in parts of four seasons (1954–59), hitting .249.

TAYLOR, Pete
Location unknown

Pete pitched in only one game for the St. Louis Browns in 1952. He departed 0-0.

TAYLOR, Sammy
Woodruff, SC

A six-year catcher (1958–63), Sammy spent his first five seasons with the Cubs. In his final year he hopped around with the Mets, Reds, and Indians. In 473 games he batted .245. Sammy first entered professional baseball in 1950, but did a four-year hitch in the Navy before returning to the game.

TAYLOR, Tony
Manager of Peninsula in the Carolina League

The most illustrious career of the players named Taylor in the 1950s belongs to Cuban-born Antonio Sanchez Taylor. He first arrived with the Cubs in 1958. Tony was traded to the Phillies in 1960, and became one of the more popular players in that team's history during the 1960s as the second baseman. He was with the Tigers in the early 1970s before returning to the Phillies to finish with a .261 average in 2,195 games. He garnered a total of 2,007 base hits.

TEBBETTS, George "Birdie"
Cleveland Indians special assignment scout

Birdie is not a good example of catchers having their big league life cut short by the nature of the position. In 1,162 games, he was never at another position in a trek which spanned 1936–52 with the Tigers, Red Sox, and Indians. He was the regular in over 100 games for the Red Sox in

both 1948 and '49. In his final two seasons, he was a
backup to Jim Hegan for Cleveland. His final major league
base hit in '52 game him an even 1,000 for his career.

He managed the hard hitting Reds' teams of the mid-
1950s, and the Braves and Indians during the 1960s. Although spending just a little over three years with the Red
Sox, he was voted the team's all-time catcher in 1969.
                                                     .270

TEED, Dick
    L.A. Dodgers scout
    Enfield, CT

In 1953 Ben Hogan took the USGA Men's Open and the
Masters. Dick "teed off" as a pinch-hitter for the Brooklyn
Dodgers in one game. He missed the ball (struck out) and
was never called upon to play another round.

TEMPLE, Johnny
    Columbia, SC

The Cincinnati Reds of the 1950s featured home-run hitters like Kluszewski, Post, Bell, and a young Frank Robinson. Leadoff man Johnny Temple contributed only a few,
but more often than not was on base ahead of the home-run
swingers. In his first seven seasons from 1952–58, he had
seven homers—an average of one a year. Then in '59 he hit
eight. He helped set the table with a .300 average in three
of those years. During the early 1960s he was with the Indians, Orioles, and Astros before returning to the Reds as a
player-coach in '64, his final season. But that was mostly
as a coach, as he played in just half a dozen games because
a new "kid" on the block by the name of Rose had taken
over at second. Overall, Johnny swung for a .284 average
in 1,420 games.

In the early 1970s he was a sports director for a Houston
TV station, then was an executive assistant to the Governor of South Carolina.

TEMPLETON, Charlie
    Location unknown

"Chuck" had a 10-game career (1955–56) with the Dodgers, losing his only two decisions.

TERRY, Ralph
    Club professional at golf course
    Larned, KS

Ralph first came up to the Yankees in 1956. A year later, the stylish right-handed pitcher was "farmed" to the Kansas City A's, but returned to enjoy some productive years with the Yanks in the early 1960s.

Terry was 16-3 in 1961 and 23-12 in '62 when he led the A.L. in victories, starts and innings pitched. However, he is best remembered for serving up the decisive home run to the Pirates' Bill Mazeroski in the seventh game of the 1960 World Series. In the 1961 Series, he was charged with the loss in game two, as the Yankees beat the Reds in five games.

Ralph capped his fine '62 campaign by beating the Giants twice in the Series, including the decisive seventh game, which he won, 1-0.

After the Yanks' pennant-winning '64 season, Ralph moved on to Cleveland and then returned briefly to Kansas City before concluding his career with the Mets in 1966 and '67. In '67 he had five strikeouts in three innings with the Mets—just enough to boost him into the "1,000 strikeout club" with an even 1,000. Overall, Terry posted a 107-99 record in 338 games.

TERWILLIGER, Wayne
    Texas Rangers coach

"Twig" went by his middle name of Wayne instead of his first (which would make his name a tongue twister—Willard Terwilliger). A star shortstop at Western Michigan University, Wayne played in the majors as a second baseman with the Cubs, Dodgers, Senators, New York Giants and Kansas City A's (1949–60). In 666 games, he compiled a .240 average.

Wayne coached with the Washington Senators and Texas Rangers in the late 1960s and early 1970s, then managed in the minors for most of the next decade before returning to coach with the Rangers.

TESTA, Nick
> Physical education instructor at Lehman College; pitches batting practice for the Yankees and Mets

Nick was a catcher in one game with the S.F. Giants in 1958. Twenty years ago he was featured in a lengthy article by Bill Libby in *The Fireside Book of Baseball.* The article, titled "Portrait of a Baseball Failure" reported, "He brims with desire, but not big league talent, and there are many more of his kind around than there are Mantles and Musials."

Nick's hobby is body building. He has done some bullpen catching with the Yankees.

TETTELBACH, Dick
> St. Louis Cardinals baserunning coach in spring training; vice president of the Copeland Co.
> Woodbridge, CT

A graduate of Yale, Dick captained the baseball team at the Ivy League school in 1950. Originally Yankee property, he was in several games with them in 1955, but spent most of the year in Denver in the American Association, where he hit over .300. He did this despite once being responsible for all three of his team's outs in one inning; he popped up and hit into a double play. Traded to Washington, he was in the Senators' opening day lineup in 1956, and homered for his first major league hit against his former team in front of President Eisenhower. Dick was with Washington in 1956–57.   .150

THACKER, Moe
> Part owner and supervisor of a chain of Long John
> Silver Seafood Shoppes
> Louisville, KY

Moe came up as a catcher with the Cubs in 1958. Thacker
also spent his days behind the dish at Wrigley Field from
1960–62, and had his last lick with the Cardinals in 1963.
.177

THIEL, Bert
> Self-employed in the Forest Products business
> Marion, WI

Maynard "Bert" Thiel, a right-handed chucker, was struggling to make the pitching staff of the Boston Braves in
1952. In four games he was 1-1.

THIES, Jake
> Florissant, MO

Vernon Arthur "Jake" Thies came up in 1954 as a Pirates'
chucker. Jake departed 3-10 in 34 games with the Bucs in
1954 and '55.   3-10

THOMAS, John "Bud"
> Assistant superintendent of schools
> Sedalia, MO

John Tillman "Bud" Thomas boasts a .350 lifetime average in the major leagues as a shortstop with the St.
Louis Browns in 1951. He was 7-for-20 (including a home
run) in 14 games in his brief exposure to big league pitching.
   At this writing, John is working toward a doctorate at
the University of Missouri.

THOMAS, Frank
    High school lecturer for ICM school of business
    Pittsburgh, PA

A long-ball-hitting 16-year performer (1951–66), Frank
took over where Ralph Kiner left off as the home-run hitter on the lowly Pirates teams during the 1950s. He had a
career high of 35 homers and 109 RBIs in his final season
with the Bucs in '58. The '58 Pirates moved up to second,
but he was traded to the Reds in '59. To his regret, he
would never play on a pennant winner. In 1962 he became
the one power hitter on the expansion Mets with 34
roundtrippers (including two in a game for three straight
games on August 1st, 2nd, and 3rd). Earlier in the year on
April 29th he had the distinction of being hit by a pitch
twice in one inning.
    A "record" which may never be challenged is one for
catching fast balls with his bare hands. During pre-game
warm ups he won bets from several players (including
Willie Mays), that he could catch their hardest throws
from the pitching mound with his bare hands.
    Good fortune came his way when he was sold from the
Mets to the league-leading Phillies during the '64 season.
Unfortunately, he broke his thumb and the Phillies folded.
Frank got into a fight with Richie Allen during batting practice before a 10-8 loss to the Reds on July 3, 1965. Following
the game (in which he hit a game-tying home run as a pinch-
hitter), he was placed on waivers. His 1,766 games were spent
with the Pirates, Reds, Cubs, Mets, Phillies, Astros, and
Braves. He played over 1,000 games in the outfield, 394 at
third base, 271 at first base, and 4 as a second baseman.
    Before turning to pro ball, Frank studied for the priest-
hood. He averaged .266, with 286 home runs.

THOMAS, George
    Assistant baseball coach at the University of Minne-
    sota
    Burnsville, MN

A 13-year outfielder from 1957–71, George also played
every infield position and caught. He was in just one game

during 1957, and then one again in '58 with the Tigers before returning in 1961. Thomas enjoyed his greatest success near the end of his career with .353 and .343 averages as a part-time player with the Red Sox.

George was a player-coach with the Bosox during the 1969–70 seasons. A $25,000 bonus player out of the University of Minnesota, Thomas finished with a .255 average.

THOMAS, Keith "Kite"
Franchisee for 19 Pizza Huts in North Carolina
Wilmington, NC

"Kite" made the big time as an outfielder for the Philadelphia A's and Senators in 1952–53. After hitting .233 in 137 games, he disappeared into the sky. He said, "I'm a franchisee for 19 Pizza Huts—18 too many."

THOMAS, Leo
Bartender
Alameda, CA

Leo hit .212 with the Browns and White Sox between 1950–52. The third sacker appeared in 95 games.

THOMAS, Valmy
Director of the Bureau of Recreation
St. Croix, Virgin Islands

A catcher (1957–61), Valmy is the only player in big league history who played for at least five years and played in a different city in each of his big league seasons. In 1957 he was with the N.Y. Giants, then in '58 with the Giants in San Francisco. He spent '59 in Philadelphia with the Phillies, then was with the Orioles in Baltimore the following year, and finished in '61 with the Indians in Cleveland. Valmy was the first man from the Virgin Islands to play in the big leagues.　　　　　.230

THOMPSON, Charles "Tim"
   St. Louis Cardinals scouting supervisor

A catcher in a few games with the Dodgers in 1954, Tim
spent most of his playing time with the Kansas City A's in
1956–57 before playing his final four games with the Tigers in 1958.   .238

THOMPSON, Don
   Realtor—Preferred Properties
   Asheville, NC

An outfielder with the Boston Braves (1949) and Brooklyn
Dodgers (1951, 1953–54), Don's career batting average of
.218 exceeds by one the 217 games he played in.

THOMPSON, Hank
   Died September 30, 1969, at age 43, in Fresno, CA

Hank broke in with the St. Louis Browns in 1947 as the
second black player in A.L. history (after Larry Doby). In
1949, he became the first black player for the New York
Giants. When he batted against Don Newcombe of the
Dodgers that season, it marked the first time in major
league history that a black batter faced a black pitcher.
   A left-handed hitting third baseman, Thompson hit two
inside-the-park home runs in a game in 1950. His best seasons were 1953 (a career-high .302 average with 24 homers) and 1954 (26 homers, 86 RBIs) for the N.L. champion
Giants. Included in his 26 homers were three in one game
on June 3rd. In the World Series, Hank helped the Giants
to a four-game sweep of the favored Indians by hitting .364
and drawing a four-game record of seven walks. He wound
up his career with the Giants in 1956 with a .267 average
for 933 games.
   Following his career in baseball, Hank served time in
prison for robbery. Following parole, he was working with
youngsters in Fresno when he suffered a fatal heart attack.

THOMPSON, John "Jocko"
Government sales coordinator for General Binding Corp.
Rockville, MD

"Jocko" began a 41-game march as a southpaw chucker with the Phils in '48. When it was over, in 1951, "Jocko" was 6-11.

THOMSON, Bobby
Westvaco Corporation in New York City
Watchung, NJ

"The Giants Win the Pennant . . . The Giants Win the Pennant . . . The Giants Win the Pennant," cried New York Giants' broadcaster Russ Hodges. October 3, 1951, remains one of the most memorable dates in baseball history. Both prior to and following his "shot heard 'round the world," Bobby (a Glasgow, Scotland born outfielder) hit other clutch and dramatic home runs. The final day of the classic '51 season he hit a key homer to tie the score against the Boston Braves in a game the Giants needed to win to force a playoff with the Dodgers. In the first playoff game, his two-out, sixth-inning homer (also off Ralph Branca) erased a 1-0 Brooklyn lead.

Possibly even as dramatic, although less significant, was a homer he hit during a 1952 season contest at St. Louis. The Cardinals were leading, 6-3, with two out and the bases loaded in the bottom of the ninth when Thomson connected for a 7-6 Giants' win.

His trade to the Milwaukee Braves following the '53 season helped the Giants to another N.L. pennant, as Johnny Antonelli came to the Polo Grounds and became a 20-game winner. The Dodger Slayer returned to the Giants again for the last half of the '57 season, the team's last in New York. Bobby also played for the Cubs, Red Sox, and Orioles at the end of his career, which terminated in 1960 with a .270 average. He walloped 264 home runs in 1,779 games (most of them in the outfield), but 184 as a third baseman—his original position—in 1946 when he came to the Giants.

In 1969 he was named to the Giants' all-time outfield

with a couple of other pretty fair players named Mel Ott and Willie Mays.

When asked what he did after he hit his immortal clout he answered, "After the game I went to the 'Perry Como Show' and then went home and had a quiet celebration with my family and friends in Staten Island. The next day we had to open the World Series with the Yankees so I had to be ready."

THORPE, Bob
Waveland, MS

Benjamin Robert Thorpe came up as an outfielder with the Boston Braves in 1951. He was with the team the following campaign, and also in '53 (the Braves' first year in Milwaukee). He sang his tune to a .251 average.

THORPE, Bob J.
Died March 17, 1960, at age 25 in San Diego, CA, electrocuted while working as an apprentice electrician

When Bob J. Thorpe arrived with the Cubs in 1955, "The Mickey Mouse Club" began a long television run with Annette Funicello. Bob J. had no record in just two games that year, but the right-hander had won 28 games in the Class C California League the previous season (completing 32 of the 33 games he started). He then became the first player in Cubs' history to advance to the majors from the Class C ranks—no "Mickey Mouse" move.

THRONEBERRY, Faye
Professional trainer of hunting dogs
Colliersville, TN

The older brother of "Marvelous Marv," Faye was never known as "Fabulous Faye." He was an outfielder in parts of eight seasons in the A.L. with the Red Sox (1952, 1955–57), Senators (1957–60), and Angels (1961).

This dog trainer bow-wowed for a .236 average.

THRONEBERRY, Marv
> Lite Beer commercials; former glass company foreman.
> Memphis, TN

There was nothing funny about Marv to pitchers in the American Association in the mid-1950s when he hit 118 home runs over a three-year period at Denver in the Yankees' organization. He made his debut in a Yankee uniform in '55, going 2-for-2 with 3 RBIs in his only game that year. He then was with the Yankees in both the 1958 and '59 seasons. After stops in Kansas City and Baltimore, he joined the expansion Mets in early 1962 and became the symbol of the team's futility, especially after owner Joan Payson commented, "Wasn't that Marvelous of Marv?" following one of the 16 home runs he hit that season.

On June 17, 1962, Marv's triple against the Cubs went for naught in the first game of a doubleheader when the Cubs appealed that he not only missed first base, but missed second also! .237

THURMAN, Bob
> Central Scouting Bureau

This Kansas native joined the Reds as a backup outfielder in 1955 on a team that included such sluggers as Frank Robinson, Gus Bell, and Wally Post. From 1955–59, Bob hit .246 in 334 games while displaying power of his own on occasion, especially in 1957 when he hit 16 homers despite playing in just 74 games.

TIEFENAUER, Bobby
> Philadelphia Phillies pitching instructor

Bob worked in 179 games between stints in the minors from 1952–68, compiling a 9-25 record with all his appearances coming out of the bullpens of the Cardinals, Indians, Astros, Braves, Yankees, and Cubs.

TIPTON, Joe
  Salesman for Lonnie Russell Leasing (Ford Co.)
  Birmingham, AL

Joe's big league menu consisted of 417 games and a .236 average as a seven-year catcher (1948–54) with the Indians, White Sox, Philadelphia A's, and Washington Senators.

TOMANEK, Dick
  Millwright, B.F. Goodrich Chemical Co.
  Avon Lake, OH

Dick's father always said that if his son ever made it to the majors and pitched in Cleveland, he would walk the 20 miles from the family home in Avon Lake to see him pitch. Dick made it and in '53 his dad walked to Municipal Stadium where he saw the left-hander beat the Tigers in his big league debut. Overall, Dick pitched for the Indians ('53, '54, '57, '58) and Kansas City A's (1958–59). He was 10-10 in 106 games.

TORGESON, Earl
  Lumber company salesman and supervisor of logging operations
  Everett, WA

As a youngster in Snohomish, Washington, Earl idolized the original "Earl of Snohomish," Earl Averill. Late in 1941 Averill was at the end of a career which would later gain him entry into Cooperstown. He was on the Seattle club in the PCL and was joined by the 17-year-old Torgeson, who had been signed out of high school. Torgeson reached the majors in 1947 as a first baseman with the Boston Braves. In the '48 World Series he was the top hitter in the "Fall Classic" at .389. His finest season was in 1950 when he hit .290 and scored a league-leading 190 runs. He was with the Phillies from 1953–55 before switching leagues when he played for the Tigers and another World Series team—the White Sox—in '59. Earl swung his powerful stick with the White Sox and Yankees in 1961, his final season. Briefly during the 1960 campaign a teammate on the White Sox was Earl Averill—the son of the original Earl of Snohomish. .265

TORRE, Frank
   Senior vice president
   Rawlings sporting goods
   St. Louis, MO

A slick-fielding first baseman, Frank was with the Milwaukee Braves (1956–60) and Philadelphia Phillies (1962–63), hitting for a .273 average in 714 games. He took over for Joe Adcock at first base when Adcock broke his leg in 1957. In one game on September 2nd of that season, he scored a record six runs. His brother Joe broke in with the Braves in 1960, Frank's final year with the team.

TREMEL, Bill
   Employed with S.K.F. Ballbearings
   Altoona, PA

This right-handed chucker flew in with the Cubs in '54. Between 1954–56 Bill was 4-2 in 57 games with the Cubs— all out of the bullpen.

TRIANDOS, Gus
   Owner, Diamond Mail Service
   San Jose, CA

A slow-footed but heavy-hitting catcher, Gus originally broke in as a first baseman with the Yankees in 1953. He was one of the early stars with the Orioles after the franchise shift from St. Louis. Primarily a first baseman with them in '55, he became a fixture behind the plate in Baltimore the next several seasons. His 30 home runs in 1958 tied an A.L. record held by Yogi Berra for most home runs by a catcher in a season. Also in '58, he had the only stolen base of his career in his only attempt to pilfer a bag. Triandos also played for the Tigers, Phillies, and Astros in the early 1960s before finishing with a .244 average.

Gus has the distinction of being the first man to catch no-hitters in each league. He was on the receiving end of Hoyt Wilhelm's masterpiece against the Yankees in 1958 as a member of the Orioles, and was behind the dish for the Phils in 1964 when Jim Bunning pitched his perfect game against the Mets.

TRICE, Bob
Weirton, WV

Bob became the first black to ever play for the Philadelphia A's when he joined them late in the '53 season after winning 21 games at Ottawa in the International League. The right-hander remained with the A's for a few games into the 1955 campaign after the franchise shifted to Kansas City.   9-9

TRIMBLE, Joe
Plant manager for Coca-Cola Bottling Company of New England
Fall River, MA

Joe tossed a couple of games for the Red Sox in 1955. He barely broke a sweat for Pittsburgh two years later where his pitching career ended at 0-2.

TROSKY, Hal, Jr.
Sales supervisor
John Hancock Mutual Life Insurance Co.
Cedar Rapids, IA

Hal was born Harold Arthur Troyavesky, Jr., in Cleveland, in September 1936, as his father was concluding his most outstanding season in the majors as a first baseman with the Indians.

Hal Jr. was a right-handed hurler who won his only decision in two games with the 1958 White Sox.

TROUPE, Quincy
> Manager of a home for the elderly
> Los Angeles, CA

Do you remember Quincy, who played in six games for the Cleveland Indians in 1952? A former top-flight catcher and manager in the old Negro Leagues, Quincy had a book published about his life in the Negro Leagues. .100

TROUT, Dizzy
> Died February 28, 1972, at age 56
> Harvey, IL

A colorful right-handed pitcher, Paul "Dizzy" Trout spent most of his playing days with the Tigers (1939–52). Trout's 20 wins paced the A.L. in 1943, but his finest season came in '44 when he won 27 to combine with teammate Hal Newhouser's 29. It was the closest that two pitchers on the same team came to winning 30 since 1904 when "Iron Man" McGinnity won 35 and Christy Mathewson 33 for the Giants. Despite the combined 56 wins of Trout and Newhouser, the Tigers missed out on the A.L. pennant by one game to the St. Louis Browns. Dizzy was able to console himself with league-leading figures in ERA at 2.12, games completed (33), games started (44), innings pitched (352), and shutouts (7). He even hit .271 with five of his career-total 20 home runs.

In 1945 he was an 18-game winner, including four the final week and a half as the Tigers won the A.L. flag. He then was a winner in game four of the World Series as Detroit beat the Cubs. Pitching against the Yankees in 1950, he was the winning reliever in a contest where all 19 runs were accounted for by home runs. The biggest of the 11 homers was his grand-slam blast, leading the Bengals to a 10-9 victory.

Trout became a Tigers' broadcaster and appeared to be retired after pitching with the Red Sox in '52. But five years later, after an impressive showing in an Old-Timers game, he signed with the Orioles. Dizzy pitched in two games with them before retiring for good with a 170-161 record and fine 3.23 ERA. He was doing public relations work for the Chicago White Sox at the time of his death. His son Steve is currently pitching for the Cubs.

TROWBRIDGE, Bob
Died April 3, 1980, at age 49 in Hudson, NY

1956: The Four Lads were "Standing on the Corner" while Bob was standing on the mound as a rookie chucker with the Milwaukee Braves. He stayed in the Brew City until 1959, and was 7-5 for the World Champion Braves. After a brief stop in Kansas City in 1960, Bob was standing in the unemployment line.   13-13

TRUCKS, Virgil
Ex-director of civic center and recreation dept.
Leeds, AL

"Fire" was 177-135 in 517 games in an A.L. career that lasted from 1941–58. The hard-throwing right-hander threw a pair of no-hitters in the Class C Alabama-Florida League in his first year in pro ball in 1938. Throwing no-hitters in every league he ever pitched in, he also had one in the Texas League and in the International League while working his way up to the majors. In 1945 he joined the Tigers after being released from military service in time to pitch and win the second game of the World Series over the Cubs.

A 19-game winner in 1949, Virgil was the A.L. leader in both strikeouts (153) and shutouts (6). Then in 1952 he had his first "poor" year with an ignoble 5-19 mark. However, the five wins included a pair of no-hitters, a one-hitter, and a two-hitter. The second no-hitter that year came late in the season against the champion Yankees, and for a few innings he wasn't working on a no-hitter at all as Phil Rizzuto had been credited with a base hit on a ball Tigers' shortstop Johnny Pesky failed to handle in the third inning. Later in the game, the official scorer, John Drebinger, changed the scoring from a base hit to an error on Pesky.

Traded to the St. Louis Browns, Trucks was 5-4 early in '53 when he was traded to the White Sox where he won 15 games for his first 20-game season. He also pitched for the A's and Yankees near the end of his career. Virgil coached for the Pirates in 1963 and has scouted for the Atlanta Braves.

TSITOURIS, John
  Car salesman at Griffin Chevrolet
  Monroe, NC

John began a big league run bridged between Detroit ('57), K.C. (1958–60), and the Reds (1962–68). The right-hander compiled a 34-38 mark, his best season coming in '63 when he went 12-8, with three shutouts.

TUCKER, Thurman
  Insurance business
  Oklahoma City, OK

A look-alike for comedian Joe E. Brown, Thurman was a flychaser with the White Sox (1942–47) and Indians (1948–51). He departed with a .255 lifetime average. In the 1948 World Series, he went 1-for-3 for the Indians.

TURNER, Earl
  Pittsfield, MA

Earl was behind the dish in 42 games for the Pirates in 1948 and 1950.   .240

TURLEY, Bob
  Securities business
  Dunwoody, GA

"Bullet" Bob was originally with the St. Louis Browns (1951 and '53) and then the Orioles in '54 before becoming the key figure in a 17-player deal with the Yankees. His big year came in 1958 when he went 21-7 and was the Cy Young award winner. Turley also starred in the World Series after being knocked out of the box in the first inning of the second game by the Braves.

After a 14-victory season with the anemic Orioles in '54, Baltimore denied all rumors of ever trading him, but eventually did in the colossal 17-player swap.

The Yankees originally thought they had signed him out of high school in the late 1940s, but after a tryout

camp, the wrong R. Turley was signed. It was Bob's uncle
Ralph, just two years older than Bob.   101-85

TUTTLE, Bill
    Peoria, IL

Bill was signed by the Tigers off the Bradley University
campus where he also played football. He was with
Detroit briefly in '52 before becoming the team's regular center fielder starting in 1954. Tuttle also played for
Kansas City (1958–61) and Minnesota until '63. In his
11-year stay he hit .259 in 1,270 games, with his finest
season coming in 1959 when he swatted an even .300 for
K.C. A fine defensive outfielder, he twice led the A.L. in
putouts and assists. Tuttle didn't suffer from "Triakai-
dekaphobia," the fear of the number 13, as he wore that
number during his career.
    Born on Independence Day, Bill once lived in Indepen-
dence, Missouri.

U

UMBRICHT, Jim
    Died April 8, 1964, at age 33 in Houston, TX

This big right-handed chucker out of the University of
Georgia made his debut with the Pirates in 1959. He was
also with Pittsburgh briefly in both 1960 and '61 before
going to the expansion Astros. Jim had some nifty days
working out of the Houston bullpen in both 1962 and '63,
with an 8-3 mark in 69 games, and an ERA under 3.00.
Overall, 9-5 in 88 games. The Astros have retired his uniform number 32. Jim died of a brain tumor while still active in the majors.

UMPHLETT, Tom
> Self-employed—furniture building hobby
> Ahoskie, NC

Tom started with the Red Sox as a 23-year-old rookie in 1953. He hit .283, replacing Dom DiMaggio in center field. Following the '53 campaign, Umphlett was traded to the Senators in a deal that saw Jackie Jensen go to the Red Sox. While playing in the nation's capital, Tom tailed off to .219 and .217 seasons, and was soon an ex-major leaguer.
> .246

UPRIGHT, Dixie
> Kannapolis, NC

Even with a guy named Upright, the St. Louis Browns were downright terrible in 1953, when they lost 100 games. Used exclusively as a pinch-hitter with the Brownies that year, "Dixie" (whose given name is Roy) appeared in nine games, going 2-for-8, including a home run.
> .250

The Upton Brothers
UPTON, Bill
> Retired; previously managed bowling lanes
> La Mesa, CA

Bill pitched in two games with the Philadelphia A's in 1954, giving up one run in five innings before rolling out of the big time.
> 0-0

UPTON, Tom
> Math professor at Compton Junior College
> Downey, CA

"Muscles," as he was sometimes called, broke in with the Browns as a shortstop in 1950 where he spent two seasons. He flexed his muscles for the last time in '52 with the Senators.
> .225

URBAN, Jack
Painting company
Omaha, NE

A right-hander with the K.C. A's (1957–58) and Cardinals ('59), Jack traveled with a 15-15 record.

USHER, Bob
La Mesa, CA

Bob had his swan song in '57. An outfielder with the Reds (1946–47, 1950–51), Cubs ('52), and Senators ('57), Bob batted .235.

VALDES, Rene
Havana, Cuba

Rene pitched in five games with the last edition of the Brooklyn Dodgers in '57, without costing the Dodgers too many games, going 1-1.

VALDIVIELSO, Jose
Sports Director, WNJU-TV (Channel 47)
Newark, NJ

In 1955 Jose began as a shortstop with the Washington Senators where he played in 1955–56 and 1959–60. His final days were spent in Minnesota in '61. Jose's father was a football player at Boston University in the early 1930s, then returned to Cuba to teach physical education.
.219

VALENTINE, Corky
  Policeman
  Atlanta, GA

Harold "Corky" Valentine had an unusually short jog
with a winning record, going 12-11 and 2-1 with the Reds
in 1954–55. This Valentine was most likely heartbroken
as his rather promising career came to a close after two
campaigns.   14-12

VALENTINE, Fred
  Construction company draftsman
  Washington, DC

Fred broke in with the Orioles in 1959. A one-time football
star at Tennessee A&I, he was in Baltimore in '63. The
flychaser then moved to the Senators from 1964–68 and
also spent a part of the '68 season back with the Orioles.
                                                         .247

VALENTINETTI, Vito
  New York State court system
  Mount Vernon, NY

Vito never starred in *The Godfather*. He was a second baseman on the Manhattan Aviation High School team with
Whitey Ford (who was a first baseman-outfielder) in the
mid-1940s. After attending Iona College, Vito was with
the White Sox in '54 and the Cubs in '56 before returning
to the A.L. with the Indians, Tigers, and Senators. Valentinetti finished 13-14 in 108 games.

  In recent years he has pitched batting practice for both
the Yankees and Mets when the teams are home. Vito
probably made them an offer they couldn't refuse.   13-14

VALENZUELA, Benny
  Manager of Reynosa in the Mexican League

This third baseman played in just 10 games with the Cardinals, hitting .214 in 1958.

VALO, Elmer
    Philadelphia Phillies scout

Born in Ribnik, Czechoslovakia, Elmer came to the
United States as a boy, and had a lengthy career as an
outfielder. It was one that should have spanned four decades. Late in the 1939 season he was called up to the
Philadelphia A's. On the final day of the season he
walked as a pinch-batter. However, a young writer
named Red Smith (the scorekeeper that day), pointed
out to A's manager Connie Mack that Elmer hadn't officially been signed to a contract, and the A's would be
subject to a fine by the Commissioner. Thus Valo's
name was never entered into the scorebook.

Among his distinctions are two bases-loaded triples in
one game (in 1949). He is the only player to ever play on
two different major league teams which suffered a 20 or
more game losing streak—the '43 A's (20), and the '61
Phillies (23). Three separate times he moved with a
team in a franchise shift. He went with the A's from
Philadelphia to Kansas City after the '54 campaign,
with the Dodgers from Brooklyn to L.A. following the
'57 season, and traveled with the Senators to Minnesota
after 1960.

His career total of 90 pinch-hits ranks Elmer among the
all-time leaders. Overall he hit over .300 five times, compiling a .282 average in 1,806 games.

A Cleveland Indians coach in 1963–64, he has since been
a hitting instructor, and now scouts with the Phillies.

VAN BRABANT, Ozzie
    Electrical maintenance worker at Wayne State Uni-
    versity
    Royal Oak, MI

Canadian-born Camille Oscar Van Brabant didn't stick
around long, going 0-2 with the Philadelphia and Kansas
City A's in 1954–55.

VAN CUYK, Chris
    Retired; formerly with Portland Cement Co.
    Tampa, FL

A 6'6" southpaw hurler, big Chris rolled a 7-11 mark in 44 games with the Brooklyn Dodgers from 1950–52. His older brother, Johnny Van Cuyk, had no decisions in seven appearances with the same Dodgers from 1947–49.

VANDER MEER, Johnny
    Retired; former Schlitz brewery company sales manager
    Tampa, FL

To youngsters just beginning to follow baseball in the fifties, the name Johnny Vander Meer was legendary for his 1938 back-to-back no-hitters for the Reds. It would be surprising to learn that his overall mark in 346 games pitched stood at 119-121.

Johnny's first no-hitter in '38 was over the Boston Braves (known as the Bees at the time), 3-0, in Cincinnati. Four days later in the first night game ever played in New York at Brooklyn's Ebbets Field, he no-hit the Dodgers, 6-0. It was the first no-hitter ever thrown at night. Among those witnessing the feat were recently-retired Babe Ruth and Olympic hero Jesse Owens. Vander Meer did not yield a base hit until the fourth inning of his next start when Debs Garms of the Boston Braves (the victim of his first no-hitter), connected.

Johnny pitched for the Reds from 1937–49 and for three straight years in the early forties he led the N.L. in strikeouts. In 1946 he was involved in the longest scoreless game in major league history (19 innings). He threw shutout ball for the first 15 innings of the marathon. He finished with the Cubs ('50) and Indians ('51).

VAN DUSEN, Fred
    Stamford, CT

Frederick William Van Dusen, a name which seems to belong in the society page rather than a box score, was

in only one box score. A New York City high school star
in the mid-fifties, Fred made just one pinch-hitting
appearance as an 18-year-old with the Phillies in
1955.   .000

VAN NOY, Jay
        Owns automobile agency
        "Jay's Quality Cars"
        Logan, UT

An outfielder by trade, Jay made his six-game debut with
the Cardinals in 1951. Van Noy was a Brigham Young
University assistant football coach in 1958.   .000

VARGA, Andy
        Belleville, KS

This southpaw appeared in three games for his home town
Cubs in '50 and '51. He finished at 0-0.

VARGAS, Roberto
        Altamesa, PR

A chucker with the Milwaukee Braves in 1955, he had no
decisions in 25 games. Vargas evidently made brief stops
to the mound as he pitched just 25 innings.

VARNER, Buck
        Steamfitter and welder
        Hixson, TN

Glen Gann "Buck" Varner made it into two games with
the 1952 Senators. Today the former outfielder reminisces
about his day in the sun while residing on Varner Road in
Hixson, Tennessee.   .000

VEAL, "Coot"

   Salesman for Macon Mine and Mill industrial supplies
   Macon, GA

Orville "Coot" Veal was a shortstop with the Tigers in the
late 1950s, and with the Senators, Pirates, and Tigers
again in the early 1960s. Coot played college basketball at
Auburn University.   .231

VERBAN, Emil

   Realtor, farmer, chairman of a bank
   Elkhart, IL

Known as "Antelope," Emil was the Cardinals' regular
second baseman in 1944 and '45. As a 29-year-old rookie in
'44, he led the Cardinals, batting .412 in the World Series
win over the cross-town Browns. He remained as the regular second baseman in '45 while rookie Red Schoendienst
played the outfield. Red moved to the pivot position in '46,
and Emil moved to the Phillies. He also played for the
Cubs before closing with the Boston Braves in 1950.   .272

VERBLE, Gene

   Runs a general store
   Concord, NC

A shortstop, Gene appeared in 81 games with the Senators
in parts of 1951 and 1953.   .202

VERDI, Frank

   Managed San Jose in the Class A California League in
   1983; managing on Triple-A level in 1984

Frank's cup of coffee was "instant" as he appeared in one
game at shortstop with the 1953 Yankees and made no
trips to the plate.
   In 1959, playing with Miami in the International
League, his team played a game in Havana, Cuba. Plastic
liners usually protect batters from pitched balls, but in
Frank's case, the liner saved him from serious injury not

from a pitched ball, but from a stray bullet from the stands.

VERNON, Mickey
  New York Yankees scout

President Eisenhower's favorite player, Mickey first appeared with the Senators in 1939. When he finally departed he had competed in four decades, finishing with the Pirates in 1960. In between, he hit for a .300-plus average four times, including a pair of A.L. batting titles in 1946 (.353), and in 1953 (.337).

It is Mickey Vernon, not Lou Gehrig (as would be expected), who holds the major league record for most games played at first base. He appeared in 2,237 games at first base compared to the 2,136 of the "Iron Horse." Vernon also played for the Indians, Red Sox, and Braves during his long tenure, but it was with Washington that he spent most of his playing time, and was voted that team's all-time first sacker in 1969.

Mickey has remained in baseball the past two decades as a manager for the Senators in the early 1960s, a coach with the Pirates and Cardinals, and as a hitting instructor for the Royals and Expos.

On Opening Day in 1954, Mickey had quite an experience playing for the Senators in front of President Eisenhower. He remembered, "In the tenth inning, against Allie Reynolds and the Yankees, we had a man on first and none out. After we tried a bunt and failed, I hit one over the right field wall. Just as I got to home plate, a Secret Service man grabbed my arm and took me over to see President Eisenhower. He said to me, 'That was a nice job. Congratulations.'" Actually, the President had started to leave his seat and go onto the field, but the Secret Service stopped him and brought Vernon over to the President's box.

A slick-fielding first baseman, he could play first base in a tuxedo (it was often said). After 2,409 games, Mickey parted with a .286 average. If he follows the footsteps of Minnie Minoso, baseball fans may catch one more glimpse of Mr. Vernon.

VERSALLES, Zoilo

> Collects workman's disability insurance in Minneapolis, MN (injured his back as a player in 1968)

"Zorro" first came up with the Senators in 1959. The Cuban shortstop went to Minnesota with the franchise, and put together one outstanding year in 1965 when he was named A.L. MVP with league-leading totals in doubles, triples, and runs scored. The catalyst of the Twins' offense that season, he also led the A.L. in total bases and, would you believe, strikeouts!

Following the '65 season, it was all downhill as he moved to the Dodgers, Cleveland, Washington and Atlanta Braves. He played for one year in the Mexican League in 1970, and he was barely 30 years old when his playing days culminated. Overall he hit for a .242 average in an even 1,400 games.

VIRDON, Bill

> Montreal Expos manager

Bill was voted N.L. Rookie of the Year in 1955 when he began with the Cardinals. Traded early the following year, he defied the so-called "sophomore jinx" by responding with his finest season, at .319 for Pittsburgh. He was a fixture in the Pirates' outfield through 1965.

He managed in the minors in 1966 and '67, then returned to the Pirates as a coach in 1968. Virdon played briefly that year, just long enough to hit a home run for his final major league hit.

He replaced Danny Murtaugh as manager of the Pirates in 1972, only to be later replaced by Murtaugh. Virdon also managed the Yankees before taking over the helm of the Astros. Although he never played a game for the Yankees, Bill was originally Yankee property.

Virdon has the distinction of being the only Yankee manager since the opening of Yankee Stadium in 1923 never to have managed the pinstripers in that ballpark. He piloted the Yanks in 1974–75 when they played at Shea Stadium while Yankee Stadium was undergoing renovation. .267

VIRGIL, Ozzie
   San Diego Padres coach

Ozzie was the first player from the Dominican Republic to
play in the majors. He played all over the diamond in his
nine-year stay, mostly as a third baseman (although he
played every other position, except pitcher).

   He was originally with the New York Giants in 1956–
57. He also spent time with the Kansas City A's, Orioles,
Pirates, and Giants again (in San Francisco). He was the
first black to play for the Tigers. Virgil's son, Ozzie Jr.,
was a catcher with the 1983 N.L. pennant-winning Phillies.
Ozzie was a Giants' coach from 1969–72.   .231

VOISELLE, Bill "Ninety-Six"
   Parke-Davis capsule plant
   Greenwood, SC

Bill is best remembered for wearing No. 96, the name of
his home town. He had a fine rookie season with the New
York Giants in 1944, when he won 21 games and led the
N.L. in strikeouts and innings pitched. He was a 13-game
winner for the 1948 N.L. champion Boston Braves, as it
wasn't all "Spahn and Sain and pray for rain." Voiselle
concluded with the Cubs in 1950.   74-84

VOLLMER, Clyde
   Semi-retired; owns two taverns
   Cincinnati, OH

Clyde broke in with his home town Reds in 1942 with a
home run in his first major league at-bat. He has a few
other noteworthy distinctions in a career which ended
with the Senators in 1954. Vollmer shares the big
league record for most plate appearances in a nine-
inning game (with 8) on June 8, 1950, while playing for
the Red Sox.

   In July 1951, as a member of the Red Sox, he was baseball's hottest hitter with 13 homers and 30 RBIs for the
month. During one seven-game stretch, he had 16 RBIs
and knocked in the game-winning run 6 times. He also hit

what still stands as the latest-inning grand-slam homer, a
16th-inning blast in that same '51 season.   .251

WADE, Ben
   L.A. Dodgers director of scouting

Originally with the Cubs in 1948, Ben had his finest season as a member of the 1952–53 Dodgers. As a part-time
starter and reliever he won 18 games those two years for
the N.L. champions. The right-hander also pitched for the
Cards and Pirates in the mid-fifties. His older brother,
"Whistlin" Jake Wade, was a lefty chucker with several
American League teams from 1936–46.   19-17

WADE, Gale
   Electrician
   Nebo, NC

The lights went out for this electrician after a brief
19-game career. The outfielder hit .133 in parts of 1955
and '56 with the Cubs.

WAGNER, Leon
   Professional actor; automobile salesman
   Altadena, CA

"Daddy Wags" was a colorful long-ball-hitting outfielder.
He came up with the S.F. Giants in 1958, then played for
the St. Louis Cardinals in 1960 before having his most productive season with the expansion L.A. Angels in 1962
when he hit a career high 37 homers with 107 RBIs. He
also played for the Indians and White Sox in the mid-1960s
before finishing back in San Francisco in 1969.
   Among his acting parts was a role in "Bingo Long's
Traveling All Stars," a story of the old-time Negro barn-

storming team. Yankee announcer Bill White calls Leon "a black Dusty Rhodes." Wagner collected 211 round-trippers and had a .272 average.

In the early sixties Leon used to own a clothing store. His popular logo was "Buy Your Rags at Daddy Wags."

WAHL, Kermit
       Director of admissions
       Chapparal College
       Tucson, AZ

Kermit was a utility infielder with the Reds during the mid-forties and also played with the Philadelphia A's and St. Louis Browns in 1950 and '51. A graduate of the University of Indiana, this South Dakota native lives on East Speedway in Tucson. After he took his last lap, he drove away with a .226 average.

WAITKUS, Eddie
       Died September 15, 1972, at age 53 in Boston, MA

This smooth fielding and steady hitting first baseman had a fine career, hitting for a .285 average in 1,140 games. Yet, he will always be remembered for being shot in the chest by Ruth Ann Steinhagen, a deranged admirer, early in the 1949 season in Chicago.

Originally with the Cubs in 1941, he returned in 1946 after the war and remained with them until traded to the Phillies following the 1948 season. He was hitting over .300 early in the '49 campaign when the shooting incident occurred. He returned in '50 to play every game for the N.L. champion Phillies. He was with the Orioles in 1954–55 before closing with the Phillies in '55.

WAKEFIELD, Dick
       Probate court consultant—helps to appraise estates
       Dearborn Heights, MI

Baseball's first bonus baby, Dick was signed for $52,000 out of the University of Michigan by the Tigers. In his first full season (1943), he hit .316, with league-leading totals of

200 hits and 38 doubles. He was at .355 early in '44 when he was called to military service. In his comeback bid with the Tigers after the war in 1946, he never returned to his early form.

While Wakefield was stationed in Hawaii during his military tour of duty, he met Ted Williams. As the story goes, he bet the "Splendid Splinter" that he would hit more homers, drive in more runs, and hit for a better average when they returned from the war. His big league playing time in the fifties consisted of three pinch-hitting appearances for the Yankees in 1950, and three more for the N.Y. Giants in '52, hardly a threat to Mr. Williams.

Dick's father, who died the year Dick broke into the majors in '41, was a catcher for Washington and Cleveland from 1905–07. After 638 games, Dick exited with a .293 average.

WALKER, Harry "The Hat"
    University of Alabama baseball coach
    Birmingham, AL

"The Hat" and his brother "Dixie" (Fred) were both solid-hitting outfielders in the N.L. during the 1940s. "Dixie," who first came up with the Yankees in 1931, had most of his success as "The People's Cherce" (long before "The People's Choice" became a TV hit in the '50s) in Brooklyn. He won the N.L. batting crown in 1944 with a .357 mark, and last played in the majors in 1949.

Harry came up with the Cards in 1940. He hit .412 in the '46 Series, and it was his base hit which brought Enos Slaughter around from first base with the winning run in the seventh and deciding game. Early the following season he was traded to the Phillies for outfielder Ron Northey. Harry's .363 average that year gave him the N.L. batting title, the first player to win it while dividing the season between two teams. Playing for the Cubs in '49 he was dealt to the Reds in a trade, again for Northey.

Walker rounded out his playing days with the Cardinals in 1950 and '51 prior to taking over as manager for their International League team at Rochester. When Eddie Stanky, "The Brat," was fired during the '55 season,

Harry became the St. Louis manager and also appeared in 11 games. His brother, who had been a coach under Stanky at St. Louis, then took Harry's place at Rochester. Walker later became the manager of the Pirates and the Houston Astros in the late 1960s and early 1970s, and has also been a hitting instructor for the Cardinals and Astros.

Harry and Dixie were the second set of brothers from the Walker family to play in the biggies. Their father, Ewart, also known as "Dixie," was a pitcher for the Senators from 1909–12. His brother Ernie was an outfielder with the St. Louis Browns from 1913–15. The Walker brothers (Harry and Dixie) are the only sibs in baseball history to each win a batting title.   .296

WALKER, Jerry
Pitching instructor in New York Yankees organization

This right-handed chucker was an 18-year-old bonus player with the Orioles in 1957 when he won his only decision, a ten-inning, four-hit shutout 1-0 win over Washington. After spending most of the '58 campaign in the minors, he returned in '59 for his first full season, and it turned out to be his finest, with an 11-10 mark and an ERA under 3.00. Among his victories was a 16-inning 1-0 shutout over the A.L. champion White Sox. He was also the starter and winner for the A.L. in the second All-Star Game that season making him the youngest to ever start and/or win the prestigious mid-summer event.

His pitching fell off to 3-4 the following year, but his .368 batting average was the best in the majors among pitchers. Later he was with the Indians and Kansas City before having his career end at age 25 in 1964 with a 37-44 mark in 190 games. With the Indians in '63, he was credited with just one save out of the bullpen, but that came in relief of Early Wynn's 300th career victory.

He has been in the Yankee organization as a minor league manager, a pitching instructor, and scout in recent years.

WALKER, Al "Rube"
   Atlanta Braves coach

Rube was to Roy Campanella as Charlie Silvera was to
Yogi Berra. He was the backup catcher on the Dodger
teams of the 1950s. Walker was with the Cubs from 1948
until traded to Brooklyn in 1951. Like Silvera (who saw
very little action playing behind Berra), Walker also
picked up his World Series check four times in five years
from 1952–56. He was the catcher during the '51 playoff
with the Giants due to a thigh injury to Campanella. Rube
completed his career as a player-coach for the Dodgers'
first team in Los Angeles in 1958.

After managing in the minors for a few seasons, he
joined former teammate Gil Hodges at Washington as a
coach for the Senators, then went to the Mets as a coach
when Hodges took over as the team's manager. Walker
has remained a Mets' coach ever since.

A brother, Verlon Walker (also called "Rube"), never
played under the big top, but was a coach for the Cubs during most of the 1960s.   .227

WALL, Murray
   Died October 8, 1971, at age 45 in Lone Oak, TX

Murray was out of the University of Texas where he
pitched for an NCAA championship team and also played
basketball. He signed with the Boston Braves in 1950, appearing in one game that year. Seven years later he returned with the Red Sox, winning all three of his decisions.
Along with a 3.33 ERA, he hit for a .333 average. In '58 he
was an ace out of the Red Sox bullpen with 8 wins and 10
saves. The following year he spent his final season with
Boston. He played with the Senators for one game, and
then was back again with the Red Sox.

Wall was traded to the Senators for Dick Hyde. But
since Hyde was unable to pitch because of a sore arm, the
deal was cancelled and Murray was returned to the Red
Sox after pitching only one game for the Senators.   13-14

WALLS, Lee
   New York Yankees coach

Ray L. "Lee" Walls was initially with the Pirates as a
19-year-old outfielder in 1952. He spent his first full season in '56 and was then traded to the Cubs, where he had
his finest year in 1958 with a .304 average and 24 home
runs. In the early 1960s, he was with the Reds and Phillies
before spending his final three years mainly as a pinch-
hitter for the Dodgers from 1962–64.

   A San Diego native, he had been a batboy for the Padres
of the Pacific Coast League in the mid-1940s.   .262

WALSH, Jim
   Olyphant, PA

"Junior," as he was known, was a right-handed hurler
with the Pirates in 1946 and from 1948–51. He established
a record of sorts by winning exactly one game for four consecutive years from 1948–51 with Pittsburgh. His '49 victory was a shutout.   4-10

WALTERS, Bucky
   Retired; former coach with the Braves and Giants
   Glenside, PA

William Henry "Bucky" Walters was not a significant
part of the 1950s, since he pitched in just one game with
the Boston Braves in 1950. However, in the late 1930s and
1940s, the right-hander was one of the premier hurlers
with Cincinnati while going 27-11 in '39, and 22-10 the following year. He captured the ERA crown both seasons. In
1944 he was a 23-game winner.

   Pitching for the Reds on Aug. 26, 1939, Bucky beat the
Dodgers in major league baseball's first televised game.

   He became the Reds' manager late in the '48 campaign
until he was released in 1949.

   His overall pitching mark stands at 198-160, including
42 shutouts. Bucky began as a third baseman in 1931.

WARD, Preston
    Las Vegas, NV

"You oughta be in pictures." Preston, who strongly resembled Gregory Peck, had his first taste of honey with the Dodgers in 1948. His next stop was with the Cubs in '50 before spending 1953–56 with the Pirates. At the end of the decade, Ward logged time in the junior circuit with the Indians and K.C. A's.

    The year 1956 was great for Gregory Peck as he made *The Man in the Gray Flannel Suit* and *Moby Dick.* Preston had a whale of a season in '58 when he hit for a nifty .284 clip, split between Cleveland and K.C. In 744 games, Preston played first base, third base, and the outfield.
                                            .253

WATERS, Fred
    Manager at Elizabethton in Appalachian Rookie
    League

Fred is the only major leaguer ever named Waters, and he wasn't around too long. With a birthdate of 2-2, he compiled an exact mark of 2-2 in 25 games with the Pirates, giving up 55 hits in 56 innings of work during the '55 and '56 seasons in Pittsburgh.

WATLINGTON, Neal
    Mercantile business; tobacco and cattle ranch
    Yanceyville, NC

Julius Neal Watlington was in 21 games as a catcher with the Philadelphia A's in 1953, hitting .159.

WAUGH, Jim
    Union City, IN

Jim checked in with the Pirates in 1952. Gone after the '53 season before his 20th birthday, the teenage chucker left at 5-11.

WEATHERLY, Roy
Steel company employee
Beaumont, TX

Cyril Roy Weatherly was known as "Stormy." There was certainly some thunder in his bat in his major league debut with Cleveland in 1936 when he had four hits. He hit .335 that rookie year. Roy remained with the Indians until 1942, then was with the Yankees in 1943 and '46. Roy weathered the storm until 1950 when he made his last appearance with the N.Y. Giants.   .286

WEBSTER, Ray
Insurance business
Yuba City, CA

Ray began his 47-game tour in 1959 with the Indians. The infielder closed with the Red Sox the following year at .195.

WEHMEIER, Herman
Died May 21, 1973, at age 46 in Dallas, TX

Herman entered the majors out of high school in 1945 with his home-town Cincinnati Reds. He had his best season in his first full year in the biggies, going 11-8 in 1948. Following five consecutive losing campaigns (in which he led the league in bases-on-balls three times), Herman escaped the jeering of his home-town "fans" when he was traded to the Phillies. In 1956 the right-hander joined the Cardinals, a team he had been 0-14 against. Wehmeier then had a pair of winning years for them, including an opening day win back in Cincinnati in 1957.

At the time of his death, he was testifying as a witness in a trial involving theft from a shipping company where he held an executive position.   92-108

WEIK, Dick
>   Supervisor in catalog department for Sears, Roe-
>   buck
>   Tinley Park, IL

"The Wild One" with Marlon Brando was an attraction in
'54, the last year of this wild man's career. A lanky 6'3"
right-hander known as "Legs," Dick was with the Senators (1948–50), Indians ('50 and '53), and Tigers ('54). Apparently control problems kept Dick from stardom as he
issued 237 free passes in just 213 innings. When Mr. Weik
took his last walk from the mound, he was 6-22.

WELLMAN, Bob
>   Los Angeles Dodgers scout

A first baseman-outfielder, big Bob's birthdate of 7-15-25
resembles the numbers in his total statistics with the Philadelphia A's in 1948 and '50, as he was 7-for-25 in 15
games. He attended Indiana University on a football scholarship before signing to play professional baseball.   .280

WELTEROTH, Dick
>   Sheet metal, roofing, and heating business
>   Williamsport, PA

A native of Williamsport, Pa. (the site of the Little
League World Series), Dick saw action in 90 games as a relief pitcher with the Washington Senators, going 4-6 from
1948–50.

WERLE, Bill
>   Baltimore Orioles scout

This southpaw gave it a "whirl" with the Pirates (1949–
52), Cardinals ('52) and Red Sox (1953–54). "Bugs" finished 29-39. One of the all-time pitching greats at the University of California, Bill went 25-2 for the Golden Bears
as a collegian.

WERLEY, George
>   President of the Wenzel Tent and Sleeping Bag Co.
>   St. Louis, MO

The "Do-Wop" sound in music swept the country in
the mid-fifties when this eighteen-year-old right-hander
worked in one inning for the Orioles in '56.   0-0

WERTZ, Vic
>   Owned a successful beer distributorship in Detroit,
>   MI, at the time of his death on July 7, 1983, at age 58

This bald, chunky outfielder-turned-first baseman, had a
lengthy career from 1947–63. In over 1,800 games Vic
slammed out 266 homers and hit .277. But what he is most
remembered for has nothing to do with his offensive production.

As a member of the Indians in the '54 World Series,
Wertz hit a titanic wallop to deep center field in the Polo
Grounds that was snared by Willie Mays with his back to
home plate. The famous catch has gone down in WS annals
as one of the greatest ever. However, more miraculous
than the Mays' catch was the recovery Vic made from his
polio attack in the '55 season. He showed his mettle by returning in '56 to hit a career-high 32 homers for the
"Tribe."

Vic spent most of his days with the Tigers (1947–52), Indians (1954–58) and Red Sox (1958–61). He also made brief
stops with the Browns, Orioles, and Twins. Wertz returned
to Detroit for a few seasons at the twilight of his career. In
'62 with the Tigers, his 17 pinch-hits led the A.L. in that
category.

On September 14, 1957, while playing for the Indians,
he drove in 7 runs in two consecutive innings against the
Red Sox at Fenway Park. The RBI barrage tied a then-
major league record established by George Sisler in 1925.
Vic's big day came on a grand slam in the first inning, followed by a three-run round-tripper in the second frame.
His power display went for naught as the Red Sox nipped
the Indians, 13-10, in a Fenway fiasco.

WESTLAKE, Jim
  Paper company salesman
  Sacramento, CA

Just as Beaver Cleaver tried to follow in the footsteps of
his older brother Wally, Jim Westlake did likewise. Ten
years younger than brother Wally, his big league life was
short as he struck out as a pinch-hitter for the Phillies in
1955 in his one lone at-bat.

WESTLAKE, Wally
  Construction work
  Sacramento, CA

Wally, Jim's older brother, lasted ten years as an outfielder (1947–56) with some of his best years coming in the
late forties with the Pirates. After stays with the Cardinals and Reds in the early fifties, he joined the Indians in
1952 and hit for a career high .330 as a part-time player in
1953. He was also a member of the '54 Indians. Westlake
was with the Orioles and the Phillies at the end of his career in which he hit .272 in 958 games, 957 more than
brother Jim.

WESTRUM, Wes
  Atlanta Braves scout

A light-hitting but fine defensive catcher, Wes spent his
entire 11-year run (1947–57) with the New York Giants. In
1950 he blasted 23 four-baggers and had a fielding percentage of .999. On June 20th he had his biggest day, clouting
three homers and a triple.

  Westrum moved to San Francisco with the franchise in
'58 as a coach. He later returned to "The Big Apple" as a
coach, then manager of the Mets. Wes went West again to
coach the Giants before becoming a scout.   .217

WHEAT, Lee
Athletic director at Broward Community College
Fort Lauderdale, FL

Lee reached the majors as a right-handed pitcher with the
A's in Philadelphia and Kansas City in 1954–55. His entire career with them consisted of 11 games, in which he
lost both his big league decisions.

WHISENANT, Pete
Replaced as manager of Albany (Eastern League) during 1983 season

Pete was an eight-year outfielder with the Boston Braves
(1952), St. Louis Cardinals ('55), Chicago Cubs ('56), and
Cincinnati Reds in the late 50s. He then drifted around the
A.L. with the Indians, Senators, and Twins in 1960–61 before finishing with the pennant-winning Reds in '61.

In 1957 he was 8-for-20 as a pinch-hitter for the Reds.
Five of Pete's eight emergency hits were home runs, and
oddly, three were against Vinegar Bend Mizell of the
Cards.   .224

WHITE, Bill
New York Yankees announcer

A first baseman who had his finest seasons with the Cardinals in the early 1960s, Bill broke in with the N.Y. Giants
on May 7, 1956, with a home run in his first at-bat. After
military service he rejoined the Giants in San Francisco in
1958 with Orlando Cepeda holding down White's previous
job. Bill was traded to the Cardinals in 1959 and became
an outfielder as Stan Musial was playing first base. He
took over the first base position in 1960 and hit over the
.300 mark four times, including a career high of .324 in
1962. On July 5, 1961, Bill had a three-homer game and
several weeks later on July 17–18, playing in back-to-back
doubleheaders, he collected 14 base hits.

White was with the Phillies from 1966–68 then departed
in '69, returning to the Cardinals. In 1,673 games he hit
for a .286 average.

WHITE, Charlie
    Vancouver, BC

Charlie emerged as a catcher with the Milwaukee Braves
in '54 where he began a 62-game trip that ended the following year.   .236

WHITE, Ed
    School teacher and former coach at Lakeland high
    school
    Lakeland, FL

A star running back and receiver for the University of
Alabama in the late forties, his home run gave the Crim-
son Tide the NCAA baseball championship. In three
games with the White Sox in 1955, the outfielder was
2-for-4.   .500

WHITE, Hal
    Retired; former Kansas City scout
    Corning, NY

Hal was a right-handed flipper with the Tigers (1941–43,
1946–52), Browns ('53), and Cardinals (1953–54). He was
46-54 in 336 games with his finest year coming early when
he was 12-12 with four shutouts in 1942. However, in limited action in '49 he won his only decision in 9 games and
hurled 12 scoreless innings.

WHITE, Sammy
    Golf pro
    Hanalei, HI

An All-American basketball player at the University of
Washington in the late 1940s, Sam had a tryout with the
NBA Minneapolis Lakers.
    He was the number one catcher for the Red Sox through-
out most of the 1950s. White was behind the plate in over
100 games every year from 1952–59 before wrapping up
his career in the early 1960s with the Braves and Phillies.

Sam made one of the most colorful home run trots in big league history on June 11, 1952. After hitting a ninth-inning grand slam at Fenway Park to defeat "Satchel" Paige and the Browns, he completed his home run jog by crawling halfway home from third base. He finished his run by kissing home plate.

On June 18, 1953, he scored a record three times in one inning during Boston's 17-run marathon frame as they beat Detroit 23-3. Like his close friend and one-time room-mate with the Red Sox, Frank Sullivan, Sammy is today a golf pro in Hawaii.   .262

WHITMAN, Dick
>   San Jose water works maintenance manager
>   Campbell, CA

This one-time University of Oregon athlete was an out-fielder with the Dodgers (1946–49) and Phillies (1950–51). His 12 pinch-hits led the N.L. in 1950 as a member of the pennant-winning Phillies. Recalling that '50 season, Dick says, "I came from the Dodger organization, so it was a thrill beating that club."   .259

WIDMAR, Al
>   Toronto Blue Jays pitching coach

Al was with the Red Sox (1947), Browns (1948, 1950–51), and White Sox ('52). The right-hander collected all his deci-sions in his three years with the Browns, going 13-30. To-day, he has helped turn around the records of the Blue Jay pitchers from those similar to the 7-15 mark Al struggled through in 1950.

WIEAND, Ted
>   Plumbing and heating contractor
>   Slatington, PA

Franklin Delano Roosevelt "Ted" Wieand was born in 1933 a few months after the inauguration of FDR. "Ted" was a nickname he picked up after ex-president "Teddy" Roosevelt.

Ted lost his only decision in six games with the Reds in 1958 and '60.

WIESLER, Bob
Anheuser-Busch employee
St. Louis, MO

Bob made his debut with the Yankees in 1951, but soon entered military service. He did not return to Yankee Stadium until 1954 when he posted a 3-2 record.

The following year he appeared in 16 games for the pinstripers before he was traded to the Senators where he finished in 1958 at 7-19. While in the minors (1949–51) he led his league in strikeouts for three straight years.

WIGHT, Bill
Atlanta Braves scout

Bill, who was born in '22, wound up with several double-digit figures in a big league career which spanned 1946–58. He was 77-99 overall, with 66 complete games. He had 2-2, 7-7, and 6-6 seasons along the way. At the plate he had 55 base hits.

Originally with the Yankees, he was a 20-game loser with the White Sox in '48, but then won a career-high 15 games the following season. During the early 1950s he was with several other A.L. teams (Red Sox, Tigers, Indians, and Orioles) before breaking away with the Reds and Cardinals in the N.L.

WILBER, Del
Detroit Tigers scout

A catcher with the Cardinals (1946–49), Phillies ('51), and Red Sox (1952–54), Del ended with a .242 average in 299 games. Following his playing days, he coached with the White Sox in the mid-fifties, then became a manager in the minors. He was also a coach for the Senators and Texas Rangers in the early 1970s.

During his career, Del hit just 19 home runs, but on August 27, 1951, he had three in one game, accounting for all his team's runs off Ken Raffensberger and the Reds in a 3-0 win. During the '53 season with the Red Sox, he had three consecutive pinch-hit homers.

WILHELM, Hoyt
New York Yankees scout

One of the great relief pitchers in the game of baseball, Hoyt holds all-time records with 123 wins in relief, games pitched (1,070), and games finished (651). Overall he was 143-122 plus 227 saves. All of this was accomplished despite a ten-year delay in reaching the majors after first signing a pro contract in 1942.

Hoyt homered in his first big league at-bat in 1952, but is not remembered for his hitting. He never hit another home run in the next 20 years. In that outstanding rookie season for the New York Giants, Wilhelm's baffling knuckleball appeared in 71 games. He had a 2.43 ERA to go with his 15-3 record and .833 winning percentage—all three of which were league-leading figures.

He was nearly 50 when he retired in 1972. The knuckleball king also pitched for the Cardinals, and Indians (1957–58), Orioles (1958–1962), White Sox (1963–69), Cubs, Angels, Braves, and Dodgers near the end of his career. Late in the '58 season with Baltimore, he hurled a no-hitter on September 20th over the Yankees, the last no-hitter pitched against the Yanks.

During World War II, Hoyt received a Purple Heart for injuries incurred.

WILHELM "Spider"
Inspector in fire prevention bureau
Baltimore, MD

No relation to Hoyt, "Spider's" big league itch—er—hitch, lasted 7 games as a shortstop with the Philadelphia A's in 1953. He did go 2-for-7.   .286

WILKS, Ted
    Court bailiff
    Houston, TX

Ted was 17-4 for a league-leading .810 winning percentage
with the Cardinals in his first season. During the 1946–47
campaigns with the Cardinals, he was undefeated, going
8-0 in '46, and 4-0 in '47 over a 77-game stretch. He was
credited with a save in the sixth and final game over the
Browns in the '44 World Series. In 1949, the right-hander
was the N.L. leader in appearances (59) and in saves (9). In
1951 with the Pirates, his 13 saves paced all N.L. relief
pitchers. He completed his journey with the Indians in
1952–53.   **59-30**

WILL, Bob
    Bank executive
    Chicago, IL

This banker out of Northwestern University invested six
years of his life with the Chicago Cubs (1957–58, 1960–63).
Bob kept his figures most efficient with 9 home runs and 9
triples. He scored 87 runs and had 87 RBIs.   **.247**

WILLEY, Carlton
    Philadelphia Phillies scout

Called up to the Milwaukee Braves in June '58, Carlton
helped the Braves to the N.L. pennant with his 9-7 mark.
Despite his late arrival, he had a league-leading four shutouts. That was his only winning season in a career which
saw him spend his last three years (1963–65) with the expansion Mets.   **38-58**

WILLIAMS, Billy
    Oakland A's batting coach in 1983

Although Billy starred in the 1960s and early 1970s as a
Cubs' outfielder, he did debut in 1959, hitting .152 in 18

games. However, he usually hit for a higher average, including a league-leading .333 mark in 1972. He was the "iron man" in the majors, playing in a N.L. record of 1,117 consecutive games from 1963–70. That mark was broken by Steve Garvey of the San Diego Padres early in the 1983 season.

In 1903 Kid Elberfeld had all four of his team's hits in a game against the A's Rube Waddell. Billy had several games in which he was the only Cub hitting that particular day. On Sept. 5, 1969, he had a pair of doubles and two homers for the only four Cub safeties off the Pirates' Steve Blass. The next year, his two singles were the only Cub hits off the Braves' Phil Niekro, and in 1961 his two singles were the only hits off Warren Spahn when the Cubs faced the Braves. He broke up five no-hitters in his career.

Given a "day" at Wrigley Field on June 29, 1965, he was 5-for-9 in a doubleheader sweep over the Cardinals, as he didn't disappoint his fans. Among the records he holds are home runs in two consecutive games with five in September 1968, and a record four straight doubles on April 9, 1969.

Like his long-time Cub teammates Ernie Banks and Ron Santo, Billy also missed an opportunity to play in a World Series. He did have a chance at the end of his career playing in Oakland in 1975, but the A's lost the A.L. playoff to the Boston Red Sox. One of the more underrated players in the last 30 years, his overall stats include a .290 average in 2,488 games with 426 home runs among his 2,711 base hits.

WILLIAMS, Davey
    Service station
    Dallas, TX

Davey spent his entire six-year gallop as a second baseman for the New York Giants (1949, 1951–55). He had his finest year in '53 hitting .297, but had his career shortened by an ailing back at just age 27.

He was a Giants' coach in 1956–57 and later managed in the Texas League.   .252

WILLIAMS, Dick
San Diego Padres manager

Dick Williams' name has become well known in baseball during the past decade and a half. As a rookie manager he took the Red Sox from ninth place to the A.L. pennant in 1967. Dick had a stormy but successful tenure as manager with Charlie Finley's Oakland A's in the early 1970s, leading the club to World Championships in 1972 and '73. He managed the California Angels and Montreal Expos before taking over at San Diego in 1982.

In a 13-year trip, he was generally a utility-type player used mostly at third base and in the outfield. He also dabbled around first and second base. Dick originally was with the Dodgers (1951–54) and was 1-for-2 as a pinch-hitter in the '53 World Series. From the mid-fifties until 1964 he was with the Orioles, Indians, Orioles again, K.C. A's, a third tour with Baltimore, and finally the Red Sox. His 16 pinch-hits in 1963 with Boston were the most in the A.L.

On Aug. 30, 1958, Dick played all three outfield positions for the Orioles in a game against the Red Sox, and failed to collect a single putout or assist as Baltimore defeated Boston, 7-2.   .260

WILLIAMS, Don
Williams Brothers Enterprises
Garrett Park, MD

During the 1950s, the O'Briens were not the only set of twins signed by the Pirates. Don Williams and his identical twin Dewey were inked in 1953, and were together for a few years in the lower minors before Dewey, a right-handed pitching prospect, developed a sore arm and was released.

Don eventually worked his way up and had no decisions in 8 games with Pittsburgh in 1958–59 and 3 games with K.C. in 1962. The following year, another Don Williams pitched in three games with the Twins without a decision.

WILLIAMS, Stan
    Cincinnati Reds pitching coach

Stan made his debut with the L.A. Dodgers in 1958 with a two-hit shutout over the Cubs in his first major league start. He was the winning pitcher in the second playoff game over the Braves in '59.

Williams won a career high 15 games in '61, but then in 1962 he walked in the eventual winning run as the Giants rallied to win the third and final playoff game for the N.L. pennant.

Stan pitched for the Yankees in 1963–64. After a time in Cleveland in the late 1960s, he joined Minnesota and was the ace of the Twins bullpen in 1970 with a 10-1 mark, plus 15 saves in 68 games. Previously he had pitched for both the Dodgers and Yankees in World Series games, but missed a chance at playing for a third WS team when the Twins were beaten by the Orioles in the A.L. playoffs. Stan pitched six scoreless innings of relief in the playoff series. He concluded in 1972 after stops with the Red Sox and Cardinals.   109-94

WILLIAMS, Ted
    Red Sox hitting instructor; public relations for Sears fishing equipment
    Islamorada, FL

Possibly the greatest hitter in major league history, Ted broke into the biggies in 1939 with the Red Sox.

A four-decade player (1939–60), Williams spent his entire 19-year career with the Red Sox, missing five seasons due to military service in WW II, and the Korean Conflict (as a flyer in the Marine Corps).

Among his many accolades include two triple crowns and six batting titles. He was baseball's last .400 hitter when he batted .406 in 1941 without the benefit of the sacrifice fly rule.

Ted's superstar career was filled with drama and controversy. His three-run homer in the ninth inning of the 1941 All-Star Game gave the A.L. a 7-5 win. In 18 All-Star contests he batted .304 and posted a record 12 RBIs. Williams' clout off Rip Sewell's "ephus" pitch in the '46 All-Star Game is now legend. Other dramatic four-baggers among his lifetime 521 include the one he hit in the last game before returning to the military in 1952, and his homer against the Indians in his first time at bat as a pinch-hitter late in '53 upon returning from Korea.

His penchant for the dramatic was evident on September 28, 1960, when he homered against Jack Fisher in his final at-bat.

Notorious for his feuds with the Boston press, he not only wasn't elected MVP in '41, but he was also snubbed in '42 and '47 when he won triple crowns. In '47, one sportswriter failed to give him even one vote among the top ten.

Ted's hitting achievements are monumental. However, he rates his 2,019 career base-on-balls, or nearly four full seasons of walking, as "my proudest record." In 1940, Williams pitched in one game, giving up one run in two innings of relief.

Inducted into the Hall of Fame in 1966, Ted managed the new Senators to their only winning season in Washington in 1969 when they went 86-76. Off the field, Ted is an avid fisherman. "The Kid," as he was also known, finished with a .344 average. His uniform number 9 is the only one retired by the Red Sox.

WILLIS, Jim
School principal
Boyce, LA

Jim broke in with the Cubs in 1953. The following year the right-hander departed 2-2 after 27 games.

WILLS, Maury
Ex-Seattle Mariners manager

How to Steal a Pennant was the title of Maury's biography, and along with aid from Koufax and Drysdale, he helped the Dodgers steal four pennants (1959, '63, 1965–'66).

He had to wait in the minors several years before finally reaching the big show with the Dodgers in '59. Despite a belated start, Maury finished with 2,134 base hits, compiling a .281 average in 1,942 games.

Four six straight years, Wills was the N.L. leader in stolen bases, including a record-setting 104 in 1962. He was with the Pirates in 1967–68 and the expansion Expos in early '69, before returning to the Dodgers where he closed shop in 1972, just a few years before his son "Bump" arrived with the Texas Rangers.

Maury and Bump made history as the first father-son combination with a father managing against his son (after Maury took over as the Mariners' skipper late in the 1980 season).

WILLS, Ted
Otis Orchards, WA

Ted pitched in parts of four seasons (1959–62) with the Red Sox. The lefty, who spent his collegiate days at Fresno State, also wore the uniforms of the Reds ('62) and the White Sox ('65).   8-11

WILSON, Archie
Purchasing and traffic manager
Fruehauf Corp.
Decatur, AL

Archie, an outfielder, played in four games for the 1951 Yankees, who signed him as a bonus player out of the University of California. The following year Archie was busy traveling, as he played for the Yanks, Senators, and Red Sox.   .221

WILSON, Artie
Automobile salesman
Portland, OR

Artie was featured in a chapter of Roger Kahn's book, *A Season in the Sun.* One of the stars in the Negro leagues during the 1940s, he was past 30 when he had a chance to play in the big time with the N.Y. Giants as an infielder in

1951. After appearing in 19 games and hitting for a .182 average, he was sent to the minors upon the recall of a young outfielder named Willie Mays. Artie hit over the .300 mark in the Pacific Coast League for several years during the 1950s.

WILSON, Bill
Cerritos, CA

This flychaser was with the White Sox (1950, 1953–54), Philadelphia A's ('54), and K.C. A's ('55).   .222

WILSON, Bob
Supervisor in support services for the Dallas, TX, Independent School District

Bob was over the .300 mark four times at the Triple-A level in the Dodgers' system during the 1950s, but didn't get a good chance to show what he could do with the big club, going 1-for-5 in three games during their first year in L.A.   .200

WILSON, Duane
Valley Center, KS

During the fifties, Duane Eddy and "The Rebel Rousers" had teenagers wild with emotion. Unfortunately, chucker Duane Wilson and the Red Sox couldn't do likewise for Boston fans in 1958.   0-0

WILSON, Earl
Manufacturer's representative
Detroit, MI

The big right-hander first came up with the Red Sox in 1959, and in the early 1960s was a regular in the Boston starting rotation. A few weeks after Bo Belinsky had thrown his celebrated no-hitter early in the 1962 season, Earl no-hit Belinsky and the Angels, 2-0, at Fenway Park.

In the process, he hit a home run for one of Boston's two runs.

Originally a catcher in the Red Sox organization, Earl ranks among the all-time home-run leaders for pitchers with 35. Four times he led big league hurlers in homers.

Traded to the Tigers during the 1966 season, he had his biggest year as a 22-game winner for the Tigers in 1967.

121-109

WILSON, George "Ted"
Died October 29, 1974, at age 49 in Gastonia, NC

George Washington Wilson was named after our first President. A native of Cherryville, North Carolina, he was an outfielder for the White Sox (1952), N.Y. Giants (1952–53 and '56), and Yankees ('56). Things weren't a bowl of cherries for George, who was axed with a .191 average.

WILSON, Jim
Director of major league baseball's Central Scouting Bureau

Jim almost saw his career (1945–58) come to an end before it began. With the Red Sox in 1945, he was hit by a torrid Hank Greenberg line drive while on the mound. He recalled, "The ball was hit so hard it fractured my skull and put a dent in it one-fourth of an inch deep."

Somehow he recovered, but in May of 1947 he had a leg fractured by another line drive. He was up and down between the minors and the St. Louis Browns and Philadelphia A's in the late '40s.

From 1951–54, the right-hander was with the Braves in both Boston and Milwaukee. In June of '54 he pitched in just a few innings for the Braves and was placed on waivers with no takers. Given a starting assignment on June 12th against the Phillies and their ace Robin Roberts, Jim hurled a no-hitter for a 2-0 win. A few weeks later he was named to the N.L. All-Star team. The following season he was with the Orioles. With the White Sox in 1957, he was a 15-game winner with a league-leading 5 shutouts.

Overall 86-89 in 257 games, he previously was a vice-president with the Milwaukee Brewers before being named to head the Central Scouting Bureau.

WILSON, "Red"
    President of United Bank of Westgate
    Madison, WI

Bob "Red" Wilson was the Big Ten Conference's MVP on the gridiron in 1949 for the University of Wisconsin Badgers. He then played in the big top from 1951 to 1960, and was a catcher with the White Sox from '51 until traded to the Tigers early in 1954. His last season was spent with the Indians. Red's best year was in '58 with Detroit as he hit .299 in the only year that he caught in over 100 games. Wilson was an assistant football coach at Wisconsin during the 1950s in the off season while he was still in baseball.   .258

WINCENIAK, Ed
    Industrial engineering department supervisor, Republic Steel
    Chicago, IL

Ed was a popular guy around his home town as he played 32 games for the Cubs in 1956–57. The infielder strolled out with a .209 average.

WINDHORN, Gordy
    President, House of Beverages
    Danville, VA

Gordy never played organized baseball as a youth, but was signed to a pro contract after attending a tryout camp with a friend. He was the batting champ in Denver in the American Association in 1958. The flychaser then played in a few games with the Yankees in '59. In '61 Gordy was with the Dodgers briefly. The following year he joined the Kansas City A's and the expansion Los Angeles Angels.
                                     .176

WISE, Casey
Orthodontist
Naples, FL

The Cubs scooped this infielder out of the University of Texas in 1953. Kendall Cole (Casey) Wise was with them in 1957, the Braves in 1958–59, and the Tigers in 1960. This Casey struggled at-the-bat with a .174 average.

WITT, George
High school teacher
Tustin, CA

A Long Beach State graduate, "Red" was a right-handed pitcher for the Pirates (1957–61) and the expansion Angels and Astros (1962). Overall he had an 11-16 mark in 66 games. But in '58 things looked very promising as he had a 9-2 record, including three shutouts and a sparkling 1.61 ERA with Pittsburgh.

WOJEY, Pete
Safety director, Alabama Dry Dock and Shipbuilding Co.
Mobile, AL

Born Peter Paul Wojciechowski, "Wojey" fit into box scores more easily. A right-handed hurler, Pete was 1-1 for the Dodgers in 1954 and had no decisions with the Tigers in 1956–57.

WOLFE, Ed
Location unknown

"Terry and the Pirates" had a short voyage on the tube during the fifties. This Pirate was marooned after pitching in three games with the Bucs in 1952.   0-0

WOOD, Ken
Insurance agent
Charlotte, NC

Between 1948–53, Ken spent parts of several seasons with such teams as the Browns, Red Sox, and Senators. When he departed in '53 he took along a .224 average.

WOODESCHICK, Hal
Salesman, Zep Manufacturing
Houston, TX

This southpaw chucker made his debut with the Tigers in 1956. He then made stops with the Indians ('58), Senators (1959–61), and Tigers again ('61) before becoming the workhorse of the Astros' bullpen.

In 1964 he was just 2-9 in 61 appearances (all out of the bullpen), but his 23 saves topped the N.L. The year before he won 11 and saved 10 with a glossy 1.97 ERA for Houston. From 1965 until his final season ('67) he was with the St. Louis Cardinals (being a member of the 1967 N.L. and World Series champions).   44-62

WOODLING, Gene
Benefits from oil wells on his property; part-time scout for Cleveland Indians; raises horses
Medina, OH

A native of Akron, Ohio, Gene was originally an outfielder in the Indians' organization, playing in Cleveland in 1943 and after World War II in '46. He was with the Pirates in '47. After hitting .385 for San Francisco in the PCL in 1948, he became part of the Yankee monopoly (1949–53) as he played on five straight A.L. and World Series champions. He contributed .300-plus seasons in both 1952 and '53, and in 26 World Series games hit for a .318 mark.

Following the '54 season, Gene journeyed to Baltimore, Cleveland, and then back to the Orioles before playing for the Senators in the early 1960s. His swan song came in 1962 under manager Casey Stengel and the expansion

Mets. Some called him "Old Faithful" because of his timely clutch hitting.   .284

WOODS, Jim
   San Bruno, CA

Jim got the chance to play for his home-town Cubs. The Chicago native was just 18 when he appeared in several games for the Cubs in 1957. In 1960 and '61 the third baseman played with the Phillies.   .207

WOOLDRIDGE, Floyd
   Owns Wooldridge Construction
   Greenfield, MO

Floyd pitched in 18 games for the St. Louis Cardinals in '55. He disappeared with a 2-4 mark.

WORKMAN, Hank
   Attorney for a Los Angeles law firm
   Santa Monica, CA

The Yankees tried a great number of people at first base between Lou Gehrig and Bill Skowron. One you probably don't remember is Hank Workman, who appeared in only two games, going 1-for-5 in 1950.   .200

WORTHINGTON, Al
   Lynchburg Baptist College baseball coach
   Lynchburg, VA

"Red" arrived on the scene in July 1953. The right-hander with a great natural slider immediately hurled back-to-back shutouts in his first two starts, a pair of 6-0 wins over the Dodgers and Phillies.

After struggling the rest of that season and early in 1954, he was back in the minors. He returned to the Giants, and in the late fifties was with them in San Francisco. Al made his final starting assignment in '59, then drifted around between the minors and the Red Sox,

White Sox, and Reds, before finding himself in 1964 as an effective relief pitcher with the Minnesota Twins. He helped them to the A.L. pennant in 1965 with 10 wins and 21 saves. In his next to final season in pro ball in 1968, his 18 saves were the most in the A.L. Overall he was 75-82, with an additional 110 saves in 602 games. He was a pitching coach for the Twins in the early 1970s.

WRIGHT, Ed
> Exxon station owner
> Dyersburg, TN

Henderson Edward Wright appeared in 101 games with a 25-16 mark off the mound. The right-hander was with the Boston Braves (1945–48), and Philadelphia Athletics (1952) in his last major league season.

WRIGHT, Mel
> Pitching coach for the Montreal Expos when he died in 1983 at age 55

Following the Astros' playoff victory over the Dodgers for the N.L. Western Division championship in 1980, ABC announcer Bob Uecker was in the Houston clubhouse for the celebration. There, next to Uecker, stood a middle-aged man only a few would recognize. We refer to Astros' pitching coach Mel Wright. As a former chucker himself, Mel wasn't interviewed too often. He was with the Cardinals (1954–55), and Cubs (1960–61), compiling a 2-4 log with an ERA over 7.00 in 58 games—all out of the bullpen. Mel was also a pitching coach for the Cubs and Pirates.

WRIGHT, Roy
> Employed with North Georgia Electric Power Board
> Fort Oglethorpe, GA

If you don't remember Ed and Mel, you probably don't know about Roy, who started one game for the 1956 New York Giants. Three innings, five runs, and eight hits

later—before his big league pitching career ever left the
ground—it was over.　　　　　　　　　　　　　　　　0-1

WRIGHT, Tom
　　　Department store credit manager
　　　Shelby, NC

Unlike Ed, Mel, and Roy, Tom was not a right-handed flipper. He did throw righty, but hit lefty and played in the
outfield. He was with the Red Sox briefly in the late 1940s,
then had his finest year, hitting .318 in 1950 for the Bosox
in limited playing time.

　　From 1952–56, Tom drifted around the A.L. to the St.
Louis Browns, White Sox, and Senators. Dividing the '52
season between the Browns and White Sox, his 10 pinch-
hits were the most in the A.L. In 1949 he led the American
Association in hitting with a .368 average.　　　　.255

WYNN, Early
　　　TV commentator, Chicago White Sox

Early did not win early in his career. He struggled to
win number 300 late in his career, but in between he
won plenty. "Gus," as he was known, was feared by
opposing hitters because of his brushback pitches. As a
nineteen-year-old Senator in 1939, he lost his only two
decisions. Throughout most of the 1940s he struggled as
a member of the Senators, losing a league-leading 17
games one year and going 8-19 in 1948. But the following campaign he became a member of the Indians.
Along with Feller, Lemon, and Garcia, the Tribe had a
formidable mound machine for several years. Early was
a 23-game winner in '52 and again in '54, as the Indians
ended the Yankees' dynasty. In '59 his 22 victories for
the White Sox paced "The Hose" to their first A.L. flag
in 40 years. He was named the Cy Young Award winner
for his efforts.

　　The right-hander passed the 20-year mark and entered
his fourth decade when he finally looked to be at the end of

the trail at age 42 in 1962, one victory short of career win
No. 300. Released by the White Sox, he hooked up with the
Indians, and in July 1963 (after several attempts), he
achieved win number 300. Among the all-time leaders in
numerous pitching records, he ranked first in one—most
bases-on-balls allowed (1,775) surpassed by Nolan Ryan in
1981.

Early is the only pitcher to both hit and give up a
pinch-hit grand-slam home run. He hit one in 1946 as a
member of the Senators, and served one up to Bob Cerv
in 1961.

With a career mark of 300-244 in 691 games, Early was
elected to the Hall of Fame in 1972. During the 1960s he
coached with the Indians and Twins, and was a minor
league manager in the early 1970s.

WYROSTEK, Johnny
Mayor of Fairmont City, IL; carpenter by trade

An outfielder from 1942–54, Johnny spent his first two
seasons with the Pirates. In 1946–47, the flychaser
made his living as a member of the Phillies. Before he
made his last stop with the Phils (1952–54), Johnny
played with the Reds (1948–51). His finest season came
in '51 when he hit .311. He split the '52 season with the
Reds and Phils.   .271

WYSE, Hank
Union electrician
Tulsa, OK

Hank was with the Cubs from 1942–47. The right-hander
was a 22-game winner in '45 for the pennant-winning
Cubbies. In the WS he was the starter and loser in game
two to the Tigers. A three-run homer by another "Hank,"
named Greenberg, led to his 4-1 defeat. In 1950–51, he was
with the Philadelphia A's and Washington Senators in the
junior circuit.   79-70

Y

YEWCIC, Tom
New England Patriots offensive backfield coach
Arlington, MA

For Tom, 1954 was a giant year. Not only did he quarterback the powerful Michigan State Spartans to a victory in
the Rose Bowl, but he was also the MVP of the College
Baseball World Series. Turning to professional baseball,
he played in one game as a catcher for the Detroit Tigers in
1957. He then switched to pro football, and from 1961 to
1966 he played in the American Football League.

YOCHIM, Len
Pittsburgh Pirates chief roving scout; scouting A.L.
teams
New Orleans, LA

Len pitched with the Pirates in 1951 and again in '54,
going 1-2 in 12 games. His brother, Ray, hurled in four
games without a record for the Cardinals in 1948–49.

YOST, Eddie
Boston Red Sox coach

One of the more familiar names from the 1950s, Eddie
Yost is best remembered as the steady third baseman for
the Washington Senators. "The Walking Man" might
have been a Yankee, but he turned down an offer to sign
with them and enrolled at New York University. He joined
the Senators out of college and never spent a day in the minors.

Yost first joined Washington in 1944 and drew the first
of 1,614 bases-on-balls he would rack up in his 18 years.

Only Babe Ruth, Ted Williams, Mickey Mantle, Mel Ott, and Carl Yastrzemski had more free passes. From 1947–58 he was the Senators' third baseman and played in 838 consecutive games before having his streak snapped in 1955 by a case of tonsillitis.

In 1959 and 1960 Eddie was with the Tigers. In '59 he led the A.L. in runs scored with 115, and also led the league in walks for a sixth time. He walked out with the expansion Angels in 1961–62. Yost then coached for the Senators until 1967 when he joined the New York Mets. Never making it into the World Series as a player, he made it as a coach twice with the Mets.

"The Walking Man" didn't always look for a freebie. He led off games with home runs 28 times. This was a record until 1975 when Bobby Bonds hit his 29th roundtripper to start a game.   .254

YOUNG, Bobby
    Construction company
    Baltimore, MD

Trivia buffs recall Bobby as the last second baseman for the St. Louis Browns. A native of Maryland, he was also the Orioles' first second baseman in 1954, following the Browns' shift to Baltimore. He had previously played for the Baltimore team in the International League in 1949–50 after breaking in with the St. Louis Cardinals in 1948. He also played for the Indians (1955–56) and Phillies ('58).

In a memorable 1952 game in which Bob Cain outdueled Bob Feller in a battle of one-hitters, Bobby tripled off Feller in the first inning, and evenutally scored the game's lone run.   .249

YOUNG, Dick
    Payroll supervisor—Western Farmers Association
    Lynnwood, WA

The namesake of the well-known New York baseball columnist, Dick played in 20 games as a second baseman with the Phillies in 1951–52. In '54 the Phillies sent Young and

cash to the Brooklyn Dodgers for Bobby Morgan. However,
Young never saw action with the "Bums."   .234

YUHAS, Eddie
      Retired; formerly employed with Anheuser-Busch
      Winston-Salem, NC

In 1952 Eddie posted a 12-2 mark as a 28-year-old Cardinal
rookie. The following year he was in just two games for the
Cards without a decision.

YVARS, Sal
      Stockbroker
      Valhalla, NY

A New York City native, Sal was a reserve catcher for the
New York Giants from 1947 until he was traded to the
Cardinals during the 1953 season. He completed his playing days in St. Louis in 1954.
      During the Giants '51 season, he hit .317 in 25 games.
But in the World Series against the Yankees, he had a
chance to be a hero in his only appearance. In game six,
with the Yankees up three games to two and the score
4-3, Sal came up as a pinch-hitter with the tying run on
second base. He lined a shot into right field that was
caught by Hank Bauer for the final out. Had the ball
fallen and the Giants gone on to win the game, a well-
rested Sal Maglie might have proved troublesome for the
Yanks in the seventh game. Reliving Bobby Thomson's
immortal blast, Sal recalled, "I was in the bullpen when
Thomson hit the home run. It put a hell of a good down
payment on my house." The stockbroker has been associated with Little League and Babe Ruth League baseball for several years.

Z

ZANNI, Dom
    Insurance agent
    Massapequa, NY

Dom's career started and ended on high notes. In his first and only appearance with the San Francisco Giants in 1958, he was the winning pitcher in relief. Most of his 9-6 record (in 111 games) was accumulated with the White Sox ('62) and Reds ('63). In his final campaign (1966) he worked 7 scoreless innings in 5 appearances, and also picked up a base hit in his only at-bat.

ZARILLA, Al
    Oakland A's scout

"Zeke" was a ten-year outfielder with the St. Louis Browns, Boston Red Sox, and Chicago White Sox. At the end of his career he had a second run with the Browns and Bosox. Al helped the Browns to their only A.L. pennant, swatting .299 in 1944. Following a .224 season in '47, he hit for a career-high .329 in 1949. On July 13, 1946, he hit two triples in one inning for the Browns.

Traded to Boston during the '49 campaign, he joined Ted Williams and Dom DiMaggio in forming an all-.300 hitting outfield in 1950. Al hit .325, and on June 8th he garnered four doubles and a single when Boston massacred the Browns, 29-4. And believe it or not, he failed to collect an RBI that day.   .276

ZAUCHIN, Norm
    Hart Hanks Company account executive
    Thomas Acres, AL

This big first baseman arrived with the Red Sox briefly in 1951, then again from 1955–57. He was then employed by

the Senators (1958–59). In '55, following the illness and
untimely death of Harry Agganis, Norm took over as the
regular Red Sox first baseman and responded with his best
year, collecting 27 home runs and 93 RBIs. On May 27,
1955, Norm banged out three homers and 10 RBIs in leading the Red Sox to a 16-0 rout over the Senators.   .233

ZERNIAL, Gus
> Manages real estate investments for a company called
> Maranatha
> Fresno, CA

Big Gus, who was known as "Ozark Ike," was an 11-year
outfielder from 1949–59. Originally with the White Sox, he
was traded to the Philadelphia A's in '51, and became the
first player since 1915 to lead the league in home runs (33)
and RBIs (129) in a season divided between two teams. In
one four-game stretch Gus hit 7 homers.

He hit a career-high 42 four-baggers in '53, but lost out
to Al Rosen by one for the A.L. home-run title. He remained with the A's through their first three years in
Kansas City before finishing with the Tigers in 1958–59.
His 15 pinch-hits were the most in the A.L. in '58.

Gus, who was a sportscaster in Fresno for several years
before going into an automobile dealership, closed at .265
with 237 home runs.

Concerning his moniker "Ozark Ike," the story goes
that Fred Haney (who was broadcasting games for the Hollywood Stars) referred to Gus as "Ozark Ike." Although
Zernial was from Texas, it apparently was close enough for
Haney.

ZICK, Bob
> Waterloo, Belgium

A Chicago native, Bob was a right-handed pitcher who
worked in 10 games for his home-town Cubs with no record
in 1954. There is a humorous story involving Cubs' manager Stan Hack and Zick. When Bob reported to the Cubs
during the middle of the season, he announced to manager

Hack, "I'm Zick," and Hack reportedly replied, "I haven't been feeling so well myself."

ZIMMER, Don
Chicago Cubs coach

When Don joined Brooklyn in 1954 he was considered to be Pee Wee Reese's eventual replacement at shortstop for the Dodgers. For a brief time he was (until Maury Wills arrived). Don was with the Dodgers for the remainder of the decade, long enough to be a part of both the 1955 and '59 championship teams.

Married at home plate while playing in the Eastern League in 1951, he almost died in the batter's box several years later when he was hit on the head by a pitch in 1953 while playing at St. Paul in the American Association. He was unconscious for nearly two weeks and required two brain operations.

Always the fighter, Don was in the big leagues the following year, but in 1956 he was hit on the jaw by a pitch, causing another setback, The scrappy infielder was with the Cubs, Mets, Reds, and Dodgers again in the early 1960s, before making his exit with the Senators in 1965.

Don managed in the minors in the late 1960s, then went on to coach (Expos, Padres, and Yankees) and manage (Padres, Red Sox, and Rangers) in the '70s and '80s. His son Tom, a former catcher in the Cardinals' organization, manages in the minors.   .235

ZOLDAK, Sam
Died August 25, 1966, at age 47
Mineola, NY

Sam was in the A.L. for nine seasons (1944–52). He came up with the pennant-winning Browns in '44 and remained in St. Louis until traded to the Indians during the 1948 season. The southpaw won 9 games as a spot starter and reliever in the second half of the season in '48 to help Cleveland to the A.L. flag. He was with the Indians through 1950, before closing with the Philadelphia A's in 1952.   43-53

ZUPO, Frank
    Cocktail lounge manager
    Burlingame, CA

"Noodles" Zupo followed in the tradition of Italian ball-players coming out of the San Francisco Bay area. Signed out of high school as a catcher by the Orioles, he joined the big team as a teenager in 1957. Between games of a doubleheader he was warming up the Orioles' starting pitcher for the nightcap. "Kids will be kids," and Frank was teasingly faking throws in the direction of the umpires. Ump Ed Hurley didn't take kindly to this, and after a warning, he ejected Frank from the scene.

In a 16-game career (1957, '58, '61), Frank hit .167.

And now—for all of you who are not quite sure who "Zuverink" is . . .

ZUVERINK, George
    Insurance business
    Bankers Life of Nebraska
    Tempe, AZ

George's career spans the decade, as he was originally with the Indians in 1951–52 and Cincinnati briefly in '54, before becoming a member of the Detroit Tigers. The right-hander pitched reasonably well that year, and his hometown fans in nearby Holland, Michigan planned a day in George's honor at Tiger Stadium. The plans had to be changed because George felt it would be a jinx to hold it on a day he was scheduled to pitch. George tossed an 11-inning, 3-hit shutout, winning 1-0.

The following season (1955), after going 0-5, he was placed on waivers by the Tigers and was picked up by the Orioles. It was with Baltimore that he became one of the most respected relief pitchers in the A.L., leading the circuit in appearances in both the '56 and '57 seasons. In '56 he also led the A.L. in games saved. Overall George was 32-36, plus 40 saves in 265 games.

SPECIAL ACCLAIM

For the 1,500-plus players who made it into a major league game during the 1950s, there were probably another 15 million who wish they had. Some just missed, never getting the call from Triple A. The majority saw their careers end in Little League. One who didn't deserves special mention.

BAUMER, Jim
   Philadelphia Phillies Vice President of Player Development and Scouting

As an 18-year-old out of high school in 1949, Jim played in 8 games as a shortstop for the White Sox, going 4-for-10, including a double and a triple. A dozen years later, Jim played in ten games as a second baseman for the 1961 N.L. champion Cincinnati Reds. Jim hit .206 in 18 career games, missing the entire decade of the fifties.

As so many of us wonder where the fifties went, we're sure Jim Baumer feels the same way.

Bibliography

Alicoate, Jack (ed.). *Yearbook of Motion Pictures 1957*. New York: The Film Daily, 1957.

Baseball Encyclopedia. New York: Macmillan, 1974, 1979.

Benaugh, Jim. *Incredible Baseball Feats*. New York: Grosset and Dunlap, 1975.

Berger, Phil. *Where Are They Now?* New York: Popular Library, 1978.

Borst, Bill. *Baseball Through a Knothole*. St. Louis: Krank Press, 1980.

Brown, Bob and Phil Itzoe. *Baltimore Orioles 1974 Yearbook* (20th Anniversary Edition). 1973.

Davids, L. Robert. *Great Hitting Pitchers*. Virginia: Society for American Baseball Research, 1979.

Eckhouse, Morris and Carl Mastrocola. *This Date in Pittsburgh Pirates History*. New York: Stein and Day, 1980.

Einstein, Charles. *Willie's Time*. New York: Lippincott, 1979.

Gipe, George. *The Great American Sports Book*. New York: Doubleday, 1978.

Goldberg, Hy. *Who's Who in the Big Leagues*. New York: Dell Sports, periodical, Vol. #1, No. 4, 1958.

Hollander, Zander, and David Schulz. *Sports Nostalgia Quiz Book #3*. New York: Signet Books, 1979.

Horsley, Edith. *The 1950s*. Hong Kong: Bison Books Ltd., 1978.

Irving, Elliot. *Remembering the Vees—Richmond Virginians 1954–1964*. Virginia: Cumberland Printing, 1979.

Jennison, Christopher. *Wait 'Til Next Year*. New York: Norton, 1974.

Kahn, Roger. *The Boys of Summer*. New York: Harper & Row, 1971.

Karst, Gene, and Martin J. Jones, Jr. *Who's Who in Professional Baseball*. New Rochelle: Arlington House, 1973.

Kiersh, Edward. "Where Have You Gone?" *Newsweek* (Inside Sports), April 1981.

Leglar, Charles. *Balls and Strikes Forever.* FCL Distributing, 1978.

Lewis, Allen, and Larry Shenk. *This Date in Philadelphia Phillies History.* New York: Stein and Day, 1979.

Lowenkrin, Hank. *Best Baseball Stories.* New York: Grosset and Dunlap, 1975.

McBride, Joseph. *High and Inside.* New York: Warner Books, 1980.

Marazzi, Rich. *The Rules and Lore of Baseball.* New York: Stein and Day, 1980.

Neft, David, Roland Johnson, Richard Cohen, and Jordan Deutsch. *The Sports Encyclopedia: Baseball.* New York: Grosset and Dunlap, 1977.

Obojski, Robert. *Bush League.* New York: Macmillan, 1975.

Reichler, Joe (ed.). *Baseball Encyclopedia.* New Jersey: Macmillan, 1979.

Rainovic, Al. *The Diamond Report.* West Allis, Wisconsin: ARR Features, 1976–1979.

Salant, Nathan. *This Date in New York Yankees History.* New York: Stein and Day, 1979.

Smalling, R.J. and Dennis W. Eckes. *Baseball Address List.* Laurel, Maryland: Den's Collectors Den, 1980.

Stern, Chris. *Where Have They Gone?* New York: Grosset and Dunlap, 1975.

Sugar, Bert Randolph. *Who Was Harry Steinfeldt and Other Baseball Trivia Questions.* Chicago: Playboy Press, 1976.

Terrace, Vincent. *Complete Encyclopedia of TV Programs 1947–79,* Vol. 2. New York: Barnes, 1980.

Townsend, Doris. *This Great Game.* New Jersey: Prentice-Hall, 1971.

Turkin, Y. and S.C. Thompson. *The Official Encyclopedia of Baseball.* New York: Dolphin Books, 1977.

Walton, Ed. *This Date in Boston Red Sox History.* New York: Stein and Day, 1978.

_____. *Red Sox Triumphs and Tragedies.* New York: Stein and Day, 1980.